BECOMING BELAFONTE

Mark Crispin Miller, Series Editor

This series begins with a startling premise—that even now, more than two hundred years since its founding, America remains a largely undiscovered country, with much of its amazing story yet to be told. In these books, some of America's foremost historians and cultural critics bring to light in our nation's history episodes that have never been explored. They offer fresh takes on events and people we thought we knew well and draw unexpected connections that deepen our understanding of our national character.

By Judith E. Smith

BECOMING BELAFONTE

BLACK ARTIST, PUBLIC RADICAL

University of Texas Press
AUSTIN

Printed in the United States of America
First edition, 2014

Requests for permission to reproduce material from this work should be sent to:

Permissions
University of Texas Press
P.O. Box 7819
Austin, TX 78713-7819
http://utpress.utexas.edu/index.php/rp-form

♾ The paper used in this book meets the minimum requirements of ANSI/NISO Z39.48-1992 (R1997) (Permanence of Paper).

LIBRARY OF CONGRESS CATALOGING-IN-PUBLICATION DATA

Smith, Judith E., 1948- author.
Becoming Belafonte : black artist, public radical / by Judith E. Smith.
pages cm — (Discovering America)
Includes bibliographical references and index.
ISBN 978-0-292-72914-8 (cloth : alkaline paper)
1. Belafonte, Harry, 1927- 2. African American civil rights workers—Biography. 3. Musicians, Black—United States—Biography. 4. Actors, Black—United States—Biography.
I. Title. II. Series: Discovering America series.
ML420.B32S55 2014
782.42164092 —dc23
[B]

2014006424

doi:10.7560/729148

For the 1940s radicals of Belafonte's generation, for my 1960s generation who took it to the streets, and for all the new ways our children are finding to "carry it on"

CONTENTS

ACKNOWLEDGMENTS
- ix -

INTRODUCTION
- 1 -

From Harlem, Jamaica, and the Segregated Navy to New York City's Interracial Left-Wing Culture, 1927–1948
- 8 -

Black Left, White Stage, Cold War: *Moving into the Spotlight, 1949–1954*
- 55 -

Multimedia Stardom and the Struggle for Racial Equality, 1955–1960
- 110 -

Storming the Gates: *Producing Film and Television, 1957–1970*
- 176 -

AFTERWORD
- *251* -

ABBREVIATIONS FOR NOTES
- *257* -

NOTES
- *261* -

INDEX
- *333* -

ACKNOWLEDGMENTS

Harry Belafonte appeared on the periphery of my research on Lorraine Hansberry for my book *Visions of Belonging*, but as the first black Hollywood movie producer, he emerged as a critical player in new research on representations of racial citizenship in Hollywood filmmaking between 1949 and 1965 that I began as a fellow in the Charles Warren Center's Film and History seminar in 2002–2003. Untangling the threads of his screen persona, his musical celebrity, and his work for television moved him to center stage and prompted this book.

Extraordinarily generous friends and colleagues helped me along the way. The brilliant scholarship of Rachel Rubin taught me new ways to read, and how to listen to and think deeply about music and culture; her steadfast support infused this project from the very beginning. Ron Cohen's historical research on folk music and the Left is foundational for all who venture into these fields; he generously directed me to research, sources, and personal contacts, and encouraged my work at every turn. I have relied on pathbreaking scholarship on the black left by Mark Solomon, Robin Kelley, and Jim Smethurst, and on their friendship and encouragement as well. My fellow travelers in postwar cultural history Dan Horowitz and Ruth Feldstein, and in the wartime and postwar literary left, Mary Helen Washington and Alan Wald, have frequently shared research and insights over many years. I am also the grateful beneficiary of a generous group of people willing to share historical memories with me, sometimes in multiple conversations: Harry Belafonte, Burt D'Lugoff, Taylor Branch, Oscar Brand, Irving Burgie, Len Chandler, Robert DeCormier, Olga James, Chiz Schultz, and Alice Spivak.

The work of documenting Belafonte's extensive public record was made possible by the collective resources of many scholars, friends, and librarians. I want to thank those who led me to research materials I drew on in writing *Becoming Belafonte*: Taylor Branch, Margaret Burnham, Lizabeth Cohen, Ron Cohen, Nancy Cott, Elena Tajima Creef, Nancy Falk, Crystal Feimster, Ruth Feldstein, Dayo Gore, Molly Geidel, Andrew Hannon, Dan Horowitz, Evan Joiner, Ahmed Kathrada, Alice Kessler-Harris, Kimberly Lamm, Randy MacLowry, Sarah Malino, Jeffrey Melnick, Mark Crispin Miller, Georgia Parker, Steve Ross, Rachel Rubin, Steve Schewel, Chiz Schultz, Toru Shinoda, Terry Signaigo, Maren Stange, Tracy Heather Strain, Lynnell Thomas, Mary Tiseo, Susan Tomlinson, Shane Vogel, Alan Wald, Lary Wallace, Tom Zaslavsky, and Seyna Bruskin. Particularly helpful were collections at the Academy of Motion Picture Arts and Sciences, University of Southern California Cinematic Arts Library, UCLA Film and Television Archives, New York's Paley Center for Media, the Schomburg Center for Research in Black Culture, the Tamiment Library and Robert F. Wagner Labor Archives at NYU, and the Library of Congress's Motion Pictures, Broadcasting and Recorded Sound Division. Special thanks to the expert guidance of Kristine Krueger at AMPAS, Ned Comstock at USC; Lauren Pey at John F. Kennedy Library, Diana Lachatanere and staff at Schomburg Manuscripts, Archives and Rare Books and the Moving

Image and Recorded Sound Divisions; Peter Filardo and Sarah Leila Moazeni at Tamiment Library; Bryan Cornell at Recorded Sound Reference Center and Josie Walters-Johnson, Motion Picture Division, Library of Congress.

While teaching full-time, I was able to temporarily employ a far-flung network of graduate students to help me track down additional research materials: Joey Fink located Taylor Branch's interviews with Belafonte housed at the University of North Carolina; Tad Suitor went through Apollo materials at the Smithsonian National Museum of American History; Heather Vermeulen combed through the Langston Hughes and Carl Van Vechten papers in the James Weldon Johnson collection at the Beinecke Rare Books and Manuscript Library at Yale; Brittany Adams reviewed materials at UCLA's Film and Television library. For many years, I have been able to rely on the extraordinary and meticulous research expertise of Michael Beckett, who knows how to locate any kind of source and productively comb through newspapers both pre- and post-digitizing. My ability to research extensively in the black press has been considerably expanded by his skills. Pembroke Herbert and Sandi Rygiel at Picture Research Consultants, Ron Cohen, and Michael Beckett were tremendously helpful in locating and gaining rights to some of the photographs reproduced here.

My colleagues in American Studies at University of Massachusetts, Rachel Rubin, Lynnell Thomas, Bonnie Miller, Aaron Lecklider, Marisol Negron, Jeffrey Melnick, Phil Chassler, Patricia Raub, Paul Atwood, and Shauna Manning, have made our department a very stimulating environment for thinking about Belafonte, even when our work responsibilities compete with writing projects. Along the way I have also benefitted from scholarly conversation and companionship offered by Crystal Feimster, Mary Frederickson, Karen Miller, Virginia Reinburg, Sharon Strom, and Susan Tomlinson. A sabbatical leave granted by the University of Massachusetts Boston in 2011–2012 gave me the space for full-time writing, during which many scholars and friends responded graciously to research queries: my thanks to Martha Biondi, Celia Bucki, Paul Buhle, Irving Burgie, Jelani Cobb, Ron Cohen, Robert DeCormier, John D'Emilio, Tom Doherty, Lew Erenberg, Eric Foner, Crystal Feimster, Mary Frederickson, Vicki Gabriner, Molly Geidel, John Gennari, Keith Gilyard, Van Gosse, Aram Goudsouzian, Jim Green, Matthew Jacobson, Geoffrey Jacques, Tammy Kernodle, Aaron Lecklider, Robbie Lieberman, David Levering Lewis, Randy MacLowry, Jeffrey Melnick, Ethelbert Miller, Paul Mischler, Milt Okun, Leah Rosenberg, Rachel Rubin, Dave Samuelson, George Schuller, Toru Shinoda, Jim Smethurst, Faith Smith, Mark Solomon, Alice Spivak, Lawrence Squeri, Maren Stange, Michelle Stephens, Tracy Heather Strain, Susan Tomlinson, Penny Von Eschen, Alan Wald, and Mary Helen Washington.

Early comments on several chapters from Dan Horowitz, Barbara Lewis, Jim Smith, and Christina Simmons provided helpful direction, and Revan Schendler helped me cut an earlier draft. Generous readings of the whole manuscript by Mari Jo Buhle, Paul Buhle, Ron Cohen, Robert DeCormier, Ruth Feldstein, Geoffrey Jacques, Ann Holder, Dan Horowitz, Robin Kelley, Jeffrey Melnick, Rachel Rubin, Lois Rudnick, Mark Solomon, and Jim Smethurst caught important mistakes and improved the book's final form. Being able to consult frequently with Rachel Rubin, Ann Holder, and Jeffrey Melnick, and their extra eleventh-hour readings of the revised manuscript, were particularly important in the finishing process. I am especially grateful to Mark Crispin Miller, editor for the Discovering America series, and Theresa May, editor in chief at University of Texas Press, for their early and continuing enthusiasm for this book, and to Robert Devens for expert guidance through publication. I also want to thank my colleague

Brian Halley, UMass Press editor, for sharing his expertise on the publishing process.

My long-distance extended family, Beth Smith, Sarah Malino, Debbie Smith, Jim Smith, Lois Feinblatt, Patty Blum, and Jeff Blum, have lived through this project with me and kept on the lookout for Belafonte sightings. In New York and New Haven, Ben Blum-Smith and Diane Henry, Sarah Blum-Smith and Drew Hannon, and Laura Blum-Smith and Ed Underhill provided dinner companions on research trips and listened to endless Belafonte stories, and I look to them as discerning cultural critics and astute editorial consultants. My housemates, Noel Jette and Alan Zaslavsky, have once again generously accepted more piles of papers, files, movies, and music overflowing onto our dining room table, and have also contributed cultural and political insights throughout the research and writing of this book. When he used to play the guitar as parent help at the various day care centers that helped us raise our children, Larry Blum made sure that "Jamaica Farewell" was part of the local pre-K repertoire. Larry and I have learned so much from each other as our scholarly interests in the historical processes and moral dimensions of racialization have converged, and I cherish sharing our work as well as our home lives. His constant interest in and engagement with *Becoming Belafonte* have sustained me.

BECOMING BELAFONTE

INTRODUCTION

Today Harry Belafonte is most commonly known as a singer of "Day-O," sometimes called "Banana Boat Song." New York Yankee fans have heard the song reverberate throughout the stadium; new generations have encountered its memorable presence in Tim Burton's 1988 film *Beetlejuice* and have heard it sampled in recent releases by rap artist Lil Wayne and popular singer Jason Derulo. (Other Belafonte hits, such as "Mary's Boy Child" and "Jump in the Line," have shown up in mixes by hip-hop, ska, dance, and R & B artists from the United States, Jamaica, and England, such as Ginuwine, Pitbull, Prince Buster, Bounty Killer, and Shaft.) In the late 1950s, Belafonte was labeled as the "King of Calypso." Show business headlines trumpeted his sex appeal for women fans across the color line by promising to reveal "why girls are wild about Harry." Photographs of appearances with the civil rights leader Martin Luther King, Jr., linked Belafonte with the call for integration.

But the prevalence of these one-note characterizations has concealed a much more complex figure, a multitalented artist, questing radical intellectual, and relentless political provocateur. The "King of Calypso" was also the first black artist to head a Hollywood film production unit. Martin Luther King's friend and associate was involved in efforts to confront Jim Crow segregation as a part of social justice campaigns at home and abroad years before and after the era of King's leadership. In contrast with Belafonte's appearance as a supporting actor in various accounts of popular music, civil rights, and Caribbean culture in the United States, and in Hollywood, this study features Belafonte's leading man performance on multiple stages—in nightclubs and concert halls; on Broadway, television, and film sets; and up front at rallies and demonstrations.[1]

The aim of *Becoming Belafonte* is to reintroduce this peerless cultural figure in all his dimensions, shining a spotlight on Belafonte's emergence as a working black artist and public radical from his early musical performances in the second half of the 1940s through his rise to stardom in the 1950s and his *uses of celebrity* in the 1960s. I focus on how he crafted a public persona that enabled him to navigate the minefields of racial discrimination, anticommunist blacklisting, and the demands of stardom while still speaking out on issues of racial and social justice and putting his career and body in jeopardy to support major expressions of black resistance.

Two versions of Belafonte's personal story have appeared recently: his 2011 memoir, *My Song*, written with *Vanity Fair* writer and biographer Michael Shnayerson, and a 2011 film documentary, *Sing Your Song*, produced by his daughter Gina Belafonte. As a form, memoirs fall between fiction and nonfiction. Both *My Song* and *Sing Your Song* offer invaluable and well-crafted narratives of Belafonte's chosen memories of his own life, shaped primarily by his decisions about what to reveal, to confess, to memorialize, to celebrate.

The aims of a historical account of Belafonte's "becoming" are different from the personal and individual reckoning of memoir and documentary. With the exception of Muhammad Ali, it is hard to think of another African American figure of the 1950s and 1960s who so successfully translated popular success and acclaim into such a broadly ambitious national (and international) agenda. What *Becoming Belafonte* offers, then, is an archeology of the years during which Belafonte began to figure out how to spend the cultural capital he accrued as a popular singer and actor in order to take on some of the most pressing social issues of his time.

Belafonte's "becoming" was part of a larger theatrical, musical, and political story. While his memoir and documentary chronicle his acting efforts, musical career, and political activism, there is much more to say about the exhilarating social, cultural, and political world of New York arts radicals between the late 1940s and the late 1960s that provided the context in which Belafonte came of age and became a star. Born into a Harlem West Indian working-class family, a high school dropout and a WWII navy vet, Belafonte transformed racial anger and street rage into an artistic, intellectual, and political vision that could sustain him through decades of performance and activism.

Belafonte's chosen music repertoire, of American and international folk songs, work songs, and calypsos, constituted his first form of artistic expression. His calypsos drew on diverse Afro-Caribbean and Latin American musical traditions, and his recording success accelerated an already well-established process of musical exchange in the Caribbean and between the West Indies and New York. He chose music that exposed the color line as a tool of white supremacy. His songbook revealed black history as a source of cultural wealth, and black and white working people's determination and creativity as fueling resistance around the world.

On stage in the 1950s, Belafonte's musical charisma and repertoire were inseparable from his stance of racial equality. His 1956 hit recordings made this commitment tangible for wider circles of fans beyond those who heard him live. One of those fans was Ann Dunham, Barack Obama's mother, who held him up, alongside Albert Einstein and Mahatma Gandhi, as a role model for her black son. A Belafonte record was the first single bought by Patti Smith, future rock-and-roll singer-songwriter and poet, growing up in a working-class family in South Jersey. The musician and poet Gil Scott-Heron described his "debut as a vocalist" singing Belafonte's "Jamaica Farewell" while a second grader living with his grandmother in Jackson, Tennessee. Northern California high school student and Quaker pacifist Joan Baez remembered his song "Man Smart, Woman Smarter" on the first folk album in her parents' house. Soon after he arrived in New York in 1961, singer-songwriter Bob Dylan made his first professional recording playing harmonica for Belafonte, whose "radiating greatness" made him feel he had "become anointed in some way." When their guards allowed music piped into their cells in the 1970s, the South African freedom fighters imprisoned with Nelson Mandela on Robben Island liked hearing Belafonte sing "Sylvie": "She brought me nearly every damned thing, but she didn't bring the jailhouse key."[2]

Belafonte rose to national stardom in the years when anticommunist repression, surveillance, and blacklisting shut down the careers of much better-established mentors and peers. *Becoming Belafonte* decodes the forms of camouflage Belafonte had to don in order to sustain public performing momentum in the Cold War years notoriously inhospitable to radicalism. Belafonte's protective public stance was reinforced and expanded in 1960 with the appearance of music writer Arnold Shaw's "unauthorized" celebrity biography. Shaw had lost his own university teaching position as a result of anticommunist blacklisting, and his account assiduously erased any traces of Belafonte's left-wing political affiliations.[3]

The interracial radical movements that shaped Belafonte's political sensibilities prioritized the demand for racial equality as integral to fulfilling the unmet promises of postwar democracy. They viewed the work of promoting black arts and history and rejecting racial confinement as urgent for black and white allies. By the 1960s, Belafonte's efforts to maintain popular acclaim and political commitments took place amid dramatic shifts in musical tastes and civil rights demands. When integration came to seem incompatible with black power, Belafonte again had to tread carefully to convey his particular artistic and political vision.

Belafonte was unusual among his peers for his determination to leverage his triple-threat celebrity as popular performer, matinee idol, and top-selling recording artist into gaining artistic control within commercial television and film production. As a radical black artist, he was deeply aware of the power of popular cultural forms to deliver crucial messages about citizenship and national belonging. In the United States in the late nineteenth century, efforts to reinstitute racial boundaries via a new legal apparatus of Jim Crow segregation and the mass disenfranchisement of African Americans in the South coincided exactly with the emergence of the mass-culture industries of sound recording, film, and journalism. These developments resulted in the expanded and endless circulation of demeaning stereotyped images of black bodies, black voices, and black culture on records, in print, on-screen, and in radio broadcasting.[4] Belafonte grew up feeling the painful power of those degrading images. At the same time, he knew firsthand the cultural riches and modernity of black experiences that never registered in public popular culture. As a star, he dedicated his efforts to demanding and promoting new forms of black representation across popular media in music, television, and film, challenging conventions and genres audiences were accustomed to expect.

The political significance of publicly circulating racial representation was very clear to Belafonte, convincing him, along with other black arts colleagues, that postwar democracy absolutely required new forms of racial representation imagining multiracial citizenship and belonging. If African Americans were to win the double victory of World War II—against fascism abroad and racism at home—then new forms of racial representation would have to be constructed in order to displace whiteness as the norm and blackness as the problem. This task seemed even more urgent after the 1954 *Brown v. Board of Education* decision discredited long-standing arguments for school segregation and generated a fierce white supremacist backlash. Belafonte consistently drove himself to create and circulate alternative and multifaceted racial representations in music, television, and film that protested racialist exclusions and resisted racialist boundaries while celebrating black arts and culture as foundational, regenerative, and resistant to national boundaries.

How audiences did or did not recognize and respond to Belafonte's efforts as a producer helps explain his mixed record of commercial success and dismal failures in the 1950s and 1960s. Concert crowds and record and ticket sales were the central measure in the culture industries, and the measure that mattered enormously to Belafonte, despite his attraction to challenging material that might not have commercial potential. By and large, white audiences determined commercial success, but the black press closely followed Belafonte's accomplishments, public positions, and pronouncements. Analyzing the reception of Belafonte's work, and especially the *different responses* of black and white critics to Belafonte's television and film projects in the 1950s and 1960s, offers unusual access to otherwise unspoken assumptions about the character and significance of racial difference and to public debates on how best to represent racial equality.

A focus on "becoming" is by definition partial, and Belafonte's lifetime accomplishments extend far beyond these chapters. But locating Belafonte in these decades, as a creative participant in the era's theatrical, musical, and film innovation, as a critical voice in debates over race and representation, and as a visionary radical committed to making a better world, offers an intriguing alternative route to "discovering America."

FROM HARLEM, JAMAICA, AND THE SEGREGATED NAVY TO NEW YORK CITY'S INTERRACIAL LEFT-WING CULTURE, 1927–1948

Growing Up a Working-Class Black Immigrant, 1927–1944

Harry Belafonte's birth in a New York hospital on March 1, 1927, made him the first person in his family to hold U.S. citizenship. His parents were struggling immigrants who had met in 1926 in New York and married sometime before the birth of their first child. Both were the children of interracial unions unremarkable in the Caribbean. Melvine "Millie" Love was the daughter of a black sharecropper and a white Scottish overseer; she left the hills of St. Ann's Parish, Marcus Garvey's birthplace, to follow four siblings to the West Indian outpost in Harlem, supporting herself on household day work. Harold George Bellanfanti was the son of a white Dutch Jewish father and a black Jamaican mother; he worked as a cook in New York restaurants and on United Fruit Company boats making the circuit between New York and ports in the Caribbean and South America.[1]

Belafonte's childhood unfolded across various Harlem locations. He moved between the apartments of West Indian relatives and friends around West 145th Street and

Seventh Avenue. With his mother he waited at the "slave market" corner where white employers sought day workers, on the edge of the Upper East Side. He ran errands at the corner shops run by the Jewish and Italian immigrants who had arrived in previous waves of migration. He had an insider's view of the flourishing underground economy of the numbers syndicate, associated with notorious Jewish and Italian gangsters, because it supported two of Millie Love's siblings. Uniformed sleeping car porters paraded occasionally and proudly in the streets, organizing what would become the first major black union. Even years after the Jamaican born Pan-Africanist Marcus Garvey was jailed in 1925 and deported to Jamaica in 1927, Belafonte accompanied his mother to meetings of Garvey's followers, who discussed collective self-help, economic development, racial independence, and international black allegiance and solidarity. Sundays included Catholic Church services at St. Charles Borromeo, off West 142nd Street, and cheap shows featuring black performers in glorious musical revues at the Apollo Theater on West 125th Street, which opened to black audiences in 1934.[2]

Despite migrant aspirations, ingenuity, and the ceaseless hard work of Belafonte's parents, their household was precarious. Harold's employment was reliable, although he himself was not; Millie's ability to find work was less certain, and maids were always poorly paid. Their poverty was unremarkable and unrelenting. In his memoir, Belafonte recalled childhood feelings of being angry, afraid, and vulnerable, but also the generosity of neighbors and the "camaraderie of poverty." His 1950s interviews emphasized the sensory deprivations of living below working-class respectability. His family crowded into one room of a dark, six-room, cold-water flat they shared with four other families. "We were too poor to own a radio. We were hungry as kids. We didn't even have our own hand-me-downs to wear." With most of the wages spent on food and coal, "the winters were horrible." Like many struggling families, they moved frequently when they could not keep up with the rent and sometimes to elude immigration agents.[3]

Belafonte's mother brought him with her to work when employers permitted it, and otherwise left him in the care of a relative or friend. She also fell back on help from her mother, first leaving Harry with Jane Love for an extended stay in her modest two-room farmhouse in the mountains of the north coast of Jamaica in 1929 when he was eighteen months old.[4]

A quarter of Harlem residents in the early 1930s were out of work; unemployment during the Depression would eventually reach 50 percent. Harlem dwellers faced higher rents and worse housing stock than elsewhere in the city; there were few parks and playgrounds. After Belafonte's younger brother Dennis was born in 1931, their father's absences became more frequent and prolonged. Even as a five-year-old child, Harry was expected to watch the baby on Saturdays while his mother worked.[5]

By 1930, central Harlem was 70 percent black (and it would be almost 100 percent by 1940), but there were still sections where white residents continued to live. At Belafonte's elementary school, PS 186, on West 145th Street between Broadway and Amsterdam Avenue, most of the students were white. Harry responded to their racial taunts and shoves, on the way to school and in the halls, by fighting "every day." Interviewed in 1957, his mother remarked, "as long as he would defend himself like a man I wasn't sorry." Perhaps encouraged by what she had heard at the Garvey meetings, Millie inverted the epithets her son heard at school: "When the boys would yell 'Nigger' at Harry, I would tell him that we were Negro, or they could call us colored . . . We didn't care. Everyone has to have some race. But they were the niggers . . . the niggardly people who were so niggardly in their thinking." In later accounts, Belafonte emphasized the broader perspective conveyed by his mother's instruction to "never ever go to bed at night knowing there was something you could have done during the day to strike a blow against injustice and you didn't do it."[6]

Even with help from her New York siblings, Millie Love barely managed to keep the family together, and she sent Harry back to live with her mother for the 1934–1935 school year. He was far away in March 1935 when Harlem was the scene of spontaneous street attacks against white-owned businesses on West 125th Street, sparked by rumors of police brutality against a teenager caught shoplifting a cheap penknife. On this stay, Harry was old enough to explore the island beyond his grandmother's farm and to run errands by himself in a nearby village. He traveled with relatives and neighbors to the nearest market in Brown's Town, and to the larger market at Ocho Rios, where he watched United Fruit Company employees collect bananas, sugarcane, and mangoes grown by the locals.[7]

Music was part of everyday life in New York's black neighborhoods, recorded music commonly spilling from radios and Victrolas into hallways and out windows, and live music jumping in dance halls, bars, and clubs.[8] When the family was able to afford a radio, Millie and Harry sang along, harmonizing to Tin Pan Alley songs that pop vocalists crooned over the airwaves. In their regular trips to the Apollo, they listened to hot swing bands led by Cab Calloway and Duke Ellington, and to the powerful performances of Billie Holiday and Ella Fitzgerald. For a brief period, Millie's cultural aspirations for her son included renting a piano and managing the cost of weekly lessons with a respected neighborhood music teacher, before giving in to Harry's defiant resistance.[9]

The Depression made it difficult for a domestic worker to support two children in the mid-1930s; in 1936, after ten years in New York, Millie returned to Jamaica to look for work, with nine-year-old Harry and five-year-old Dennis in tow. But falling prices for sugar and wage cuts had heightened local tensions, and unemployment was rising on the island, too. By 1938, the unemployment rate in the capital would approach 50 percent. After several weeks of being unable to find work in Kingston, Millie arranged for the children's board, enrolled them in schools, and returned by herself to New York. Harry and his brother remained in Jamaica until 1940, when Millie brought them back to New York, perhaps worried that the outbreak of war would leave the British colonies vulnerable.[10]

Being in Jamaica for this period, largely on his own, gave Belafonte a special perspective on black life in a British colony. In 1957, Belafonte recalled it as "a lonely time": sometimes he and his brother were with their grandparents, but most often they boarded and were schooled separately.[11] The formal education that Belafonte received in Jamaica provided him with a close-up view of British class and cultural norms and the presumptions of imperial supremacy.

Belafonte observed the varied color palette of West Indian society when among his Jamaican relatives: "If you could see my whole family congregated together, you would see every tonality of color from the darkest black . . . to the ruddiest white. . . ." Color ranking was enmeshed in Jamaica's class hierarchy, and Belafonte discovered its painful ramifications when he boarded with his mother's sister and her white Scots civil-servant husband. When guests came to dinner, Harry's relatives sent him to eat in the kitchen, along with another child who was also considered too brown, lest their darker skin lower the family's light-skinned status.[12]

While Belafonte was living in Kingston, fierce economic and political battles took place in the streets. By the late 1930s, underpaid and laid-off laborers from the countryside were streaming into Kingston. There were increasing confrontations between the minority white elite and black workers in the plantation and port sectors, as well as in civil service. Strikes were common, with organizers associating workers' rights with racial equality. In May 1938, the police attack on striking sugar factory workers sparked riots around the island, including Kingston, where Belafonte witnessed what he later described as a "violent peasant uprising . . . with guns booming and English troops moving in to quell them."[13]

Musical variety was part of everyday street life in Jamaica. Peddlers sang their goods for sale; politicians sang to attract an audience before delivering a speech. Wandering near the wharf, Harry could hear bands playing the Jamaican mento music then popular for tourists arriving on cruise ships. Mento fused Afro-Caribbean and Latin rhythms with the unifying beat of Trinidadian calypso, in both an informal rural style and a more urban, polished dance-band style, sometimes with topical lyrics. By the 1930s, calypso and mento, like other genres of music, spread via commercial recordings and live performance. Their forms and melodies reflected musical influences from other Caribbean islands, Latin American song, and New Orleans–style jazz. Commercial recordings of Trinidadian calypso outsold mento in Jamaican music stores, and Kingston sales of calypso surpassed those in Trinidad. A 1940 observer described the outcome: "Commercialism is no respecter of tradition. Calypso is fast becoming a kind of international Caribbean swing."[14]

When Belafonte returned to Harlem in 1940, he was thirteen and Harlem was crowded and tense, especially along its borders. After the attack on Pearl Harbor, labor shortages lessened unemployment, but a third of residents of central Harlem remained jobless or on relief. The push for wartime unity superseded campaigns for social reforms to address racial inequality. In August 1943, the simmering tensions in Harlem ignited after the arrest of a young black soldier who had been involved in an altercation with a white police officer. Thousands of residents took to the streets, smashing white-owned businesses, and sparing black-owned stores and Chinese laundries, in a rampage against racial confinement and economic exploitation. As the black writer and poet Langston Hughes wrote in 1944, most black people lived where "the rooms are too small, the ceilings too low, and the rents too high."[15]

Looking for cheaper rents in buildings that did not rent to blacks, in a neighborhood of Irish and Greeks, Millie Love turned the racial indeterminacy of her family's physical appearance to her economic advantage: she claimed to be Spanish.[16] Her sons had to manage the challenges of racial passing as they crossed through white territory to sit in crowded mixed classes in the local junior high school, PS 43. Belafonte's racial masquerade as "Frenchy," from Martinique, got him admission to the white boys' lunch table, but he remembered that "having to listen to the kids telling anti-Negro jokes and act like a disinterested third party" left him feeling that he didn't belong anywhere. He would look back on this time as a period of "alienation and racial confusion."[17]

When Harry began high school at George Washington High School in the Bronx in the fall of 1941, he gravitated to the black kids. His mother encouraged him to feel "fierce racial pride"; he later described the pressures of "constant awareness of race, and the daily challenge to fight based on race" in battles between rival black and Puerto Rican street gangs. Although he found the classes difficult, he managed to pass the first semester. Then, to his mother's great disappointment, he quit school. He worked at jobs available to a nonwhite high-school dropout: delivering groceries and moving produce at a local market, pushing racks of clothes in the garment district, and delivering clothes and operating a pressing machine in an uncle's tailor shop. One available alternative to these low-wage jobs was service in the wartime military, so in March 1944, just after his seventeenth birthday and with his mother's permission, he enlisted in the navy.[18]

From Street Rage to a Political Vision, 1944–1945

Belafonte's time in the navy introduced him to the kind of contemporary debates about racial inequality that transformed his political imagination. Intense conversations had been taking place in black communities in 1940 and 1941 about whether to support the "white man's war." Ignoring vocal protest from African American civil rights leaders and their allies, the military strengthened its commitment to segregation in the armed forces. In practice, this meant *expanding* segregation as part of an enlarged wartime military. Segregated Red Cross blood banks were a particularly egregious rejection of science in concession to white supremacy.

The pressing question was how to get the campaign against Jim Crow segregation onto the national agenda. Even before Pearl Harbor, the black labor leader A. Philip Randolph organized local chapters of a March on Washington movement to plan nonviolent civil disobedience to push for desegregation of the military and defense industries. In February 1942, the *Pittsburgh Courier*, a national black newspaper, began to publicize what it called the Double V campaign, a strategy to mobilize the national goals of the fight against fascism in Europe in order to legitimate and build momentum for the fight against white supremacy at home.

Watching the film *Sahara* in a New York theater in December 1943 had offered Belafonte a heroic vision of a black soldier's fight against fascism: Rex Ingram plays a Sudanese officer, allied with the British in North Africa, who kills a German fighter pilot. Although the navy was the most obdurate branch of the military in confining black recruits to menial duties, cracks in its white supremacist practices had begun to appear. Belafonte enlisted at a time when the navy commissioned its first black officers and its first antisubmarine vessel was manned for combat with black sailors. He went through basic training at the newly built all-black Robert Smalls unit at the navy's boot camp at the Great Lakes Training Center near Chicago.[19]

In the segregated navy, Belafonte found a world of class, ethnic, and cultural diversity far beyond what he had known in the Harlem West Indian community. Interviewed in the 1950s, he dated his interest in "Negro culture" to the experience of meeting soldiers who "each came from different parts of the country . . . and had something different to contribute." He had engaged political discussions with college-educated soldiers who pushed him to understand how racial discrimination operated, and would have to be challenged, as part of a national system. "The Southern boys took the attitude that we in the North had run away from the Negro problem and left them to face it alone," Belafonte later explained. His time in the navy was "like taking a deep breath."[20] A friend lent him Du Bois's autobiographical *Dusk of Dawn* (1940), which illuminated how racial difference was shaped by the social heritage of slavery and discrimination ("a black man is a person who must ride Jim Crow in Georgia"). His training continued at the U.S. Navy's Storekeepers School on the grounds of Hampton Institute in Virginia. There Belafonte met and began to date Marguerite Byrd, a psychology major from a respectable and comfortably middle-class black family in Washington, DC. Byrd had grown up assuming racial progress was a gradual outcome of education and effort, and she later recalled their courtship as "one long argument about racial issues."[21]

In 1944 and 1945, the black press publicized arguments among leading black intellectuals that racial discrimination was part of foreign policies supporting colonialism and imperialism around the world. A. Philip Randolph, historian Rayford Logan, and scholar, writer, and NAACP leader W. E. B. Du Bois all called attention to the discrepancies between the 1941 Atlantic Charter's call for national self-determination, the 1944 Bretton Woods agreements ignoring the millions under colonial rule, and the failure of the 1944 Dumbarton Oaks Conference to take up issues of self-government. Without addressing colonial self-determination, Randolph wrote in the spring of 1944, WWII was "a war to continue 'white supremacy,' the theory of Herrenvolk, and the subjugation, domination, and exploitation of the peoples of color. It is a war between the imperialism of Fascism and Nazism and the imperialism of monopoly capitalistic democracy."[22] Du Bois's critique of Dumbarton Oaks, *Color and Democracy: Colonies and Peace*, published in May 1945, asked how could the United States, with its "Negro problem," claim the mantle of world leadership, especially on questions of democracy, given its "legal recognition of race hate, which the Nazis copied in their campaign against the Jews"? How could a "union of nations keep the world's peace . . . so long as these nations are divided in interest over the control and possession of colonies"? African American journalists covering the founding meetings of the United Nations in San Francisco in April 1945 questioned whether wartime commitment to anticolonialism would be sustained and how it would be applied to domestic civil rights.[23]

The segregated military kept many black soldiers stateside, including Belafonte. In Virginia, a run-in with his commanding officer sent him to military prison for two weeks, where he observed superior conditions for Nazi prisoners of war. His training as a storekeeper yielded only a position with munitions loaders. By luck his crew avoided the most dangerous assignment for black sailors, loading live munitions onto ships at Port Chicago, part of the navy fleet city in the San Francisco area where just months before, hundreds had been killed or injured by an explosion. Spending his last months in the service handling live munitions at a navy weapons station in New Jersey, he finished his eighteen-month stint in December 1945, with no particular skills, and outraged by much he had seen. From his fellow soldiers he had gained new intellectual and political frameworks for resisting the racial status quo, and he later recalled his new sense of urgency to figure out how "to organize . . . what would we become when we got out of there? How could we help make things different?"[24]

Left-Wing Black and Interracial Politics and Culture, 1946–1948

Not yet nineteen when he returned to New York in December 1945, Belafonte sought out settings where conversations about dismantling white supremacy and "making things different" were taking place. The combination of labor and civil rights insurgencies, the extensive federal theater and writing projects, and the expansive growth of the new culture industries of radio and sound film after 1935 had provided fertile ground for rethinking and reshaping representations of American democracy. Depression-era disillusionment with the capitalist system and the impact of the alliance with the Soviet Union in fighting Hitler showed up in the results of a poll conducted by *Fortune* magazine in 1942 suggesting that one-quarter of respondents favored socialism, with another 35 percent maintaining an open mind about it. With national acquiescence to Jim Crow so deeply entrenched, a 1942 editorial in the *Chicago Defender*, another national black newspaper, argued that the fight against segregation would require battle on "economic, political, and cultural fronts," emphasizing "the fight on the cultural front" as "one of the most important."[25]

For a brief period during the war, the vision of a labor-led movement against fascism and Jim Crow segregation had coincided with national goals. The groups supporting continuing New Deal social programs and FDR's 1944 re-election ranged from the Communist Party USA—reconstituted as the Communist Political Association in 1944—to liberal Republicans who lost their candidate when Wendell Willkie dropped out of the race (and died shortly after). Although FDR's last electoral victory was his narrowest, and conservatives were poised to dismantle the New Deal and roll back civil rights and labor protections that were passed during the war, many of the broad progressive alliances and coalitions that constituted the post-1935 Popular Front left remained intact and committed to extend African American citizenship rights and to dismantle segregation.[26]

A chance encounter led Belafonte into the intoxicating world of New York's black left-wing theater, the first place he found some of what he was looking for "to make things different." After being discharged from the navy, he returned to his mother's apartment on Amsterdam Avenue, where she now lived with his brother, her new husband, and their two children. Belafonte found work with his stepfather, who worked as a maintenance man for a group of buildings in Harlem, helping him fire furnaces, haul out ashes, and overhaul plumbing. In January 1946, in exchange for hanging her venetian blinds, one tenant, Clarice Taylor, tipped him with a ticket to the closing performance of the American Negro Theater (ANT) production of *Home Is the Hunter,* in which she had a starring role. The dissenting black theater associated with ANT represented a new realm of social possibility for Belafonte. Seeing his first "legitimate play," performed by talented black actors, was a powerful and formative encounter.[27]

Most "legitimate" theater productions cast black actors only as maids and butlers; all-black singing and dancing productions provided other theatrical employment. In the late 1930s, some left-wing writers and directors had mounted productions that began to chip away at theatrical segregation and cast leading black actors: the New York Federal Theater Project's Harlem Unit production of a black-cast *Macbeth,* directed by the young Orson Welles and set in Haiti, and another play about the slave uprising in Haiti. Playwright Shirley Graham, who later married W. E. B. Du Bois, had directed a Chicago Federal Theater Project (FTP) production of black playwright Theodore Ward's play *Big White Fog,* which debated Garveyism, capitalism, and socialism as black political strategies.[28] What Belafonte saw on the ANT stage suggested the power of theater to challenge demeaning forms of racial representation and to dramatize political alternatives.

The ANT company introduced Belafonte to an institution devoted primarily to nurturing black talent and creativity but also committed to a cosmopolitan interracialism. Founders Frederick O'Neal and Abram Hill had set up ANT in 1940 in the basement of the 135th St. branch of the New York Public Library as a cooperative, with the actors sharing expenses and contributing a 2 percent tithe on their earnings from outside productions. In a 1940 letter to a friend, aspiring actress Ruby Dee characterized its politics: "And I mean progressive." ANT's mission was to encourage black creativity and produce new black drama, but the group was also open to the work of white playwrights with social concerns and dramatic range that would expand opportunities for black actors. ANT hired white teachers and accepted white actors and technicians committed to its goals, which, as stated by founder Hill, were to "break down the barriers of Black participation in the theater; to portray Negro life as they honestly saw it, to fill in the gap of a Black theatre which did not exist." Its production of *Anna Lucasta* in August 1944 provided ANT's breakthrough success, drawing large audiences in Harlem before moving to a two-year run on Broadway. Later Belafonte would describe the play's retelling of *Anna Christie,* written by white screenwriter Philip Yordan and adapted for a black cast by a white director, Harry Wagstaff Gribble, as "dancing around the issue of our true condition."[29]

The play Belafonte saw, *Home Is the Hunter,* was ANT's first postwar production. Dramatizing the struggle between a returning Nazi-sympathizing vet, his progressive wife, and the labor leader with whom she allies herself, the play emphasized the parallels between Nazi racialism and right-wing antilabor politics. Eleanor Roosevelt attended its premiere. Although reviewers for mainstream white, left-wing, and black newspapers concurred that a lack of subtlety and clumsy stagecraft marred the production, they recognized the play's social commentary and praised the acting, especially that of Clarice Taylor and Maxwell Glanville. The *Amsterdam News* reviewer noted that the playwright, the modern art dealer and critic Samuel Kootz (whose gallery had recently hosted a one-man show of Romare Bearden) had "snatched copiously from the transcript of the United Auto Workers–General Motors negotiations for his material" and "managed to squeeze in some sharp and deserved barbs at Nazism."[30]

Whatever its dramatic inadequacies, *Home Is the Hunter* may have compelled Belafonte because of its political relevance. The *Amsterdam News* and the *New York Age* described it as a "new anti-fascist play" dealing with "the problems of returned soldiers, industrial unrest, and America's continued fight against fascism." The use of this language revealed a continuing effort to link the fight against Nazism and the fight against white supremacy, a framework that was circulated initially by the black press and the Popular Front Left in the mid-1930s and was reiterated within efforts at home-front mobilization during the war.[31]

In interviews conducted in the 1950s, Belafonte emphasized ANT's collective atmosphere as part of its appeal. When he went backstage to thank the actors, one of them asked him to hold a rope for a minute, and at 3:00 a.m. he was still there, helping them strike the set. "I liked . . . the group feeling. Everybody wanted this theater to work, man; they were all pitching in to help. And it kind of rubbed off on me." Belafonte and his benefactor, Clarice Taylor, were among the young actors whom Ruby Dee described as part of impromptu parties that followed rehearsals, "warm and joyous times with people who felt like family, who felt like my first real friends." At these parties, in the spring of 1946, Ruby Dee remembered that Belafonte "would get up and sing along with the music on the radio." Undeterred by people teasing him and rolling their eyes, "he'd strike his singer's pose, laugh along with us, and keep on singing."[32]

Belafonte did not formally enroll in the ANT-sponsored training program, headed by the actress and teacher Osceola Archer, housed in a borrowed Greenwich Village space at 215 West 11th Street. But hanging around the company, he made friends with ANT student Sidney Poitier, who was just his age and who had lived until he was fifteen on Cat Island and in Nassau in the Bahamas. Belafonte caught the eye of Archer, who cast him "because they needed a 'type' for a certain role" in a February 1946 touring production of ANT director Abram Hill's satire on black bourgeois pretensions, *On Strivers Row.* Archer also cast him in a student production of Frank Gabrielson's light college-life drama, *Days of Our Youth,* which ran for a few days in June 1946. Later Archer would comment that although Belafonte "was just a boy, inexperienced and untutored . . . on stage the electricity and the tremendous appeal came through even then."[33]

Belafonte's most significant experience with ANT was performing the part of the flawed Irish revolutionary Johnny Boyle in a production of Irish Communist Sean O'Casey's play *Juno and the Paycock* in July 1946. The

Harry Belafonte (seated at left) in a scene from ANT production of On Striver's Row *(1946). (Courtesy of American Negro Theater Alumni Photograph Collection, Photographs and Prints Division, Schomburg Center for Research in Black Culture, the New York Public Library, Astor, Lenox and Tilden Foundations.)*

black actors' use of West Indian accents added a new dimension to O'Casey's critique of British imperialism. The *Daily Worker* review credited Belafonte as one of the actors who had successfully revealed the "strength, weakness and frustration drawn by O'Casey."[34] Later in the 1950s, although to claim in public any association with the Left was to risk being blacklisted, Belafonte signaled the political significance for him of appearing in *Juno*. "When I stepped out onstage, I knew I had really truly found the feeling and the thing I wanted to do—I wanted to be an actor and communicate to large masses of people. Here was a chance for me to communicate like I'd never communicated before in my life." Without using overt left-wing language, he described the potential of left-wing popular theater and his

Harry Belafonte (third from left) in a scene from ANT production of Juno and the Paycock *(1946). (Courtesy of American Negro Theater Alumni Photograph Collection, Photographs and Prints Division, Schomburg Center for Research in Black Culture, the New York Public Library, Astor, Lenox and Tilden Foundations.)*

own conversion from individualism to solidarity. "My life had always been such a solitary one, you know. I'd never had any childhood friends or guys I bummed around with. But now this was going to be my destiny, and my way to be with people."[35]

Finding Paul Robeson and Arts Activism

His casting as Johnny Boyle brought Belafonte into contact with Paul Robeson, who was then at the height of his career as both a performer and an advocate for the expansion of multiracial democracy. Robeson had broken through many racial barriers as an all-American college football player, Phi Beta Kappa Rutgers University graduate, lawyer, world-famous concert singer, and actor. His performance as Othello in 1943—in the longest Broadway run of a Shakespeare play—directly challenged the segregationist norm that prohibited love between a white woman and a black man, onstage or off. Robeson used his celebrity to publicly support labor, wartime antifascism, and decolonization and to press for the dismantling of Jim Crow. For Belafonte, Robeson's intertwined artistic and political commitments were formative.

During the war, the national call for unity had increased invitations to Robeson to appear at rallies and on the radio, not only as a singer but also as a citizen-statesman. He spoke at a Labor for Victory Rally in 1943, on broadcasts commemorating Lincoln's birthday in 1944, and at the opening of the United Nations (UN) in 1945. Many admirers, black and white, lavishly praised his artistry, political activism, and internationalism. Sponsors of Robeson's public forty-sixth birthday celebration in April 1944 included a range of celebrated artists, from composer–band leader Duke Ellington and jazz musicians Count Basie, Teddy Wilson, and Mary Lou Williams to dancer Pearl Primus and comedians Zero Mostel and Jimmy Durante. Greetings arrived from the baseball legend Babe Ruth, the Broadway wordsmith and producer Oscar Hammerstein II, writers and playwrights Theodore Dreiser and Lillian Hellman, and a host of national social reformers, politicians, and religious leaders. Just a few months earlier, Robeson had received the Spingarn Medal, the NAACP's highest honor, which cited his "active concern for the rights of the common man of every race, color, religion, and nationality" and his "distinguished achievement in theater and on the concert stage."[36]

Robeson attended one of the ANT performances of *Juno* and came backstage to meet and congratulate the actors. Belafonte later described Robeson's generous response: "Sean O'Casey was a good friend of his. And he couldn't wait to get back to England and meet up with his friend to tell him of black people doing [his play], how magnificent his play really was," and how the Irish had failed to evoke "the deeper resonances." Robeson's chosen path as a performer who used his public prominence to fight against fascism and for racial equality inspired Belafonte.[37]

In addition to offering artistic encouragement, Robeson introduced Belafonte to the interracial left-wing political organizing that prioritized the dismantling of white supremacy as central to progressive social change. In 1946, Robeson remained in demand as a prominent spokesperson for the labor–civil rights coalition that had supported FDR and the social safety net identified with the New Deal, articulating the political goals espoused by Popular Front organizations such as the National Negro Congress (NNC) and its successor organization, the Civil Rights Congress (CRC). These groups opposed conservative attacks on labor rights and the segregationist violence directed against black veterans and civil rights activists, challenged the national acquiescence to Jim Crow, and agitated for the establishment of a permanent Fair Employment Practices Commission (FEPC).[38]

Robeson and Du Bois together chaired the Council on African Affairs (CAA), an organization that supported decolonization and made the connection between the struggles of African Americans, movements for Indian independence, Nigerian trade unions, and opposition to legally mandated apartheid in South Africa. At numerous rallies and meetings, Robeson articulated the postwar concerns Du Bois had formulated in *Color and Democracy*, speaking out against U.S. foreign policies that supported colonial empires and increased the polarization between the United States and the Union of Soviet Socialist Republics (USSR).[39]

Robeson's rally appearances integrated politics and culture. At one CAA rally in June 1946 in Madison Square Garden, nineteen thousand people came to hear Robeson link struggles in the United States to those in other parts of the world. They also listened to jazz musicians, a black gospel quartet, white and black folksingers presenting a history of the connections between African and African American music, and Robeson performing with the Congress of Industrial Organizations (CIO) chorus.[40]

Robeson helped lead the Independent Citizens Committee of the Arts, Sciences, and the Professions (ICCASP), which grew out of a group organized to support Roosevelt's reelection. Other conveners from the arts included actors Canada Lee, James Cagney, Gene Kelly, José Ferrer, and Orson Welles, alongside Ellington, Hammerstein, and composer Aaron Copeland. ICCASP members met in subcommittees for theater, radio, film, literature, music and art, as well as science and technology, medicine, and education. Its platform supported "full employment and a decent standard of living in post-war America; the extension of democracy in the United States; extension of democracy abroad," and worldwide peace through the agency of the UN. One of ICCASP's specialties was producing events in the style of the CAA rally, using entertainers to enliven political rallies by supporting the speeches with related skits and music. Robeson's radical activism in this period did not diminish his popularity; he drew huge crowds in Harlem and his concert in June 1947 would sell out Lewisohn Stadium.[41] Robeson showed Belafonte how to connect cultural work with political activism: where to go, whom to work with, and how to "make things different."

By August 1946, demonstrations and mass meetings around the country in Chicago, Philadelphia, New York City, and Washington, DC, protested the "rising tide of fascist terror" against black veterans and citizens in the South and the North. Belafonte was in Washington, DC, around Labor Day in 1946, combining a visit to Marguerite Byrd with participating in "a youth protest group marching on the White House."[42] This action may have been con-

Paul Robeson (second from left) picketing with members of the Baltimore NAACP in front of Ford's Theater, Baltimore, to protest the theater's policy of racial segregation (1947). Behind Robeson is the composer Earl Robinson. (Courtesy of American Negro Theater Alumni Photograph Collection, Prints and Photographs Division, Schomburg Center for Research in Black Culture, the New York Public Library, Astor, Lenox and Tilden Foundations.)

nected to the Civil Rights Congress's first campaign, a petition to unseat Theodore Bilbo, the rabid white supremacist conservative senator from Mississippi who led the southern filibuster to oppose the FEPC. Belafonte may also have been involved with a Washington, DC, action by hundreds of black and white members of the United Negro and Allied Veterans of America (UNAVA), the largest association of black veterans formed because segregation excluded blacks from mainstream organization such as the American Legion and the Veterans of Foreign Wars. UNAVA, convened in April 1946 as an interracial advocacy group, shared the broad vision of the CRC, bringing members to the Capitol in September 1946 with demands to pass antilynching legislation, repeal the poll tax, and unseat Bilbo.[43]

Belafonte was present at the ICCASP-organized Madison Square Garden rally on September 12, 1946, pressing a ticket to the event into the hand of the young African American actor Ossie Davis when they bumped into each other on the street outside. Speakers at the event challenged the Cold War direction of Truman's foreign policy and his lack of support for the Fair Employment Practices Commission and protested what appeared to be increasing racist violence. The February shooting of two black veterans at the hands of Long Island police; the lynching in July of two black couples in Monroe, Georgia; and the February blinding of the black solider Isaac Woodard, still in uniform, by a South Carolina police officer galvanized concern that wartime hopes of social transformation were running aground in the face of Jim Crow's intransigence. The celebrity actor-director Orson Welles, prodded by the radical black *Amsterdam News* cartoonist Oliver Harrington, who was then publicity director for the NAACP, had been calling attention to the Woodard case on weekly national radio broadcasts through the summer.[44]

Robeson, featured speaker, demanded government action to stop "this swelling wave of lynch murders and mob assaults against Negro men and women." Rally entertainers included the comedian Zero Mostel, the dancer Pearl Primus, and the CIO chorus. In his featured speech, Secretary of Commerce Henry Wallace, Roosevelt's former secretary of agriculture (1933–1940) and vice president (1941–1944), challenged Truman's "get-tough-with-Russia" foreign policy. This speech led to his firing from Truman's cabinet and ultimately to his candidacy for president in the Progressive Party campaign the following year. Wallace's refusal to engage in Cold War posturing and his commitment to desegregation crystallized debate over the direction of U.S. postwar policies: prioritize the social reform legacy associated with FDR or follow the lead of an increasingly hawkish Harry Truman?[45]

Stage Left, 1946–1948

In the fall of 1946, at the age of nineteen, Belafonte gambled on training in the performing arts. Seeking out the theatrical Left, he enrolled in the innovative Dramatic Workshop, affiliated with the New School for Social Research in Greenwich Village. Belafonte didn't have a high school diploma, but he was able to talk his way into the college-level program and use his GI benefits to pay the tuition. He left his mother's apartment in Harlem to move in with people he met through ANT, first on Bleecker Street and then in the Eighties, off Central Park West.[46]

The Dramatic Workshop was a magnet for actors who wanted to learn the techniques of 1930s radical theater. The New School had a history of offering refuge to artists fleeing fascism; the Dramatic Workshop was established in 1940 to support the work of Erwin Piscator, a prominent left-wing German theatrical producer, theorist, and colleague of Marxist playwright Bertolt Brecht and Communist composer Hans Eisler. Piscator's politically inspired innovations in Berlin in the 1920s and 1930s were well known in U.S. left-wing theatrical circles, and they had provided an important model for the use of projected film and documentary technique in the Federal Theater Project's Living Newspapers in the late 1930s. Stella Adler and Mordecai Gorelik, former members of the left-wing Group Theatre, taught acting and set design. Piscator taught directing, and his wife, Maria, dance.[47]

The Dramatic Workshop was a nearly all-white world, but a number of its members were Jewish and came from ethnic working-class backgrounds. Although Belafonte was one of only a few black students in that period, some of his classmates were also working-class WWII veterans with GI benefits. Among them were Walter Matthau, Rod Steiger, and Bernard Schwartz (later renamed Tony Curtis). These artists would carry into the 1950s the spirit of the 1930s Popular Front stars: ethnic, working-class musicians and actors such as Benny Goodman, Artie Shaw, Frank Sinatra, Billie Holliday, Count Basie, Paul Muni (Meshilem Meier Weisenfreund), Rita Hayworth (Margarita Carmen Cansino), Sylvia Sidney (Sophia Kosow), Charlie Chaplin, and Joan Crawford (Lucille LeSueur). Bea Arthur was from a middle-class family, but she too had served in the military, in the Women's Reserves of the Marine Corps. Another student at the Dramatic Workshop, Marlon Brando, classified 4F, also from a middle-class family, had taken classes in 1943–1944, and then appeared in two Broadway plays: the long-running hit play *I Remember Mama* (1944) and *Truckline Café* (1946). By the time Belafonte enrolled in the program, Brando no longer attended classes regularly, but he was a charismatic presence in its social world and became friends with Belafonte. Brando took lessons in Afro-Cuban dance and drumming at the black anthropologist-choreographer Katherine Dunham's School of Dance; Belafonte guided him uptown to Harlem jazz clubs.[48]

The Dramatic Workshop aspired to produce cutting-edge left-wing drama of social engagement and theatrical experimentation. Piscator insisted that "it is the business of the theatre to deliver a social message," while at the same time offering "a magnificent evening in the theater." While Belafonte was training, the Dramatic Workshop mounted the first American production of Jean-Paul Sartre's *The Flies* and Robert Penn Warren's first stage adaptation of his Pulitzer Prize–winning 1946 novel, *All the King's Men*. In Belafonte's theater-history course with John Gassner—who years earlier had taught ANT founder Abe Hill at Columbia—Workshop students presented a "March of Drama Repertory," staging passages of plays in "open rehearsals" punctuated by lectures and discussions.[49]

Taking part in the Dramatic Workshop immersed Belafonte in left-wing and experimental theater of the 1930s and 1940s. Encountering the classic works of the literary Left encouraged Belafonte to rethink and revalue his own experiences, turning the indignities of poverty, racism, and colonialism into the basis of a powerful social and economic analysis. Later he would describe playwrights Clifford Odets and Arthur Miller as "great social thinkers" and note the influence of stories by Sholem Aleichem and other plays by Sean O'Casey. These writers "put me in touch with worlds that I did not know, made me see how relevant these people were to my world—and how relevant I was to theirs. This was the culture that captivated the mind of a young black kid, born in poverty in Harlem, growing up in the plantations of Jamaica."[50]

Belafonte's hopes for the future were focused on mastering acting and stagecraft, but singing and musical theater were also part of his Dramatic Workshop experience. Visiting instructors from Katherine Dunham's dance school gave demonstrations for students in Gassner's theater class. One of these teachers was the white dancer Julie Robinson, a close friend of Brando, who would later become Belafonte's second wife.[51]

The presence of dance and music in Dramatic Workshop curriculum resulted from the experimental cross-fertilization between different creative arts and the integration of classical and popular forms. This mixture was characteristic of progressive theatrical ferment in this period, in both mainstream Broadway productions and left-wing entertainment. Music and dance were widely understood to be popular art forms that celebrated the creativity and resilience of ordinary people; they could supplement proud noncomedic genres in which black artists performed resisting visions of racial equality that might educate white audiences and inspire black ones.

New hybrid forms of musical theater fusing political expression with musical idioms from vaudeville, Tin Pan Alley, and jazz had been one of the hallmarks of left-wing culture since the late 1930s. This development was exemplified by Marc Blitzstein's 1937 labor opera, *The Cradle Will Rock*; Harold Rome's 1937 ILGWU Labor Stage presentation of the musical revue *Pins and Needles*, which ran for three years on Broadway; Langston Hughes's 1938 Harlem Suitcase Theater staging of *Don't You Want to be Free?*, a "poetry play . . . with music, singing and dancing"; and Duke Ellington's 1941 musical revue–history of black America, *Jump for Joy*.[52] Richard Rodgers's and Oscar Hammerstein's seamless dramatic integration of music, ballet, and story in the 1943 production of *Oklahoma!* led to a record-breaking five-year run on Broadway. Hammerstein's 1943 updating of Bizet's opera *Carmen* as *Carmen Jones*, a wartime star-crossed romance between a black soldier and a black factory worker, ran for nearly two years.

Belafonte's performing experience at the Dramatic Workshop included singing. For an adaptation of Steinbeck's 1937 novella-play, *Of Mice and Men*, the director Peter Frye, associated previously with various left-wing theater groups, including the Workers' Lab Theater, the Theater of Action, and Michael Chekhov's acting classes, added an extra character, "a singing wayfaring stranger who links the scenes." He proposed an opening with the wayfarer singing "Goodnight Irene," the signature song of the Louisiana musician and ex-convict Huddie Ledbetter, who had begun to perform and record in New York in 1935. Frye learned this song in the summer of 1938, when Ledbetter, known as Lead Belly, performed at the interracial Camp Unity, a vacation resort in the Communist cultural orbit, where Frye served as social director. After an experienced white actor–folksinger initially cast as the wayfaring stranger quit the Workshop, without hesitation Frye offered the part to one of the new students, "a tall, slender, very beautiful black boy. I said to him one day, 'Harry can you sing?'" To open the show and to cover scene changes, the wayfaring stranger appeared out of a darkened corner of the stage and sang Depression-era songs of migrant labor as well as Woody Guthrie and Lead Belly tunes. Belafonte later commented that the demands of inhabiting this character taught him to command the stage through song.[53]

For a 1947 Dramatic Workshop revue called *Middleman, What Now?*, about returning soldiers, Belafonte performed an original song. He had written "Recognition" in the style of cabaret blues, a fusion of jazz and political cabaret associated with left-wing musical performances, in particular the late 1930s music of Billie Holiday and Josh White at the interracial Greenwich Village nightclub Cafe Society.[54] Its original lyrics referred to black veterans facing Jim Crow ("They won't let me forget I'm dark"), borrowed Du Bois's famous formulation ("My color's put a veil on me"), and like Billie Holiday's rendition of "Strange Fruit," protested the persistence of lynching. Its refrain demanded recognition for a man who intended to take his place in the unfolding freedom struggle. The actress Ellen Holly, then a high school student from a middle-class black family, remembered hearing Belafonte sing "Recognition" at a winter 1947 benefit for the *New York Amsterdam News*. While she was dazzled by his physical beauty, she "experienced the song as a revelation," sung with "burning intensity."[55]

Belafonte had reason to imagine he might find a place onstage. During the theater seasons of 1945–1946, and 1947–1948, while he was a Dramatic Workshop student, a number of Broadway productions provided new openings for black actors. These included dramas calling attention to racial inequality (*Deep Are the Roots, Strange Fruit, On Whitman Avenue*, and *Jeb*) and classical drama with an all-black cast (*Lysistrata*). Revivals and new musicals like *Show Boat, Carmen Jones,* and *St. Louis Woman* also offered star roles for black performers. In December 1946, Duke Ellington's music transformed John Gay's satirical ballad opera of inverted social hierarchy, The *Beggar's Opera,* into *The Beggar's Holiday,* featuring a white gangster and a black chief of police that overturned Broadway racial casting conventions.[56] Yip Harburg, Burton Lane, and Fred Saidy's 1947 musical, *Finian's Rainbow,* featuring an interracial cast and a satirical critique of southern conservative racial politics, had a long and successful Broadway run. Langston Hughes and Kurt Weill collaborated on an opera version of Elmer Rice's popular 1927 tenement drama *Street Scene,* which opened in January 1947. Katherine Dunham's company followed its 1945–1946 production of a "musical play of the West Indies" with a 1947 Broadway production of *Bal Negre.*[57] Not all of these productions were commercially successful, but to an aspiring black actor, they offered hope that the theater was becoming less constrained by conventionally stereotypical racial representation.

New York Musical Insurgencies

As a student, Belafonte was exposed to a broad range of musical styles. Left-wing composers and lyricists wrote across the genres, from Broadway show tunes, pop standards, cantata-styled choral pieces, and cabaret blues to jazz ballads. Left-wing rallies and benefits featured an expansive and eclectic range of musical performance, from labor choruses to jazz, country blues, gospel, and the American vernacular musical traditions loosely grouped as "folk music." Because their performance added a visual and aural challenge to norms of segregation, the participation of black artists was a particularly crucial aspect of these events. The black performers who stood with white friends and allies to publicly oppose injustice and inequality expanded the power and appeal of the cultural front.

In 1946, Belafonte was particularly drawn toward two forms of musical innovation, bebop jazz and folk music, showcasing black artistry and cosmopolitan cultural exchange. Almost all of the big swing dance bands, white and black, were disbanding because of the rising cost of travel and shifting habits of leisure entertainment. Louis Jordan's hard-driving jump blues was one of the new forms pioneered by black musicians who had previously played in the big bands. The innovation Belafonte found most compelling was bebop, which broke with the conventions of swing to experiment with harmonics, use of dissonance, and polyrhythmic interplay between soloists and rhythm sections. Beginning in after-hours sessions in Harlem clubs during the war, after 1944 bebop experimenters Kenny Clarke, Thelonious Monk, Dizzy Gillespie, and Charlie Parker had moved down to clubs on 52nd Street that were already known for hosting small-combo Dixieland and small-group swing.[58]

The bebop scene did not respect racial or ethnic boundaries. The move to 52nd Street meant that bebop's uptown musical experimentation, highlighting black modern urbanity, became more accessible to white musicians and to both white and black jazz fans.[59] Bebop musicians valued the broadened exposure: Dizzy Gillespie later recalled that "it took some time, but 52nd St. gave us the rooms to play and the audiences," especially in its heyday in the late 1940s. White enthusiasm for hot swing during the war had resulted in a crackdown on mixed dancing at Harlem's popular Savoy Ballroom, a prohibition on the Savoy hiring white bands or advertising in white newspapers, and a temporary closure in 1943. Bebop clubs' informal interracial interchanges, onstage and off, raised hackles and sparked police harassment on the grounds of "promiscuous mingling." Bebop musicians employed another form of "promiscuous mingling" in their experimentation with African and Afro-Cuban rhythms. Gillespie, who had worked with the Cuban jazz trumpet player Mario Bauzá in Chick Webb's big band in the 1930s, was especially identified with Afro-Cuban jazz after he began to work with the great Cuban percussionist Chano Pozo who had moved to New York in September 1947.[60]

Belafonte spent many nights at the Royal Roost, a club around the corner from the Dramatic Workshop's main theater, at the time when the jazz scene was migrating from 52nd Street to Broadway. The Royal Roost was a club particularly identified with bop, and it cultivated an interracial youth audience. The white promoter–booking agent Monte Kay, who had been running after-hours jam sessions of musicians since the early 1940s, joined with the late-night deejay, white jazz fanatic "Symphony Sid" Torin, bringing top musicians, including Charlie "Bird" Parker, Miles Davis, Fats Navarro, and Dexter Gordon, to play off-night concerts there. Kay instituted a bleacher-seating policy designed to attract young people, black and white; for a modest cover, they could listen without buying a drink. These sessions at the club, promoted through print and radio ads, soon drew crowds. Symphony Sid, whose broadcasts from the Three Deuces on 52nd Street were popular in Harlem, began to broadcast live from the Roost when the club started to book bop artists nightly in June 1948. Saxophonist Lester Young wrote the show's theme song, "Jumpin' with Symphony Sid." The Roost's set-up minimized distance between artists and audience; one fan remembered "a complete rapport . . . we were members of the same cult." Symphony Sid's broadcasts broadened the fan base, as he invited the radio audience to come right into "the House that Bop Built, the Royal Roost, the Metropolitan Bopera House" to enjoy the musicians' innovations.[61]

After finishing at the Dramatic Workshop, Belafonte hung out at the Royal Roost, and sometimes even "did my homework in the club when I had an analysis due for the theater." There he talked with Charlie Parker and with Lester Young, who had just finished a bruising stint in the military. Both Monte Kay and Lester Young attended a Dramatic Workshop performance in which Belafonte sang. He was close enough to the musicians to run errands for them. Trumpeter Kenny Dorham recalled that in December 1948 it was Belafonte who delivered Bird's request that Dorham substitute for Miles Davis in their Roost gig.[62]

The cultural politics associated with bebop, its effort to create music in live performance that could not be "covered" by white musicians, its demonstration of rich African American creativity, musical artistry and sophistication, and its interracial collaboration all appealed to Belafonte. He would later comment that he "saw jazz not only as an expression of ourselves but also an expression of our protest." One 1948 jazz critic identified this protest as opposing the "monopoly control of music, and the commodity-like exploitation of the musicians." Jazz and swing had been the dominant popular music of the CIO, and radicals in the jazz world resisted Jim Crow whenever they could.[63]

Many jazz musicians made these connections with protest explicit when they performed at rallies and benefits connecting labor, antifascism, and civil rights throughout the war and in the months following the peace. For example, Duke Ellington was a sponsor of a benefit concert highlighting the history of jazz at Town Hall for the American Committee for Yugoslav Relief in January 1946, and he was on the board of directors of the ICCASP in June 1946. Charlie Parker and Dizzy Gillespie were among those performing at a "Salute to Negro Veterans," a benefit concert kicking off a national conference of the radical interracial veterans' organization UNAVA, at Town Hall on May 31, 1947. Mercer Ellington, Duke's son, had been among those at the founding convention of UNAVA in Chicago the previous spring.[64]

The other form of musical innovation compelling Belafonte was the folk repertoire drawing on regional and international vernacular music, which he encountered at many events associated with the issues he cared about. This music was performed by black musicians such as Lead Belly, former Piedmont street musicians Josh White, Sonny Terry, and Brownie McGhee, and Trinidad-born calypso singer Lord Invader (Rupert Grant). White musicians publicly identified with a folk repertoire included Oklahoma dust-bowl poet Woody Guthrie, Harvard-educated song collector Pete Seeger, Arkansas labor song leader Lee Hayes, and Illinois ballad singer Burl Ives.[65]

Vernacular music, circulating more broadly by the mid-1930s, had gained in popularity on recordings and on radio during World War II. The migration of defense workers relocated listeners who were accustomed to regional sounds, and in some cases it created musical audiences willing to cross the color line in centers of industrial production such as Detroit, Chicago, San Francisco, and Los Angeles. Soldiers also expanded their musical range in various directions. In his time in the army, Pete Seeger found that he could lead enlisted New Yorkers and southerners in singing what he referred to as "common denominator songs": these included "Latin and calypso songs, blues, old pop tunes, and hillbilly songs." Stationed in Liberia, Georgia-born Ossie Davis, was thrilled to hear calypso songs, which he recognized as "topical, funny, and satirical, just like the calypsos I had heard and loved" in Harlem in the late 1930s. Belafonte's future songwriter Irving Burgie, the Brooklyn-born son of a Barbadian mother and an African American father, learned music theory and alto sax from another black Brooklyn solider stationed with him in Burma, broadening his musical exposure beyond the Tin Pan Alley, jazz, blues, and pop songs he absorbed from the radio.[66]

The term "folk music" was attached to many different kinds of white and black musical production in the

1940s. The music industry publication *Billboard* observed new commercial vitality for the white-performed western and southern music it now grouped within in the category of folk, as a polite substitute for prior labels of "hillbilly" and "old time music." "Folk Music" included the traditional American and Anglo-American ballads sung on radio and record by white artists Richard Dyer-Bennett, Burl Ives, and the popular female vocalist Jo Stafford. It encompassed the Piedmont-style blues performed and recorded by black artists Josh White, Sonny Terry, and Brownie McGhee. "Folk" described the music Josh White and the Golden Gate Quartet were invited to sing for Franklin and Eleanor Roosevelt at the White House on several occasions after 1940, prominently reported in *Ebony*. The left-wing Almanac Singers, then including Guthrie, Seeger, and Hayes, performed topical songs they called "folk songs" for unions, on picket lines, and at rallies. The radio sound track for a CBS series *This Is War* in 1942 consisted of the mountain ballad "Old Joe Clark" turned by Woody Guthrie into "Round and Round Hitler's Grave."[67]

In New York, Trinidad-based calypso music, including the topical verses emerging from competitions between calypso singers, was promoted as folk music. Starting in 1934, Paul Robeson's concert repertoire had included what he called international folk songs—Russian, Jewish, Irish, Scottish, Welsh, Finnish, and Mexican—which he spoke of as "the music of basic realities, the spontaneous expression by the people for the people of elemental emotions." Contemporary cantatas, such as Earl Robinson's "Ballad for Americans," with which Paul Robeson had dazzled audiences on CBS radio in November 1939, and *The Lonesome Train*, a cantata written by Robinson and Millard Lampell about Lincoln's death but played frequently on the radio after FDR's death in April 1945, were also categorized as folk music.[68]

These various genres of folk music circulated commercially and informally. Small record labels—such as Moe Asch's early Asch, Disc, and Stinson labels—and commercial operations such as Decca were actively recording all these categories of music. Radio disc jockeys and jukeboxes, cultivating local racial cultures and ethnic musical tastes, played the recordings. Vernacular musical exchanges facilitated by the military's enforced migrations and heterogeneity persisted as a musical sensibility. When Belafonte's future musical director, army veteran and Juilliard music student Robert DeCormier, spent time with soldier buddies after the war, "singing folk music was always a big part of that."[69]

Folk had also migrated to Broadway's musical theater in the 1940s, with varying degrees of acceptance and success. Robeson and Josh White had appeared in a very short-lived performance of a folk musical, *John Henry*, in 1940. *Sing Out, Sweet Land*, "a Salute to American Folk and Popular Music"—written and conducted by the left-wing composer Elie Siegmeister, with musical performances by Juanita Hall and Burl Ives—opened in 1945. Alan Lomax named 1946 "the year that American folk songs came to town," commenting that "there is likely to be a ballad singer in Scene 1 of any of the new Broadway shows nowadays." The central plot of the successful 1947 Broadway musical *Finian's Rainbow* relied on the audience's familiarity with left-promoted folk musicians and music. A black sharecropper named "Sonny" performed the harmonica music that opened the show; the character was played by Sonny Terry himself. The male romantic lead, "Woody," appeared onstage carrying a guitar. The stage directions connect this Woody to his real-life counterpart, describing him as "wearing the navy blue garb as a merchant seaman . . . back from fighting fascism" and speaking in a "Talking Union Blues rhythm."[70] Belafonte himself had sung the music of Lead Belly and Guthrie in the Dramatic Workshop's production *Of Mice and Men*.

Folk singing and performance flourished as part of the social world of the New York Left during Belafonte's Dramatic Workshop years, in part through the efforts of the new music organization People's Songs. Pete Seeger, Woody Guthrie, and Alan Lomax, just coming out of the military in late 1945 and early 1946, were interested in using music to support radical organizing. Seeger and his friends convened People's Songs as a means to bring together singers and musicians from various racial and ethnic backgrounds to build on the momentum for labor unions and radical protest connected with the wave of strikes initiated after the war by auto and electrical workers, meat packers, coal miners, and teachers.

People's Songs gained attention and members through public performances, formal concerts, and informal weekly gatherings that got audiences involved in the singing. The first publicly advertised People's Song "Hootenanny" took place in March 1946, featuring Lead Belly, Sonny Terry, Brownie McGhee, Woody Guthrie, Lee Hayes, Alan Lomax, and the CIO chorus. In an early mission statement, the group wrote, "We believe that songs should be concerned with more than just 'June-moon-croon.' There is a need for songs about things in the world about us, and songs expressing the deepest aspirations of all the people for freedom and equality." Seeger himself wanted to be part of a singing labor movement: "Just as every church has a choir, why not every union?" He imagined a collaboration of "every kind of musical expression which can be of use to people's organizations: folk, jazz, popular, or serious cantatas for union choruses."[71] People's Song spaces provided an interracial meeting ground where people looking for like-minded radicals might find one another. Robert DeCormier, then a member of the CIO chorus, was at Juilliard when he met Harry Belafonte, who was just starting at the Dramatic Workshop. "We were both hanging out in the same places . . . wherever folk music was, if Lead Belly was doing something, if Woody Guthrie was doing something organized by People's Songs, he was there, I was there."[72]

People's Songs embraced calypso, a form that was brought to New York by Trinidadian musicians who had come to record in the late 1930s and had stayed on. When *Time* wrote about a People's Song hootenanny in April 1946, the reporter likened the atmosphere to "the spontaneity and enthusiasm of the competitive chants of calypso singers in Trinidad." Lord Invader's version of "And God Made Us All," was published in the *People's Songs Bulletin* in July 1946; in November, "Walk in Peace," written by Los Angeles–based Trinidad-born calypso singer Sir Lancelot, was featured as People's Song of the Week.[73]

People's Songs events routinely showcased black as well as white performers collaborating on programs variously billed as a "Union Hoot," "Freedom Hoot," and "State of the Nation Hoot," all protesting racial inequality. These were formal performances, often with a period at the end when performers encouraged the audience to join in. Coverage of People's Songs in Baltimore's black newspaper, the *Afro-American*, emphasized its interracial mission to provide new songs for "Americans of all races, creeds and colors" that would tell of "their battles against discrimination, against a rising cost of living . . . the acute housing shortage . . . [and] reactionary legislators" in Congress. The accompanying picture was of Seeger and Lomax with Lord Invader. The article prominently featured black musicians who were "members and performers" in People's Songs—"Brownie McGhee, singer, Sonny Terry, blind harmonica player from North Carolina . . . Huddie Ledbetter, king of the twelve-string guitar"—and others who would appear on upcoming programs: Big Bill Broonzy, "famous calypso singer" Rupert Grant [Lord Invader], Josh White, and his friend and bass player Sam Gary. The People's Song publicity director interviewed for the article (identified as "Felix Landau, white") emphasized that the organization's musical range, including "fine arts composers and pop song writers." Other black musicians contributed ballads, New Orleans barrelhouse blues piano, prison songs, and country blues to People's Songs weekly concerts in August and September 1946.[74]

People's Songs relied on a range of musical traditions to represent "freedom." A "Songs of Freedom" Hootenanny at Town Hall in New York City on May 12, 1946, included a program of "American soldier songs of the Revolution and the Civil and World Wars; Negro spirituals, work songs and blues; calypsos; a song of the natives of the Mariana Islands; and Scottish, Irish, Jewish and Chinese folk melodies voicing the spirit of freedom." The performers included Josh White, Lord Invader, Pete Seeger, and Lee Hayes.[75]

Peoples Songs intentionally juxtaposed black and white music as folk genres in a series of "Midnight Special" Town Hall concerts, organized by Alan Lomax. "Blues at Midnight" on November 9, 1946, featured Big Bill Broonzy, Sonny Terry and Brownie McGhee, along with McGhee's brother and his band. "Strings at Midnight," on December 7, 1946 presented a musical dialogue between Seeger's banjo versions of mountain ballads, blues, and square dances and Carlos Montoya's guitar versions of Spanish *fandanguillos, mulerias,* and flamenco ballads. "Calypso at Midnight," on December 21, 1946, showcased the hit calypso tunes popularized by jump blues singer Louis Jordan and others but here performed by New York–based Trinidadian performers, band leader Gerald Clark, Lord of Iron, and MacBeth the Great, along with Lord Invader. Spring concerts in 1947 presented spirituals, mountain music, and, most successfully, "Honkytonk Blues at Midnight," introducing southern low-down blues performed by Big Bill Broonzy, Memphis Slim, and Sonny Boy Williamson.[76]

People's Songs encouraged support for labor militancy. The September 1946 People's Songs record, *Songs for Polit-*

ical Action, produced in collaboration with the CIO's Political Action Committee, protested inflation and segregation with songs such as "A Dollar Ain't a Dollar Anymore," and "No, No, No Discrimination." Concert-style performances and weekly sing-alongs took place in New York union halls, such as the Fraternal Clubhouse on 48th Street, where the Greater New York CIO convened, and on the top floor of 13 Astor Place, the building owned by Local 65 of the Warehouse and Wholesale Workers Union, where New York's United Public Workers met.[77]

The multiple musical traditions Belafonte discovered in these Left and labor venues deepened his understanding of black and working-class history and culture. He remembered that when he saw Lead Belly, Josh White, and Bill Broonzy, he felt that he "began to hear the black voice in song in a way I'd never heard it before. I'd heard it in gospel. I'd heard it in spiritual music. I'd heard it, certainly, singing the refined music of the cultural world that Marian Anderson and Paul Robeson sang, but never quite the way I heard them sing about the plight and the conditions of working people." Later, he reflected on what these songs taught him: "I had no tradition. . . . I did not come from the black church. I didn't come from workers in the dust bowl. I didn't come from miners. I hardly really knew who I was."[78]

Performing Progressive Politics

Still supported by his GI Bill stipend, Belafonte did not yet need to make a living within the heady world of theater, music, and politics. He had resumed his relationship with Marguerite Byrd, now doing graduate work in education in New York, continuing their "long argument about racial issues." When he rode the subway, Belafonte was offended by the presumptive whiteness of advertisements, and he challenged their message by writing on them, "What about Negro hands?" and "What if your skin is yellow or black?"

He used posters calling for "tolerance" as an invitation to broadcast that "there is prejudice in America!" Byrd saw Belafonte's subway writing as an ineffective protest. The black middle-class norms of racial uplift, stability, and respectability within which she had been raised clashed with the oppositional spirit and sexual experimentation characteristic in the left-wing circles associated with arts and theater in which Belafonte now moved. Byrd lived in a teachers' dormitory connected with the Bethany Day Nursery where she worked. She and Belafonte frequented separate social universes, although their differences did not interfere with their pursuing a courtship.[79] The prospect of marriage increased the pressure on him to make a living in the theater.

Working hard at the actor's craft did not enable Belafonte to support himself as an actor. He watched as his white classmates were offered parts on stage and screen. Theatrical roles for black actors were scarce: the postwar promise of theater introducing new kinds of black characters was not fulfilled beyond those few plays depicting the wrongs of racial discrimination. Black playwrights faced many obstacles in getting their work staged; parts for black actors did not expand significantly beyond those roles as maids and butlers. Canada Lee's "color-blind" casting as the presumptively white Daniel de Bosola in the British restoration drama *Duchess of Malfi* in the fall of 1946 was publicly admired but not repeated.[80] Black actors got parts in a few all-black or majority-black productions, such as the short-lived *Lysistrata*, in which Sidney Poitier made his Broadway debut, and the musical *Lost in the Stars*, an adaptation of Alan Paton's *Cry the Beloved Country* that provided significant roles for Todd Duncan and Julian Mayfield.

Belafonte did get a small part in *Sojourner Truth*, one of ANT's last productions, directed by Osceola Archer. This play, exploring the life of the nineteenth-century abolitionist and women's rights advocate, opened in April 1948, in the Kaufman Auditorium of the 92nd Street YMHA (now known as the 92nd Street Y), before moving to the ANT space in the Elks Club on 125th Street. Belafonte hoped that this role would be significant for his career. Although not on Broadway, it was a commercial production, and a step beyond his student work. The lead actress, Muriel Smith, had won critical acclaim for her starring role in the long-running stage production of *Carmen Jones*, but *Sojourner Truth* had only a modest run, and the critical response to it was tepid. *New York Times* critic Brooks Atkinson admired Smith's performance in the title role, but he saw "little theatrical skill in the writing" and "only a feeble sort of theatre skill in the staging." The *Phylon* reviewer Miles Jefferson pronounced Smith's performance "superb" but concurred with Atkinson's overall assessment, dismissing the production as "trifling."[81] Unable to attract theatrical works consistent with its mission, ANT moved toward dissolution.

Whatever his talent, Belafonte realized that "the only thing they would let me read for was Uncle Tom parts." It was almost impossible "for a man who's got brown skin to walk in the stage door of the theater."[82] In striking contrast to Belafonte's obstructed path, his Dramatic Workshop friend Bernard Schwartz caught the attention of a Hollywood talent scout, signed a movie contract, and began to develop a successful career as Tony Curtis.[83]

Belafonte's distinctive gifts were much more visible in his appearance as the black preacher in a People's Song Town Hall concert on February 14, 1948, "For Lincoln and Liberty," orchestrated by Canadian-born Oscar Brand, People's Songs member and producer of WNYC's weekly broadcast, *Folk Song Festival*. The program featured the composer-folksinger Earl Robinson and the CIO chorus, conducted by Robert DeCormier, performing Robinson and Millard Lampell's folk cantata *The Lonesome Train*.

Based on the last chapter of Carl Sandburg's acclaimed biography of Lincoln, Lampell's text painted Lincoln's foes as political ancestors of opponents to the New Deal, Lincoln's supporters embodying the goodness of ordinary people, and his death a prescient warning that "until all men are equal and free, there will be no peace."[84]

When he was cast as the black preacher, Belafonte was not a People's Songs "insider."[85] Brand and DeCormier were familiar with Belafonte's musical range, through either People's Songs events or more informal socializing, and it suited what they were looking for in the part, even though Belafonte had no formal musical training and did not read music.

Afterward, both Brand and DeCormier agreed that Belafonte made a "powerfully frenetic preacher" in an event they characterized as a "huge success." For Belafonte this role exemplified the potential of folk music performance to expand the possibilities of racial representation. To New York's newspaper-reading public in 1952, he would name the preacher's song he sang in *Lonesome Train* as the piece best satisfying the "sense of personal responsibility" that Belafonte felt as a black performer to convey "Negro life with as much dignity as I can give it."[86]

Performance opportunities such as *Sojourner Truth* and *Lonesome Train* enlarged Belafonte's sense of his own abilities, introduced him to wider audiences, and made his choice to pursue acting more legitimate to Marguerite—but it didn't put food on the table. Belafonte competed to be a disc jockey on a radio show in Woodside, New York; someone else was hired. He auditioned to be on staff at the Fur Workers Resort in White Lake, New York. But Henry Foner, head of the union, turned him down because he didn't sing opera.[87] With his roommate Alan Greene, Belafonte spent time helping to stage plays and sing-alongs at a union retreat called Beaver Lodge. When he and Marguerite married at City Hall in June 1948, Beaver Lodge provided them with honeymoon accommodations in exchange for Belafonte's work on that summer's entertainment staff.[88]

By 1948, many of those in Belafonte's circle were drawn to the Progressive Citizens of America (PCA), a third-party movement with racial equality a central tenet of a platform that critiqued the postwar compromises of both the Democratic and Republican Parties. In response to Truman's firing of Henry Wallace from the cabinet in September 1946 and then the fall congressional elections that united the conservatives in both parties in Congress to continue the offensive against the New Deal, many World War II–era radicals turned to the PCA. The third-party platform stood against segregation, the poll tax, lynching, and increased military spending for the Cold War and supported the FEPC, national rent control, and federal aid to education.

Both its political stance and the ICCASP subcommittee structure that grouped members according to arts and literature eased the path for many of New York's black artists and writers to support the PCA at rallies and conferences in 1947 and then to publicly support Henry Wallace's candidacy for president in 1948. This group included Paul Robeson and W. E. B. Du Bois; the writers Shirley Graham, Theodore Ward, Willard Motley, and Langston Hughes; the artists Jacob Lawrence, Ernest Crichlow, and Charles White; and the celebrity performers Lena Horne and Canada Lee.[89]

Political divisions sharpened. From March to June 1947, Truman had articulated what came to be known as the Truman Doctrine in foreign and domestic policy, instructing his attorney general to compile a list of so-called subversive organizations allegedly sympathetic to communism, a tool to establish the "disloyalty" of members and supporters of those groups. The 80th Congress passed the antilabor Taft-Hartley legislation, severely constraining union militancy and the labor movement's political clout by prohibiting wildcat strikes, solidarity strikes, secondary boycotts, and mass picketing. Taft-Hartley required union leaders to sign noncommunist affidavits, or loyalty oaths, and enabled states to pass so-called right-to-work legislation. In October 1947, the House Committee on Un-American Activities subpoenaed a number of left-wing Hollywood directors and screenwriters to publicly question their political beliefs and associations. Liberals divided on domestic and foreign policy issues; some wanted to stand for labor and civil rights and to oppose militarism and escalating hostilities with the Soviet Union. Many of those who held the latter position took the leap of faith to support Wallace's third-party campaign.

The Wallace movement created an interracial public alliance that attracted national black interest. The former secretary of agriculture had consulted with a group of black leaders—including Du Bois, Robeson, Graham, and the sociologist E. Franklin Frazier—before announcing his candidacy. Central to his campaign was an uncompromising language of social equality and racial justice. Stumping in the South, Wallace defied Jim Crow ordinances, refusing to speak to segregated audiences, sleep in segregated hotels, or eat in segregated restaurants. Although many African American leaders and voters, including the NAACP leadership, stood by Truman and the Democratic Party, other prominent African Americans endorsed Wallace. Wallace supporters included some of the black newspaper publishers, the dean of Howard's medical school, and Bishop R. Wright. The distinguished lawyer, civil rights activist, and lifelong Republican Charles Howard gave the keynote address at Wallace's nominating convention in Philadelphia, using the opportunity to call for immediate desegregation of the armed forces. Carrying a pennant supporting Wallace's candidacy was a student delegate, a recent graduate of Antioch College in Ohio and an accomplished musician and singer named Coretta Scott. World heavyweight champion Joe Louis contributed a hundred dollars to the campaign.[90] At the University of Wisconsin, the aspiring playwright Lorraine Hansberry became the chairman of her campus chapter of the Young Progressives of America.[91] In New York City, the campaign attracted Harry Belafonte.

People's Songs performers actively campaigned for Wallace, writing and circulating songs that criticized segregationist backlash and compromises, Cold War militarism, the retreat from the New Deal, and efforts to undermine unions. Alan Lomax became the campaign's musical director, and members organized concerts to raise money. Pete Seeger and Paul Robeson traveled with Wallace; Lead Belly, Brownie McGhee, Duke of Iron, Lord Invader, and Sir Lancelot were among those who sang at Wallace events.

The integration of politics and cultural expression in the Wallace campaign provided opportunities for young performers like actor Harry Belafonte and singer-conductor Robert DeCormier at a time when it was hard to find work in the arts. Following the appealing cultural strategy utilized by ICCASP, organizers sought entertainers for campaign stop political rallies. Progressive Party organizer-turned-historian Curtis MacDougall wrote that never before had there been "anything like this participation in public affairs of outstanding persons in the arts." MacDougall described traveling "caravans" for the Wallace campaign as consisting mostly of young people: "There was always a folk singer, a folk singer who played his guitar or banjo and led the singing of catchy progressive songs. Others in the group, which usually ranged from four to six, put on dramatic skits with political morals."[92]

Robert DeCormier, the choral director of Camp Unity in the summer of 1948, was part of an interracial caravanning group sent to St. Louis, where they were arrested after trying to be served at a restaurant. Belafonte worked with a caravan group associated with the Young Americans for

Wallace in New York. He remembered bringing musicians from the Royal Roost into the campaign: "As I got to know Charlie Parker, and to talk, it was just around 1948, when the Young Progressives of America, which I belonged to, were mobilizing people. And Robeson was on his march. And I went out and conned these guys into coming in and playing for our rallies. Charlie Parker went with me many a night to Brooklyn and to Harlem just to play before Du Bois spoke and before Robeson spoke. And once he did it, he began to say, 'Hey, Harry man, you get any more of them gigs, call me.'"[93]

Wallace rallies, described as a "combined revival and song fest," drew big crowds in New York City. One New York-area Progressive Party rally filled Yankee Stadium on September 10: "48,000 Hear Wallace Assert Prejudice Will Fail in South" according to the headline in *New York Times*. The mostly young crowd, according to one reporter, clapped and swayed to the "hot music" that opened the program; when Robeson sang "Let My People Go" and "Old Man River," they "listened in silence and then roared applause." Robeson's speech, described as "a bitter tirade" against racial oppression, "brought the crowd to its feet with thunderous applause." Pete Seeger had them singing and clapping along with a gospel hymn. Black actor-singer-dancer Avon Long, who had played Sportin' Life in the 1940s revivals of *Porgy and Bess,* did a parody of "It Ain't Necessarily So"; the crowd responded with groans and boos at his mention of the major party candidates, Harry Truman and Thomas Dewey.[94] Wallace addressed a primarily black audience in Harlem at a rally at the Golden Gate Ballroom on October 29, 1948.[95]

White and black musicians Burl Ives, Earl Robinson, Pete Seeger, Josh White, and Sir Lancelot campaigning for Wallace associated the third-party effort with folk music.[96] However, vocal and musical support for Wallace came from a range of musicians identified with different kinds of music: Yip Harburg, Jay Gorney, and Harold Rome associated with Tin Pan Alley, Broadway, and movie songs, as well as Marc Blitzstein and Aaron Copeland, composers of symphonic music. And some of the people billed as folksingers also played and sang across the genres of jazz and blues.

By November 2, the electoral quest of the Wallace movement was lost. Despite challenges from Left and Right, Truman decisively defeated Dewey with a majority of labor and black support, holding together the elements of the New Deal Democratic coalition one more time. Strom Thurmond, then governor of South Carolina—who led southern segregationists in a states'-rights Dixiecrat alternative to the Democratic Party, after Truman and the Democratic Party platform moved toward desegregating federal employment and the armed forces—won slightly more of the popular vote than Wallace and took the electoral votes of four southern states. As the House Committee on Un-American Activities continued its investigations, political attacks against progressive causes gained momentum. Reflecting anti-Soviet foreign policy, restrictions began to appear in film and broadcasting, public employment, liberal associations, and labor unions excluding individuals and organizations affiliated in any way with the Communist Party or its positions. The hallmarks of 1930s radical coalitions—support for labor, civil rights, antifascism, and decolonization—now became evidence of "un-Americanism."

The failure of the Wallace campaign left People's Songs in financial straits and divided New York's labor movement and its black organizations. But New York's American Labor Party, whose endorsement brought Wallace half of his support, much of it from New York City's black and Puerto Rican communities, continued to field candidates in New York races and to gain in votes in black-populated areas.[97]

The "progressive" common sense that persisted even after Wallace's defeat continued to inspire Belafonte's political imagination at the same time as the worlds of black arts, jazz, and folk music enlarged his cultural imagination. By the end of 1948, his GI benefits had run out and he had no regular means to support a household. His wife's modest teacher's pay was their only regular income, and she was pregnant. During the fall, Marguerite continued to live in the teachers' dormitory at the Bethany Day Nursery; Harry stayed with her when he could, otherwise camping out with relatives and friends and working part time pushing a clothes rack in the garment district. In December 1948, she returned to her parents' home in Washington, DC, to await the birth of their child.[98] How could he move toward the future he passionately sought—the political relevance, cultural vitality, and social connectedness he found in theater?

BLACK LEFT, WHITE STAGE, COLD WAR

Moving into the Spotlight, 1949–1954

Introducing the Jazz Singer, 1949

On the stage of the Royal Roost, Belafonte found his chance to earn a living through expressive art rather than the blue-collar laboring of his family and class. By 1948, weekly bop concerts had become nightly shows, and by the end of the year, the Roost was a center of bebop, with repeated engagements for Charlie "Bird" Parker's quintet, including Miles Davis, and live broadcasts of their sets by Symphony Sid on late-night radio. Belafonte longed to act, but he needed work, especially with a child on the way. Soon after the New Year, Monte Kay, the white jazz aficionado who booked the Roost's acts and who had seen Belafonte's student performances, invited him to sing jazz standards between sets. Kay asked Al Haig, the white pianist playing with Bird, to help Belafonte arrange a repertoire.

When Belafonte stepped up to the microphone on Tuesday, January 18, Parker and the musicians playing with him—Max Roach on drums, Tommy Potter on bass—remained onstage to back up the hesitant singer. The Roost crowd responded enthusiastically, and Monte Kay offered him a week's work, singing in the intermissions, at union-scale pay. The seventy dollars a week was almost twice as much as he had ever earned. Two nights later, "Introducing Harry Belafonte" appeared on the tickets for "Symphony Sid's Bop Concert" between the main acts, big-name rhythm and blues vocalists, and jazz groups.[1]

Belafonte's limited repertoire then included conventional jazz standards such as "Pennies from Heaven" and "Skylark." But it also included "Recognition," the song Belafonte had written for a Dramatic Workshop production, which associated his own performance with the struggle against Jim Crow: "I'm gonna put my shoulder to the wheel of freedom and help it roll along."[2]

Recognition as a performer is what he got. Although his voice was untrained, Belafonte projected something powerful and compelling onstage. His personal magnetism, the racial demands he voiced via his song, and his own lucky break became part of his story from the beginning. Writing about Belafonte at the end of that first week, Billy Rowe, the New York–based theater critic for the *Pittsburgh Courier*, called him a "modern Cinderella man." Rowe emphasized the obstacles facing a black actor on Broadway and referred to Belafonte's plea "for his and his race's cause" in "Recognition." The enthusiasm of the Roost audience was "amazing," Belafonte "sensational." Symphony Sid also urged radio listeners to come hear this "Cinderella Gentleman" who went from pushing a clothes rack in the garment district to "packin' 'em in at the Roost." A few weeks later, a reviewer for *Down Beat*, the premier magazine for jazz fans, wrote that "Roost patrons took to the newcomer immediately." Kay kept extending Belafonte's contract; the job eventually lasted for twenty-two weeks.[3]

In 1949 New York, Belafonte's Royal Roost job provided a lucky break in the spotlight and decent pay, but it wasn't the theater, and it wasn't steady. Although the music industry was much more open than the theater to black artists, black musicians found themselves confined to specific genres, especially jazz, blues, and gospel, and the most reliable work required constant travel between one-night appearances. On the road outside major cities, musicians often could not eat and drink where they played. What helped sell records were radio broadcasts and appearances on the new medium of television that could lead to multiweek gigs at nightclubs and hotels. However, despite the overlapping of black and white musical tastes in response to popular big band swing and jazz, broadcast opportunities were much more available to white than to black musicians.[4]

Working at the Roost, where he had been a regular, cushioned Belafonte's break into show business: he began to sing among sympathetic performers and their supporters who saw themselves as part of an interracial jazz scene alternative to music making driven by the bottom line. After that first week, Monte Kay and Symphony Sid offered to manage Belafonte as a professional singer, with the understanding that no money would change hands until he was established. They introduced him to a publicist, Virginia Wickes, whom he would pay to drum up interest among music critics and entertainment columnists.

Jazz vocalists were gaining attention as they moved from accompanying big bands to being a central attraction. Billy Eckstine's romantic, string-backed ballad singing provided a standard against which Belafonte was judged. Belafonte was not sufficiently trained to engage in the harmonic improvisation associated with bebop singers, but instead delivered "his wares in a straight manner." Perhaps prompted by Kay and Wickes, reviewers identified other dimensions of Belafonte's performance that captivated the audience: "His personality is appealing, and his stage presence superior to better established singers."[5]

Only a month after Belafonte first sang at the Roost, Kay and Symphony Sid slipped him in as an intermission singer

Publicity photograph autographed to a musician, ca. 1949. (Courtesy Ron Cohen Collection; photograph copyright © Morgan and Marvin Smith.)

at a Carnegie Hall "Bop Concert" featuring Woody Herman and Nat King Cole's Trio.[6] Two weeks later, Symphony Sid staged and emceed a series of weekly shows at Harlem's Apollo Theater. He included Belafonte along with artists like the esteemed Palladium dance hall musicians Machito and his Afro-Cubans.[7]

Left-wing politics fit comfortably into the jazz circuit; during Belafonte's gig at the Roost, events sponsored by radicals offered him other opportunities to perform. He was a featured attraction of a two-night "Free and Equal Hootenanny" at the Yugoslav American Home on West 41st Street at the end of January, along with a new group called The Weavers (Pete Seeger, Lee Hayes, Fred Hellerman, and Ronnie Gilbert), who had just started to sing together professionally.[8] When Alan Lomax staged "New York: A Musical Tapestry" at Carnegie Hall in an effort to shore up the depleted finances of People's Songs in early March, Belafonte was part of a lineup that included jazz musicians, blues and folksingers, a Latin band, a Peruvian soprano and trio, and two Palestinian dancers.[9] Although unable to forestall the shutdown of People's Songs, the well-attended event did mark Belafonte's first featured appearance on New York's most famous music stage.

On the success of his performance at the Roost, Belafonte headlined a Young Progressives event in memory of FDR at the Manhattan Center, a prominent midtown venue, in April 1949. The black and white radicals who had been drawn to the presidential campaign of Henry Wallace were still active, determined to maintain public pressure for desegregation, voting rights, and antilynching legislation, despite accusations of disloyalty.[10] In his speeches at this time, Wallace warned about the dangers of the Cold War: opposition to civil rights and labor movements had resulted in "far more peril from the right than the left," he declared. One April leaflet announcing the Manhattan Center event promised a speech by Wallace in addition to "razzle-dazzle entertainment," which included Belafonte.[11]

Belafonte's fellow performers at this event were Artie Shaw and Eddie Condon, who had led swing and jazz bands since the 1930s. Both supported progressive issues and had challenged the color line by showcasing interracial collaboration. On the leaflet for the "Salute to FDR" event were the names of Wallace, in large type, followed by the top-

"...we have just begun to fight."
SALUTE TO
FDR
SPEAKER: HENRY A. WALLACE
PROGRAM: ARTIE SHAW
FRED ROBBINS
JACK GILFORD
HARRY BELEFONTE
ART HODES
HERB WARD
SLICK JONES
PEE WEE RUSSEL
EDDIE CONDON
Adv. .75
Door 1.00
APRIL 11th · 7:30 P.M. MANHATTAN CENTER
34th Street and 8th Ave., N. Y. C.
YOUNG PROGRESSIVES OF NEW YORK · 570 Seventh Ave., Room 1003

Leaflet for Salute to FDR event, Manhattan Center, New York, April 18, 1949. (Courtesy Tamiment Library, New York University.)

billed entertainers—Shaw, New York bop deejay Fred Robbins, comic actor Jack Gilford, and Belafonte. Condon and other jazz musicians appeared in slightly smaller type. Jack Gilford had contributed to left-wing political entertainment for years, including performances at People's Songs events, union festivities at 13 Astor Place, and at rallies for Wallace and the Independent Citizens Committee of the Arts, Sciences, and the Professions (ICCASP).[12] Belafonte's appearance at this kind of political event enhanced his visibility as a jazz performer.

Recognition, Jazz Protest, and Danger from the Right

By 1949, records were an increasingly important means to popularize hits and to promote vocalists on radio, and on jukeboxes catering to the tastes of local clientele.[13] Monte Kay and Symphony Sid decided to launch a Roost record label with Belafonte singing his protest song "Recognition" and an original pop song, "Lean on Me," written by his friend Allan Greene. In April, Monte Kay arranged a recording session with trumpeter Howard McGhee, who worked as a sideman for Charlie Parker, and tenor sax player Brew Moore, who worked with Machito, backing up Belafonte. Symphony Sid gave "Recognition" significant airtime on his radio show; according to music writer Arnold Shaw, Sid "played it as if it were 'The Star-Spangled Banner.'" Many New Yorkers bought the single, but it had few sales outside the city.[14]

By the time Harry and Marguerite's first child, Adrienne, was born in Washington, DC, in May 1949, Belafonte's jazz singing was bringing in money, but unevenly. His publicist, Virginia Wickes, served as one of Adrienne's two godparents, indicating Belafonte's immersion in his new life. But working in nightclubs entailed financial insecurity and late-night hours, undermining a conventional family life. The twenty-two weeks at the Roost were nearly over, and although in the spring Monte Kay had raised Belafonte's weekly pay to two hundred dollars, the club soon shut down, unable to renew its lease. Belafonte found a fourth-floor walk-up one block above Harlem in Washington Heights, not far from where his mother lived, and Marguerite rejoined him in New York, accompanied by her mother, who would take care of the baby while Marguerite returned to the teaching job that reliably supported their household.[15]

However financially precarious, working in jazz clubs

fell below the radar of anticommunist scrutiny, an advantage for a radical black artist. Just as Belafonte was getting started, entertainment columnists, church and veterans groups, and conservative consumer groups were joining congressional committees at the local and national level to define "American" as unquestioning enthusiasm for the Cold War and opposition to organized support for refugees, labor, or desegregation. The burgeoning culture industries of broadcasting and film, already unlikely to employ black performers, were the first targets of these groups, who threatened consumer boycotts and urged that individuals associated with supposedly "un-American" positions be blacklisted.[16]

Between 1947 and 1949, many of the supporters of the postwar black Left so generative for Belafonte came under attack. On the East Coast, three former FBI agents named themselves the American Business Consultants (ABC) and published *Counterattack*, a weekly newsletter that monitored the culture industries for suspected Communists. Particularly incensed by the star power of celebrities who had publicly identified themselves with progressive causes, and by their access to rapidly growing radio and television audiences, ABC targeted radio commentators, film actors, and directors, many of whom were subsequently fired.[17] Newspapers publicized the growing number of groups on the attorney general's list. Association with the still-legal Communist Party USA, at the top of the list, constituted the most dramatic evidence of alleged "disloyalty," but the list also included groups such as ICCASP and United Negro and Allied Veterans of America (UNAVA), which had sponsored rallies and meetings Belafonte could well have attended.

Belafonte and other black artists faced a real dilemma. Beyond a narrow range of black-identified genres and black venues, opportunities were few. Radicals led the organizations demanding racial equality. These were precisely the groups in the glare of anticommunist scrutiny. Belafonte's youth, for a time, protected him; the generation of artists who preceded him were the first to feel the heat. Most had not been members of the Communist Party, but because the party supported civil rights militancy and encouraged black arts, they had worked closely and performed at benefits with many people who were.

Folksinger Josh White, who appeared frequently on radio and in the national press, began to distance himself from the interracial nightclub Cafe Society, where he had frequently performed when its owner, Barney Josephson, came under investigation. He had taken his name off the People's Songs advisory board by the summer of 1947. Paul Robeson and the actor Canada Lee, who had appeared on Broadway and in two Hollywood films as well as on radio, were frequently accused of disloyalty for their support of Henry Wallace's Progressive Party campaign, as well as for their militant opposition to conservative congressional initiatives, Jim Crow segregation, and HUAC.[18]

There were many black radicals in Belafonte's world who continued to publicly express their criticisms of the Cold War and domestic anticommunism. At the end of March 1949, the *New York Times* invited renewed scrutiny of Cold War critics by publishing the list of sponsors for the Left-supported Cultural and Scientific Conference for World Peace. The list included prominent black ministers and lawyers as well as intellectuals Du Bois and Alphaeus Hunton; writers Langston Hughes, Theodore Ward, and Shirley Graham; Robeson, Lee, and other actors and musicians. When *Life* magazine published an article about the conference in early April, its two-page photo spread, headlined as "Dupes and Fellow Travelers Dress Up Communist Fronts," included a picture of Langston Hughes, who had supported the conference, and also of black composer Dean Dixon and Harlem minister-politician Adam Clayton Powell, Jr., who had not.[19]

The harassment of black radicals intensified in late April when remarks made by Paul Robeson at a World Peace Congress in Paris were misquoted and widely publicized as asserting that American Negroes, treated as second-class citizens in the United States, would never go to war against the Soviet Union. Although there was some debate in the black press, many leaders distanced themselves from Robeson. HUAC planned a round of hearings to pressure black figures to denounce him. Early in July, it summoned Jackie Robinson, the first black player in Major League Baseball, to appear. That same week, syndicated columnist Ed Sullivan, previously a supporter of Canada Lee, turned on him, excoriating him as a Communist sympathizer.[20]

Lee became virtually unemployable, but rather than abandon racial militancy, he held firm: "I don't care what names they call me. Nothing or no one can force me out of the struggle my people are making in this country for democracy which only exists for some. . . . Should I put an end to my fight for civil rights for my people because I'm tarred with a red brush?" A few days later, Lee called a press conference at the Apollo, where he announced his readiness to "talk against racial or religious discrimination" and "to participate in any program that was designed to make the world a better place to live in, no matter what organization or political party was listed as a sponsor."[21] In practice, standing with the black Left to oppose racial discrimination meant questioning the legitimacy of the blacklist.

Organizing to Get Black Artists on Air and Stage

At his press conference, Canada Lee announced that he would participate in an upcoming event at Harlem's Theresa Hotel—called by the Committee for the Negro in the Arts (CNA), a left-wing black arts advocacy group organized in 1947—to "expose racial discrimination in the radio and television fields." This was an area of urgency for black performers, especially in 1949, when the broadcast networks were pouring financial resources into the new medium of television. It was not yet known whether television would extend radio's racist stereotyping and exclusionary employment practices or open doors to introduce black talent to a new white and black mass audience.

Harry Belafonte added his name to the call for this CNA conference "On Radio, Television and the Negro People." The brochure advertising the conference featured a photograph of white actors Freeman Gosden and Charles Correll "blacked up" as their radio characters Amos 'n' Andy; the accompanying text demanded action to challenge the "distortions" and attacks on the Negro people circulated by the mass media. It demanded an end to racial discrimination in all broadcast employment, performance, *and* production.[22] Signing on to the CNA conference call, Belafonte joined a talented group of black artists and leaders, people who had long been publicly identified with these issues as well as many who had not: jazz and classically oriented musicians, conductors, artists, stage and screen actors, professors, writers, and performers from the worlds of ballet, tap, and modern dance. Nearly half the sponsors were black; white allies included many progressive actors, artists, writers and editors, composers, musicians, lyricists, and arts and media trade unionists who supported civil rights and postwar labor movements, and opposed escalating tensions with the Soviet Union.[23]

CNA and the broadcasting conference built on earlier organizational efforts by the arts, theater, literature, music, and broadcasting subcommittees of ICCASP and the cultural committee of the National Negro Congress. These groups had been active in supporting public demands for desegregation, raising money for scholarships, providing mentorship to help young black students train in music and

Cover of Call to a Conference on Radio, Television and the Negro People, Hotel Theresa, July, 9, 1949. (Courtesy Tamiment Library, New York University.)

the arts, and presenting performances for Negro History Week. After the demise of ANT, many of its underemployed members joined CNA's theater committee. Robeson's artistry, political engagement, and commitment to black culture provided a "guiding spirit" for many in CNA, and the organization provided a meeting ground for arts radicals active in the 1930s and 1940s to mentor younger artists like Belafonte.[24]

The CNA broadcasting conference attracted unusual attention in the mainstream media. *Variety* quoted from Canada Lee's speech, which appropriated Churchill's naming of the ideological division of postwar Europe to protest the effects of minstrelsy and de facto segregation in hiding the circumstances of ordinary black Americans. "A virtual Iron Curtain exists against the entire Negro people as far as radio is concerned. Where is the story of our lives in terms of the ghetto slums in which we must live? Where is the story of jobs not available? Who would know us if he had to know us only by listening to Amos and Andy, Beulah, Rochester, and minstrel shows?" The conference's protest against broadcast employment discrimination drew a considerable audience: "300 radio and TV writers, actors, directors, representatives of unions and colored organizations."[25] A number of the creative and politically engaged people attracted to CNA's dissent would remain friends and associates with Belafonte for years to come.[26]

By the end of the summer of 1949, red-baiting of black artists had become frightening. A violent assault by local branches of the Veterans of Foreign Wars and the American Legion shut down Paul Robeson's outdoor concert in Peekskill, New York. Robeson was not physically hurt, but while the local police looked on, anticommunist crowds burned a cross, smashed the stage, torched chairs, stoned cars, and sent a dozen concertgoers to the hospital. A rescheduled concert took place the next week, with a protective cordon provided by white and black trade unionists from the Fur and Leather Workers, the United Electrical Workers, and the Longshoremen. Robeson sang a short program, but then white mobs stoned the estimated twenty thousand concertgoers as they tried to leave. The mobs focused their rage on black attendees, who composed roughly a quarter of the audience. The union men providing security were trapped between a rock-throwing crowd and the local police, who prevented them from returning to their buses. Vehicles were overturned, windows were smashed, and more than 150 Robeson supporters required medical treatment. A wire recording made that day captured the hostile crowd shouting, "Hey, you white niggers, get back to Russia!" and "Jews, Jews, Jews!" State and local public officials blamed the violence on Communists, for "fomenting racial and religious hatred." Belafonte watched angry conservatives force the towering Paul Robeson, CNA's shining light, from the pubic stage.[27]

Singing Jazz and Pop

Belafonte did not yet face pressure to limit his political activism; opportunities to sing continued to come his way. Monte Kay wangled him two recording sessions, in New York in July and December 1949, with Capitol, the new Los Angeles–based label started by singer-lyricist Johnny Mercer. Capitol had become a major player in the popular music business, recording Paul Whiteman and his orchestra and popular ballad singer Jo Stafford. Mercer and Capitol had made stars out of Nat King Cole's trio by marketing them as mainstream pop, outside the "race record" category. Monte Kay, who produced Belafonte's Capitol sessions, nudged him in the direction of pop and away from jazz, with orchestration provided by Pete Rugolo, the New York music director at Capitol. Naming Belafonte "vocal find of the year" the *Pittsburgh Courier* noted that syndicated show business columnists had praised him as the "male Lena Horne" (Walter Winchell) and "the newest sensation" (Earl Wilson). In early September, Belafonte, billed as "Capitol Records' newest singing star," joined the lineup for a CNA-sponsored jazz concert at Town Hall with Charlie Parker, Erroll Garner, Bud Powell, and Miles Davis. In October, Belafonte was a featured artist in a "Horizons in Jazz" concert at Carnegie Hall, on a bill with Dizzy Gillespie's band and Al Haig, Tommy Potter, and Max Roach.[28]

Belafonte broke into network television in the fall of 1949 on a short-lived black-cast variety program. Musical variety was among radio's most commercially successful genres, and by the fall of 1948, both Milton Berle and Ed Sullivan had shown that a vaudeville variety format could be successfully adapted to television. In this period, when television was broadcast only to local markets, network programs in New York tested the potential profitability of black entertainers.[29] One experiment, variously called *Uptown Jubilee, Harlem Jubilee,* and *Sugar Hill Times,* was broadcast live and hosted by Apollo emcee and New York area musical and radio performer Willie Bryant. The regulars were other popular Apollo entertainers and newcomer Belafonte. On the air in September and October 1949, the show was scheduled opposite Milton Berle's popular *Texaco Star Theater,* but it couldn't compete with Berle's antics and his special guests, nationally recognized black performers such as Bill "Bojangles" Robinson, Duke Ellington, and baseball star Jackie Robinson. Rescheduling *Sugar Hill Times* against ABC's musical quiz show *Stop the Music!* yielded no better results; it was canceled in October.[30] For the moment, the television door slammed shut.

Monte Kay continued to feature Belafonte as an opener at Birdland, the club named for Charlie Parker where the party was scheduled to move after the Roost shut down, but trouble over a liquor license delayed its opening until December. The Orchid Room, a club on 52nd Street, picked up the "remnants of the Birdland show" at the end of September, including Belafonte. He got another week at the Apollo in November, but Apollo audience enthusiasm was shifting to groups with rhythm and blues hit records.[31] When Birdland finally opened in December, Symphony Sid was set up to broadcast nightly; the first booking included Charlie Parker's quintet, Lester Young, and Belafonte. By the end of January, the programming had switched from a "Dixieland to Bop" cavalcade that included Belafonte to a "cooler brand of jazz," where his talents did not fit.[32] Jazz employment remained an uncertain proposition

Between Jazz and Folk

Without the musical chops for improvisation, Belafonte found nightclub singing unsatisfying artistically and politically. Looking for race-conscious political and artistic conversation, he found a group of black musicians, artists, dancers, and writers who met informally after midnight on weekend nights at the 28th Street apartment of artist and former Dunham dancer Frank Neal and his wife, Dorcas. Other regulars at the Neals' salon included painter and playwright Charles Sebree, who had directed Belafonte in *Juno* in 1946; singer-actor Brock Peter, who had made his stage debut with a small part in the 1943 Broadway version of *Porgy and Bess*; aspiring writer James Baldwin; and musician and composer Billy Strayhorn, who had worked with Duke Ellington since 1938. Dorcas Neal later described these gatherings as a place where "people could be the artists they were and be dealt with like artists. They faced a lot of the same problems and lot of the same questions regarding their place in the world, which was white." Former Dunham dancer and choreographer Tally Beatty remembered talking about "every kind of art. . . . A Black gathering, very socio-political. We had all worked with prominent white people, and we had done well with them, up to a point. At the salon, we could discuss our observations and frustrations together, and argue about them." Brock Peters emphasized the mutual support: "We were all daring to try to have careers in an arena where everything was structured against the possibility of having a career. And we got fuel from seeing each other and comparing notes and laughing about things and gossiping about things as they looked from our perspective."[33] Being part of these discussions surely fueled Belafonte as well.

While taking any paid jobs he could get singing jazz and pop standards, Belafonte explored musically. He hired the experienced swing and jazz composer Fred Norman to arrange some pieces, and tried out his voice accompanied by a quartet of singers. He rehearsed with a flautist, a bass player, and two classically trained guitarists: his former ANT colleague Millard Thomas and Thomas's student Craig Work.[34] Belafonte didn't want to limit himself to the jazz he could be paid to sing; during a Birdland engagement, he asked to try out a folk song encore—the answer was no. Undeterred, Belafonte plotted with Work and his friend, novelist Bill Attaway, to pull off an impromptu performance. After Belafonte had finished his planned set, Attaway distracted attention from Work's guitar-laden entry. Work came up to the microphone and "spontaneously" started playing a folk tune, "A Rovin'," then Belafonte joined in. The audience, expecting jazz, was surprised, and not particularly responsive. A *Variety* reviewer commented that Belafonte was "OK, if not particularly standout" singing "romantic standards."[35]

Belafonte's musical passions extended far beyond the jazz and pop repertoire he was now allowed to sing—more along the lines of a Town Hall concert featuring jazz alongside blues, folk songs, ballads, and calypsos that Alan Lomax helped to organize in memory of Lead Belly at the end of January.[36] Monte Kay, interviewed in the late 1950s, remembered that Belafonte's "concern with the lyrics of songs made him a kind of oddball among music people. The jazz set was concerned mainly with melody and melodic variation . . . Pop singers . . . did not make too much of a fuss about the words." Belafonte, on the other hand, "was lyric conscious. He was intent about what the words said." His political convictions made him uncomfortable singing only "to the ladies, one mushy love song after another."[37]

Performing at left-wing events gave Belafonte more musical freedom and the opportunity to be "lyric conscious."

In early 1950, he appeared in a series of programs in Harlem sponsored by the CNA. Actress Ellen Holly, then a Hunter College student, recalled that CNA created a musically and dramatically eclectic laboratory "where up and coming actors like Harry Belafonte worked out repertoire." CNA provided a performance space where black artists could take risks and challenge and sustain one another's aspirations, sometimes with the support of white allies.[38]

CNA's capacious vision of black history and black arts permeated the Negro History Week programs it sponsored in 1950. At the 135th Street Library, Belafonte sang in a variety program that ranged from classical music, to Haitian folk music performed by Haitian guitarist Franz Casseus, to Afro-Cuban poetry. The audience understood Belafonte's plea for "Recognition" and would have been familiar with the spiritual he sang and had recently recorded, "Sometimes I Feel Like a Motherless Child," popularized by the Fiske Jubilee Singers and recorded by Robeson in the 1930s. The previous evening at the library, actors including Frank Silvera and Alice Childress had presented a "History of the Negro People through Literature and Music." A few days later, the dancers and choreographers Archie Savage, Donald McKayle, Jane Dudley, and Sophie Maslow performed a dance concert at the Harlem Children's Center on 134th Street, accompanied by spirituals including "Motherless Child."[39]

Even as the Cold War heated up, Belafonte and other CNA artists remained committed to promoting black arts and radical dissent in public. After Communist forces took over China in December 1949, the rhetoric pitting the "free world" against an international Communist conspiracy gained political currency. In February 1950, Senator Joseph McCarthy claimed to have evidence that the State Department was "infested with Communists." Belafonte was not personally a target of anticommunist scrutiny at this time, and he continued to participate in CNA-initiated protests and perform at left-wing events.[40] In March 1950, he sang "Recognition" at an event raising money for the Caribbean Labor Congress. Along with other sympathetic entertainers, he performed in Distributive Workers District 65's Saturday Night Club, a variety revue for union families, held on the top floor of the union's building at 13 Astor Place. Belafonte was featured in notices for a folk concert series in April and also at 13 Astor Place, sharing the stage with calypsonian Duke of Iron and folksinger Oscar Brand. On a visit to a Harlem-church-supported fresh air camp in the summer of 1950, Belafonte joined in a rousing duet of "John Henry" with Juilliard-trained Irving Burgie, one of the camp song leaders.[41]

Belafonte's nightclub employment and record sales limped along unsteadily. After a second recording session in December 1950, Capitol dropped its option to renew his contract. Marketed as "blues," his single "Close Your Eyes" had not crossed the color line.[42] The singles "Whispering" and "Sometimes I Feel Like a Motherless Child" had garnered only a "fair" rating in *Metronome*. Reviewers characterized the collaboration between singer and orchestra as uneven, and Belafonte's singing on "Motherless Child" as "school-girl anguish." Ratings improved only marginally for other Capitol singles in July, and none sold well.[43]

When Belafonte could find work onstage, his personal magnetism in live performance generated a much stronger response than the recordings. In May he landed five weeks at the interracial nightclub Cafe Society in Greenwich Village, featuring a wider range of musical genres than in the jazz clubs. Watching Belafonte's live performance, the reviewer for *Variety* deemed Belafonte "a vocalist of promise" and "a warbler of great sensitivity when he tackles ballads"; his performance of "Recognition" conveyed "the feeling of a spiritual." *Metronome*'s Barry Ulanov, who had had a lukewarm response to the recordings, now praised Belafonte for confronting the audience "with a bolder stance and a more vigorous voice to go with it." Ulanov described Belafonte as having "given up the fight for 'Recognition' in favor of a handsome selection of standards," delivered with "languorous phrasing." He approved of the singer's technique "in the groove known as cool."[44]

To sing folk music during this period was to risk attracting right-wing political surveillance and sometimes blacklisting. New York-area performers were a particular target of ABC's *Counterattack.* After The Weavers appeared on a new NBC TV variety show *Broadway Open House* at the end of May, the newsletter blasted them.[45] Two weeks later *Counterattack* distributed its book-length report, *Red Channels: The Report on Communist Influence in Radio and Television,* to networks, advertising agencies, and sponsors. Organized alphabetically, it listed appearances at state and national congressional hearings and documented affiliations to "suspect" organizations, going back to the mid-1930s.[46]

Counterattack had been watching and writing about People's Songs musicians since September 1947; folksingers Oscar Brand, Richard Dyer-Bennett, Burl Ives, Alan Lomax, Earl Robinson, Pete Seeger, and Josh White, and jazz artists Hazel Scott and Artie Shaw were among the writers, directors, actors, and musicians listed in *Red Channels.*[47] The project to expose communism became even more urgent a few days later. Tensions over the Allies' political division of the Korean peninsula after World War II resulted in military action by the Communist government in the North against the U.S.-supported government in the South, and the commitment of U.S. troops to fight on the side of South Korea.

Being listed in *Red Channels* had a devastating impact on folk performers more well known than Belafonte. The less famous ones were not called to testify before Congress, but they were only able to keep working by distancing themselves from the Left. Josh White and Burl Ives were nationally prominent and more vulnerable. In an effort to salvage his career, White volunteered to appear before HUAC in September 1950. He made an effort to stand by his protest against "injustice and discrimination and Jim-Crowism" and he did not reveal the names of his former comrades. But his "friendly" description of having been "played for a sucker" gave legitimacy to the anticommunist investigations. In May 1952, Burl Ives agreed to appear before the Senate Internal Security Subcommittee and he was willing to name names.[48]

Although The Weavers were listed in *Counterattack* and then in *Red Channels*, their pathway was not immediately blocked. Orchestra leader and musical director for Decca Records Gordon Jenkins heard the group singing "African chants and Israeli horas [circle dances] and hymns and Christmas carols" during a six-month engagement at the Village Vanguard beginning December 1949, and arranged to record them. Their versions of the Israeli folk song "Tzena, Tzena, Tzena" and Lead Belly's "Goodnight Irene" reached the pop charts by July 1950. They followed this early success with other songs written by Woody Guthrie and taken from Carl Sandburg's *American Songbag* collection. A string of hits led to lucrative bookings in nightclubs across the country in the fall of 1950. The Weavers agreed to follow their manager's recommendation not to appear at left-wing events, but before long, the *Counterattack* listing began to have its desired effect. A contract to appear on a network TV show was withdrawn—an ominous sign that the group's crossover into commercial success could be halted.[49]

Belafonte, still moving under the anticommunist radar, appeared singing jazz at Birdland in August 1950.[50] He signed with Jubilee Records, a rhythm and blues label that had recorded the first black vocal group successful in the white pop market. Belafonte's two Jubilee sessions between August and December were arranged by Fred Norman, associated with 1940s big swing bands. They were produced by Jack Rollins, then an inexperienced Broadway theatrical producer, who had grown up in Brooklyn and was the son of a Jewish garment worker. The first session featured Belafonte singing a ballad and the title song from a recent movie, accompanied by a small combo of jazz musicians. On the second session, Belafonte recorded four songs that revealed the new musical directions he had been exploring with Craig Work and others: quirky arrangements, with a backup vocal quartet, "the Belafonte singers."[51]

During this period, Belafonte got one more chance at professional acting, winning a part in a Theater Guild production of a new play, *Head of the Family*, by a black playwright, George Norford. The only black correspondent for the army weekly *Yank* during World War II, Norford had studied playwriting at Columbia and at the New School. Try-out reviews referred to Belafonte among the twenty "outstanding Negro actors," including former ANT actors Fred O'Neal and Rosetta Le Noire, and cast members of the Broadway production of *Porgy and Bess*, Avon Long and Etta Moten. In an effort to sidestep contentious debates over desegregation, the publicity described the play as "a heart-warming and clean-cut American comedy" with "no controversial overtones," dealing with "no prejudice." The actors appeared in a number of try-out performances in Westport, Connecticut, but to Belafonte's great disappointment, the play did not make it to Broadway. Etta Moten later recalled that while they were working on this play, Belafonte wanted to discuss postwar black politics, particularly the connection between "Negro life" and Africa.[52]

In December 1950, Belafonte headed to Miami Beach for his best-paid engagement to date, singing pop standards as part of late-night "one for the road" entertainment at the foul-mouthed comedian Martha Raye's Five O'Clock Club. Jim Crow rules required him to stay in a cheap motel on the black side of town; he needed a pass for a black taxi driver to drive him there and back, since white taxi drivers wouldn't pick him up and black people weren't allowed to hail cabs. He was required to carry a police pass to be out after a nine o'clock curfew enforced only for black people, and another card to be allowed to perform at the club.[53]

The contrasts, for Belafonte, were stunning—between New York's interracial Left theater and jazz scene and the unbridgeable divide separating Miami Beach from the black district, Overtown; between the personal authority and magnetism especially appealing to women he conveyed onstage, and the threat to white womanhood that white supremacy defined him as embodying offstage; between the wide-ranging lyrical and dramatic possibilities of folk music and what felt like the narrow confinement of the pop standards he was paid to sing. The club manager offered him a second week, but Belafonte turned it down—shocking behavior for a young entertainer hoping to make his way as a singer. However, Belafonte was finished with the world Monte Kay had opened to him.

Black Arts Radicals in Greenwich Village and Harlem, 1951

Having rejected his uneven prospects as a pop singer, Belafonte now turned to the black and interracial Left of New York's Greenwich Village. His friends, writer Bill Attaway and actor Ferman Phillips, came up with the idea to start a restaurant, as a means to support themselves while developing their respective crafts and eluding the public harassment of 1940s radicals. Belafonte devoted his savings to support the venture, a small restaurant they called the Sage.[54] Although it ultimately failed financially, the restaurant and the contacts he made there supported Belafonte's professional turn to folk music performance.

Belafonte was one of many black performers losing hope

of making a living through the limited opportunities onstage. By 1948, Gordon Heath, the widely admired star of a successful and long-running 1946 Broadway play, had abandoned the United States, moving first to London and then Paris. There he and his partner opened a nightclub, where they sang folk songs, spirituals, and the blues. The only work Brock Peters could find was touring with Leonard de Paur's infantry chorus and a cabaret act. And Belafonte wasn't the only aspiring actor to open a restaurant. Although Sidney Poitier had worked steadily in the traveling company of *Anna Lucasta* in the late 1940s and had already played two substantial parts on-screen, he now was unemployed. With the manager of Harlem's Hotel Theresa, he opened an uptown barbecue grill, Ribs in the Ruff, at 127th Street and Seventh Avenue.[55]

Belafonte and his partners chose a location in the heart of Greenwich Village, on Seventh Avenue just south of where Grove and Fourth Streets and Christopher Street and Washington Place met. It was near Cafe Society, a few blocks south of the Village Vanguard's poetry, jazz, and folk music scene, and a few blocks north of the Cherry Lane Playhouse. None of the partners knew anything about running a business. During the eight months it was open, the Sage never broke even, but it did provide a gathering place for artists, actors, and writers, which, like Cafe Society and the Village Vanguard, respected no color line.[56]

Greenwich Village was New York's "celebrated refuge" of artistic and sexual freedom, with its cheap rents and twisting streets, its cafés and nightlife. People who were drawn to Village bohemianism, including black intellectuals and artists, rejected conventional boundaries and embraced a racially and sexually expansive cosmopolitanism. In a 1949 essay, *Ebony*'s New York bureau chief, Allan Morrison, quoted a black Greenwich Village writer reminding readers, "The Negro is no interloper here." But those who sought release from Harlem's racial confinement traded the comforts of presumptive blackness for the tension of living among a white majority.[57]

After the war, there was competition for scarce housing, price inflation, and a backlash against the interracial mixing and nonnormative sexuality that had flourished earlier. Morrison's interviews with black Greenwich Village writers, artists, and musicians suggested that former "acceptance had turned to resentment." Verbal and physical attacks by gangs of white youths "hell-bent on violence against Jews, Negroes, homosexuals, and Communists" became more common. Black Greenwich Villagers told Morrison that people who spoke "for equality and artistic freedom" had been "dissipated, diverted, or silenced..." The artist Beauford Delaney, who had lived since 1933 in a loft on Greene Street, observed that black people still wanted to move to the Village, despite the increasing late-night "anti-Negro hooliganism," which he saw directed at "the artistic type of Negro" and at "colored men escorting white women."[58] Many African American writers and poets would eventually adopt the position taken by some of the Harlem Renaissance modernists, that bohemia ultimately failed black artists and intellectuals; but in the 1950s, Greenwich Village continued to attract black radical experimentation.[59]

The legal consequences for involvement with activities and organizations that were supported by the Communist Party became more severe when Congress passed the McCarran Act in September 1950, which required these organizations to register with a Subversive Activities Control Board and added the Senate Internal Security Committee to the existing surveillance system. Even President Truman, who established his own loyalty program in 1947, vetoed the McCarran Act, calling it "the greatest danger to freedom of speech, press, and assembly since the Alien and Sedition Acts." Unfortunately, there was enough anticommunist sentiment in Congress to override the president's veto. Alan Lomax, who had been under FBI investigation for his ties to the Left since 1942, departed for Europe in September 1950 and stayed out of the country for eight years. Paul Robeson's passport was held and then revoked, with serious economic consequences for his livelihood, which was dependent on revenues from performances around the world. Robeson's response was to found *Freedom,* an alternative black monthly newspaper, as a means to keep his own voice and news of the black Left in circulation. *Freedom* published its first issue in January 1951. In February, W. E. B. Du Bois was indicted for circulating the Stockholm Peace Appeal, a petition calling for world peace. When the nearly eighty-three-year-old founder of the NAACP was arraigned in handcuffs in Washington, DC, Belafonte was among those protesting in New York, in front of the federal courthouse in Foley Square.[60]

As Belafonte later recounted, the Sage restaurant provided a refuge where he, his partners, and their devoted customers could work out a new song, argue about socialism, and "anguish over the best way to fight segregation." They kept the restaurant open for those eight months by relying on loans from customers, credit extended to them by friends who waited to cash checks, and cash infusions from poker wins.[61]

During the time he was involved with the Sage, Belafonte continued to participate in Committee for the Negro in the Arts events countering the mainstream invisibility of black arts and artists. A yearly masked ball and fund-raising brunch at the Savoy Ballroom, with arts and theater celebrities judging the best costumes, drew attention to "outstanding Negro performers": those who were already well known, such as writer Langston Hughes, actress Fredi Washington, jazz musician Mary Lou Williams, and playwright Theodore Ward; and those for whom CNA members sought wider recognition, such as artist Charles White, singer Hope Foye, and dancer Janet Collins. In May

1951, Belafonte and Poitier were among the group of honorees. The arts and music chapters of CNA concentrated on raising funds to support scholarships for black talent. In July 1951, Bill Attaway was part of the literature chapter, calling for creating jobs in publishing and advertising for black writers.[62]

CNA's theater division addressed mainstream theater's exclusionary whiteness with two strategies. One entailed pressing Broadway producers to expand opportunities for black actors. The other was to stage its own theatrical productions. In September 1950, CNA opened its version of a Harlem community theater in Club Baron, a jazz nightclub on Lenox Avenue at 132nd Street.[63] Its first production, "Just a Little Simple," consisted of short theater pieces and musical numbers. The variety entertainment featured several dramatic vignettes involving Jesse B. Semple, the character Langston Hughes created in 1943 for his columns in the *Chicago Defender*, adapted for the stage by ANT actor, teacher, and writer Alice Childress. It also included Childress's first original play, *Florence*, depicting the encounter between a southern black domestic who wants to support her daughter's acting ambitions and an established white New York actress who assumes that the place of black women is in service. The "Simple" revue paid all its actors and musicians at union scale and ran for several months. By April 1951, Poitier had taken over the part of Jesse B. Semple.[64]

The *Chicago Defender* described the CNA's musical revues at Club Baron as a showcase for black performers. Belafonte's appearances gave him the chance to experiment. At a benefit for Mississippi death-row prisoner Willie McGee, found guilty by an all-white jury for the alleged rape of a local white woman, Belafonte performed the song Gillespie had first done in 1947, "Cubano Be, Cubano Bop."[65] Louis "Sabu" Martinez, the Puerto Rican drummer who had joined Dizzy Gillespie's band after the death of drummer Chano Pozo, accompanied Belafonte. According to critic Geoffrey Jacques, this piece marked "the marriage between Cuban American dance music and African American jazz." At the McGee concert, Belafonte, accompanied by Craig Work, also performed his version of "Brown-Skinned Gal," a calypso originally recorded in 1946 by the calypsonian King Radio (Norman Span) that commented on the sexual consequences of the American military presence in Trinidad during World War II. Work also accompanied a Jewish singer, Mort Freeman, on songs from the European resistance. Belafonte, Work, and Poitier appeared in another variety show at Club Baron in June 1951, a benefit for the fledgling organization Domestic Workers Local 149.[66]

While the Sage remained open, Belafonte continued to explore musically. He jammed with a conga drummer and a pianist at the loft of jazz clarinetist Tony Scott, a Sage regular who became a close friend. Guided by producer Jack Rollins, he continued to practice with Millard Thomas, Craig Work, and the three men and one woman who made up the Belafonte Folk Singers. Belafonte and these singers appeared in a few guest slots on television. Their version of the folk song "Venezuela," the most innovative of the Jubilee sides, was Belafonte's first recording to be reviewed enthusiastically in *Metronome*: "The five voices, backed by only a flute, a tambourine and two guitars, create an exciting Latin atmosphere."[67]

Belafonte and his musician friends were drawn to music that crossed genres and national boundaries—the popular island music Belafonte had heard in Kingston in the 1930s, Latin and Afro-Caribbean jazz, and the many traditions of People's Songs. Scott worked with Belafonte so intensely on a call-and-response version of "John Henry" that the sculptor who lived below Scott's loft banged on the ceiling in protest. In September 1951, Scott participated in an eclectic jazz and folk roundtable at the Music Inn in Lennox, Massachusetts, where musicians, critics, and ethnomusicologists explored the folk genealogies of jazz in ragtime, Afro-Caribbean rhythms, field hollers, street cries, gospel, and blues. Pete Seeger, who had performed in 1950 at a Music Inn folk festival, told an interviewer from *Metronome* in the fall of 1951 that "nothing but good can come from contact with other forms."[68]

For the music he now wanted to perform, Belafonte concentrated on the black, diasporic, and labor song traditions he had heard from Paul Robeson, Lead Belly, Josh White, Woody Guthrie, and various Kingston and New York iterations of mento and calypso. His friend Bill Attaway, whose two published novels illuminated the social consequences of migration, class exploitation, and racial discrimination, encouraged Belafonte to view folk songs as a body of social knowledge, a collective resource open to all. With Attaway's support, Belafonte immersed himself in listening to field recordings, many collected by Alan Lomax and preserved at the Library of Congress. Belafonte and his friends worked to transform and reclaim songs he discovered in these collections. He and Attaway revised some of the lyrics; Work and Thomas "tinker[ed] with melodies" to create new arrangements. Rollins, who formally assumed the position as Belafonte's manager in 1951, rented a rehearsal studio above the Lyceum Theater, where he had an office. He and Belafonte shared an interest in stagecraft; he worked with Belafonte on sharpening his performance and deepening its dramatic force.[69]

Singing folk music would draw on Belafonte's strengths: acute sensitivity to sound and rhythm, deep intellectual curiosity and profound historical sympathy, lithe physicality and personal animation. His untrained voice and not having learned to read music would no longer hold him back. "When I was a jazz singer, I found I had nothing to contribute to the field," he told an interviewer in the 1950s. "In folk music, on the other hand, I can use my voice and my dramatic training. . . . Going into folk music was originally a study of tradition, of my own people's tradition, an attempt to find a culture in which I could learn and the structure within which I could function."[70]

The most advantageous setting to debut the new songs would be the Village Vanguard, stepping-stone to success for Josh White, Lead Belly, and The Weavers. Jack Rollins knew the owner, Max Gordon, who chose the acts for the Vanguard and his uptown nightclub, The Blue Angel; he asked Gordon to take a chance. But Gordon, who knew Belafonte from the jazz clubs and called him "a handsome man singing three pop tunes, not bad, not good," turned Rollins down. Not giving in, Rollins pressed Gordon to hear Belafonte audition with a chain-gang song, a calypso, and a work song. Gordon found Belafonte's versions unoriginal and uninspiring, compared to those performed by Lead Belly and the many calypsonians who had played at the Vanguard. But Rollins somehow persuaded Gordon to give Belafonte a trial run. For opening night on October 26, 1951, Tony Scott, his future wife, Fran Settele (whom he had met at the Sage), and Attaway did what they could to pack the room, sending postcards to everyone they knew: friends, Sage customers, likely CNA associates, mailing lists of Negro organizations.[71]

Folk Songs, Work Songs, and Calypsos: October 1951

By all accounts, Belafonte's Vanguard performance was electric, and it marked the beginning of a hugely successful career as a musical performer. The dubious Max Gordon saw something in Belafonte's live performance that he had not imagined from his audition. He described the audience that first night as "spellbound," Belafonte's presence like "an explosion, an unexpected but an instantaneous explosion." Singing with guitar accompaniment freed Belafonte to use his hands, his face, and his body to inhabit and convey the world invoked by a song. Later Craig Work would describe how Belafonte's "magic" made Work "invisible": "Everyone was instantly . . . absorbed in Harry's aura."[72]

From that first performance at the Vanguard, Belafonte's repertoire of "folk songs, work songs, calypsos" kept faith with the political vision of the otherwise besieged popular front Left. He chose pieces that revealed racial history as a source of cultural wealth and the color line as a tool of white supremacy, songs that trespassed racial and national boundaries to show the creativity of black and white working people around the world. The capaciousness of the folk category also provided some cover for Belafonte as he stepped into the spotlight. Folksingers continued to entertain at events that championed labor and civil rights and to face red-baiting. But folk songs sung by popular vocalists with no political associations were also becoming hits. A *New York Times* reviewer wrote in 1948 that pop vocalist Jo Stafford's turn to singing American folk songs might be just the ticket to widen the appeal for folk music to those "who were not hobbyists in this field, perhaps even to her juke-box set fans." In addition to The Weavers' hit version of Lead Belly's "Goodnight Irene," other renditions by Frank Sinatra, Stafford, and country singers Moon Mullican, Ernest Tubb, and Red Foley ranked high on the pop charts, with Tubb and Foley's duet also reaching No. 1 on the country chart.[73]

Three weeks into their Vanguard booking, Belafonte and Work broke into national TV with a guest appearance on the variety show *Cavalcade of Stars*, hosted by entertainer Jackie Gleason. The syndicated New York entertainment columns that appeared in newspapers all over the country applauded Belafonte's "debut in his new calling" and his chance at the "front-line coin and prestige" (*Variety* lingo) that had eluded him as a pop singer. "Now the young man is established and will have no more worries about an open door on Broadway. They're all open now."[74]

However, appearing on national TV also brought Belafonte his first public red-baiting from *Counterattack*. His face "may have been new to many in the TV audience," warned the newsletter, "but it has undoubtedly been seen by many Communists and fellow travelers" at functions of the CNA, "the Party's Negro cultural front, since the start of the Korean War."[75] From here on, Belafonte knew he was being watched.

Early reviews compared Belafonte favorably to other folksingers with successful nightclub careers, especially Josh White, but also to Richard Dyer-Bennett and Burl Ives. Josh White had a polished cabaret-style act: smooth, stylized, seductive. Dyer-Bennett and Ives both relied on the musical range and quality of their voices, with simple guitar accompaniment, drawing their material from the Anglo-American song tradition. Belafonte's playlist of work and folk songs included some identified with White, but the calypsos were his addition. His musical style and appeal were inseparable from his uncompromising stance, personal beauty, and emotional expressiveness. Reviewers called attention to his "feeling" for the material, and the power of his "total package": "how his baritone, his facial expressions, and bodily movements become part of the words and music, and the result is a rich dramatic portrayal."[76] This "total package" created Belafonte's charisma and distinguished him from his peers.

Metronome's jazz reviewer Barry Ulanov raved about how Belafonte "moves and tears his way through a remarkable variety of songs, American Negro and Brazilian Negro, America's white and European." A Broadway columnist provided more details of his musical range, "from the early American folk and work tunes, to songs from Israel, Afro-Brazilian numbers, sea chanteys, Calypsos, and tunes from the British isles."[77] Belafonte did not seek to embody one particular cultural tradition but instead presented himself as a black world citizen who drew from and respected multiple traditions. Protesting racialized boundaries and resisting white supremacy by rejecting the segregation of musical genres had international implications.

In his choice of words, Ulanov exposed some of the larger debates about how the term "folk" was being interpreted at the time. He deemed Belafonte's folk repertoire as of "greater depth than is generally supposed," music that involved "art and artists," in contrast with music he denigrated as produced by "incompetent primitives." Ulanov saw folk "as the best music that man has made and hasn't signed, the best of the music of the primitive and untutored." As opposed to "music that has been prettied and fussed and turned tastelessly indoors in the past," Belafonte had added "a beat and a boom." Ulanov's praise associated Belafonte with the jazz he admired but in masculinized and racialized terms.[78]

When Belafonte performed calypsos at the Vanguard in 1951, he associated himself with music familiar to New Yorkers in a variety of settings. The boasting trickster's satirical and sexually playful lyrics and the Afro-Caribbean and Latin American orchestration in recorded calypso music had traveled with West Indians to New York and had become part of the musical soundscape in Harlem, San Juan Hill, and black and West Indian neighborhoods in Brooklyn.[79] Travel to the Caribbean exposed white tourists to the music. By the late 1930s, some of the Trinidad-born calypsonians were expanding their audiences by adding North American themes and references to their songs. Many more white and black Americans heard calypso after the U.S. military built its base in Trinidad in 1941. As one white travel writer wrote in 1947, "American soldiers who packed the calypso tents nightly during the war were always rewarded with a calypso or two about themselves," sometimes critiquing the American occupation at the same time. Harlem theaters specialized in calypso: Duke of Iron was a favorite of Apollo audiences. But calypsonians had also appeared regularly at the Vanguard after 1939, and newspapers covered calypso as an ingredient of Village bohemianism. In the early 1940s, several Hollywood adventure films had used Sir Lancelot and other musicians to enhance a Caribbean setting; he sang "Ugly Woman" in *Happy Go Lucky* in 1943.[80]

Calypso had not reached radio's broader public, because most of its lyrics failed the broadcast standards of "good taste," with the notable exception of a 1934 broadcast in which Trinidadian singers performed on the *Rudy Vallee Show.* But by 1945 and 1946, several calypsos had become best-selling records and jukebox hits, especially the Andrews Sisters' Americanized and cleaned-up version of Lord Invader's "Rum and Cocoa-Cola," a pointed commentary on the local impact of the U.S. occupation, and Ella Fitzgerald and Louis Jordan's rhythm and blues version of "Stone Cold Dead in the Market." Nat King Cole recorded "Calypso Blues" in 1949. By then, separate black and white American audiences converged in one large calypso market. A 1946 Town Hall concert organized by Alan Lomax, "Calypso at Midnight," had shined the spotlight on Trinidadians singing popular calypsos and other songs, including MacBeth the Great's versions of "Hold 'Em Joe" and "Man Smart, Woman Smarter," songs that would later be identified with Belafonte. Duke of Iron, Lord Invader, MacBeth the Great, and Sir Lancelot had made calypsos part of the mix at many People's Songs and Progressive Party events in the late 1940s.[81]

Belafonte did not have the vocal resonance or concert presence of Robeson. He did not convey the experiential authority or musical ingenuity of southern-born blues performers, such as Lead Belly, Big Bill Broonzy, Sonny Terry, and Brownie McGhee, or possess the facility with wordplay of the Trinidadian calypsonians. But his juxtaposition of folk songs, work songs, and calypsos renewed each form. His clearly articulated calypsos, absent the island costumes, instrumentation, and dance, became more lyrical and accessible. The folk aegis offered a way to represent calypso as akin to other forms of black and nonelite culture, repositioning the music apart from colonial associations with "native" inferiority or tourist-driven exoticism.[82]

Belafonte's intensity and dramatic authority made his audiences feel they were hearing the music for the first time, engaging directly with a world that came alive through his performance. Max Gordon observed that Belafonte gave himself fully to each performance. And the bookings flowed in. According to Craig Work, audiences at the Village Vanguard, the Blue Angel, the Apollo, and Birdland all embraced the new folk and calypso repertoire. When Work received his draft notice in 1952, Millard Thomas, Belafonte's friend and Work's teacher, stepped in as accompanist.[83]

Ignoring *Counterattack*'s warning, Belafonte continued to appear with other CNA activists to feature diasporic black culture, history, and protest and to demand work opportunities and recognition for black artists in the culture industries. He and Poitier were proposed as vice-chairmen when CNA convened a two-day constitutional convention at the end of January 1952.[84] A special "Evening in the Arts" event at the end of the convention featured Belafonte, Poitier, Robeson, and the actors Clarice Taylor, Alice Childress, and William Marshall. Belafonte's repertoire included a rendition of the "Negro Preacher's Song" from *Lonesome Train*, which he had performed with such power at a People's Songs concert four years before. At the end of February 1952, many of these same artists participated in a Negro History Festival sponsored by Robeson's *Freedom* newspaper. Belafonte, Poitier, and the writer John O. Killens narrated a pageant written for the occasion by Lorraine Hansberry and Childress. Timed in coordination with the South African antiapartheid "Defiance of Unjust Laws" campaign, CNA presented Childress's play, *Gold through the Trees,* depicting blacks in the United States, Haiti, British West Indies, and South Africa struggling to free themselves from racial oppression: it opened at Club Baron on April 7, 1952.[85]

Although Belafonte's earnings still barely covered his expenses—which included paying his guitarist at union scale and fees to his manager Rollins and publicist Wickes—he had almost found a way to support himself and his family by making art that was personally and politically meaningful. "What I am doing now makes me the happiest guy in the world . . . saying to an audience, 'here's Negro life with as much dignity as I can give it," he told the *New York Post* in April. Avoiding language that would flag him as a leftist, he echoed the People's Songs critique of pop lyrics: "Singing about love, moon and June meant nothing to him." To gesture toward his political intent, artfully disguised, Belafonte described the song he had sung in the 1948 *Lonesome Train* performance as a "haunting Negro folk song written about the death of Abe Lincoln" to exemplify "what I can best offer you as a Negro artist."[86]

Appearing at the upscale Blue Angel, "a class niterie" according to *Variety,* provided important show business exposure. Rollins broadened Belafonte's visibility with guest spots on radio and on network television. He negotiated a new recording contract with RCA Victor, the largest record company in the country. Belafonte's new prominence could also burnish the prestige of the CNA, who advertised him as a "recording star" when they listed him, along with Poitier, as regular performers for "Showtime at the Club Baron" on Thursdays in April. By early May, columnist Dorothy Kilgallen reported that MGM was screen-testing the "folk balladeer" for a dramatic role, which the *Chicago Defender* explained as the result of impressing "Holly notables, including Dore Schary" (then studio chief at MGM) who saw him at the Blue Angel.[87] All the pieces seemed to be falling into place.

Red Scare for a Rising Black Star

A Hollywood film would raise Belafonte's national profile, but it could also attract unwanted right-wing political scrutiny. HUAC had reopened its hearings on Hollywood and the entertainment industries in March 1951. In early February 1952, Harvey Matusow, a Communist Party member who had worked in the People's Songs office in 1948 and who became an undercover informer for the FBI in 1950, became a key government witness offering testimony about The Weavers and other People's Song folksingers. A few years later, Matusow would admit that much of what he claimed was unsubstantiated, and he went to jail himself for conspiring with U.S. attorneys to give false testimony and perjuring himself under oath. But at the time, The Weavers lost bookings, and scrutiny of Left-oriented folksingers intensified. Hope Foye, the black concert singer who had appeared at People's Songs and Progressive Party events and had been scheduled to sing with Robeson at the first Peekskill concert, was called before McCarran's Internal Security Committee at the end of February. Not long after, in an effort to "admit his mistakes," Burl Ives volunteered to appear. The actor Canada Lee, forced out of work since early 1951 and unable to clear his name, died in early May at the age of forty-five, just before he was scheduled to appear in front of HUAC.[88]

In this politically charged atmosphere, Belafonte began to face hard choices. Paul Robeson, barraged by anticommunist public censure, was just finishing a fifteen-city fund-raising tour for *Freedom*, the Council on African Affairs, the National Negro Labor Council (a new formation of left-wing trade unionists), and the CNA. The tour fell short of its goals. Although some unions and churches were willing to sponsor concerts, public authorities pressed municipal venues to cancel the bookings. Local supporters fought in court and scrambled to find black churches and outdoor spaces where Robeson could perform. The FBI filmed the audiences who attended his concerts.[89]

A turning point for Belafonte came at the end of Robeson's tour. Belafonte was ready to join Robeson onstage to sing at an NNLC rally in New Jersey, but Robeson worried that appearing with him would cut off careers just beginning to be established. Labor organizer (and future mayor of Detroit) Coleman Young remembered Robeson advising Belafonte *not* to perform. "You don't need [to sing] to prove your support of me," Robeson reassured him. According to Young's account, Belafonte wept, but followed Robeson's counsel.[90] Robeson's generous concern to shield younger artists guided Belafonte's way forward.

That anticommunism had begun to isolate the larger-than-life Robeson from his audiences was tragic to his followers, including Belafonte, who realized that navigating treacherous political waters would require a caution he had not yet practiced. Robeson's commitments constituted a crucial and perhaps sometimes burdensome yardstick against which to measure himself. Rather than attaching his name to a petition, showing up at a rally, or participating in a benefit, Belafonte would have to speak primarily through his performance.[91]

From New York to Hollywood, 1952

Singing in nightclubs in New York, Philadelphia, Chicago, Las Vegas, and Los Angeles; recording songs for national sales through RCA; appearing on film, radio, and television; taking part in a musical revue on Broadway: in each of these career-building settings, Belafonte had to deal with difficult situations outside his control. Travel meant being cut off from sustaining relationships, and it required him to manage various forms of racial segregation. Anti-communist blacklisting caused distrust among former friends and allies, who found themselves unsure whom to trust and how to handle interrogation while remaining true to core political convictions.

Belafonte's film debut resulted from an experiment at MGM, *Bright Road,* "the first non-musical movie made with an all-black cast on the lot of a major studio." In the early 1950s, there was little studio interest in films that dealt with race. Any connection to labor, civil rights, and social critique courted controversy and unwanted scrutiny. The major studios had been weakened by the antitrust decision in the late 1940s, which severed control of production from exhibition. But making films with black characters might prop up the studios' sagging bottom lines by extending movies' appeal to black ticket buyers.[92]

MGM planned *Bright Road* as an inexpensive second feature. For black artists, however, *any* studio film involved high stakes, since screen opportunities were so limited and racial representations so constrained. Based on a short story by black writer Mary Elizabeth Vroman, *Bright Road* told the story of a thoughtful but nonconforming fourth grader (Philip Hepburn) who tested the skills of a new teacher (Dorothy Dandridge) and her supportive principal (Harry Belafonte).[93]

The project was full of contradictions from the start. The main roles in this "nonmusical" film were played by musical performers without extensive dramatic résumés. The film's trailer introduced Dandridge as a glamorous nightclub performer and featured Belafonte singing. Its publicity aimed for mainstream appeal, promising that it "makes no protest [and] files no complaints."[94] Even so, any film about a black schoolchild would resonate with the five legal challenges to race-based school segregation then working their way through the courts, challenges that

Principal Belafonte and teacher Dandridge in a publicity still for Bright Road *(1953). (Courtesy of Academy of Motion Picture Arts and Sciences.)*

were joined and would be resolved in the Supreme Court's *Brown v. Board of Education* decision in 1954.

Even this low-budget film required its actors to pass a loyalty clearance. Belafonte and Dandridge were eventually able to clear this bar, despite documentation of left-wing political sympathies. Belafonte explained his Caravan for Wallace performances as paid employment and promised to avoid further affiliations of this kind.[95] For the school principal to sing a folk song strained credibility, and the quick shoot offered him little opportunity to learn screen acting. *Ebony*'s cover photo of Belafonte in the company of Tony Curtis and Janet Leigh intimated Hollywood stature. In the studio workplace, and Los Angeles more generally, it was clear to the black actors that they had only temporary visitors' passes when they ventured outside of Los Angeles's black institutions and neighborhoods.[96]

When *Bright Road* opened months later, Belafonte's

character didn't make much of an impression on the white critics, as indicated by a headline in the *Los Angeles Times*: "'Bright Road' Touching Film Story of Children." A Los Angeles preview audience of black sorority members was unenthusiastic, and a syndicated article from the American Negro Press reported that "critics were divided" on whether Belafonte's acting was stiff or charming.[97]

Heading from Hollywood to a nightclub engagement in Las Vegas plunged Belafonte back into the Jim Crow arrangements he had hoped to leave behind in Miami. Performing at the Thunderbird, he was not allowed in its dining room, casino, bar, or pool. Black performers on the road frequently had to cope with the discord between being the object of personal adulation onstage and humiliat-

At the premiere of Bright Road, *Belafonte lights a cigarette for actor Leslie Scott, then starring in the Broadway revival of* Porgy and Bess. *55th Street Playhouse, New York, April 17, 1953. (Courtesy of Photographs and Prints Division, Schomburg Center for Research in Black Culture, the New York Public Library, Astor, Lenox and Tilden Foundations.)*

ing exclusion off stage.[98] Musical performance in Las Vegas fronted for the primary business of gambling, with a sideline in sex. In the late 1940s and early 1950s, when the casinos began to attract more people from the South and the East, racial segregation reorganized urban space and the resort hotels, and black entertainers could find lodging only on the west side of town.[99]

As Belafonte moved from city to city, the intensity of his performance grabbed the attention of different and class-stratified audiences: at the "boisterous" Boulevard in Queens, the "square" Coconut Grove in Los Angeles, the "chi-chi" Blue Angel in New York, and the "posh" Black Orchid in Chicago. Reviewers emphasized "s.a." (sex appeal) and fan enthusiasm, reporting that "bobby-soxers" were making off with life-size advertising photographs. Even following an engagement by the more widely known Josh White, Belafonte held his own, singing a work song identified with White and adding his own version of a calypso. "He electrifies the place with his opener, 'Timber.' However, he really gets the crowd going with his 'Birds and Bees' ["Man Piaba"]." Writing for *Down Beat,* Don Freeman called his performances "transformative" and his appeal universal: "He hits all audiences the same way—hits them with such truth and honesty that the differences between people seem to vanish." By November 1953, jazz writer Nat Hentoff judged Belafonte's "command of the audience" as "electric and complete." His playlist continued to cross genres and national boundaries: the preacher's song from *Lonesome Train;* "Scarlet Ribbons," a contemporary ballad that had provided a recent hit for Jo Stafford; "Hava Nagila," the Israeli wedding song he learned from his Sage and CNA friend Mort Freeman; and the calypso hits "Hold 'Em Joe" and "Matilda."[100]

Recording was the key to more reliable income as a performer and higher fees at nightclubs, but Belafonte could not initially communicate his personal charisma in this medium. The record companies were interested in finding formulas for hits, and Belafonte had little say at his first RCA session in early April 1952 at the Manhattan Center (where he had sung for the Young Progressives in 1949). Rather than to try to capture what was distinctive about Belafonte's sound, the RCA producer backed him with strings, piano, accordion, drum, and a chorus of male singers. This was an approach similar to what Decca had used on early recordings of The Weavers. Belafonte's first single consisted of "A Rovin'," the folk song he and Craig Work tried out at Birdland, and "Chimney Smoke," a pop-styled folk song.

Belafonte worked to bring his studio sound closer to what he was able to convey in performance, with assistance from the folk song collector and sound engineer Tony Schwartz. Belafonte's friend Tony Scott played the flute on his next RCA session, where they recorded versions of "Timber," "Shenandoah" (an early-nineteenth-century American song recorded by many, including Robeson), "Scarlet Ribbons," and "Man Smart, Woman Smarter," previously performed by New York calypso singers.[101] In the rest of the country, reviewers couldn't quite place what they heard on "Timber" and "Man Smart." One in Madison, Wisconsin, remarked that Belafonte sang "with a foreign accent" and with "much feeling." Even the *Chicago Defender* struggled to define his "different 'pop' approach," calling it "unusual," "unique," "weird," and "exciting."[102] Belafonte had a long way to go to produce musically intelligible "hits" for national audiences.

Without substantial sales, Belafonte had to accept his RCA producer's suggestion in February 1953 to record "Gomen Nasai," a Japanese pop song that might attract "novelty" interest but was far afield from his chosen repertoire. Belafonte brought in new orchestration for his next recording of the calypso "Matilda" and the folk song "Venezuela." He added three clarinets, three fiddles, three drummers, including an Afro-Cuban drummer, and a carefully selected vocal group of men and women that included Ray Charles, whose songs were topping the rhythm and blues charts but who had not yet crossed over into popularity with white audiences. Still, no real hits for Belafonte.

Strains in the Spotlight, 1953–1954

By early 1953, the increasing pressures on Belafonte became evident as entertainment columnists began to track his missed performances due to "laryngitis": three in January and three in May. Belafonte did not have the training to conserve his voice, but this was also a time when blacklist pressures escalated for former friends and CNA colleagues Robert DeCormier and Ruby Dee and writer Langston Hughes. Targeted musicians and actors managed as best they could, with the help of modest off-Broadway productions and cultural programs for left-wing unions.[103] In sharp contrast, Belafonte enjoyed growing success. Ed Sullivan invited him onto *Toast of the Town* in October 1953, and as a singer of folk songs, in December he debuted on the Broadway stage in a sprawling variety revue called *John Murray Anderson's Almanac.*

Sullivan's tightly controlled guest spots provided critical access to national audiences, invaluable exposure for black performers. Most genres of television programming had become decidedly whiter after the coaxial cable enabled national live broadcasting and corporate sponsorship imposed segregationist limits to reassure southern markets. Ed Sullivan saw himself and his show as a central promoter of black talent, claiming in *Ebony* that television was "just what the doctor ordered for Negro performers" because it was "always flattering to the Negro performer whose vitality and wonderfully expressive face registers remarkably well." Belafonte's initial appearance on *Toast of the Town* suggested that the avid anticommunist Sulli-

Belafonte with Ed Sullivan, 1956. (Courtesy of the Everett Collection.)

van was willing to accept Belafonte's explanation of his political history, though it also set off suspicions among some on the left that Belafonte may have turned on former colleagues.[104] Introduced as a "youngster" with a "tremendous surge" and as a "Victor recording star," Belafonte sang the pop ballad "Scarlet Ribbons" and his version of "Matilda," after which Sullivan praised his "tremendous talent."[105]

Belafonte's acoustic presentation of his original riverboat work song "Mark Twain" stopped the show onstage

Belafonte photographed by Carl Van Vechten, February 18, 1954. (Courtesy of the Carl Van Vechten Trust, Beinecke Library, Yale University.)

in *John Murray Anderson's Almanac*, a standout amid the combination of satirical sketches, physical comedy, singing and dancing, beautiful scenery and costumes. His version of "Hold 'Em Joe" added calypso to the show's representation of carnival in a big production number building to the finale. *New York Times* drama critic Brooks Atkinson named Belafonte's "Mark Twain" as the show's "high point in theatrical artistry." What Belafonte contributed was "original, imaginative, and stunning," a counterbalance to what he viewed as the show's weak musical score. The black arts connoisseur Carl Van Vechten photographed Belafonte, in his *Almanac* costume and street clothes, to add to his portrait gallery of distinguished New York writers and performers.[106]

Belafonte's notices outshone those of the show as a whole. The *New York Times* music critic wrote that the drama critics judged him as the show's "shining light," even in production numbers that drew "the listener's attention away from the singer's individuality and intensity," because his "furious conviction is like a jolt in a show dedicated largely to light entertainment." The extravagant critical praise anticipated the Tony he was awarded at the end of March 1954, for Distinguished Featured Musical Actor, the first awarded to a black actor.[107] Belafonte was performing nightly in this show when the Supreme Court announced the *Brown* decision, abandoning the legal fiction that "separate" was "equal." (Robeson's publication *Freedom* warned its readers that "Popular Movement Needed to Enforce Court Decree" if segregation was to actually be dismantled.)[108]

By the end of 1953, Belafonte was anointed as a rising star by *Billboard*. He appeared alongside Jackie Gleason, Liberace, and Frank Sinatra on a newly created honor roll: "Box Office Hits of 1953 Point to 1954 Headliners."[109] Belafonte had more money than he ever had before, and could look forward to future high-paying bookings. With the assistance of CNA colleague and actor Frank Silvera, he bought his family a two-story attached house with a yard in a white neighborhood across from Randall's Island in Elmhurst, Long Island.[110]

Belafonte's heightened visibility and success revived the interest of his right-wing critics. In early January 1954, *Counterattack* blasted him as a "Communist fronter," citing appearances with Robeson for the left-wing union District 65, for CNA, and for *Freedom*, at events for the National Council of Arts, Sciences and Professions and the Young Progressives of America, seared by the "rosy hue" of entertainers connected with the Village Vanguard. Belafonte's next scheduled appearance on *Counterattack*-booster Ed Sullivan's show one week later was now in doubt. But after Belafonte met with Sullivan, he appeared as announced.[111]

Belafonte's defense appeared in *Counterattack* the following month: he had never been a member of the Communist Party or "knowingly" associated with any Communist front. "As a Roman Catholic, a Negro, and an American he hates Communism and everything it stands for." He was just a paid entertainer for progressive organizations, didn't remember attending meetings, and supported the CNA because he thought it "was devoted to the advancement of Negro culture." Taking note of his prior film industry clearance and his promise to "exercise extreme care in his future associations," *Counterattack* let the case rest.[112]

But surveillance continued. The FBI came to Queens to interrogate Marguerite about Belafonte's associations with Robeson and Du Bois. A HUAC investigator confronted Belafonte with details that could only have come from a political acquaintance-turned-informer. By the summer of 1954, the CNA and the NNLC were designated as "subversive" organizations on the attorney general's list.[113] Mounting pressure made it increasingly hard to know whom to trust.

Belafonte turned for guidance to two new friends, a progressive psychiatrist and her financier-writer husband, both of whom had shown interest in civil rights and the arts. They had met him the previous summer at the White Mountain Seven Arts Festival in New Hampshire, where Belafonte was singing and Janet Alterman Kennedy, a psychiatrist who had published research on "Problems Posed in the Analysis of the Negro Patient," was lecturing. Her husband, Jay Richard Kennedy, who had recently published a well-reviewed novel of Hollywood intrigue, approached Belafonte as a fellow lover of folk music. When he first met Janet Kennedy, Belafonte later recalled thinking to himself, "I'd like to call you. I'm up to deep shit with problems in my life."[114]

In the spring of 1954, dealing with self-alienation and personal uncertainty, he began five-day-a-week psychoanalysis with her. When she asked him questions about Robeson and Du Bois, he assumed she shared his concerns for them. She encouraged him to turn to her financially savvy and successful husband for help in managing his earnings and his career. Jay Richard Kennedy listened to Belafonte speak about his work and money-related concerns and promised, "You never have to worry again. I know all the parts and I'll put that to rest. What other meaning does life have except in the service of things that you believe in . . .?"[115] Even while Belafonte was still represented by Rollins, Kennedy took over management of his bookings, and by the end of the year, it was Broadway news that Belafonte and Rollins had "called it a day."[116]

The contrast for Belafonte between his phenomenally successful, physically draining nights and the considerably less glamorous domestic daytime had never been sharper. Even though Belafonte was now working steadily in New York rather than traveling—he was performing a nightly show at La Vie En Rose after appearing in *Almanac*—he often stayed over with Tony and Fran Scott in midtown. Belafonte's publicity featured a conventional family life, and Marguerite become pregnant with their second daughter, Shari, who was born in September. But their marriage, already premised on leading quite separate lives, became even more frayed. The adulation of fans, the exploding financial remuneration, and uncertainty about his work left Belafonte distraught. A *Newsweek* interview captured his restless, unsettled, and self-critical state. "I don't want to be a pretty, pretty boy. I don't care for glamour. I guess I'd still rather act than be the greatest singer in the world."[117] He was the only recognized performer who did not appear at the Plaza Hotel dinner where the Tony Awards were presented. Marguerite attended in his place.[118]

By the time plans were announced for a major studio production of the black-cast opera *Carmen Jones*, Belafonte was the obvious choice to play the leading man. Director Otto Preminger saw the production as an opportunity to use the new wide-screen CinemaScope technology to feature black entertainers as sexy and sophisticated movie stars. When Belafonte signed at the end of April 1954, his contract stipulated top billing in screen credits and first-class airfare from New York to Los Angeles for him, his wife, and their child.[119] Marguerite and Adrienne may not have used their tickets. Spending the summer in Hollywood working on the film, Belafonte became involved in a significant relationship with Julie Robinson, the beautiful Katherine Dunham dancer and dance teacher from a left-wing Jewish family who had previously dated his friend Marlon Brando. New York newspaper readers who were following the buzz before *Carmen Jones*'s October opening might have spotted a picture of Belafonte and Robinson among the photos of the stars arriving at a party at Preminger's house.[120]

Carmen Jones employed a gifted group of black artists pleased to be involved in a film that aspired to art, with an extensive budget for production and promotion. They hoped the production would show off their talents: star qualities of the leads, Belafonte and Dandridge; the voices of the classically trained singers Olga James and Brock Peters, Belafonte's friend from the Neals' New York salon; the style of nightclub performers Pearl Bailey and the young Diahann Carroll; and the expressive dancers, including Carmen De Lavallade and the young Alvin Ailey. Although they were disappointed that the producers insisted that opera singers dub Belafonte's and Dandridge's singing, and that "aspects of the plot and characters and situations were every bit as stereotyped as the 'dees,' 'dems' and 'dats' that filled the dialogue," they were proud that superb black performances filled the screen. Belafonte later described *Carmen Jones* as the first "black film," not just a film with black characters.[121]

But the actors all knew their access to Hollywood was just temporary. Diahann Carroll later described how "we were the only black people on the lot. The producers, production staff and crew were quite polite and professional but there was absolutely no camaraderie on or off the set, no sense of shared purpose. The unspoken assumption seemed to be that we were outsiders, in town only a short while to do our 'black' feature film . . . and when it was over we would go back to wherever we came from and no one would ever see us again."[122] Before its New York opening, when Belafonte was asked if he thought the film would lead to more work for black actors, he was direct: "Not really." The best it could do was to work "symbolically," proving that "there's no corner of the human drama Negroes cannot play." Like his fellow artists, he did not have the illusion that Hollywood was "geared to pioneering of this sort."[123]

Appearing in *Carmen Jones*, the first all-black film to be a commercial success, Belafonte and Dandridge gained status as "movie stars" and as a new film couple.[124] They received mostly rave reviews, even without being allowed to sing; everyone agreed that they "sizzled the movie screens." The film itself prompted a more complex response. Was it a "triumphant wedding of music, drama, and film," "a grand opera, a grand show," or "emotionally superficial, inconsistent with the depth of its theme"? Was it as "commercial as a bright new dollar and artistic in the best sense of the word" or "a sex melodrama with longhair music and a mad conglomeration of bizarre show"? Film critic Bosley Crowther was struck by the incongruities between the opera's extravagant theatricality and the realist effects of the film's military and urban settings. In the midst of explicit battles over segregation, a reviewer for one of Los Angeles's black newspapers worried about the stereotypical costs of what he called the "gimmick" of modernizing a classic opera with an all-black cast: "These inanities, these absurdities, become direct reflections upon Negroes. They become 'traits' because nobody else is around to shoulder the blame."[125]

Interviewed in the middle of filming *Carmen Jones*,

Soldier Belafonte and factory worker–temptress Dorothy Dandridge in publicity stills for Carmen Jones *(1954). (Courtesy of the Academy of Motion Picture Arts and Sciences.)*

Belafonte seemed to be floundering. In an effort to maintain an identity other than that of movie star, he announced ambitious plans as a collector of folk songs. When work on the film was over, he intended to follow Alan Lomax's path on a "tour [of] prison camps and penitentiaries in the South . . . for the purposes of recording songs sung by prisoners." He hoped to use these songs as the basis of what he called "an Evening of Negro Folklore and Music," for a fall tour produced by Paul Gregory and Charles Laughton. He would appear as "singer, narrator, and magician," backed by a forty-voice chorus.[126]

When the filming was over, what Belafonte actually did was to fulfill a nightclub commitment and then head back to New York. RCA had released his first long-playing album, featuring Belafonte finally sounding like his acoustic performances, with work songs including "Mark Twain," ballads, Anglo-American folk songs, and the calypso-styled "Man Piaba." He was there for the birth of and baptism of his daughter Shari, whose godparents were Frank Silvera's wife, Ann, and Tony Scott. A few days later he appeared again on Sullivan's *Toast of the Town,* singing "Mark Twain" and "Hold 'Em Joe." In this period he and Marguerite began to face the possibility that his relationship with Julie Robinson might end their marriage.[127]

The opening of *Carmen Jones* at a theater near Times Square was seen by millions in twenty-four cities across the country: this was the first premiere from New York to be transmitted coast to coast on network television and radio. Many of the stars who attended were captured on newsreel footage, which marked the film's status as a Hollywood production. The film's director and stars were out in force; also attending were Broadway stars, producers and directors, New York nightclub stars, and important black politicians.[128]

Harry Belafonte did not attend the premiere. On October 28, he was on the road, escaping from family life and its complication. Rather than staging his proposed "Negro Anthology," he was on a grueling fifteen-week tour with a light musical revue, *3 for Tonight,* sharing the stage with a white husband-and-wife dance team, Marge and Gower Champion. They performed ninety-four shows in thirty-six states across the country, playing to full houses in modest locales—school auditoriums and gymnasiums and concert halls—across the country. Belafonte, the only featured black artist, sang fourteen songs from his repertoire.[129]

Many of the show's performances were scheduled in segregated towns, despite the producers' promises to avoid them. Although the three stars hoped to stir audiences when physical contact between the three of them "desegregated" the stage, Jim Crow rules in public accommodations frequently separated Belafonte and guitarist Millard Thomas from the rest of the cast and musicians. They were relegated to "colored" bathrooms, drinking fountains, waiting rooms, hotels, and boardinghouses, with respite only when they could arrange to be hosted by local black families. Belafonte wrote in March 1955 that he had been determined "to face whatever conditions existed, in order to go out there on stage and cause white Southern audiences to accept a Negro performer in a mixed cast."[130]

When *3 for Tonight* arrived back in New York, enthusiastic ticket buyers lined up to see Belafonte, whose rave reviews again outstripped those of the production. A caricature drawn by show business cartoonist Al Hirschfeld heralded the opening. One New York theater critic wrote that "the producer Paul Gregory did not need three for tonight as long as he's got Harry Belafonte for tonight. . . . There's no getting away from . . . the power, the command, and the magnetism of the irrepressible Mr. Belafonte." Whatever his personal turmoil, Belafonte delivered stunning performances night after night, showing audiences what another critic described as the "fanaticism of the dedicated artist," losing himself in the "fiery intensity" of his singing.[131]

Belafonte continued to speak of his hopes for a "Negro Anthology," which would include a program of folk songs and readings from Langston Hughes and Paul Laurence Dunbar.[132] Even as he was celebrated, Belafonte was far from calling the shots. For now, that personal project was beyond his grasp. He had reached the top, singing and recording folk music, performing on stage, screen, and records, but he felt politically isolated, personally lost, and professionally out of control.

Later he would describe this as a period of breakdown, manifest in attacks of laryngitis and retching, although it was also a time of major breakthroughs. He was torn between remaining on guard against racist rejection and becoming seduced by the warmth, praise, and financial rewards of fan adulation. He felt intense pressure "as the spokesman for my race" that came with his token success as a black man in white world. "I felt I didn't deserve this success. At the same time I had a tremendous drive to deliver."[133] He was "desperate for relief," but there was no relief in sight.

MULTIMEDIA STARDOM AND THE STRUGGLE FOR RACIAL EQUALITY, 1955–1960

Representing the Race after *Brown v. Board of Education*

The timing of Belafonte's rising celebrity was inextricable from its historical moment: the months following the 1954 U.S. Supreme Court decision banning segregation in public schools that marked a national shift away from acquiescence to Jim Crow. The radical black sociologist and journalist Horace Cayton, reading about the court decision on the subway in New York, found himself "shocked" by the "magnitude of the decision." He imagined "a large hole . . . [in] the dike of segregation, through [which] would soon pour a torrent. Would this widen the breach so that eventually it would cause the collapse of the whole structure?"[1]

Cayton, covering the UN for the *Pittsburgh Courier*, understood the court's decision in the context of the decolonization occurring around the world in the years after World War II. He had long assumed that "the United States would find it impossible to maintain a caste society in this modern world desperate for freedom." The legal record shows that the *Brown* judges were indeed affected by Cold War competition for nonaligned nations, but that day

Cayton's mind was set on the coming changes, "long overdue." Because the "Supreme Court had just ruled that I was an American citizen with the rights and privileges of a citizen," he vowed to seize those rights, marching straight into the barbershop at Grand Central Station rather than travel to Harlem for a haircut. After that, he "threw over all my former compliance with any so-called color line and for the first time I felt free to go any place, provided I had the money to pay the bill."[2]

Southern black and white responses to a verdict that overturned the racial separation cornerstone of public education were not immediately visible to national media audiences. Mainstream newspapers and radio stations continued to feature blackface minstrelsy and black criminality rather than to cover potential noncompliance with the color line. But the black press followed developments closely.[3] Within weeks of the decision, white southerners across the South formed White Citizens' Councils (WCC) to defy the ruling and inflict economic damage and vigilante punishment on black people associated with challenges to segregation. Some institutions and school systems prepared to comply with the court's order; in May 1955, a few black students signed up to attend the all-white Central High School in Little Rock, Arkansas. But the tenacity of Jim Crow norms enforced by violence was harshly exposed at the end of that summer when Emmett Till, a fourteen-year-old black youth from Chicago visiting relatives in Mississippi, was found brutally murdered, reportedly for whistling at a white woman.

The most unexpected turn of events was the broad working-class participation in a surprisingly effective boycott of the segregated buses in Montgomery, Alabama, beginning December 1, 1955, organized after the arrest of Rosa Parks, seamstress and local NAACP activist, who had refused to yield her seat to a white passenger. For weeks and months, the boycotters and community leaders who supported them, including a young minister new in town, Dr. Martin Luther King, Jr., held meetings and organized alternative forms of transportation. City buses rolled nearly empty through Montgomery. Outraged white responses included calls for "massive resistance" to the court decision.[4] In March 1956, nearly one hundred congressmen across the South and Southwest signed "A Declaration of Constitutional Principles" in defense of segregation.

"Up South" in New York, black radicals followed the news of the boycott. When they heard that newly visible southern black activists were being targeted by white supremacist groups, they began to mobilize support. One supporters' group, In Friendship, was instigated by Ella Baker, Harlem branch leader of the NAACP, and two trusted political colleagues—nonviolent civil disobedience activist (and former Josh White backup singer) Bayard Rustin and left-wing lawyer and fund-raiser Stanley Levison—with some help from labor leader A. Philip Randolph. In Friendship brought together allies from progressive unions, local civil rights campaigns, and churches to raise money for those engaged in this confrontational and dangerous new phase of southern activism.[5]

After the court outlawed segregation, many African American writers and artists felt increasing urgency to address the mainstream erasure of black experience, what Lorraine Hansberry described as "the historical and cultural obliteration" when "Europe becomes the world" and the "Grace Kelly–Marilyn Monroe monotyped 'ideal' [is] imposed on the national culture . . . eradicat[ing] all evidence of negro culture anywhere." They wanted to displace the stereotypes of minstrels and maids, sexual predators and sexualized primitives, and reintroduce black people as ordinary citizens possessing equal rights to public space in schools, workplaces, and neighborhoods. But there was no consensus on how to celebrate the riches of black culture, traditions, and modernity while continuing to challenge white supremacist definitions and policing of racial boundaries. Campaigns for expanded citizenship exerted pressures to conform to middle-class norms and sexual respectability.[6] All-black productions like *The Head of the Family* and *Bright Road,* which aspired to "avoid controversy" in their representations of Negro life, now seemed to concede too much to segregation.

These were the circumstances in which Belafonte found himself, a popular performer on stages across the United States, prized guest on network television variety shows, and bona fide movie star following his charismatic performance in *Carmen Jones,* on-screen into 1956 at neighborhood theaters and drive-ins.[7] He was now a force to be reckoned with in the music industry. Belafonte's success reflected a shift in American popular music when, according to cultural historian Brian Ward, "young whites increasingly turned to black music and its derivatives for entertainment." The most commercially successful forms of black music, for black and white audiences, were black rock and roll, and after 1956, what Ward categorizes as a sweeter form of black pop.[8] But Belafonte's repertoire of folk music also became commercially successful in the crossover pop market, offering audiences of "steelworkers, symphony patrons, bobby-soxers and school children" a black alternative to rock and roll.[9] By 1957, Belafonte singles appeared at the top of the pop charts, but his greatest success was in the sale of albums, a relatively new format purchased primarily by consumers with more discretionary income, and responsible for an increasing share of industry revenues.[10]

Belafonte's celebrity in one medium promoted it in others. His first long-playing folk album, *Mark Twain,* had been released in 1954, but in January 1956 it rose to third place on the *Billboard* charts; the folk album *Belafonte,* released in 1955, was at No. 1 for six weeks, from February 1956. *Calypso,* which had originated in a television segment broadcast October 1955, was released at the end of May 1956, rose to the top of the album charts by June, and stayed there for thirty-one weeks, becoming the first album by a solo performer to sell a million copies.[11] Buying and playing his records gave audiences a tangible connection to what he and his music represented. A survey of New York–area male and female high school and college students reported in *Billboard* in December 1956 found that although more students ranked Elvis Presley, Frank Sinatra, Teresa Brewer, and Doris Day as their favorite singers, Belafonte had "the highest percentage of record buyers." Perhaps when students at Marquette, a Jesuit university in Milwaukee, Wisconsin, petitioned to replace Presley with Belafonte in the jukebox in the student union, they wanted to reclaim the union for the civil rights promise associated with his music.[12]

Belafonte's performances in primarily white venues reinforced his association with changing racial dynamics. He knew that he represented, in the language of the day, "the Negro in America"; for years he had been thinking about how to use his performance to "help bring about . . . a greater feeling of respect for my race." When he guest wrote Dorothy Kilgallen's syndicated column "The Voice of Broadway" in May 1955, the caption under his photo read "Harry Belafonte: Facing the Race Problem." At this time, black writers who had access to mainstream media framed their opposition to segregation very carefully in order not to fuel the segregationist claim that integration caused violence. Belafonte used this column to applaud the "gigantic strides in the sphere of equal social and artistic acceptance" over the last twenty years, while also emphasizing that there were "many barriers to be broken down, many prejudices to be met and conquered." He noted that the special treatment he received as a celebrity did not negate "frequent, blunt, harsh reminders that I am a Negro and that my race still has a long way to go to its goal of receiving equal recognition." He paired the warm reception of *3 for Tonight* by young southern university students with the series of "humiliation after humiliation" he and Millard Thomas had faced in finding places to sleep and eat. He accepted a personal burden of responsibility, writing that "Negro performers can help [eliminate barriers] by continuing to perform in the South," by "conduct[ing] themselves in a manner to win respect."[13]

Performing Race in Folk Music

In popular usage, the term "folk music" remained imprecise. A journalist writing in 1952 observed that folk music was becoming "extremely hard to classify," identifying its presence in popular music (Burl Ives), country (Gene Autry and Eddie Arnold), and "art" music (Béla Bartók)." All these examples associated folk music with white performance, ignoring black performance of folk music altogether.[14]

Folk music associated with the Left and People's Songs tended to feature black folk musicians and to celebrate interracialism. In the early 1950s, blackness and folk music intertwined in new ways. Southern blackness was associated with a folk past, with recognizable "traditions" and "authenticity." In contrast, jazz, the music that Belafonte had turned away from, was seen as black *and* modern. But renewed interest in the sources of jazz, especially in field hollers, spirituals, and urban and rural blues, expanded the visibility of black-identified folk genres. The encounter between country and city and black and white had produced jazz and constituted its modernity. Both black and white jazz musicians valued folk sources as contributing to jazz's hybridity and crossing of racial boundaries.[15]

The idea of separate black and white traditions in folk music was also challenged by Harry Smith's 1952 *Anthology of American Folk Music,* which interspersed urban and rural forms representing the music's multiracial origins. Smith emphasized the importance of modern technology in circulating folk music by drawing his selections from commercial music recorded between 1927 and 1932. The new long-playing (33⅓ RPM 12″ disc) format made it possible to juxtapose music that had previously been marketed separately as "race music" and "hillbilly." Smith refused any racial classification, identifying his selections as "ballads, social music, and songs."[16] His musical curation emphasized the cross-fertilizations made possible by commercial recording.

Belafonte's repertoire of work songs, folk songs, and calypsos also mixed tradition and modernity, black particularity and folk universality. Recasting himself as a folksinger, his publicity emphasized his theater background and his study of the popular uses of folk songs rather than racial authenticity. "To folk music he brings a fine voice and dramatic training . . . and a perspective of the enduring value of the music that is of, by, and for the people. . . . He doesn't look on traditional folk songs as relics of the past but as a living art form with distinctive melodies and words with meaning . . . songs which recall history and yet have meanings for today."[17] In 1955, Belafonte collaborated with his friend Tony Scott, combining acoustic guitar and jazz accompaniment to inject what Scott called a "jazz feeling" into his sound "whenever it seemed natural and spontaneous." Interviewed in the 1950s, Scott proposed a meeting ground between jazz and folk: "Folk material always has a pronounced rhythmic beat, partly because much of it is sung by groups of people. Distinct rhythms make it easy to keep together. Also some folk material is sung in connection with dances."[18]

Belafonte's formulation of folk music was also politically circumspect. Publicity identified the presence of folk in his repertoire as a *new* discovery, reflecting the influence of his new manager Jack Rollins and his research at the Library of Congress. These accounts avoided disclosure of his musical experimentation in left-wing settings in the late 1940s that could fuel red baiters. Presenting folk as a new artistic preference, following a commercial run as a pop singer, might protect him from the forces that had driven Paul Robeson from the stage.[19]

Reviewers praised the expressive qualities and range of repertoire that Belafonte brought to folk performance. "Belafonte brings out the emotions—humor, pathos, sheer joy—in folk music, projecting these emotions so that anyone . . . can feel and understand and be moved," one critic wrote, contrasting the "earthy vitality" of Belafonte's folk repertoire with "Tin Pan Alley product" or "contrived 'Oklahoma' brand of precious folksiness."[20] Others described him as "synthetic" in folk singing, a "passionate minstrel," "a self-made folk singer" who presented the music as a "living art" rather than himself as an "arty or folksy singer." A college student reviewing Belafonte's first album of recorded folk songs wrote that "he does them in a style so original in nature that with each listening, the performance comes alive again and again with the listener finding something new and exciting."[21]

Still, some white reviewers foregrounded racial difference in their assessment of Belafonte. Music critic Howard Taubman wrote that his style had the "ring of authenticity" because he transformed the songs "in his own image. . . . When he sings 'Mark Twain' he makes you feel the weight of the Mississippi riverman's labor as well as the struggle of the human personality to dominate it." Taubman emphasized Belafonte's presumed racial heritage when he called attention to "ferocity" in his singing of the "tragic ballads of his people" that made "this aspect of this Negro artist's work memorable." He also remarked on the "vivacity" of Belafonte's calypsos, his "good ear for the sound of the words and the rhythm of the music" from his "early years in the West Indies."[22]

Although he did not explicitly project Belafonte's blackness as racial authenticity, drama critic Brooks Atkinson interpreted Belafonte's post-*Brown* performance in *3 for Tonight* with the white dancers Marge and Gower Champion as suffused with a "mission," presumably desegregation. Belafonte was "apocalyptical" and sang "with the fierce conviction of an evangelist," Atkinson wrote. "The fate of the world hangs on his ability to convince the audience that each song is a vital part of the human experience." In contrast, drama critic Wolcott Gibbs, adopting what he imagined to be a color-blind aesthetic, described Belafonte's performance of the spiritual "Take My Mother Home" as a "landmark in melodramatic bad taste"; he dismissed Belafonte's "clenched, Rodinesque posturing," with its claims of "supernatural emotional significance."[23]

Folk music's vernacular range attracted interest from black and white listeners; it also drew black musicians to a liminal space that was not racially confined.[24] Singing folk music rather than a more racially identified genre such as jazz or blues carried an implicit endorsement of interracialism, and it often entailed a turn toward white audiences.

In the late 1940s, blues musician Big Bill Broonzy, for example, continued to perform for the black audiences who came to hear him in black clubs and had been buying his blues recordings since the late 1920s. But he also gained a new white ticket-buying audience of politically engaged folk music fans who heard him perform at an interracial folk song revue, "I Come for to Sing," on concert stages, at college campuses, and at a prestigious Chicago jazz club. By the early 1950s, most of the bookings Broonzy could arrange entertained white jazz aficionados in Europe and white folk enthusiasts in the United States. Working as a solo performer on an acoustic guitar, Broonzy now presented himself as bearing witness to southern black poor rural life, as a historian of the blues' musical form, and as

Folk music's escape from racial confinement, ca. 1955: folk singer (Ramblin' Jack Elliott) on a Sunday afternoon in Washington Square, Greenwich Village; and a musician in a Greenwich Village café/folk club.
(Jack Elliott photo by George Pickrow/Three Lions; café photo by Weegee (Arthur Fellig), International Center of Photography. Both photos courtesy of Getty Images.)

a sharp critic of American racism, commercially recording his old song "Black, Brown and White Blues" in 1952.[25]

As a black performer whose repertoire intentionally bridged black-identified work songs and calypsos, Anglo-American and international folk songs, Belafonte walked both sides of the line between tradition and modernity. He emphasized folk as originating among common people and expressing their sharp insights. He distinguished these songs from mainstream commercial music, "bent to fit a machine made mold," and from the classical canon: "They mean a whole lot more to me artistically and emotionally than an opera or any other kind of singing." He presented himself as a folk collector, learning songs from the Library of Congress and the St. Louis Folk Festival, traveling with a tape recorder in the United States and Mexico, and referring to his "precious tapes which were made in prisons, on freighters." One reporter described him as "wistfully" recalling "Jamaica as a wonderful hunting ground for music never heard before that was true and gloriously reflective of its imaginative civilization." At the same time he acknowledged that folk music there was also vulnerable to the forces of tourism and modernization, "carried away to be readapted to other rhythms, influences and uses."[26]

As an alternative to authenticity, Belafonte offered variation, revision, and his own creative appropriation. "I search long and hard for the material I feel is right for me, and then, as any creative artist does, I dig and probe. I try to get it right on the inside of it until it becomes uniquely my own."[27] His performance attire was a compromise between formal nightclub dress and theatrical costuming. Wearing open-necked shirts and tight black trousers, he became "the first singer in the history of the Copacabana Nightclub in New York to perform in shirt sleeves," explaining that "I can't see myself singing work songs about chain gangs in a dinner jacket."[28]

Racial Boundary Crossing on the Nightclub Circuit

Belafonte's success garnered prize bookings in nightclubs and hotels where earnings were guaranteed irrespective of the gate, but in these swanky venues, audiences were rich and "white only" was the norm—with the necessary exception of the waitstaff and performers. In some places Belafonte was the first to desegregate a stage. Whenever he could, he used his celebrity status to challenge the color line more generally and to open spaces for other black artists. Belafonte was the first black performer at the Cocoanut Grove Lounge at the Hotel Ambassador in Los Angeles in 1953, in the Empire Room at the Waldorf Astoria in New York, and at the Palmer House in Chicago in 1955. Belafonte's contract to perform at the Eden Roc Hotel in Miami in 1955 stipulated that all the facilities of the hotel would be open to him, making him the first black person to cross Miami Beach's sharply enforced color line.[29] Belafonte's appearances on radio and television, film and Broadway, his "whirlwind success in top NYC nightspots" and his "firsts" were followed closely and covered with pride in the black press as cracks in the edifice of segregation.[30]

Being the first to cross the color line often entailed being seen as a black interloper in spaces defined by white exclusivity. At the Empire Room at Chicago's elegant Palmer House, when the maître d' first encountered Belafonte waiting to go onstage, he saw only a young black man and threw him out.[31]

Belafonte looked for openings where even small violations of racial segregation might expand the possibilities for broader forms of recognition and access. Traveling in 1955 in Las Vegas with Tony and Fran Scott, who had begun working as Belafonte's musical conductor and secretary, Belafonte had political allies who provided cover when he made a display of swimming and gambling in the formerly segregated pool and casino. Playing at the Copacabana in New York and at the Empire Room at the Waldorf, Scott brought black sidemen to play with the previously all-white house orchestras, desegregating the bandstand. In one Waldorf performance, Belafonte asked Scott to sing a duet with him on an encore: their physical closeness enacted interracial intimacy, after which Belafonte introduced the interracial orchestra as "in Technicolor."[32] Organized black hotel workers at the Waldorf signaled their special appreciation. During Belafonte's engagement in the fall of 1955, they petitioned and won for him an honorary membership in Local 6, the Hotel and Club Employees Union. The scroll they presented to him expressed pride in their shared union commitment, working-class backgrounds, and connections to the West Indies.[33]

Challenging Black Exclusion on Television

During the years in which Harry Belafonte was a sought-after guest on televised musical variety shows, most television programming was "white only." For example, the popular genre of live television drama favored supposedly unmarked "everyman" characters, but in 1952, African American actor Frederick O'Neal, founder of the American Negro Theater, estimated that less than four-tenths of one percent of the actors on television were black. Black neighbors and family members alerted each other whenever black performers were scheduled to appear, not wanting anyone to miss the rare chance to see "Colored on TV."[34]

Television appearances gave Belafonte access to a mass audience, both black and white, and greatly enhanced public visibility and authority. Although white variety programs were interested in "hot" black talent, performers had little control over their appearances. They had to play by the rules of the networks, the sponsors, the blacklisters, and individual variety hosts. Belafonte did what he could to take advantage of the openings he was offered. His initial forays—in the all-black Apollo-type musical showcase that couldn't compete against a white-hosted variety program in 1949 and as a guest on Jackie Gleason's variety show *Cavalcade of Stars* in 1951—gained him some exposure but no opportunity to challenge prevailing race-based limitations.

For example, Belafonte's appearance on *Cavalcade* was sandwiched between a short comedic *Honeymooners* skit with Gleason as the bus driver Ralph Kramden and a sketch featuring Gleason as Joe the Bartender. Belafonte and Craig Work, billed as "appearing now at the Village Vanguard in New York," accompanied the featured June Taylor Dancers. Costumed to match the dancers in stage-show Calypso garb and adopting a pronounced island accent, Belafonte crossed the stage leading a donkey and singing the calypso "Hold 'Em Joe," an adaptation of a song first recorded in Trinidad in the 1920s.[35] The performance veered between exoticism and caricature; still it attracted unwanted attention from *Counterattack* two weeks later: "How many Communists recognized Harry Belafonte on 'Cavalcade of Stars'?"[36]

Invitations to appear on variety shows poured in between 1953 and 1956, and Belafonte appeared several times on Ed Sullivan's star-making *Toast of the Town*, as noted in Chapter 2. In addition to requiring anticommunist clearance, Sullivan insisted on exerting absolute control over his guests' performances, imposing strict time limits that often required drastic cuts. Facing the challenge of how to present popular recorded music for an audience of viewers rather than listeners, television's common solution was for hit songs to be presented as three-minute skits. This format was highly restrictive for a performer with Belafonte's range and aspirations.[37]

Television's unacknowledged concessions to white supremacy were gaining notice. In the fall of 1955, the editor of the *New York Herald Tribune* weekly *TV and Radio Magazine* referred to guest shots for Negro stars, including Belafonte, as throwing "a bone from time to time." Faye Emerson, a 1940s film actress who had a second career hosting television, wrote in 1955 that "No matter what anyone tells you, there is a color line drawn in television . . . [T]here has been no major series starring a Negro," identifying *Amos 'n' Andy*, as "simply Uncle Tomism."[38]

The television special following the final live performance of *3 for Tonight* in June 1955 showed Belafonte what artistic control over a block of television time might enable. He began to formulate his own creative ambitions for television, describing for Emerson a television spectacular depicting the history of the Negro in America, a new format for his planned "Negro Anthology."[39]

After appearing that August on the *Colgate Comedy Hour*, timed to compete with Sullivan, Belafonte was offered a contract for several more shows. This time he negotiated for a longer time slot and a sustained thematic approach to the musical selections. With the help of Bill Attaway, then writing for NBC and assigned to the show, Belafonte planned the first segment to feature work songs. When Attaway brought along singer, composer, and folklorist Irving Burgie, who was then studying and performing Caribbean folk music, Burgie reoriented their thinking and provided the direction that would result in the hit album *Calypso*.[40]

Like Belafonte, Burgie was associated with the folk music Left and with the popularization of calypso music. He had followed a path from learning music theory—from a fellow black soldier stationed in Burma during World War II—to studying voice and music at Juilliard, University of Arizona, and University of Southern California. He gravitated to folk music, singing at left-wing venues and interracial camps, including the Chicago South Side Community Arts Center beginning in 1951 and Camp Unity in 1953, where the arts staff included Lorraine Hansberry, her husband, Robert Nemiroff, and CNA actor Julian Mayfield. Burgie began a job singing at a new calypso-themed nightclub, the Blue Angel in Chicago, in January 1953. Having grown up in Brooklyn, the son of a Barbadian mother (whom he would later identify as a Garveyite) and an African American father, he knew those double entendre–laden tourist calypsos that nightclub guests expected. But he had also developed a political and historical interest in Caribbean music as a whole, exploring black diasporic musical borrowings in "merengues from Santo Domingo; mentos from Jamaica; ring games, shouts, ceremonials, and rituals from Haiti." He saw his study of Caribbean folk music as allied to the study of folklore and performance by Katherine Dunham, the Trinidad-born dancer Pearl Primus, and the Haitian-born dancer Jean-Léon Destiné. In the period before he began to write songs for Belafonte, Burgie formed a group that sang calypsos, mentos, and songs from Haiti, Cuba, the Dominican Republic, and Puerto Rico, named by the Village Vanguard's Max Gordon as Lord Burgess and the Sun Islanders when they played there in 1954. As Lord Burgess, Burgie also played and sang at Festival House and Music Inn in Lenox, Massachusetts, and performed with the Jamaican mento singer Lord Flea in Miami.[41] His musical and political sensibilities had a lot to offer to Belafonte's project.

Sustained exploration of a black musical genre was a novelty on television. Publicity for the "Holiday in Trinidad" *Colgate* show, broadcast October 2, 1955, promised "an integrated musical trip thru the West Indies." The black press emphasized that Belafonte would have "complete say about the style and presentation of the half-hour segment . . . on an important show to be aired nationwide." Belafonte's five songs, all written by Burgie, included his version of a Jamaican work song, "Day-O (Banana Boat Song)," revised with a dramatic a cappella opening callout that would become indelibly attached to his persona from then on. The show itself was limited by a white-oriented variety framework, with the Caribbean islands as tourist havens captivating the show host, Jack Carson, but the powerful music and coordination between script and song in the extended segment generated great excitement. In contrast, Belafonte's television acting debut one week later, on *General Electric Theater* with Ethel Waters in a boxing drama, "Winner by Decision," adapted by Attaway from a story by Budd Schulberg, received little press attention.[42]

Belafonte, Attaway, and Burgie thought that an "integrated musical trip through the West Indies" had the makings of an innovative LP. Even before the show aired, Belafonte announced plans for an album of "Island and Calypso songs."[43] Assuming a limited commercial appeal for such an album, RCA producers opposed the idea. But Belafonte got a green light from George Marek, the label's Austrian-born Jewish creative head of Artists and Repertory.[44]

Within two weeks of the broadcast, Belafonte began the process of recording these songs and others in the album that would become *Harry Belafonte: Calypso*. He gathered Scott and a group of musicians, including Burgie's colleague, Jamaican pianist and pennywhistle player Herb Levy, and Haitian guitarist Franz Casseus, who had played with Belafonte at a CNA Negro History event in 1950. The chorus of singers included actor Brock Peters, whom Belafonte had known since the late 1940s; *Finian's Rainbow* cast member Margaret Tynes; and Charles Colman and Sherman Sneed, performers in various revivals of *Porgy and Bess*. Irving Burgie played the guitar and sang in the recording sessions, and Attaway wrote the liner notes. When it was released in 1956, *Calypso* zoomed to the top of the charts. Its sales and its duration as a best-selling album made music history.[45]

The same night "Holiday in Trinidad" was broadcast,

another precedent-shattering program appeared on television screens. Immediately after the variety hour, the *Philco-Goodyear Playhouse* featured a live television drama starring a black actor. In "A Man Is Ten Feet Tall," Sidney Poitier played the character of an exemplary black longshoreman who teaches a white loner (Don Murray) how to stand up to the arbitrary authority of the white waterfront boss (Martin Balsam). An Associated Press TV reviewer, Charles Mercer, sent out a congratulatory article over the wire service, remarking on the experience of watching two black stars, Belafonte and Poitier, back-to-back on network television. Mercer criticized network "timidity" and "fear of the Southern market" that kept them from featuring more "Negro performers" and devoting "serious treatment" to Negro characters. Mercer missed the racial significance of a white longshoreman being tutored in resistance by his black coworker. But he liked how Poitier's character did not represent the "Negro Problem" and appreciated his performance in portraying a man who "happened to be a Negro [living] with as much dignity and courage as many men who happen to be white constantly live with dignity and courage in innumerable TV dramas."[46]

When Belafonte was quoted in Mercer's article, he added a broader, CNA-style critique of mainstream media. Although Belafonte credited television with recognizing the Negro "much faster than the theater, radio, and the movies did," he still insisted that, given "the millions of man hours going into TV . . . Negro life does not have an adequate representation and could be drastically increased." He called for increasing black labor on television at all levels, "Negro technicians as well as of Negro performers," adding that there had not been "either a great enough exposure of established Negro talent or enough opportunities for Negro newcomers."[47]

By June 1956, with the just-released *Calypso* shooting up

the charts, Belafonte was in a position to set his own terms for performing on television. He paid his debt to Ed Sullivan for career-enhancing exposure on *Talk of the Town* by appearing on a special celebration of Sullivan's eight years of hosting television variety. Then on the day of that broadcast, Belafonte directly criticized TV's failure to feature black artists, saying that "an industry as vast and powerful as television needs the Negro and the Negro needs it." Guest appearances were inadequate. "It is not enough for a singer like 'King' Cole to just appear occasionally and sing some pretty tunes."[48]

For the next two years, Belafonte would refuse to appear on television guest spots unless they met certain conditions, turning down substantial financial offers ("No Dough-Re-Mi Man," according to a 1958 headline in the *New York Daily News*). He made an exception to appear on the Nat King Cole show in August 1957 for a nominal fee, to support the first network experiment with a black-hosted variety show, on the grounds that this show's success would "help keep TV's doors open to Negro performers." He did not accept the usual time limits of three-minute slots but held out for terms that would allow him to "select the form and content of presentation" and to create the "proper settings" for songs "taken from the ethnic sources of all nations."[49]

Celebrity Missteps

Interviewed in 1957, Belafonte described the celebrity fast track he was on as "traumatic": having learned from a young age to manage racial hostility in everyday encounters, he was unprepared for the "universal acceptance by people of all denominations in all walks of life by millions as a performer and an artist." Nor was he comfortable with constantly being on display. "All of a sudden there are crowds coming to see you, hundreds of faces looking at you wherever you go." As a performer, "you're suddenly this special kind of thing," but the fawning adoration of fans was a world apart from the expectations of daily life with a wife and two small children.[50] The combination of success, privilege, and celebrity objectification was deeply disorienting.

Harry and Marguerite Belafonte would not legally separate until sometime in 1956, but his travel and performing schedule after the fall of 1954 left him little time at home. In one estimate, he was away from New York all but six weeks in two years: his wife's account emphasized her support of his "artistic freedom" and his "terrific drive . . . to make it" that led him to stay on the road. In 1955 and 1956, gossip columns in both the mainstream and the black press tracked Belafonte's marriage and printed numerous "rift rumors." Black columnists had a stake in Belafonte's family image, noting when he was sighted with his wife and children on tour, and representing him as a "devoted family man" and "decently acting star."[51] "Family man" news items and photographs could not, however, contain Belafonte's image within 1950s heterosexual domesticity. Although an August 1956 profile of Belafonte in *Look* included separate photographs of him with Marguerite, Adrienne, and Shari, the captions identified him as "volatile, restless" and "no conventional homebody."[52]

Beginning in the spring of 1954, and more purposefully in 1955 and the first half of 1956, psychiatrist Janet Alterman Kennedy and her successful writer-financier husband, Jay Richard Kennedy, offered themselves as willing to advise Belafonte in all aspects of his life. Belafonte would have encountered psychoanalytic theory in left-wing theater, where it was integral to method acting, as well as in his friendship with Marlon Brando, who had begun analysis in 1948. Janet Kennedy listened as Belafonte explored his experiences of race-based humiliation, his rage and searing self-doubts. She quickly breached the ethical codes of her profession by encouraging Belafonte to become involved with her husband as financial and artistic adviser.

Belafonte had no preparation for handling his now-substantial earnings. "I couldn't find any way of distributing or saving a good deal of it," he later recalled. Janet Kennedy's charismatic husband seemed to know everyone and how to do everything. Janet Kennedy saw Belafonte at the couple's high-rent Beekman Place apartment; their sessions often ended with a cocktail hour with both Kennedys. They cultivated a peculiar intimacy with Belafonte, referring to him as their son and urging him to call them Mom and Dad. A friend interviewed in 1958 described Belafonte in this period as "greatly dependent" on the Kennedys, acting "like somebody spellbound. He couldn't make the smallest decision on his own; he wanted Jay Richard Kennedy to make them all."[53]

Belafonte's unease as a white-anointed black celebrity and the prominence of his interracial partnership with Kennedy were on display when he appeared in front of a largely black audience at Mahalia Jackson's Greater Salem Baptist Church on the South Side of Chicago in December 1955. At this event, he and Kennedy were jointly honored with a citation from the black-led Chicago Conference for Brotherhood for making "great contributions to the creative arts and to the advancement of interracial teamwork in America." Speaking to the crowd of three thousand, Belafonte described Negro performers who were the first to desegregate clubs and hotels and who found themselves "lonely and unhappy because their people do not know of their struggles and accomplishments." Earlier on this trip, invitations extended to Belafonte to meet Chicago's cardinal Samuel Stritch and mayor Richard Daley and an award from the city's Catholic Interracial Council marked Belafonte's stature as a black performer in a white world. Stritch praised him as "one of America's truly important artists and certainly the most important Negro artist." Belafonte used the occasion at the church to make a special public pledge, which brought the majority-black crowd to their feet: "So long as I live, I will never be a Judas to my people, for I know my people will never be a Judas to me."[54]

Jay Richard Kennedy's ambitions for Belafonte redirected him away from black communal loyalties. Belafonte's financial arrangements with his new manager included a percentage of his earnings, shares of royalties, and power of attorney over various business matters. Quickly financial and artistic decisions began to overlap. Kennedy had some stature in the arts accruing from his popular and long-running radio mystery series, the two Hollywood films, and his published novel.[55] They agreed that Kennedy would assume more involvement in Belafonte's artistic choices, which Kennedy detailed for the press as selecting and writing the singer's material, staging his nightclub act, and producing and directing his TV segments.[56]

Kennedy's grandiose show business aspirations shaped Belafonte's first spectacular failure, the musical production *Sing, Man, Sing,* which was proposed as a "musical Odyssey tracing the evolution of American music from its earliest beginnings to modern times by means of dramatic interpretation." Although he knew little about music, Kennedy masterminded the show. Press and promotional materials noted that the production was "put together as a showcase for the unique Belafonte talents," but it also made sure no one would miss the extent of Kennedy's involvement, "producing, writing, directing, and supervising every facet."[57]

In its final form, *Sing, Man, Sing* paid tribute to the immensely popular "Family of Man" show of photographs, which was on exhibit in New York during most of 1955 and which Belafonte had found particularly moving. He had made repeated visits to the Museum of Modern Art to view the photographs (and short fragments of prose and poetry serving as wall text) produced by artists in sixty-eight countries around the world. The show was curated and printed by Edward Steichen, then head of the museum's photography department, and his assistants. Its title came from a fragment of "The People, Yes," a long poem written in 1936 by the populist poet, writer, and folk song collector Carl Sandburg, who was Steichen's brother-in-law. Steichen conceived the exhibit as a cross-cultural juxtaposition of former World War II and current Cold War combatants, colonizers, and colonized. Women and men connected by various forms of kinship were portrayed at work and play, in study and courtship, from birth to death—with a room-size color transparency of an atomic explosion casting the shadow of war and destruction over all the rituals of life. The explosion image recalled California People's Songs member Sam Hinton's refrain in a 1945 song, "Atomic Talking Blues": "peace in the world or the world in pieces." Repeating prints of a smiling Peruvian flute player placed throughout the exhibition "reaffirmed the theme of hope," in the words of one reviewer. The exhibit was seen by huge audiences across the United States and throughout the world and both admired and criticized by reviewers.[58]

Powerful photographs of African Americans were a prominent feature of the exhibition, including four by black artist Roy DeCarava, who had been the head of CNA's art committee when Belafonte was active in the organization. DeCarava's own photographic project in Harlem—supported in 1952 by the first Guggenheim Fellowship awarded to a black artist and sponsored by Steichen—proposed a race-conscious version of universality. "I want to photograph Harlem through the Negro people. Morning, noon and night, at work, going to work, coming home from work, at play, in the streets, talking, kidding, laughing, in the home, in the playground, in the schools, bars, stores, libraries, beauty parlors, churches, etc. . . . I want to show the strength, the wisdom, the dignity of the Negro people. Not the famous and the well-known but the unknown and the unnamed, thus revealing the roots from which springs the greatness of all human beings. . . . I want a creative expression, the kind of penetrating insight and understanding of Negroes which I believe only a Negro photographer can interpret. I want to heighten the awareness of my people and bring to our consciousness a greater knowledge of our heritage." DeCarava's framing, and his exceptional photographs, may have given Steichen the idea for "Family of Man." What Belafonte hoped from his singing of folk music was closely related to DeCarava's mission. Because representational conventions had refused to recognize black romantic love or everyday family life, the inclusion of African Americans in the "Family of Man," along with its implicit rejection of Cold War rhetoric, may explain why the exhibit so captivated Belafonte.[59]

Sing, Man, Sing borrowed the conceptual framing of "Family of Man," captured in the lines of the Carl Sandburg poem that appeared above the entrance to the exhibition and in the prologue to the exhibition catalogue: "There is only one man in the world / and his name is All Men./ There is only one woman in the world / and her name is All Women./ There is only child in the world / and the child's name is All Children." Kennedy's version of universality diverged from the Left's celebration of black cultural resources and diasporic cultural hybridity. Assessing Kennedy's overall approach, staging, and the songs he contributed, one Washington, DC, critic recognized the show's aspirations but deplored their "stifling banality."[60]

The book for *Sing, Man, Sing,* written by Kennedy, featured a loosely framed progression from creation to the expulsion from paradise, discovery of the blues and sin, the flood, rebuilding a home and regenerating love, with salutes along the way to freedom, children, and interracial bonds. A Chicago daily reviewer concurred with the D.C. critic, describing the British actor playing the Observer as performing his "painful duty" delivering didactic narration with the effect of tying "the show together with some history-of-man banalities." *Sing, Man, Sing* featured Belafonte as He, soprano Margaret Tynes as She, with Alvin Ailey and Mary Hinkson performing the dancing parts of He and She, choreographed by Walter Nicks, a Dunham dance teacher suggested by Julie Robinson. Others on the stage were The Guitarist, Millard Thomas, and a chorus of They, carefully balanced between white and black, male and female. The story strung together new pop-styled, "undistinguished" arrangements, several calypso and spiritual-styled songs in Belafonte's repertoire ("Man Smart, Woman Smarter," "Noah," and "Hosanna"), and a new calypso by Burgie, based on Kennedy's lyrics.[61]

The tour of *Sing, Man, Sing* drew audiences; black critics praised Belafonte and the production for its prodigious array of black talent. The *Chicago Defender* reported that New York and Chicago dailies had "attacked the shows, walloped the tunes, but praised the respective stars." But the show's universalism came at a cost, with its "ballroom dancing [of a type] where race and creed are forgotten." One of Kennedy's songs, "The Blues Is Man," effectively dismissed black musical traditions, insisting that the blues "don't need a flag or race, just a lonely heart and a haunted face," exemplifying Langston Hughes's 1940 lament, "You've taken my blues and gone . . . fixed 'em so they don't sound like me."[62]

Black reporters recognized that interracial performance was especially incendiary in the post-*Brown* South, where, in April, segregationists had attacked Nat King Cole during a performance for an all-white audience in Birmingham, Alabama. Cole, with his smooth sound, was one of the earliest vocalists to cross over from black rhythm and blues charts to mainstream popularity. Some critics praised Belafonte and Kennedy for *Sing, Man, Sing* and wondered if those dismissive of the show were in fact objecting to the interracial casting. Other black reviewers emphasized the limitations of the show's message. One described the song "I Found Me" as expressing the idea that "the human race had lost its way because they had become too imbued with racial and other differences," resolved with a finale in which "Belafonte and Tynes develop the idea 'I Found Me' and 'She Found He' and 'We Found WE' and everybody, white and colored, winds up getting acquainted and shaking hands all over the stage." The Chicago review sent via the black wire service, ANP, criticized this finale as a "pompous sermon which tried to disguise itself in a mannered attitude."[63] These black critics understood Kennedy's combination of color-blind universalism and pop psychology as detracting from the powerful black pride signified by Belafonte's performance.

The vocal demands of the material, combined with ongoing psychic stress, resulted in problems with Belafonte's voice noted by reviewers in Cleveland, DC, and Pittsburgh. When the Kennedys urged him to continue performing anyway, Belafonte became aware that their stake in the show trumped concern for his well-being. Though critics had been generally positive about his own performance, their attacks on the show must have shaken his confidence in Kennedy's judgment. A *Chicago Tribune* headline warned, "Bright Belafonte Walks into Trap in This Musical." Janet Alterman Kennedy continued to cross professional boundaries between analyst and patient, arriving in Chicago to study "audience reactions to the Harry Belafonte show."[64]

After Chicago, Belafonte shifted gears. He canceled the rest of the *Sing, Man, Sing* tour, publicized his physical condition, and had surgery on his vocal chords in early June. Now questioning his entanglement with the Kennedys, he turned for legal help to a tough left-wing labor lawyer.[65]

Investigating Kennedy, the lawyer uncovered a bombshell—Kennedy had a secret prior life as Samuel Richard Solomonick, an antifascist organizer and Communist Party activist, who had been the circulation manager at the *Daily Worker* in 1938. Solomonick broke with the party in 1939, allegedly absconding with funds. Janet Alterman Kennedy had been married previously to the left-wing lawyer Stanley Levison. After Alterman had divorced Levison and married Kennedy in the early 1940s, Kennedy and Levison were business associates and remained friends; both were active in the group Businessmen for Roosevelt in 1944, until they ended their friendship and financial association in 1948.[66]

Belafonte's lawyer uncovered another startling detail about Solomonick: he was an FBI informant. In the mid-1960s, a CIA memo on Kennedy/Solomonick would describe him as having "long provided information on the Negro Civil Rights Movement and its various leaders," a "violent anti-communist" who "has been alarmed at the Communist movement into the Negro Civil Rights field and the Communist penetration into various Negro organizations." He had "been involved with various Negro leaders since as early as 1934," knowing them on a "very close personal basis."[67] Janet Alterman Kennedy's intelligence gathering was not scrutinized by the lawyer, but her husband's participation in anticommunist surveillance made her many questions to Belafonte about Robeson and the Left highly suspect. Jay Kennedy's involvement with Belafonte was likely motivated by anticommunist political intrigue and his position as an informer. Ending treatment with Janet Kennedy was relatively easy for Belafonte. Extricating himself from his financial arrangements with Jay Richard Kennedy was more complex, but their legal involvement was terminated by the end of September 1956.[68] Although suits and countersuits continued through 1957, this Kennedy era was over.

Taking Back the Reins

Despite its considerable personal costs, the Kennedy detour did not cause Belafonte irreparable career damage. After the surgery, he served as his own manager, meeting the obligations of *Sing, Man, Sing* by returning to his one-man-performance style and repertoire of work songs, ballads, and international songs, including calypsos. His *Calypso* album remained high on the charts, and his appearance at the end of June in New York's Lewisohn Stadium broke all previous attendance records, including those set by Robeson, and garnered him ecstatic critical praise.[69]

Belafonte's fall 1956 announcement of his and Marguerite's legal separation was another indication of his renewed self-determination. She left on a Goodwill Tour of the Caribbean, and Belafonte moved into a small three-room apartment on the West Side of Manhattan. In early January 1957, press photos showed Harry and Marguerite boarding a plane to Las Vegas, where Marguerite would establish residency for a Nevada divorce.[70] News of their divorce went out over the wire services on March 1, 1957, Belafonte's thirtieth birthday. Although the specific legal details remained private, they were publicized as generous financial terms and custody arrangements that would enable Belafonte to maintain his relationships with his daughters, Adrienne and Shari, now nearly eight and two and a half.[71]

Belafonte turned toward a new marriage with Julie Robinson. In addition to romantic intimacy, the relationship with Julie promised to integrate arts, politics, and family life, realms that had remained separate in his years with Marguerite. As a child of committed Jewish leftists, Robinson had grown up in the New York world of arts and politics that had deeply engaged Belafonte in the late 1940s. She had attended the Left-oriented private school in

Greenwich Village known as the Little Red School House, and Music and Art High School. As a Katherine Dunham School dance student beginning in 1944, and a Dunham teacher and dancer between 1947 and 1953, she had been involved in the project of representing diasporic black cultures, especially Afro-Caribbean dance and music. Traveling with the Dunham dancers, Julie had lived within the constraints of public segregation. Preparing for and dancing in Dunham's 1951 controversial protest ballet *Southland,* she and the other dancers confronted painful aspects of racial experience to enact the ballet's version of the rape-lynch narrative at the heart of white supremacy. *Southland* was performed only outside of the United States, in Chile in 1951 and Paris in 1953.[72]

In the summer of 1954, when Robinson met Belafonte for the second time on the set of *Carmen Jones,* she was eager to marry and have a family—a more likely prospect with Belafonte than with her then boyfriend, Marlon Brando. Moving back to New York, Robinson taught Afro-modern dance and remained immersed in dance and musical performance. As a teacher at the dance studio that replaced the Dunham School in 1955, she was able to recommend performers to Belafonte, such as the talented conga drummer Danny Barrajanos, then working as a short-order cook, who began performing with Belafonte in September 1956. She became pregnant by December 1956, and she and Belafonte married in Tecate, Mexico, shortly after his divorce became final in February 1957. Their first child, David, was born that September.[73]

Belafonte also focused on his working conditions, vowing never again to have a manager. He set up Belafonte Enterprises in 1956 as an organizational and financial management structure, hiring lawyers, accountants, and press agents to help him manage two music-publishing companies, his concert performances, and develop plans to produce motion pictures and TV shows. Now his own boss, he more directly confronted the institutional obstacles in the way of his artistic freedom. His efforts to create and circulate new forms of racial representation were up against the corporate structure of the music business and film and television industries, ruled by the bottom line. For the moment, the bottom line was not a concern to Belafonte, who was now one of the top earners in show business.[74] At this moment he was in the rare position of being able to take risks to set his own course.

Black Politics and Black Arts in a New Era of Civil Rights

The political contexts of black performance were shifting rapidly during this time of growing conflicts between challengers and defenders of racial segregation. The houses of the ministers supporting the Montgomery boycott were firebombed, as were four black churches. Boycotters faced physical attacks and harassment, and many, including Martin Luther King, Jr., were arrested, fined, and jailed. In February 1956, when Autherine Lucy tried to take her court-ordered place as a graduate student at the University of Alabama in Tuscaloosa, rioting white students and supporters of segregation convinced university trustees to suspend her on the grounds that integration caused violence.

Watching these developments, New York black radicals continued to look for ways to support the resistance. Bayard Rustin, one of the organizers of In Friendship, traveled to Montgomery to offer his counsel when leaders of the bus boycott began to be arrested. The depth of the mass movement he saw there exhilarated him. A few weeks later, in March 1956, King made his first fund-raising trip to New York. Thousands of black New Yorkers crowded into the Concord Baptist Church in Brooklyn to hear him speak.

Although King's plan in New York was to meet with

black leaders, someone directed him to the rising star and outspoken entertainer Harry Belafonte. King asked Belafonte to attend a meeting at Adam Clayton Powell's Abyssinian Baptist Church in Harlem. Belafonte stood in the back, wary of ministers and resenting mainstream civil rights organizations for having distanced themselves from the black Left, especially from Paul Robeson and W. E. B. Dubois, in the critical years after WWII. Still, he was curious about the boycott. It seemed to come out of nowhere. As he described his thinking later, "this thing that happened ... [was] not on the drawing board of the Communist Party, not on the drawing board of the NAACP, not on the drawing boards of anybody that ever professed to be committed to the plight of black people in this world." There were no precedents for "the kind of drama that was taking place in Montgomery, Alabama. I mean, who was putting all this together? Where did it come from? Who are these people? ... and Montgomery, Alabama, of all places?" [75]

In their private meeting in the church basement, King, two years younger than Belafonte, appeared to be a different kind of minister, "a human being who was doing things that were on the one hand so radical, and on the other hand, coming in under the name of the Church." King asked for Belafonte's help and admitted with humility that he had "no idea where all this will go ... It's gotten certainly larger than anything we imagined."[76]

Even after the confrontations in Montgomery and Tuscaloosa, it was still shocking when smooth popular vocalist Nat King Cole was attacked onstage that April by white supremacists belonging to an anticommunist, anti-Semitic split-off from White Citizens' Councils in the state. Cole was performing as part of a "Record Stars Parade" tour that included white acts. What particularly enraged Cole's attackers was his appearance on stage with a white female singer.[77] Cole was not physically harmed, and his personal response, as reported in the black press, was conciliatory rather than indignant. He expressed a willingness to continue playing for all-white audiences, to work within the rules of the racial status quo. "I can't understand it," he told one reporter. "Here I have not taken part in any protests. I haven't said anything about civil rights. Nor have I joined an organization fighting segregation. Why should they attack me?"[78]

Cole was sharply criticized in the black press for making an unacceptable compromise with segregation and for his failure to side with those demanding full citizenship. How could he distance himself from civil rights protest, and how could he still be willing to entertain all-white audiences?[79] The *Chicago Defender* characterized Cole's acquiescence to Jim Crow as an "insult to his race. . . . [I]f he couldn't play to a group for American citizens on an integrated basis, he should just have stayed out of Birmingham."[80] The *New York Amsterdam News* declared, "Cole Leaves us Cold," warning that "the thousands of Harlemites who worshipped at the shrine of singer Nat King Cole turned their backs on him this week as the noted crooner turned his back on the NAACP." One reader wrote that "in effect [Cole has] sided with the White Citizens' Councils in defying the Supreme Court." A woman visiting from Norfolk, Virginia, wrote, "When are we going to learn to stick together? The Montgomery bus boycott began to prove that we could." Another demanded, "Who does he think he is that he can turn his back on the very symbol of what we have been fighting for all these years?[81]

Black public sentiment registered a major shift in expectations for black performers. The three men and one woman quoted in "Sidewalk Interviews" were asked, "Should Negro artists perform before segregated audiences?" All said no. "This is everybody's fight," one man insisted. "Our top artists are the ones that can break down segregation in the entertainment field."[82] One southern black newspaper, the *Carolina Times,* did excuse Cole's conciliatory stance by noting the precariousness of black stardom: "He is NOT in a position to fight back. . . . He walks a tightrope . . . He has worked long and hard to get this kind of money . . . and the slightest wrong move could set everything in motion against him." Within a week, in response to public pressure, Cole became a lifetime member of the NAACP, though he demurred on whether he would continue to perform for all-white audiences.[83]

Belafonte jumped at the opportunity to join with new activist challengers to Jim Crow. He was angry that *Sing, Man, Sing* performances at the DAR's Constitution Hall in Washington, DC, had faced a police order to cut an interracial dancing sequence—or be shut down—and that a proposal to produce it on television stipulated there would be no interracial casting.[84] Addressing a Chicago Conference for Brotherhood, Montgomery minister, professor, and boycott organizer Ralph Abernathy declared that the "new Negro of the South . . . [was] demanding some of the milk of democracy" instead of "sucking on the pacifier." After six difficult months, the Montgomery boycotters were "not tired of walking" but "tired of being walked over." Belafonte also spoke at this rally about the opposition to interracial performance he had encountered during the tour of *Sing, Man, Sing,* and unequivocally threw his lot in with the new resistance: "I will rise or fall with my people who have been struggling so long for complete democracy."[85]

The new civil rights militancy was not as freighted by Cold War divisions or as vulnerable to red-baiting as the Young Progressives or the CNA had been. Between surveillance, legal sanctions, and the public revelations of Stalin's crimes, in February 1956, the American Communist movement was in shambles. Under pressure from anticommunists, the NAACP had adopted a formal policy of barring Communists from membership, but the New York organizers of In Friendship—Ella Baker, Bayard Rustin, and Stanley Levison—were more concerned with mobilizing support for the new grass roots resistance than with screening members' prior political affiliations.[86]

While keeping his prior connection to the postwar Left out of sight, Belafonte seized every opportunity his fame offered to support the current struggle. In doing so, he frequently drew on the political perspectives and practices he had learned in 1940s New York's radical cultural circles.[87]

In Friendship publicized the new southern struggle by organizing a Madison Square Garden benefit in May 1956. The rally drew the biggest crowd since A. Philip Randolph's 1940s March on Washington rallies. Public sponsorship of the event included the Brotherhood of Sleeping Car Porters, the NAACP, New York churches, and labor unions. Frontline southern activists addressed the crowd: E. D. Nixon, a Montgomery labor leader and NAACP official involved in the boycott; Autherine Lucy; and Gus Courts, a Belzoni, Mississippi, grocer who had been shot for registering black voters and refusing to turn over NAACP records. Other speakers included former first lady Eleanor Roosevelt, Harlem's congressman Adam Clayton Powell, Jr., Broadway stars, and representatives from New York Jewish and labor organizations.[88]

When the resources of the Montgomery bus boycotters were falling short in the fall of 1956, the In Friendship radicals found Belafonte ready and willing to help raise money. He took the lead in organizing a fund-raising concert at the Manhattan Center to mark the anniversary of the boycott on December 5, 1956. Duke Ellington and Coretta Scott King appeared with him. The money generated by the event supported the boycotters and two groups of tenant farmers who had been evicted from the plantations where they had worked after enrolling their children in formerly all-white schools in Clarendon County, South Carolina, and Yazoo, Mississippi.[89]

Belafonte used a series of interviews in the *Chicago Defender*, published in August 1956, to place himself politically in relationship to the current civil rights struggle. In the first of the three articles, Belafonte embraced the black segments of his audience, beyond the frenzied white bobby-soxers publicized in the mainstream media. He mentioned black teenagers dancing to his songs on the jukebox, children playing to "Jump Down Turn Around," a preacher who thought his version of "Great Getting Up Morning" was a "sermon in song," "the money-proud first-night audience at the Palmer House" in Chicago who witnessed his ending twenty-eight years of white-only performances, and the "middle aged and elderly women who call him son." He carefully described his male admirers as ranging from the "red-blooded men" who liked his performing without "an air of effeminacy" to "the effeminate crowd which likes him because they appreciate true art—and because he represents their ideal of what is fabulous."[90] Here Belafonte intentionally included black bohemians who challenged normative sexuality—fellow artists, friends, and former customers in Greenwich Village—as part of *his* black community.

The second *Defender* piece positioned his successful performance as drawn from black cultures: "the sights and sounds and philosophy of Harlem and New York City" and the "exposure to the power and beauty of folk songs in the West Indies." He detailed race-conscious aspirations for singing black-based folk music; "to find, interpret and project the deepest dreams and ambitions, the most poignant emotions and philosophies of the people of the West Indies, the American Negro of the day of slavery and today." Careful to position his repertoire within multiracial and international black modernity rather than to claim a color-blind universality, Belafonte told Duckett he aimed to "include the folklore of people of different strains the world over" without homogenizing by relying on the "versatility" of folk song to "illustrate the basic likeness of all men by illustrating their very differences."[91]

In the third segment, Belafonte laid out his political and artistic strategies for celebrating the riches of racial experience while rejecting the logic of racialization and embracing principled interracialism. "Belafonte Tells Ideas about Race" began with the declaration "Harry Belafonte loves being a Negro." He counterposed being "truly deeply proud of the traditions, achievements and stamina of his race" with being "truly deeply militant against bigotry in all forms." Then Belafonte spelled out what he would do to "maintain artistic integrity and public responsibility as a Negro." First, he would refuse "Uncle Tom" roles and turn down bookings where segregation was enforced. While he explicitly distanced himself from the actions of Nat King Cole, he also returned the focus to the segregationists: "I think it is more important to fight the bigots who attack Nat Cole physically than it is to attack Nat for his single unfortunate error in judgment." Second, he promised to take risks to insist on his right to critical speech; he would "not bite his tongue when people around him, colored or white, express bigotry, narrow-mindedness, or chauvinism in any form." Finally, he would work to dismantle segregationist practices by showcasing Negro writers, performing in groups that mixed black and white musicians, and appearing as part of interracial casts.[92]

The race-conscious terms that Belafonte used to explain his musical choices echoed the black arts perspective of CNA, offering diasporic black culture as an artistic gift to the world, a black aesthetic based not on racial identity but on shared cultural traditions, common experiences of exploitation, and the sustaining spirit of resistance. "John Henry is the thousands of Negroes in labor, sports, the theater and sciences who are able to achieve miracles because they know that to compete in a hostile society they have to be twice as good, twice as strong, or twice as intuitive as the white man at their side." Singing the spirituals celebrated "the great dignity and strength of the Negro people under slavery—their reservoir of spiritual power which kept them sustained and superior to suffering." "The work songs of the exploited people of Africa and the West Indies" invited U.S. audiences to recognize themselves as part of a black diaspora. He meant his repertoire to challenge the racialized assumptions that segregated art forms and to show musical forms traveling right across socially constructed boundaries: "He sings love songs because Negroes love—and laugh songs because Negroes laugh, and blues songs—because Negroes get the blues . . . he sings just songs because . . . all kinds of people of all kinds of walks of life love to hear him sing them—and that is proof that there are areas of life in which all people can commune."[93]

The combination of race pride and interracialism that Belafonte voiced in these articles reflected Belafonte's political commitments at a time of intensifying civil rights confrontations, and his complicated situation as a successful black performer who was celebrated and turned into a token of racial progress by white audiences. The *Defender* profiles describe the balance between being "deeply proud of . . . his race" and being "deeply militant against bigotry" as "a tremendously difficult and highly sensitive thing to maintain." Belafonte was "determined to do nothing, however profitable, which will disturb the great pride with which the Negro people regard him."[94] Here he set a high bar, easier said than done.

Such statements drew out critics like the African American writer Harold Cruse, an angry and disenchanted former member of CNA. Cruse was concerned about judging black excellence via mainstream white standards. According to Cruse, the "cultural arts" had allowed "a few Negroes to gain stardom and influence" by catering to "the tastes of the American majority. This majority is *white*." Operating in the white world meant "further separation from the Negro public." Nat King Cole had, in his eyes, only followed in the footsteps of many Negro stars. "What have we done . . .

with our music? ... our dance? Our own idiom? Our poetry? Our religious traditions? Our folk culture?" Black artists had "turned our backs on it because we are ashamed of it." Cruse thought black artists would only be capable of creating a "racially conscious art" when they had freed themselves of the patronage of "white folks."[95]

Belafonte was a particular target of Cruse. After reading a *New York Post* profile where Belafonte criticized Nat King Cole's having distanced himself from desegregation efforts, Cruse wrote an outraged response. Belafonte had dared to judge Cole as having "failed his test as a human being"; Belafonte's claim that he needed "more than money and a name" to be able "to sleep nights" was, according to Cruse, just an expression of privilege. He found it "indecent for upstarts like yourself to attempt any self-glorification at Nat Cole's expense," and then he engaged in red-baiting, attributing Belafonte's getting "hepped up on civil rights" as a result of "coming up through the left-wing movement." Cruse advised him to "stick to folk singing."[96] Fortunately for Belafonte, the *Post* did not publish Cruse's letter. In addition to the vitriol, Cruse's associating Belafonte with the Left might have invited more surveillance. But Cruse was beginning to distinguish between black nationalism and black cultural autonomy, on the one hand, and Belafonte's cultural nationalism and principled interracialism, on the other. It was a distinction that emerged more sharply and with heightened urgency in the years to come.[97]

Race, Sex, and Citizenship

By October 1956, Belafonte was on a plane headed to Grenada to play the character of Caribbean labor leader David Boyeur in *Island in the Sun*, a Technicolor film based on Alec Waugh's best-selling novel. Waugh's book encompassed interracial love affairs, a murder, labor disputes, and local ferment challenging British colonial authority in the postwar Caribbean. Before publication, Waugh sold rights to serial publication in *Ladies Home Journal* and condensation in *Reader's Digest.* Darryl Zanuck, for many years the studio chief at Twentieth Century Fox and the producer of many blockbuster film adaptations of controversial best-selling books, snapped up a film option early on, and he watched with delight as the book attracted vast sales and publicity.[98]

A film adaptation of Waugh's novel had the potential to introduce Americans to the Caribbean not simply as a tourist destination but as a place where black citizens resisted British colonialism and the exploitation of working people. Depicting romances across the color line would, however, run up against the prohibition of interracial marriage on-screen. Although the Motion Picture Production Code had been amended in September 1954 to end the outright ban on "miscegenation"—replacing it with the directive that interracial romance, sex, and marriage be treated "within the careful limits of good taste"—filmmakers were aware of southern exhibitors' Jim Crow practices, and had not ventured into this territory following the hesitant efforts of the 1949 race films. Before Zanuck began his work on the project, a letter from the administrator of the Motion Picture Production Code raised the "difficult question of whether or not this story constitutes an unfair portrayal of the Negro race, and whether or not the story is told in such a way that it could reasonably inflame Negro people."[99]

Zanuck confidently welcomed controversy as good for the box office. Taking charge of developing the project, he reshaped it to conform to his ideas of race, projecting the one-drop rule common in the United States onto the social order of the Caribbean. Under his supervision, the film emphasized tensions within colonialism as resulting from racial antagonism rather than the hierarchical structures of class privilege and economic inequality. Following sensational literary conventions, he assumed interracial sexual liaisons to be exceptional rather than foundational. When he began working with screenwriter Alfred Hayes in October 1955, Zanuck criticized an early adaptation by Hayes for *minimizing* racial conflict. "In this story the people were sitting on a keg of dynamite due to the explosive nature of the black-white situation in this spot," he said during a script conference. "We should tell our personal stories in the foreground while in the background would be this seething mass of black people straining against the domination of these few whites."[100]

Zanuck visualized Harry Belafonte as the perfect David Boyeur: a tough, charismatic, manipulative labor leader who could attract the love of a white woman but would never marry her because his main interest was "the welfare, present and future, of the colored people of Santa Marta." This plotting repeated the resolution of Zanuck's 1949 hit film *Pinky*, in which a mixed-race nurse "chooses" to dedicate herself to work within the confines of segregation rather than cross the color line and marry her white doctor suitor. Zanuck imagined Boyeur's position, that "he can have Mavis [the white socialite] for the asking, but he doesn't ask, he turns her down," as providing a positive dramatic resolution of their unconsummated romance. "We should get a lift from the fact that the Negro gives up the white girl he could have had, in order to devote himself entirely to the welfare of his people." In the course of another script conference the following January, writers continued to ask, "Are we saying we do or do not advocate marriage between blacks and whites?" Zanuck settled on the idea that the film could equivocate while preserving white male privilege; the love affair between a white colonial administrator and the mixed-race secretary, to be played by Dorothy Dandridge, already under contract to Fox, would be resolved in marriage; the attraction between the black labor leader and the white socialite would not.[101]

Before he signed a contract, Belafonte tried to get Boyeur's part rewritten as a genuinely dedicated labor leader. As the only significant black West Indian character, his role was central to the film's ability to depict contemporary Caribbean anticolonial politics. Black Chicago lawyer Truman Gibson, adviser to the government on racial affairs during World War II, who read an early script, also questioned Zanuck's conception: "The development of Boyeur as a cynical exploiter of his people," he wrote, "diverts attention from some of the basic reasons why people in that area now are actively and rapidly pushing towards dominion status, and also why the Caribbean world has so radically changed in the last few years."[102]

Belafonte did what he could to convey Boyeur as a dedicated leader, and both he and Dandridge tried to enact their interracial love affairs to destabilize rather than uphold segregationist rules. During the location filming in Grenada and Barbados, Belafonte, Fontaine, and Dandridge were able to add some gestures and dialogue, but Zanuck had the final control and he cut the filmed shots of even a modest kiss and any physical contact initiated by Mavis.[103]

When Belafonte was interviewed in the West Indies and later in London during the final stages of filmmaking, black newspapers reported his hopes that the film might break with Hollywood conventions. "Never before has a colored actor been able to make love to a white woman on the screen," he was quoted as saying. "This is the most important sociological film ever made. This could open the way for Negroes to play better and more advanced parts." Belafonte emphasized the incendiary aspect of the racial power inversion: "In the film Joan Fontaine is in love with me—and I reject her." Before the film was released, the black tabloid publication *Jet* described it as "the most frank portrayal of interracial love to hit the screen."[104]

As much of the opposition to *Island in the Sun* revealed, fanning fears of interracial marriage was a central tenet of

Belafonte as labor leader David Boyeur, and with Joan Fontaine as the admiring Mavis, in publicity stills for Island in the Sun *(1957).*
(Courtesy of Academy of Motion Picture Arts and Sciences.)

white supremacy that fueled segregation. Even before *Jet*'s assessment was reprinted in the White Citizens' Council newsletter, Belafonte had received hate mail with threats such as "Nigger Commie, you have overstepped the mark. Your time has come." In April and May, both *Variety* and the black press reported segregationist efforts in Virginia, Tennessee, and South Carolina to ban the film. Joan Fontaine was the target of what she described as "reviling" letters from New Jersey, Ohio, and Pennsylvania, which included dimes and quarters ("if you're so hard up that you have to work with a nigger"). Zanuck expressed confidence in the box office value of controversy by offering to pay any local fines slapped on exhibitors for showing the film.[105]

Outraged by the final-stage evasions and compromises in *Island in the Sun*, Belafonte broke with industry protocol by publicly criticizing the film and studio efforts to monitor his speech even before it hit the screens. "The tacit romance between Joan Fontaine and myself winds up with nothing," he said in a *Look* profile in early June. He revealed that the studio had "requested" him not to refer to Fontaine in public statements about the film. Zanuck's statements distanced the film from U.S. battles over desegregation, insisting that "the problems that arise in the British West Indies because of racial issues are not at all comparable to the color problem in the U.S. today." In contrast, Belafonte promoted the militant Boyeur as an exemplar: "The importance of this movie is that it tries to show a new kind of Negro living and working in the Caribbean."[106]

Critics in the mainstream and black press were divided over Belafonte's performance as stunning or stilted. Several admired the two set pieces, when Belafonte/Boyeur appears on the dock with laborers singing "Lead Man Holler" and when he dashes the political ambitions of a white plantation owner (played by James Mason) by rallying the crowd with a rousing speech. The black press also featured criticism of the film's racial sensationalism by Jamaica's British governor.[107]

The promotional campaign for *Island in the Sun* took full advantage of Belafonte's current tour, his *Calypso* album, and the romance and sexuality associated with Caribbean tourism and with him. Reports of the film, a big moneymaker, focused on controversies over its exhibition, on Belafonte's daring in criticizing it, and on the coincidence between the screen romances and Belafonte's real life. News reports of Belafonte's marriage to Julie Robinson became public knowledge in April 1957, shortly before the film was released, and a month after the announcement of his divorce.[108]

Belafonte now faced a critical storm following the public announcement of his interracial marriage. Previous attempts to shield his children from lurid publicity failed when *Amsterdam News* reporters staked out the apartment where Harry and Julie were living. Their headlines cast the second marriage as sensational racial boundary crossing: "Belafonte Leaves Negro Wife to Marry White Dancer."[109] When a photo of the new couple went out over the wire services, some white reporters assumed Robinson was black, given her years as a Dunham dancer; others identified her as white; the *New York Post* described her as "half Cherokee and half Irish."[110] The *Amsterdam News* represented the marriage to Julie as a racial betrayal, a black man demonstrating his wealth and prestige by his acquisition of the forbidden. One front-page article asked, "Why a man who has waved the flag of justice for his race so strongly could suddenly turn from a Negro wife to a white wife." Would "Negroes . . . [continue to] accept him as their idol" and would the marriage "affect his future bookings"?[111]

A huge turnout when he appeared at a Harlem fundraiser for the local YMCA confirmed that Negroes *did* continue to "accept" Belafonte, but he did not take any chances, launching his own public relations initiative. Belafonte used a profile in the *Afro-American* as an opportunity to emphasize his own family history of racial boundary crossing: "His first wife was colored, the race of his one African grandfather and Haitian grandmother. His second wife is white, the race of a French grandfather and English grandmother. He himself was born in New York of a Jamaican mother and Martinique father."[112] Extensive profiles in the *New York Post* and the *Saturday Evening Post* appeared in April, followed by stories in *Life* and *Look* in May and June, and Belafonte's own essay in *Ebony*, "Why I Married Julie," in July. These recounted Belafonte's upbringing in Harlem and Jamaica, his "single-minded, almost compulsive concentration on his work" and the "trauma" of his success, the turn to psychoanalysis, and his sense of responsibility as a "Negro performer." The profiles generally represented the marriage to Marguerite as troubled, and both partners in the new relationship as committed to black culture and the struggle for racial equality.[113]

Belafonte's essay in *Ebony* attempted to separate his political resistance to segregation from his interracial marriage by appealing to every human being's right to love. Most of the responses that readers sent to the *Amsterdam News*, the *Afro-American*, and *Ebony* followed his lead in commenting on the new marriage in personal rather than political terms. The black women who wrote expressed concern over a jilted black teacher, and the reputational injury to black women; black men noted historical precedents and expressed their approval of expanded marital possibilities.[114]

Others were willing to stand up for interracial marriage on political grounds. Alongside Belafonte's personal account, *Ebony* asked "prominent Negro leaders" and musical celebrities Eartha Kitt, Mahalia Jackson, Duke Ellington, and Sammy Davis, Jr., whether "interracial marriage hinders" integration. All said no, and redirected attention to the political struggle for racial equality. A. Philip Randolph opposed "any law prohibiting interracial marriages" as "invasions of the privacy of citizens." For Eartha Kitt, interracial marriage was used as a "convenient smoke screen" to confuse the issue of "equal rights and constitutional liberties for all Americans." The president of the National Council of Negro Women, Vivian Carter-Mason, asserted that "existing social, cultural and economic barriers [posed] the real impediments to integration."[115]

The responses to Belafonte's essay were divided between admiration and concern that he had abandoned the wife of his youth. The angriest letter was from Marguerite herself. Her challenge to Belafonte's "version" resulted in her own essay, "The Tragedy of Divorce," published the following summer.[116] Press reports in the fall of 1958 pointed to his interracial marriage as a possible explanation of his difficulties in buying Manhattan real estate—even Belafonte faced New York's housing discrimination.[117] But neither the pressure for sexual "respectability" nor the questions about Belafonte as a family man seriously derailed his public acclaim.

Dissenting in the Calypso Craze Limelight

The unprecedented national and international success of the songs Irving Burgie wrote and Belafonte performed on *Calypso*, the first long-playing record album to sell a million copies, linked Belafonte's celebrity to calypso-styled music and generated a commercial "calypso craze." Music fan magazines tagged Belafonte "the King of Calypso," a title normally reserved for the winner of Trinidad's annual carnival competition. His recording success accelerated an already well-established process of musical exchange. Anthropologist Gordon Rohlehr wrote that the reinvention of calypso since the 1930s "had propelled the calypso outward from its parochial roots in Trinidad into the US,

UK, Jamaica, the Bahamas, Surinam, Panama, Venezuela, Ghana and Sierra Leone (among other places), where singers regularly began to call themselves 'Calypsonians.'"[118] Belafonte's calypsos drew on diverse Afro-Caribbean musical traditions, including the Afro-Cuban music played in New York's jazz clubs and dance halls, important sources for the emerging sound of rock and roll.[119]

Belafonte's hits created new opportunities for other singers to record calypsos, find nightclub work, and participate in musical revues. Some of these singers had been singing calypsos since the 1940s and early 1950s, such as the Trinidadian-and-New York–based Duke of Iron, the Jamaican mento singer Lord Flea, and then folksinger Maya Angelou. Singers associated with different musical genres also tried out calypso: black folksinger Stan Wilson; Latin artists Candido, Tito Puente, and Perez Prado; jazz singers Sarah Vaughan and Dinah Washington; pop singers Rosemary Clooney and Pat Boone; and actor Robert Mitchum.[120] In April 1957, Trinidad-born dancer Geoffrey Holder produced *Caribbean Calypso Festival,* a revue with a company that included Lord Kitchener, a calypsonian from Trinidad living in London, Lord Flea, and Maya Angelou, with music arranged and conducted by Tito Puente. Hollywood tried to cash in with *Calypso Joe,* a cheaply made feature in which the singer and black-cast movie star Herb Jeffries led a group of calypso musicians, played by Lord Flea and Duke of Iron, who provided the music that unlocked romance. The musical *Jamaica,* conceived as a vehicle for Belafonte but revised to star Lena Horne, opened in October 1957 and played for two years, its score satirizing the commercialization of calypso while popularizing a Broadway variation.[121]

Although calypsos continued to appear in his performance repertoire and his recordings, Belafonte distanced himself from the "calypsomania" his album helped set in motion. He did not refer to himself as a "calypso singer" but instead reaffirmed his commitment to all kinds of folk music, announcing plans in early 1957 to record an album of "folk and contemporary blues" and describing himself as "a singer, period. I sing all types of folk material—English, Irish, Israeli—from every section of the world." He pointed out that his No. 1 singles were not calypsos: "Jamaica Farewell" was a "West Indian folk ballad," "Day-O" a "West Indian work song." He praised "true" calypso by associating its improvisation and topicality with a form popularized by the 1930s theatrical left: "It's a kind of living newspaper." And he worried about commercialization of the current craze: "It's going to become a caricature of itself once the fast-buck guys hop onto it. While disdaining the "phony, synthetic, cliché calypso material . . . flooding the market," he promised that calypsos would remain in his repertoire: "I'm going to go on singing true calypso as I see it—just as I intend to go on singing every other kind of music that carries truth in it."[122]

Notwithstanding these disclaimers, Belafonte's identification with calypso persisted, fueled by the release of a new album, *Belafonte Sings of the Caribbean,* timed to take advantage of the film's popularity. It included the calypso-styled songs written by Irving Burgie that Belafonte sang in *Island in the Sun* and other revisions of Caribbean folk songs written by Burgie, along with an older Trinidadian calypso.[123] Even some self-described Trinidadian "purists" made allowances. Although they asserted that "Jamaican variations" were not calypso, they authorized Belafonte as an American-born singer of "real calypso" when he sang "Mary Ann," Trinidad's 1945 carnival road march, and "Mama, Look a Booboo Dey," based on a song by a Trinidad calypsonian Lord Melody. However, they identified his hit single "Day-O/ Banana Boat Song" as a version of "Time for Man Go Home," a Jamaican work song long known in Trinidad, with a rhythm distinctly "not calypso."[124] Black press reports noted with pride when sales of *Calypso* seemed to eclipse Elvis Presley's popularity, even as rhythm and blues performances outdrew rival calypso shows in Brooklyn and at the Apollo.[125]

With musical celebrity came the increased pressure of rising expectations, and the demand to keep performing proven and crowd-pleasing hits. "When I stand before audiences," he told *Look* in June 1957, "I can feel their emotions surging toward me, all their energy charged with so much love. And then I think: all this can easily be turned against me if I don't give them my best."[126] The songs the crowds loved remained in his performance repertoire, but Belafonte seized the tremendous media attention garnered by his musical celebrity as a means to voice a critique of racial confinement and profit-driven commercialism.

Belafonte became bolder in his demands for more complex film depictions of black life and for more and better roles for black actors. Having promised readers of the *Defender* to "turn down Uncle Tom parts," he declined an offer to play Porgy in Samuel Goldwyn's planned film adaptation of the George and Ira Gershwin opera *Porgy and Bess*; Poitier was pressed into taking the role. The *Pittsburgh Courier* reported Belafonte's vow never to play any part in which he would "spend all his time on his knees." Later that summer he added, "All that crap-shooting and razors and lust and cocaine is the old conception of the Negro."[127] When offered the lead in a film adaptation of Eugene O'Neill's play *The Emperor Jones*, Belafonte pushed the studio to include more details of the life of Henri Christophe, the Haitian emperor who provided the model for O'Neill. Belafonte brought in John O. Killens, author of the acclaimed 1954 novel *Youngblood* and an old friend from the CNA, to prepare a treatment that would include "Toussaint L'Ouverture and all the other heroes that made history in the war against Napoleon." The deal fell through.[128]

Belafonte also made good on his promise not to "bite his tongue." Soon after *Island* opened, he was quoted as saying it "stinks," as did the other two films in which he had appeared. He referred to *Bright Road* as a "nice bland Lassie-like thing based on a story in the *Ladies' Home Journal,*" *Carmen Jones* as "bootleg Bizet," and *Island* a "terrible picture based on a terrible best-selling book." He "detested" being labeled "Hollywood's first Negro matinee idol" and the "King of Calypso." Belafonte described being "catapulted out of drama school into a series of compromises like these pictures. And into a monstrous competition among performers. And into a vicious scramble for TV ratings." He condemned Hollywood's commercial imperative, saying he "hated Madison Av. and Hollywood and the clichés of American culture" that made form central and "content secondary."[129]

Critics and fans alike were shocked. Black newspapers reported that Belafonte had "laid waste the entertainment industry," and at least one columnist complained that his "undiplomatic comments" expressed ingratitude.[130] Belafonte persisted in his efforts to expose the industry's racial timidity and the censorship and discrimination he and others encountered. "If I were a white artist I could make many motion pictures and TV spectaculars," he said, but studios "never give stories of Negro life a chance to bloom—everybody is afraid someone might get hurt."[131] These kinds of criticism were commonly voiced among CNA radicals, but they rarely appeared in public from anyone interested in acting in film and television.

Belafonte's press statements tried to revise the rags-to-riches story commonly used to describe his career. He reminded readers that his "overnight stardom" was the result of years of hard work, using a well-worn comic line that it "takes twenty years to become an overnight sensation." He also emphasized the role of chance. Sam Lacy's profile in the *Afro-American* headlined Belafonte's claim that "it was an accident" that a working-class kid who dropped out of high school, couldn't read music, never had voice lessons, and didn't even have "a really good voice" had become a star. Lacy did not accept the "accident" framework, following other critics, both black and white, who explained Belafonte's unlikely ascent by referring to the intensity of his performance and his "lyric consciousness": "I feel them. I believe in every word I sing." Lacy also credited Belafonte's broad popular appeal to his wide-ranging repertoire. "Harry Belafonte hits you with stuff right out of your own folk history—be you colored or white, mainlander or islander, city dude or country hick."[132]

In a widely syndicated interview appearing in August 1957, Belafonte proposed an alternative yardstick for success. He reminded readers that "one million dollars" gets smaller after the government takes its share (his tax bracket was ninety percent, although few paid the full amount). While admitting "the dough was a comfort," he claimed he could buy the things he really needed—a car, an apartment in New York—with much less than he was earning. Belafonte prioritized creative freedom, self-determination, and social camaraderie. "Artistically I'm still doing the kind of work I want to do, with no compromises," he claimed, "and my friends are the same ones I've had for years."[133]

With his celebrity "power to reach the widest audience imaginable," Belafonte took seriously the moral obligation to open doors for other black performers, and "to speak his mind" rather than "avoid controversy." As a black arts radical, he wanted to move on from "pictures about inter-racial relations" to stories about black life, disparaging *Island* as poorly written and directed, and "TV bigwigs" as having "no vision, no imagination." He refused to perform in the segregated South unless "it meant that the next day Negro and white children could go to school together." One reporter called attention to the contrast between Belafonte's "gay and carefree" persona onstage and the seriousness of the political convictions he expressed offstage, which

Working with Robert DeCormier. (Courtesy of Photographs and Prints Division, Schomburg Center for Research in Black Culture, the New York Public Library, Astor, Lenox and Tilden Foundations and courtesy of Sony Music Entertainment.)

he interpreted as stemming from Belafonte continuing to carry "youthful hurts of discrimination in New York City and the West Indies."[134]

Belafonte wanted to figure out how to use his celebrity position to also serve collective demands for racial equality, a mission he shared with other black arts radicals. As former CNA colleague and writer John O. Killens articulated in a letter about their collaboration, "There is so much to say to America, culturally speaking."[135]

To help him produce art that both entertained and expressed this mission, Belafonte turned to old friends from the left and to Julie Robinson Belafonte. Belafonte was now in a position to employ friends and colleagues, although the weight of his celebrity and his considerable economic power skewed their collaboration. In early 1957, he hired the talented composer and arranger Robert DeCormier, whom he had known in the late 1940s, to work with him as musical director and choral arranger. Singing spirituals and work songs with a chorus expanded Belafonte's musical range and invoked the power of collectivity. DeCormier led the recording sessions for Belafonte's next several albums, including *Belafonte Sings of the Caribbean*, and directed the interracial Harry Belafonte Singers, assembled from the worlds of theater, opera, and folk music, to back him in live performances, on television, and recordings. Leon Bibb, a black folksinger from Robeson's circle, was at the sessions for *Caribbean*, as were Brock Peters and Burgie. DeCormier and Bibb had both been blacklisted earlier in the decade. Belafonte continued to use Burgie's revisions of Caribbean folk songs and employed close friends and CNA colleagues Attaway and Killens in various writing projects. By August 1957, Belafonte had set up the structure for his own film production company, Harbel, the first independent, black-owned unit in Hollywood, and was beginning to develop ideas for films and television specials. The new black characters, narratives, and genres that Belafonte envisioned are the subject of Chapter 4.[136]

Music Superstar, Radical Activist, and World Citizen

As a celebrity Belafonte had no control over much that was written about him. Fan magazines promised to reveal

"The Complete Life Story" of "America's King of Calypso" and "Why Girls are Wild about Harry." Tabloid headlines screamed "When Belafonte Tried to Pass," and "Belafonte's Big Problem (White Women Won't Leave Him Alone)."[137]

But he *could* try to redirect some of this kind of attention by linking his name to the struggle for civil rights. He knew that his public authority was as an artist and not as a politician or an organizer, but being part of cultural political activism in the late 1940s encouraged him now to lend his name and his presence to draw attention to marches, picket lines, and fund-raising events.[138] Both his music and the constancy of his participatory support made him an important icon for protesters on the front lines. His musical celebrity contributed to and in turn was expanded by his unequivocal commitment to the new phase of struggle for racial equality.

Belafonte made careful strategic choices about political endorsements. He had worked alongside performers who contributed to the third-party Wallace campaign in 1948; by 1956, he had the clout to use his name to bargain for public support of desegregation. Although the Democratic Party nominee Adlai Stevenson was at best a moderate on civil rights, the *Pittsburgh Courier* reported him as saying he would use the power of the presidency "for compliance [with] rather than defiance" of the *Brown* decision. After two private meetings with Stevenson to discuss "issues involving U.S. Negro citizens," Belafonte publicly endorsed him in the *Chicago Defender* and appeared in a national television broadcast planned by the Democratic National Committee alongside a group of white New York and Hollywood progressives, including Orson Welles, Oscar Hammerstein II, Leonard Bernstein, Marlon Brando, Robert Ryan, and Henry Fonda. On the broadcast, Belafonte reached back into the late 1940s left-wing songbook to sing "The House I Live In" with lyrics "altered to suit the Democratic cause." A syndicated column on the black wire service reported that Belafonte had also recorded a calypso-style campaign song, "Adlai Is de Man."[139]

When presidential hopeful John F. Kennedy approached Belafonte in 1960 for an endorsement, political tensions following the stepped-up efforts for desegregation meant that their meeting was not announced publicly, as Belafonte's meeting with Stevenson had been. Stevenson backers did not find much to admire in Kennedy's record to date. Belafonte set conditions for his support and urged Kennedy to turn his attention to the civil rights insurgency associated with Martin Luther King, Jr. When Belafonte did make an eleventh-hour TV spot to endorse Kennedy, he was filmed with Jack and Jackie Kennedy and a Harlem couple in their apartment. After the candidate had responded to questions from the couple about how he would enforce the *Brown* decision and respond to the political upheaval in the Congo during the first months of its independence, Belafonte gave his endorsement. The campaign spot that appeared on television was edited to show only Kennedy and Belafonte, and was pulled after only one broadcast.[140] Belafonte also lent his name to grassroots efforts to increase progressive black political representation, heading the list of supporters of the newly formed Unity Democratic Club in the Bedford-Stuyvesant section of Brooklyn, Representative Shirley Chisholm's initial political base.[141]

Encouraged by King and the In Friendship radicals, Belafonte agreed to use his star power to lead demonstrations supporting nonviolent resistance to segregation. When Baker and Rustin organized a national Prayer Pilgrimage to Washington, DC, in 1957 to gain national exposure for the Southern Christian Leadership Conference (SCLC) and to "protest the bombings and violence in the South," Belafonte helped publicize the event, at which Mahalia Jackson sang and Martin Luther King, Jr., preached. Harry and Julie Belafonte joined Jackie Robinson—who had broken the color bar in major league baseball—Sidney and

Jackie Robinson, A. Philip Randolph (center rear, in bow tie), Julie Robinson Belafonte, and Harry Belafonte at Youth March for Integrated Schools, Washington, D.C., October 25, 1958. (Courtesy Getty Images.)

Juanita Poitier, Ruby Dee, and Sammy Davis, Jr., onstage to welcome the "pilgrims" arriving on "Freedom Trains" from cities across the country.[142]

Jackie Robinson and Belafonte led the next large mobilization organized by Rustin and others in the fall of 1958, the Youth March for Integrated Schools, with support from NAACP youth affiliates and labor unions. After a year of fierce segregationist opposition and violence directed at the nine black students who had enrolled in Little Rock's Central High School, the governor of Arkansas ordered all high schools in Little Rock shuttered for the 1958–1959 academic year. Rustin's answer to Governor Faubus was to bring some ten thousand black and white students—from colleges and high schools, even elementary schools, across the Northeast and Midwest—to Washington to demand desegregation at their schools. Their signs read "Make Democracy Work," "Integrate in '58," and "Marching for Integration."

At the head of the march, Belafonte led a delegation of six southern white students and five southern and northern black students to the White House, to pressure the federal government to commit resources necessary to achieve integration. Among the contingent of black students were Minnejean Brown, one of those who enrolled in Little Rock's Central High; a young woman who was part of a desegregation lawsuit in Norfolk, Virginia; the first two boys to attend an integrated school in Baltimore, Maryland; a student who had organized a strike at North Carolina State to defend the NAACP; and a northern representative of the Peekskill Youth Council in New York State. At the White House they were stopped by a guard—and ignored by President Eisenhower.

The many questions about Little Rock that Belafonte had fielded during his recent concert tour in Europe had heightened his consciousness of how Jim Crow was viewed outside the United States. When he and the delegation of students returned to the demonstration, Belafonte reminded the crowd that "millions, not only in America but throughout Europe, Africa, and Asia, will know of [Eisenhower's] behavior here this afternoon." A black press reporter recounted Belafonte's warning, "in a fighting but dignified voice . . . of the 'strong feeling of indignation among the students and the people of the world' when they learned of the delegation's rebuff."[143]

The follow-up Youth March and rally in April 1959—which brought an estimated twenty-six thousand young people to the Capitol carrying petitions with the names of nearly four hundred thousand others—honored Belafonte, King, and Robinson as integration leaders, along with Daisy Bates, newspaper editor and adviser to the Little Rock students. Speeches by King (who had just returned from a trip to India to study Gandhian nonviolence) and Kenyan political leader Tom Mboya (chair of the All-African Peoples' Conference [AAPC], a Pan-African independence movement) placed the U.S. freedom struggles in an international context.[144]

The Youth Marches provided the seedbed for the new student-led phase of civil rights, and Belafonte's leadership indelibly linked him with that student movement. By the spring of 1960, when student sit-ins initiated a new stage of militancy, Belafonte's name, music, presence, and support were invaluable. The Nashville sit-in students sang "Day-O" in jail in 1960; the Freedom Riders transposed its words to "Freedom's coming, and It Won't Be Long" in their cells in Parchman Penitentiary in 1961. The teachers in Mississippi Freedom schools pasted up pictures of Belafonte cut from the pages of *Ebony* to represent the spirit of the black freedom curriculum they taught in the summer of 1964.[145]

Belafonte and the students recognized one another's radicalism. The students knew they could count on him for public support and strategic counsel, bailing them out of jail, emergency fund-raising. He let them know he would watch out for them. Belafonte mediated tensions as they arose with the elders in SCLC. He also helped pay for darkrooms in Atlanta, Selma, and at Tougaloo College so that Student Nonviolent Coordinating Committee (SNCC) members could document their movement. In September 1964, he paid the expenses for a group of SNCC leaders, exhausted from the strain and dangers of voter registration work in the Mississippi Delta, to travel with him on a revitalizing trip to Africa.[146]

Belafonte often represented the civil rights and labor alliance in this period, a continuation of his involvements with left wing–civil rights labor collaboration since the late 1940s. A number of radical unions provided financial support to organize the Youth Marches, and progressive union leaders associated their names with Belafonte when they stepped up as chairs and vice-chairs for the

Addressing noon labor civil rights rally in the garment district as part of daylong events marking the sixth anniversary of the Brown *decision, NYC, May 17, 1960. (© Bettman/Corbis.)*

second Youth March he led in April 1959. Belafonte, who had sung folk music at District 65's Saturday Nightclub in 1950, agreed to be the headliner for the union's twenty-fifth birthday celebration/rally in 1958 at Madison Square Garden, where he was accompanied by a chorus of union members and received an honorary union membership as a fighter for "equality and human rights." A widely circulated AP photograph of Belafonte exhorting the crowd at a rally on the sixth anniversary of the *Brown* decision, organized by the New York Labor Council and District 65 in 1960, kept the associations between Belafonte, labor, and civil rights in the public eye.[147]

Belafonte also intertwined his celebrity with the civil rights movement when he led the list of stars at movement benefits, important sources of funds for the new direct-action phase of civil rights. Belafonte and his former CNA colleagues Sidney Poitier, Ruby Dee, and Ossie Davis were among the first to put their names down for a Night of the

Stars for Civil Rights at the Manhattan Center on April 25, 1957.[148] By 1960, Belafonte was the one approaching other singers, musicians, and actors to appear in support of civil rights protests.

Belafonte stepped up his organizational commitment in early 1960, when the state of Alabama began a series of legal maneuvers intended to stop King and the movement he spearheaded. Belafonte took charge of the Cultural Committee to Defend Martin Luther King and the Struggle for Freedom, raising money and mobilizing signatories for a full-page appeal in the *New York Times,* which then sparked a libel suit by state and local officials in Alabama. Belafonte reached out to former CNA colleagues, actors, singers, and In Friendship labor and church allies to join the appeal.[149]

By the spring of 1960, Belafonte was a headliner at civil rights events. In April he walked a picket line and led a rally in Boston to support the southern students arrested at sit-ins. In May he performed at a "spectacular night of stars" freedom rally in New York at the 369th Armory in Harlem. Sidney Poitier and Dorothy Dandridge emceed the event, which also featured Odetta singing with the Belafonte Folk Singers, jazz singer Sarah Vaughan, concert artist William Warfield, and Nigerian drummer Babatunde Olatunji, accompanied by African drummers and dancers.

The Harlem rally culminated a day of demonstrations called for the anniversary of the *Brown* decision. Simultaneous marches and demonstrations took place in Atlanta, Boston, Ann Arbor, Chicago, Montgomery, Memphis, and Biloxi. In New York, the day began with a ceremony at the Statue of Liberty, featuring Belafonte's version of "The Star-Spangled Banner," Odetta singing "Oh, Freedom," and a group of black and white students, including veterans of the sit-ins, singing "I'm on my way and I won't turn back." At noon, an estimated fifteen thousand took part in the

Belafonte joins northern students picketing Woolworth's in Harvard Square, Cambridge, to support southern students protesting segregation, April 22, 1960. (Photograph © J. Walter Green/AP/Corbis.)

union-organized rally for civil rights in the garment district, listening to Belafonte and Poitier alongside local labor leaders.

Beyond his star allure, these events showcased Belafonte's leadership. *Amsterdam News* writer James Hicks proclaimed that Belafonte had shed his "amateur status" to become a civil rights leader in his own right, having "fused and brought together the Negro 'masses' with the so-called Negro 'classes' in common cause." According to Hicks, the Armory rally brought out more Negroes in Harlem than any other in the last twenty years, and "more

Holding his son David on his shoulders on Liberty Island at a morning demonstration to mark the Brown *decision, May 17, 1960. (Photo by Richard Martin, courtesy of Photographs and Prints Division, Schomburg Center for Research in Black Culture, the New York Public Library, Astor, Lenox and Tilden Foundations.)*

white people from downtown than Harlem has seen in the past fifty years under one uptown roof." In the mid-1960s, Belafonte-led benefits at Carnegie Hall in New York, in Atlanta and Los Angeles, in Paris and Stockholm raised significant funds to sustain SCLC and SNCC.[150] In addition to what Hicks described as encouraging attendees to "rise up in indignation against injustice and take some action of their own," these events offered transcendent moments of reversal, creating spaces of racial boundary crossing and equality despite intensifying segregationist violence and continuing federal equivocation and inaction.

Drawing on the international perspectives he had developed during and after World War II, Belafonte began in 1956 to publicly identify himself as a "world citizen." He joined the campaign against nuclear testing, appearing at a 1960 Madison Square Garden rally organized by the National Committee for a Sane Nuclear Policy (SANE) with Eleanor Roosevelt and A. Philip Randolph, and then personally leading a "ban the bomb" march through the streets of New York to the UN. The *Afro-American* marked these events as "the first major demonstration in this country for world peace."[151]

As Belafonte began to tour outside the United States, his own internationalism was deepened by the heartfelt responses of diverse audiences to his wide-ranging folk repertoire ("Moods of the American Negro," "Songs of the Caribbean," and "Around the World"). On his first tour of England and Europe in 1958, he was especially touched by "excited teenagers and laughing West Indians" in London, and found himself moved by German audience enthusiasm for the Israeli song "Hava Nagila."[152]

When he was asked, he used public remarks as an opportunity to place the U.S. struggle for civil rights in a broader context. For example, he answered questions about the standoff in Little Rock by linking segregation to fascism: "If the world survived Hitler then you can be sure that the American Negro people will survive Faubus [governor of Arkansas]." And he tried to use his celebrity to advance black citizenship rights and racial equality outside the United States. Belafonte was in London just days before white youth, encouraged by right-wing antiblack immigrant rhetoric, had attacked West Indians in the North Kensington district, setting off what came to be known as the Notting Hill riots. Radical journalist Claudia Jones, an American Communist leader originally from Trinidad who had been deported to London in 1955, responded by organizing London's first Caribbean carnival a few months later. Belafonte's negotiations for a five-year contract with the BBC demanded that his performance enact black belonging. He insisted that his appearance be scheduled each Christmas Day, one of Britain's most highly viewed broadcast times. As he explained to a *London Daily Herald* columnist, he made the demand "symbolic of my belief in the greatness of my race."[153]

Having a "world" perspective made Belafonte particularly interested in new African independence movements and the potential strategic importance of linkages between liberation struggles. The day before the second Youth March, Belafonte had participated in a Carnegie Hall celebration of the first U.S. Africa Freedom Day, responding to a call from the All-African Peoples' Conference, held in Ghana the year before, and its leader, Tom Mboya. The New York celebration was organized by the American Committee on Africa (ACOA), an organization dedicated to supporting liberation struggles in Africa, growing out of an ad hoc committee publicizing the early 1950s civil disobedience campaigns led by the African National Congress to defy apartheid's unjust laws in South Africa. The program at Carnegie Hall included Tom Mboya, Belafonte, A. Philip Randolph, and Langston Hughes reciting his poetry to percussive accompaniment by Olatunji.[154]

Belafonte subsequently responded to Mboya's call for fi-

Belafonte with South African singer Miriam Makeba ca. 1960s. (Courtesy of Photographs and Prints Division, Schomburg Center for Research in Black Culture, the New York Public Library, Astor, Lenox and Tilden Foundations.)

nancial support to bring African students to study in the United States, joining with Robinson and Poitier to send out the African-American Students Foundation's appeal for funds, including to the readers of the *Afro-American*. Along with Eleanor Roosevelt, Robinson, King, and Randolph, Belafonte was an honorary chair for the 1960 Africa Freedom Day rally at Town Hall in New York, combining celebration of the eight new independent African states with a protest against "machine-gun-enforced apartheid in South Africa." He joined Lorraine Hansberry, Robinson, King, and Randolph as sponsors of ACOA's Africa Defense and Aid Fund, raising money to fund the legal defense of challengers to apartheid, to help families of prisoners, and to aid the families of the nonviolent demonstrators killed by the police at Sharpeville.[155]

In the fall of 1959, Belafonte's personal involvement with the South African antiapartheid struggle intensified after Trevor Huddleston, an Anglican bishop recalled from Johannesburg after thirteen years' working at a mission station because of his fierce opposition to the Nationalist government's racial policies, approached him in London. Huddleston asked Belafonte to help obtain political asylum in England for the young black South African writers who had worked on and appeared in Lionel Rogosin's clandestine antiapartheid film, *Come Back, Africa*. The attention the film had received at the Venice Film Festival put its writers, and the remarkable young South African jazz singer it featured, Miriam Makeba, in danger of imprisonment. Later Belafonte would describe meeting these young people and seeing the film as "an epiphany."[156]

Following this encounter, Belafonte intensified his commitment to the antiapartheid struggle. He helped Makeba negotiate a singing career in the United States. When they began appearing together beginning in early 1960, their musical performance made the connections between the U.S. freedom campaigns and the South African resistance to apartheid explicit and vivid for their audiences.[157]

Moving forward, Belafonte's celebrity would be bound up with these movements, and his forms of cultural expression would be shaped by his experiences inside and outside the United States. The resources that had enabled Belafonte to assume control over his performing career pushed him to now try to create film and television that conveyed his black arts, interracialist, and internationalist perspectives in the service of racial equality and social justice. He was at the top of his form. But how could he maintain his appeal to that broad audience—black and white, "class" and "mass," "steelworkers and symphony patrons, bobby-soxers and schoolchildren" and still find a way to use his art to do what Bayard Rustin called "speak[ing] truth to power"?

STORMING THE GATES

Producing Film and Television, 1957–1970

Between 1957 and 1970, Belafonte took full advantage of his music and film celebrity to initiate projects expressing his political vision, celebrating the foundational contributions of black culture, supporting interracialism and internationalism, and rejecting race-based confinement. But fast-changing and frequently shifting alliances in civil rights and anticolonial struggles at home and abroad shook up political certainties, and Belafonte's producing efforts sparked more controversy than acclaim.

When Belafonte entered film productions in 1957, interracial contact itself was a direct challenge to segregation. Between 1960 and 1965, despite internal divisions over tactics and intensifying white backlash, civil rights campaigns gained the political momentum to dismantle many legal obstacles to citizenship. After 1965, the focus of the freedom movement shifted from southern to northern and western cities, from voting rights to economic discrimination and police brutality, from civil rights to the Poor People's Campaign and Black Power.

By the late 1960s, the demands for black political and economic power and black cultural autonomy exposed prior assumptions that integration meant assimilating into a white world and could be achieved while leaving white-defined norms unchallenged. Previously successful strategies for achieving "freedom now" and cross-racial alliances foundered. Many forms of black assertion, from soul music and urban riots to black electoral campaigns, *opposed* efforts to address racial inequality by advancing token individuals or by advocating tolerance and colorblind universality. Analysis of economic discrimination revealed multiple structures reinforcing inequality in addition to the dynamics that supported white supremacy.

Whatever consensus had existed concerning the international mission of the United States began to come apart. For years Belafonte had supported left-wing calls for peace and banning nuclear weapons. His 1959 work to bring African students to study in the United States in order to develop leadership for the new independence movements did not provoke particular debate. In 1960, he associated himself with President Kennedy's foreign policy by becoming an advisor to the newly organized Peace Corps, modeled in part on Harlem minister James Robinson's Crossroads Africa program. Although the black press did cover the All-African People's Conference's opposition to the Peace Corps as an effort to "reconquer and economically dominate Africa," Belafonte recognized an opportunity to encourage youth internationalism. His public support for the Peace Corps emphasized its capacity to develop a cohort of young people exposed to political currents and social exigencies in the world outside the United States.[1] By the late 1960s, critics in some of the host countries, in Europe and in the United States began to question the motives and impact of Peace Corps economic development efforts.

Many citizens in countries around the world vocally challenged the U.S. military intervention in Vietnam. At home, positions hardened in support of and in opposition to the Vietnam War. Belafonte began to speak out publicly against the war in 1965. To many critics, it was becoming increasingly apparent that the cost of fighting an unjustified war was falling disproportionately on black and working-class youth, as well as forcing cuts in the social programs directing resources toward the urban poor.

At the height of his celebrity in 1956, Belafonte had promised to make career decisions in line with what then seemed like clear and self-evident goals for the black freedom struggle. The task Belafonte now set for himself, to become a producer of new kinds of film and television that might use the media to challenge the racial status quo, required considerable risk taking and would surely raise hackles. He would enter the culture industries with the deck stacked against him. He would have to work against convention and convince audiences to explore untried paths, all while the pace of change accelerated and black freedom goals diverged.

The First Black Hollywood Movie Producer, 1957–1959

Disappointed by his prior film roles but still longing to reach film's mass audience, Belafonte's move into film production put "his money where his mouth was." The establishment of his company Harbel, the first black-owned film unit producing for Hollywood, signaled boldness and audacity. At the time, there were no black people in charge of image making in the mainstream film industry. Nothing in Belafonte's experience as an entertainer, recording star, and "matinee idol" in three mainstream films translated directly into movie know-how. Even so-called independent filmmaking in the 1950s relied on financing, distribution agreements, and loan guarantees from distributors or the studios themselves, which was not very independent from the "Hollywood" that Belafonte frequently criticized.[2]

Within months of his creating a new organizational

structure for self-management, and even before he publicly introduced its film production unit Harbel in August 1957, Belafonte was already working on ideas he hoped might draw his music audience to films introducing new black characters and stories. In the late 1940s and early 1950s, he had listened to late-night conversations at American Negro Theater (ANT) and the Committee for the Negro in the Arts (CNA) arguing about how to realize full-bodied black characters, whether to emphasize centrality or marginalization in American culture, racial rage or racial pride. Not a writer himself, he now turned to his CNA friend John O. Killens, a central figure in the Harlem Writers Guild and, after the publication of his well-received novel *Youngblood* in 1954, a prominent promoter of black arts, labor solidarity, and civil rights. Belafonte commissioned Killens to develop a film treatment of the "John Henry" story and brought him along in negotiations with studio executives for a film version of Eugene O'Neill's *The Emperor Jones*.[3]

There was little precedent in film and television for black writers and artists to tell stories that expressed black subjectivity, and mainstream audiences were completely unprepared to view them. A chasm stretched between well-intentioned Hollywood films calling for "tolerance" and "brotherhood" and black demands for racial equality and citizenship. The segregationist backlash against civil rights gains gave pause to the studios considering projects that risked white ticket sales, but they also felt some pressure to draw black audiences, an increasing segment of ticket buyers.[4]

Even among those supporting the civil rights struggle, there was no consensus on how to depict racially inflected experience. In white culture, "blackness" was commonly associated with being a "problem"; universality was supposedly color blind but presumptively white. Black Left intellectuals close to Belafonte refused to imagine the opposite of racialization as whiteness, instead proposing varieties of cosmopolitan universality.[5] To overturn the "blackness as problem" framework, one writer argued for blackness as the *center* of American culture, writing that in "this ocean of Negro life, with its cross-currents and undercurrents, lies the very soul of America."[6] But when black playwrights in the 1950s attempted to put black people at the center by presenting black characters as "ordinary" and dramatizing their everyday experience, mainstream white critics and audiences could not abandon the way of thinking that opposed "racial" to "universal." When a play produced by a Negro writer with Negro characters ventured outside the confines of "Negro protest" or "Negro solidarity," a common white critical response was praise for *not* being "about Negroes." Mainstream white acclaim for Lorraine Hansberry's play *A Raisin in the Sun* (1959) identified its themes as universal by *denying* their racial significance, describing the play, in one review, as a "touching story about a tenement family and their vanishing dream."[7]

Belafonte sought ideas for film that would parallel his musical repertoire in representing black people as resisting world citizens who trespassed racial and national boundaries. For his first pitch, backed by Killens's research and writing, Belafonte proposed to desegregate the Western, a central genre of American film and a staple of cheap fiction and nighttime television. He wanted to counter the post–Civil War Confederate presence that haunted television serials and such films as John Ford's 1956 *The Searchers* by introducing black cowboys and outlaws into the racial and ethnic mixture of the borderlands. The film he outlined told the story of half brothers, one white and one black, the product of slavery's racial and sexual border crossing, roaming the frontier after 1865, to be played by Brando and himself.[8]

Harbel's First Try: *The World, the Flesh and the Devil*

Harbel's plans quickly shifted when Sol Siegel, an independent producer connected with MGM, approached Belafonte with an idea for a film then called *The End of the World.* Belafonte would star as one of three survivors, two men and one woman, of a "cataclysmic event" in a film jointly produced by Siegel and Harbel and distributed by MGM. Siegel's proposal offered Harbel a protected launch into the business, requiring a limited investment in exchange for a percentage of the profits, with the advantage of Siegel's producing experience and access to MGM resources and distribution.

The "end of the world" story, based on a novel, had been circulating around Hollywood for years; Siegel thought that casting Belafonte would add a powerful twist and box office appeal.[9] Later Belafonte described the script he saw as "written with greater honesty for two white guys, and the metaphor was laborer vs. capitalist." He signed on to play the skilled black worker who survived the disaster before seeing a completed script.[10]

Belafonte's initial public comments on *The End of the World* were carefully optimistic about Harbel's first production and its ostensibly race-neutral casting. For black actors to take parts not written for a "black type" would change the "entire focus of dramatic casting from stereotype to realistic interpretation," allowing actors to make "contributions . . . based strictly on their abilities as talented human beings" that could "enrich American life." He hoped his first independent film would be "reviewed and received by the audience solely on its merits as a movie—not a white man's movie or a Negro's movie."[11]

For the first part of the film, Belafonte's character, mine inspector Ralph Burton, carries the action and drama.

Having freed himself from a collapsed mine shaft and made his way to New York City, he wanders down empty streets and past deserted skyscrapers. In these early scenes, Belafonte powerfully conveys the survivor's skilled ingenuity and civic-mindedness as well as his existential loneliness. After shooting New York location scenes in the fall of 1957 and beginning the work on a closed set at MGM in the spring of 1958, Belafonte remained upbeat about the message of the film. He described it to a Hollywood columnist as a "realistic story" in which the interaction between the three survivors provided "a fairly definitive look into interracial relationships. . . . All three are Americans. All have been exposed at one level or another to raciality and expressions of prejudice. In the picture great value is placed on human life. Everybody has high hopes for the kind of thing this picture can bring about." Alluding to studio-enforced limits on Belafonte's romance with Joan Fontaine in *Island in the Sun,* the columnist promised viewers that "in the end there is reason to believe that Mr. Belafonte gets the girl."[12]

Uncertainty about how to end the story turned precisely on whether "Mr. Belafonte gets the girl." When Burton encounters Sarah Crandall, the white woman who is the sole female survivor (played by Swedish-born actress Inger Stevens), the camera emphasizes her fear of him. She has been watching him for several weeks without making herself known. The racial logic of the narrative flirts with crossing but then decisively maintains the color line. Because of Burton's sterling character (and because he is played by Harry Belafonte), Crandall eventually wants to "marry" him, but he is suspicious of her sense of entitlement, and he demurs. With the arrival of the third survivor, Benson Thacker (Mel Ferrer), a wealthy white man who assumes Crandall is his for the taking, the filmmakers found themselves without a cinematic resolution. They were unprepared to play out the sexual logic of interracialism, especially given the pitched battles over Little Rock school desegregation then in the news.

A studio memo detailed their racial calculations, searching for a resolution with the potential to mollify segregationists without alienating black ticket-buyers. Although the film was supposedly completed by June 1958, an August note from writer-director Rand MacDougall to Siegel considered "three possible endings."

1. Ralph Burton [Belafonte] gets the girl.
   Liable to satisfy a few customers, alienate many thousands, and most importantly do an immense harm to the progress of racial integration. It would suggest very strongly that intermarriage is the absolute answer to racial problems. That idea can only increase tension on this subject which is not our purpose.
2. Neither man gets the girl.
   Most unsatisfactory. Begs the question, in my opinion, makes the picture a target to every faction of thought on the subject of racial integration. Critics and general public alike would castigate any variation of such an inconclusive ending—Negro and white extremists would together leap on it to illustrate their opposing point of view.
3. Benson Thacker [Ferrer] gets the girl.
   Burton [Belafonte] has to give up the girl himself; initiative must be his. This is the only way to still any possible Negro protest.[13]

MacDougall and Siegel reconvened the actors for a second round of location shooting in New York in the fall of 1958. They filmed a high-speed chase on rooftops and deserted streets, with Thacker aiming a high-powered rifle at his rival but missing his shot; then Burton takes aim. The deadly chase ends in front of the UN, where first Burton

Publicity poster for The World, the Flesh and the Devil *(1959), showing Belafonte's character holding his rifle. (Courtesy of Academy of Motion Picture Arts and Sciences.)*

and then Thacker drop their weapons. Crandall reaches for Burton's hand, extending her other hand to Thacker as they walk into what a title proclaims as "The Beginning."

Belafonte was trapped by contractual obligations in yet another Hollywood evasion. He later recalled voicing objections; Siegel "wouldn't do anything to stop the vandals."

Belafonte remembered feeling that "they'd taken out the truth that would have made the film really admirable." Although Belafonte's acting and the film's representation of postatomic New York City received considerable praise, the racial concessions made him remember his first film production as "just so false."[14]

The trade reviewers thought the film's evasions would aid its marketing. *Motion Picture Herald* wrote that the "imaginative situation, extraordinarily well-acted" would "attract interest, excite controversy, and create the kind of talk which will sell tickets." *Box Office* judged that both the "story threads" of atomic warfare and "an interracial love situation" were handled "in excellent taste and should offend no one, regardless of individual morals and geography."[15]

A number of white reviewers embraced the film's segregation-driven compromises. A newspaper critic in Cleveland appreciated Belafonte's character's acquiescence to the color line, describing him as "too proud to accept the guarantee of affection by Miss Stevens. And rightly so." Another assumed that racial separation was a universal norm: "the Negro-hero pulls to a sudden stop, leaving the white girl as the aggressor, and all because our hero cannot even for a split second discard what has seared into his heart—and what is also in the hearts of millions of his white viewers as well as his colored ones."[16]

White critics who admired Belafonte's performance as the last survivor used racialized terms to describe his character. Some called Burton "Emperor" of New York, referring to O'Neill's power-crazed Emperor Jones; *Time* referred to him as a "Black Adam."[17] Two critics were startled by a scene in which Crandall orders Burton to cut her hair, exposing sexual undercurrents in this encounter between white privilege and black pride. Perhaps guided by MGM publicity that described Belafonte's character's "ra-

Ralph Burton responding to Sarah Crandall's demand that he cut her hair. (Courtesy of Academy of Motion Picture Arts and Sciences.)

cial feeling" as his "tragic inner conflict," these reviewers understood black pride as "obsession with race," which they attributed only to Belafonte's character.[18]

Other reviewers, black and white, explicitly condemned the film's concessions to segregation. A woman columnist for Cleveland's black press rejected MGM's premise that, in the face of disaster, preserving the "civilization of the past" meant preserving racial discrimination. She found it unbelievable that the last man and woman on earth would "deny himself and her[self] the pleasures of a natural relationship simply because they are of different races." Belafonte and Harbel were responsible, in her eyes, for a picture with a "weak plot" and, apart from the racial conflict, "no depth." White film critic Hollis Alpert was equally dismissive, judging the film as "radioactive silliness" and noting that "segregationist southerners and the South African government will be heartened to know that even in a relatively empty world, the race problem continues."[19]

Other white critics who praised the power of the opening scenes thought the film's overemphasis on the color line produced a "trite triangle situation" and a "mishmash of clichés." One described the film as "a silly example of how people who are obsessed with the race question tend to see everything in black and white." They hated the ending. *New York Times* critic Bosley Crowther found it "such an obvious contrivance and so cozily theatrical you wouldn't be surprised to see the windows of the buildings suddenly crowded with reintegrated people, cheering happily and flinging ticker tape." To *Nation* film critic Robert Hatch, "the trio shakes hands and the picture gives up."[20]

Black newspapers were familiar with—and often complicit in—a long history of sensationalizing interracial sex and violence. They carefully scrutinized the film's depiction of racial boundaries. Many ran a romantic photograph of Belafonte touching Stevens's face.[21] *Chicago Defender* columnists forewarned viewers that despite the film's marketing as the "first interracial romance between male Sepian and non-Sepian female star," the only personal contact between Belafonte and Stevens occurs during the haircut scene and when she takes his hand at the end. "THERE IS NO KISSING."[22] A number of the black newspapers ran publicity photographs of Belafonte and Ferrer pointing their weapons at each other.

One L.A. black newspaper critic scorned the publicity photos of Belafonte and Stevens as intended to "make Belafonte and company richer" by exploiting "that jazz about racial tensions among the last survivors on earth." As a black viewer, he didn't feel "any identification" with Belafonte. "For a few moments you're wrapped up in the picture," he wrote. "The next second you're snapped back to reality" by the "incongruities . . . of the plot" or by "some reaction . . . by the actors that seems unbelievable, even for the last three people on earth." A university-based black film critic who appreciated the portrayal of black invisibility and frustration in the early scenes agreed that when the interracial triangle appears, "a wall of simple-minded clichés obscures the true situation."[23]

The *Chicago Defender* suggested that the film appealed more to white viewers than black ones, contrasting long lines of white ticket buyers downtown with black South Side viewers leaving the movie theater "enthused *and* disturbed" and engaged in "arguments galore."[24] Within weeks of the opening, Belafonte went public with his own disappointed criticisms. "Now it's time for MGM to cringe," wrote one Hollywood columnist, who quoted Belafonte saying, "it's not a bad picture" and that everyone agreed on the "terrific quality" of the early scenes, but the movie fell apart because of the irresolution of the interracial relationship.[25] And even after the film's concessions to segregation, an organized group of "white citizens" shut down a screening at a Fayetteville, Georgia, drive-in.[26]

Harbel Take Two: *Odds against Tomorrow*

During this same period, Belafonte, with the backing of United Artists (UA), was developing another film, *Odds against Tomorrow,* over which he had considerably more control.[27] This film drew on a 1957 novel by former reporter and popular crime writer William McGivern, a combination police thriller and racial melodrama about an unlikely interracial friendship between partners in crime, hiding out after a failed bank robbery.[28] The novel creates an interior life for Earl Slater, racist white drifter from the South, but not for Johnny Ingram, black trickster from the urban North.[29] Belafonte recognized the story's potential for the film noir-styled social critique favored by Hollywood radicals.[30] A film version of *Odds against Tomorrow* could reimagine the genre by introducing a powerful black protagonist.

To adapt the novel for film, Belafonte looked Left, to the acclaimed but blacklisted screenwriter Abraham Polonsky, who was responsible for the noir films *Body and Soul* (1947) and *Force of Evil* (1948). Polonsky was living in New York and writing for television with the help of "fronts" who would sign their names to his work and transfer earnings to him. Belafonte brought McGivern's book to Polonsky and asked him to "fix it": they shared an interest in representing the costs of white supremacy and in creating black characters not defined in relation to white characters.[31] During 1958, Polonsky produced a script under John O. Killens's name.[32]

Killens had his own reasons for participating in this subterfuge. He and Belafonte shared left-wing and black arts interests; he was himself an outspoken critic of the blacklist. Signing on as the public author of the screenplay would give Killens a screenwriting credit at a time when he was trying to establish himself in film. He had already expressed interest in serving as script scout and supervisor at Harbel. In December 1957, he wrote that Polonsky might need the "special skill and understanding of a Negro writer in terms of dialogue and psychological authenticity." Killens continued to offer ideas on the script in a meeting with Belafonte and Polonsky in March 1958, and he made at least "one last suggestion" during the filming in April 1959.[33] His name on the screenplay enhanced the film's credibility and Harbel's black arts reputation.[34]

To "fix" the story, Polonsky replaced the second half of

the novel and its interracial friendship with an exploration of the circumstances driving each character toward the bank heist. As a left-wing writer, Polonsky thought that "gangsterism is like capitalism, or the other way around." He wanted to create criminals the audience could root for, because "criminals express revolt against the conventions that are destroying everybody." A successful robbery would require the characters to move beyond racially based hatreds.[35]

Polonsky transformed the black trickster character into a self-aware, successful jazz musician with responsibilities to his ex-wife and child and gambling debts to the mob. Belafonte later described Ingram's character as demanding equality "by just his presence," and as conveying heroism through "his dignity and his strength as a person." Solving a key logistical problem in the robbery plan, Ingram was a "thinking force that saw with richer clarity than the white characters." Polonsky's Ingram represented "a black man's relationship to the world that had never been seen before."[36] Because the robbery requires the three to cooperate, its setup justifies an articulation of situational equality from the ex-cop who sets the plan in motion: "Don't beat out that civil war jazz here. We're all in this together, each man equal, and we're all taking care of each other."[37] But Slater's combination of racial contempt and distrust blows the plan, and racial rage leads to everyone's destruction.

For director, cast, and crew, Belafonte looked to people he knew from the film and theatrical Left in Hollywood and New York. Renowned director Robert Wise agreed to work with Polonsky in defiance of the blacklist. Wise and Belafonte counted on the people in charge at UA to be willing to look the other way. Robert Ryan, associated with progressive causes in Hollywood since the 1940s, agreed to play the part of Slater.[38] Shelley Winters, also connected with the theater and film Left and a friend of Belafonte's, agreed to play Slater's girlfriend. Jeff Corey, a blacklisted actor turned acting teacher in Los Angeles, suggested the novice actress Kim Hamilton to play Ingram's ex-wife.[39] The production designer, German émigré Leo Kerz, had established his New York career with the help of Belafonte's Dramatic Workshop teacher Erwin Piscator. Cinematographer Joseph Brun had filmed formerly blacklisted Martin Ritt's *The Edge of the City* (1957). Editor Dede Allen, protégée of blacklisted New York film editor Carl Lerner, innovatively paced the film without a single fade or dissolve.[40] The expressionistic opening credits were produced by Storyboard Studios, the company started by blacklisted former Disney animator John Hubley with his wife, Faith. The film's original jazz score first appearing under these credits was composed by John Lewis, pianist and musical director of the Modern Jazz Quartet, and along with Duke Ellington's score for *Anatomy of a Murder*, marked a significant milestone in film scoring by black artists.[41]

The production of *Odds*, and Belafonte's role in it, was a historic event freighted with racial significance. A *New York Times* film critic pronounced the formation of Harbel as "one of the most important developments" in what he termed "the American Negro's long and drawn out struggle for equal representation on the nation's movie screens." He understood that with the backing from UA, Belafonte was now in a position of "potential influence" that was "unprecedented," in both "the Negro's fight for recognition as a performing artist" and as a "vital cultural influence in American films."[42]

Belafonte made the move into filmmaking with an explicit political cultural agenda: to drive off the screen what he called "comic strip" characterizations of black life, "the 'yassuh boss' boys, the yammering eye-rollers, the shiftless loafers." He wanted to see complex black characters beyond the stereotyped roles offered to his friend Sidney Poitier, who "always plays the . . . good and patient fellow who finally wins the understanding of his white brothers."

Proclaiming "with his eyes snapping" that "no man has a right to 'tolerate another,'" Belafonte condemned the call for tolerance as conveying "smugness" and a "sense of superiority" rather than the "equal respect" he demanded.[43]

Belafonte's "unprecedented" outspokenness and influence inspired racially coded animosity: to many critics he seemed to be getting "above his raising." Even in a *Time* magazine cover story, a former manager, most likely Jay Richard Kennedy, denigrated Belafonte as having become "an Emperor Jones." His former wife, Marguerite, impugned his hiring a white secretary as racial disloyalty.[44]

The most powerful blast came from a weekly magazine cover exposé in May 1959, distributed in the Sunday supplement of every Hearst newspaper across the country. The writer characterized Belafonte as self-important and grandiose, a phony intellectual throwing around "big words" and "parroting" other people's ideas, casting him in the shadow of Zip Coon, a stock minstrel show caricature. Labeling Belafonte's performance of folk music as "a vehicle to mix sex into anything" invoked stereotypes of hypersexualized black masculinity. The writer's explicitly racialized discourse claimed that Belafonte believed in "white superiority" and was unable to "identify" with his group because he wasn't a "pure Negro." He represented Belafonte's marriage to Julie as a racial betrayal and repeated a quote from Marguerite saying that Belafonte "really" wanted to be white.[45]

Jackie Robinson, then a *New York Post* syndicated columnist, rushed to Belafonte's defense, vehemently rejecting the concepts of "pure Negro" and "pure White." If Belafonte "wants to be white," Robinson wrote, his presence (with Robinson) at the head of the two Youth Marches and his choice of songs "from Negro life and folklore" in the United States and the West Indies was a "strange way of going about it." Robinson identified the attack as a reaction to Belafonte's "militant, uncompromising attitude

. . . on basic human rights" and support of "freedom on the march" among the nonwhite majority around the world. A sympathetic *Ebony* profile on "Movie Maker Belafonte" lauded his aspirations to transform film representations of black life and his entrepreneurship.[46] But one New York newspaper column and one *Ebony* profile could not undo the impact of such demeaning charges in such a widely circulating national Sunday newspaper magazine.

So much rested on the success of *Odds against Tomorrow.* In interviews, Belafonte tried to redirect audience expectations. He hoped moviegoers were ready to see "the Negro as he really is and not as one side of a black and white sociological argument where brotherhood always wins in the end." Belafonte wanted *Odds* to "show Negroes as they are—decent, responsible people, with the same hopes, hungers, needs, loves and problems as anyone else." Neatly reversing the usual phrase, he proposed that "beneath his white skin, the white man is no different than the Negro."[47]

Odds against Tomorrow's challenge would be to present racially conscious black characters who at the same time defied white supremacy's focus on the significance of race. Langston Hughes had proposed in 1937 that there could be "too much of race" and that Negroes in America were tired of a "world divided superficially on the basis of blood and color but in reality on the basis of poverty and power." Belafonte wanted to show black characters in conflicts "that stem from the general human condition, and not solely from the fact of his race." His strategy for equal screen representation would include black characters that mattered to the action and were not "thrown in for a racial thesis." In *Odds against Tomorrow* he promised that "no brotherly love saves everyone here."[48]

Belafonte threw himself into promotional campaigns for the film's simultaneous release in the United States and Europe: *Variety* described him as "barnstorming" on both continents. Belafonte planned concert tours to try to le-

United Artists publicity photo of Belafonte with Ed Sullivan and autograph-seeking fans, 1959. (Courtesy of Academy of Motion Picture Arts and Sciences.)

verage his musical celebrity and access to media into film bookings and ticket sales. "This is the only film to date where the Negro character could have been played by a white man," he told *Variety*. "What we are saying is that, whatever the pressure that is put on a group, if it gives in, it destroys itself." He touted the film's artistic integrity: "The story has been filmed without compromises."[49]

The film's ad campaigns explored different approaches to reach potential audiences. New York and black press ads promoted *Odds* to jazz fans.[50] Some newspaper ads pictured Belafonte surrounded by teens "just wild about Harry," encouraging Belafonte's enthusiastic young music fans to come see "another side of this versatile performer—the side of anger and rage." Other advertising directly featured racial confrontation, with photographs of Belafonte and Ryan facing off, and taglines such as "slams with a fist full of fury," "This isn't a story—it's an explosion," and "these aren't men—they're two sticks of dynamite."[51]

White and black reviewers who liked the film welcomed *Odds against Tomorrow* as a well-made story in an acknowledged genre, recognizing characters wrestling with bitterness and failure who viewed the crime deal as a last chance for autonomy and self-respect. Critics admired how the directing and acting, crisp dialogue, shock-cut editing, stark design, expressive black-and-white cinematography, and original jazz score built tension and created the sense of futility associated with film noir. Many ranked Belafonte's depiction of Johnny Ingram as his best acting performance to date.[52]

Both white and black reviewers praised the film's glimpses of black urban life rarely captured on film. They were struck by the scene in the nightclub where Ingram

Publicity still of gambling musician Johnny Ingram in Odds against Tomorrow, *(1959). (Courtesy of Academy of Motion Picture Arts and Sciences.)*

works: the vivid, discarded girlfriend, played by dancer Carmen De Lavallade; a surprisingly explicit sexual approach to Ingram by a white mob henchman; a sympathetic white boss who seems willing to bail him out until the mobsters show up; Ingram's wild accompaniment interrupting the blues singer, played by Greenwich Village nightclub favorite Mae Barnes.[53] Uncredited appearances by black New York theater colleagues Robert Earl Jones, Diana Sands, and the young Cecily Tyson enhanced this scene's credibility.

These reviewers also called attention to how the film contrasts Ingram's middle-class wife and her black and white PTA colleagues with Ingram's unreliable devotion to his wife and daughter, and his dreams of a payoff that won't require him to submit to the system. The black family appeared so rarely on film that the black press circulated publicity photos of "the 'on screen' Belafonte family" even though Ingram's screen time as husband and father was minimal, as well as pictures of Belafonte with his own children on the shoot.[54]

But reviewers disagreed sharply about the film's "racial thesis." For white viewers accustomed to Jim Crow, the mere presence of black characters other than maids or minstrel figures constituted a "racial thesis." The exhibitors' guide *Motion Picture Herald* proposed that the film could be sold "vigorously" as "suspense" *or* "racial conflict" and warned that "sharp reactions may be anticipated in certain sensitive areas." White reviewers who liked the film's crime premise rated the "race angle" as less successful.[55]

A number of white reviewers were put off by the "injection of the racial issue" into a standard bank heist; they couldn't imagine a black character as necessary to the plot. "Crime adventure and social preachment do not mix," wrote one critic, uncomfortable with deploring intolerance on the grounds that it jeopardizes an armed robbery.[56] One

Odds against Tomorrow *publicity stills: Ingram coming into his ex-wife's interracial meeting; and with his ex-wife and daughter. (Courtesy of Academy of Motion Picture Arts and Sciences.)*

Odds *publicity still of the interracial bank robbers: mastermind Burke (Ed Begley) trying to put out the fire between his accomplices Ingram and Slater (Robert Ryan). (Courtesy of Academy of Motion Picture Arts and Sciences.)*

thought that Harbel had "bitten off more than it could comfortably chew." Another referred to a "'sizeable' chip on Belafonte's shoulder," commenting that "it would be a pity if racial issues become an obsession with Belafonte because outside of them he has much to offer."[57] Others preferred the more comforting if artificial racial symmetry of *The Defiant Ones*, where the black and white criminals "came to understand and even care for each other."[58]

Black newspaper editor Almena Lomax appreciated some aspects of *Odds* but rejected its final confrontation. She cheered the "notably life-like and every-day treatment of Negro characters," and the "total absence of Negro stereotype." Her readers would be "thrilled by Belafonte's up and at 'em manliness when he is insulted because of his race by Ryan as Slater"; she was "charmed by the womanly dignity of [his wife] Kim Hamilton" and found Hamilton's "love scene with Belafonte real and heart-warming." While praising Belafonte's acting, she found it implausible that Ingram would throw away his life because of Slater. She also objected to "the allegorical ending . . . against the war and prejudice." One of her readers agreed that "Harry Belafonte is trying to do a commendable job." But he worried that the bank-heist-driven racial confrontation was too superficial: "[Belafonte] and John O. Killens will discover that this question of race is as monumental a task as war and peace."[59]

Almena Lomax's doubts about the film's plausibility were confirmed by hearing an audience member "teetering in high heels" complain "in a southern accent," "I don't know why a man who can sing like that would want to play in a picture, resurrecting that ol' mess [of race hate]." Critic Bosley Crowther worried that the film's code of honor that made Ingram a "sort of a hero" as opposed to the "hateful thug," Slater, "cannot be good for race relations."[60]

One expression of the backlash Crowther anticipated came in an angry response from a white reviewer in Salina, Kansas, who characterized *Odds* as "another phony, patronizing 'message' film." He saw Ingram's outlaw heroism in response to Slater's attacks as formulaic, the character himself "a puppet." Outraged because he thought "Negroes in films and theater seldom show anger, fear, hatred, seldom are cowardly, evil, dishonest, except in retaliation for being victimized by white men," the writer described *The Edge of the City* (1957) and *Blackboard Jungle* (1955)—both starring Sidney Poitier—and *The World, The Flesh and the Devil* as films with "patronizing puppeting" and "stereotyped Negroes." He viciously proposed his own "message film" with "the biggest blackest Black-hearted buck of a Negro the white screen has ever seen . . . to jolt the audience into understanding that a phony stereotyped view of all Negroes as demons is no more phony than the saccharine sweet stereotypes of Negroes we've been seeing on the screen."[61]

Belafonte's personal and professional stakes in his film's success were high. He admitted that, beyond his wife and family, "nothing means more to me than my ability to establish myself as an artist."[62] He must have been pleased with the positive reviews for his acting, the recognition of the film's high production values, and the attention it generated from the press. *Odds against Tomorrow* was an entry in a Canadian film festival and became a favorite of French director Jean-Pierre Melville, who made film noir crime dramas that would become models for French New Wave cinema. The *Chicago Defender* reported that it "clicked" in Australia.[63]

Despite Belafonte's dedicated efforts, Harbel couldn't deliver a hit. Although the *Defender* claimed that Chicagoans liked *Odds* because "they go 'all the way' for murder, gang and robbery pix," the genre of film noir was in decline by the late 1950s. Its black-and-white photography competed with color and widescreen. Instead of futility and mean streets, many viewers in 1959 sought the comedy of *Some Like It Hot*, family melodrama in *Imitation of Life*, spectacular feats in *Ben-Hur*, or the showy musical pleasures of *Porgy and Bess*, all playing in theaters at the same time as *Odds*.[64] In early 1960, Belafonte acknowledged that "people just didn't want it [*Odds*]" and wondered if it was because "it has an ending in which we are all destroyed." Stung by the film's weak showing at the box office, he said he wouldn't "be thinking about movies for a while."[65]

Even though Belafonte knew that his films would be judged by their commercial appeal, he was driven by the mission to make films that could challenge U.S. racial presumptions and introduce black characters as world citizens. He had floated different ideas for films that might accomplish this mission. In addition to his Civil War story, *Brothers*, and another film that would feature the "Exodusters," former slaves who migrated to Kansas after the failed promise of Reconstruction, he proposed to film outside the United States, suggesting a picture dramatizing the life of Afro-Russian poet and playwright Alexander Pushkin, to be shot on location in Russia, with Ingmar Bergman as director.[66]

Belafonte also understood the political significance of producing dramas of everyday black life, like *A Raisin in the Sun,* films "that show us just as we are—as we work, struggle, succeed, fail, live and die."[67] He wanted to make films about how "the Negro . . . contributed to the greatness of this country. He helped to build it, win its freedom, helped preserve the Union. He fought to make the world 'safe for democracy' in the First World War and helped save it from destruction in the Second."[68] Despite big ambitions to break with prior film conventions and portray the black experience in these new ways, none of these projects materialized. In the wake of the disappointing response to *Odds,* Harbel did not follow through on these producing plans.

Returning to Television on His Own Terms

Even while trying to break into film production, Belafonte maintained a full schedule of performing, touring, and recording. Now accompanied by the Belafonte Singers, a skilled choral backup group led by Belafonte's musical and political associate Robert DeCormier, he drew record crowds at nightclubs and stadiums in the United States, and on that first 1958 European tour to France, Italy, England, Germany, the World's Fair in Brussels, Sweden, and Denmark. His next albums departed from the folk and calypso repertoire, featuring smooth blues and love songs. They did not attract comparable sales. But fans loved the two live recordings from benefit concerts at Carnegie Hall in 1959 and 1960, both of which went "gold."[69]

Belafonte was torn between singing the familiar songs

that he knew thrilled audiences and experimenting with new musical forms. He knew he had to keep his marquee value high in order to protect his drawing power for civil rights benefits and rallies. He drove himself hard. Speaking to an interviewer in the fall of 1959 at the ripe age of thirty-two, he was worried about running out of time, "If the maker is kind enough to give me one hundred years, I couldn't get it all done."[70]

Television appearances offered the best opportunity to keep himself and his music in front of the widest audiences. But because Belafonte held out for control over TV time, he refused most of the many offers he received. He was now only willing to go on TV if he was in charge of the format and could feature his chosen material, performing his alternative to conventionally distorted representations of black culture.

Belafonte's chance came in November 1958, when Steve Allen—composer, jazz aficionado, comedian, and talk show host—finally induced Belafonte to appear on his show. Allen, a loud critic of rock and roll, was willing to meet Belafonte's conditions: twenty uninterrupted minutes and complete artistic control. By this point, Belafonte was a master at using this medium; reviewers wrote that the spirituals, blues, folk songs, and calypsos he drew from his repertoire brilliantly demonstrated his artistry and gave Allen's show a "tremendous lift." The outraged "vandals" who blocked transmission of the broadcast in Montgomery, Alabama, may have resented Belafonte's insistence on artistic control or simply recognized him as a provocative race-conscious entertainer.[71] Similar praise followed Belafonte's personally designed segment on the first televised *Bell Telephone Hour*; he was the artist pictured to advertise the program in *TV Guide*.[72]

The television format most amenable to Belafonte's artistic and political ambitions was the special, a one-shot broadcast that interrupted regular programming with the promise of "something different."[73] His first offer to create a "music spectacular" came from outside the country. In August 1958, Belafonte had appeared on British television singing highlights from his concert appearances, including the calypsos and "Mary's Boy Child" especially popular with London West Indians, as well as the Irish-themed "Danny Boy" and the Israeli "Hava Nagila."[74] By January 1959, the black press crowed over Belafonte's "lush" five-year contract to do three shows a year for the BBC. Finally, in August 1959, Belafonte was able to negotiate a U.S. deal to produce a television special of his own making, to be the first in a series sponsored by Revlon for CBS.[75]

Belafonte suddenly had unprecedented control over an hour of television; the network, the sponsor, and the advertising agency had no say over form or content.[76] He seized the chance to broadcast a version of the "Negro Anthology" he had first proposed in 1954, bringing the black arts spirit of a CNA variety performance to television's vast viewing audience. Rather than reproduce his own live performances of "folk songs from all over the world" or "parade a host of big names in front of a camera all dressed up" to "act in a resplendent scene," his special, *Tonight with Belafonte,* would offer "a portrait of Negro life in America, told in song."[77]

Combining Black Cultural Riches and Interracialism: *Tonight with Belafonte* and *New York 19*

Belafonte intended his "portrait of Negro life in America" to demand equality by offering a proud black history that could challenge mainstream white erasure, show defiant survival against the odds, and soothe the difficult memory of "the pain of that life." Years of live performance made Belafonte confident that he could sing material that "has protest in it" while cueing white audiences "to understand that this is a protest they are . . . invited to be part of."[78] Canadian-born Norman Jewison directed *Tonight with Belafonte*, with musical direction by DeCormier. Belafonte negotiated with Revlon for an uninterrupted format, substituting two three-minute commercials at the beginning and end of the hour for Revlon's requested six one-minute spots.

Tonight with Belafonte carried forward the black popular front legacy by featuring black artists who shared Belafonte's cultural politics. Guests included classically trained singer Odetta, identified by her folk repertoire of spirituals, prison songs, and the blues as "one of the leading exponents of music born of the Negro people"; blues guitarist Brownie McGhee and harmonica player Sonny Terry, both associated with left-wing folk music since the 1940s; modern dancer Mary Hinkson; Arthur Mitchell, the first and at that time only black dancer in the New York City Ballet; and choreographer Walter Nicks.[79] Although the performers were not individually introduced, Belafonte did briefly tribute two important artists and left-wing icons not present: Huddie Ledbetter (Lead Belly) and Langston Hughes. With the full chorus, he sang Hughes's class-conscious "Little Lyric (of Great Importance)": "I wish the rent was heaven sent."[80]

The special's musical numbers dramatized chain gang laborers' stubborn resistance, children's feisty playfulness, blues-styled love and loss, spirituals' promise of resilience. To introduce the themes of different segments, the camera directs viewers toward full-size panels featuring drawings by Belafonte's former CNA colleague Charles White, depicting a black man singing, men with hands shackled, children playing, lovers, and musicians with their instruments playing in the rain. Throughout the program, the Belafonte Singers and groups of adult and child dancers enhanced the musical storytelling. The performing groups were primarily but not only black, projecting a vision of cosmopolitan desegregation that did not require a white majority or convey assimilation to white cultural norms.

Tonight with Belafonte began with the Belafonte singers' version of the nineteenth-century folk song "Shenandoah," recorded by many white as well as black artists, playing over the opening credits, extending a spirit of American inclusion and belonging. The next three songs invoke the harshness and communality of the chain gang. When the camera reveals Belafonte, he is determinedly *not* smiling, not aiming to please or reassure the audience.[81] Instead he is defiantly self-possessed as he sings "Bald-Headed Woman" by himself in front of laboring men in shackles keeping the beat. Performing "Sylvie," a song popularized by Lead Belly, he is accompanied by the chorus. Odetta endows "Water Boy" with the extraordinary power of her voice. Children's songs identified with Lead Belly follow the chain gang pieces, reminding viewers that hard-laboring prisoners were also loving fathers and grandfathers. Acoustic guitar and the dance duet by Arthur Mitchell and Mary Hinkson accompanying Belafonte's rendition of "Suzanne" summon the expressive gifts of the blues. The full chorus singing with Belafonte and Odetta on the two final spirituals evokes intergenerational kinship and community as sustaining forces in black life.

Tonight with Belafonte was a revelation to many television audiences. White reviewers in the daily and trade press extolled Belafonte's originality and artistry in producing a "genuine television treat." UPI's TV reporter noted how the show departed from Belafonte's usual performance style: "no preaching; no bouts with Hebrew, Spanish, Italian, Calypso or jazz tunes." He recognized the focus on songs associated with Negro people as creating a "message musical" that he *did* feel invited to be part of, promising that he "got the message." Many letter writers ranked it the best program they had seen on television.[82]

In view of television's overpowering whiteness, Belafonte's achievement elated the black press. "'Night with Belafonte' Real 'Socksationaler,'" the *Chicago Defender* declared. A. S. "Doc" Young, the first black publicist in Hollywood and a writer who had been covering media for years, praised Belafonte as "magnificent," the show itself "a tremendous accomplishment."[83] "For the first time," he wrote, "a Negro performer was the production company head, as well as the star performer, in a televised spectacular seen in millions and millions of American homes. For the first time . . . a Negro production head had the major say-so about what televiewers would and would not see in this prime-time fantastic." Although a Chicago black columnist had wondered what an "all-Sepia" show with "hand-picked talent" might look like, and a black critic in Los Angeles thought Belafonte's effort to integrate the performers too obvious to "ring true," Young wholeheartedly approved of Belafonte's strategy for challenging the color line. It "was not an all-Negro show but was an integrated show," with "the bulk of the music composed of Negro-origin folk songs and spirituals." Integration in this context was not "blatant" but "as natural as a morning's sunrise."[84]

Tonight with Belafonte received high ratings and a Sylvania distinguished achievement award as "Outstanding Light Musical Program" of 1959. When Belafonte won an Emmy for Outstanding Performance in a Variety or Musical Program, he was the first black artist to be so recognized by the Academy of Television Arts & Sciences.[85]

The next few months after *Tonight with Belafonte* were the period when Belafonte intensified his involvement with King and with the young radicals sitting in at lunch counters and initiating direct action against segregation. For Belafonte to become known as "an energetic and outspoken participant" in these protest movements was the opposite of the conventional wisdom that entertainers had to play it safe to maintain their careers. But his international experiences on a three-month tour exposing him to enthusiastic audiences in parts of the world new to him—in Japan, Australia, Israel, Greece, and the Soviet Union—supported an alternative perspective.

Belafonte's arrival in Japan followed major violent anti-U.S. protests against the renewal of the U.S.-Japan security treaty; these had resulted in the cancellation of a planned state visit from President Eisenhower. Initially, Belafonte did not comment on civil rights struggles in his careful statements to the press. "I come to countries as an artist, not a politician." But Japanese audiences greeted Belafonte not as a representative of American foreign policy but as a friend whose historical experience had something in common with theirs. They were especially charmed after he added a beloved Japanese song to close his last concert in Tokyo.[86]

Emboldened by how Japanese audiences recognized and responded to him and his music, he used a *Variety* interview at the end of his time in Japan as an opportunity to make the case for declaring his support for protest. Without being explicit about his formative experiences on the left, or the costs of the silencing enforced by the blacklist, he invoked his memories of participating in postwar insurgencies as he now identified himself as a politically engaged citizen-artist who refused a separation between culture and politics. He referred to "once upon a time" when it was a "rich and common thing" for the artist "whether he was the performer, the writer, or the painter" to be welcomed in society "as an outspoken and free thinking man . . . part of an intellectual group that met in restaurants and went to meetings and participated in violent discussions." Then he took direct aim at those who were reluctant to stand up and fight for freedom now: he criticized "parlor liberals" who professed "their love for their Negro maids, chauffeurs, and hairdressers" but didn't support the sit-in students, and "professional humanitarians" who gave money to uncontroversial charities but remained silent on civil rights. Belafonte had crossed some line, no longer a polite supplicant seeking white support. He took his stand out in front as he had written to *Afro-American* readers earlier that spring, "The battle is on!"[87]

For his second television special, scheduled for November 1960, Belafonte hoped to build on this experience, to challenge racial confinement and national boundaries by featuring "international" talent, artists, and materials he had encountered on his tours.[88] However, with only limited preparation time after returning to the United States in mid-October, Belafonte narrowed his sights from international talent to a local version of internationalism. He announced instead a show he called *New York 19*, intended to play "musical tribute to Postal Zone 19, New York's melting pot of culture and the arts."[89] Showcasing the generative presence of black music within American popular music would provide another means to demonstrate cosmopolitan desegregation.

In prebroadcast publicity, Belafonte explained that postal zone 19 encompassed "Broadway, a part of the theatrical district, and the docks with big and little liners and freighters."[90] Residents from diverse racial, ethnic, and class backgrounds absorbed high and popular culture in local concert halls, jazz clubs, boxing rings, and churches. The area's musical diversity had been featured in a 1954 Folkways recording, *New York 19*, produced by sound documentarian Tony Schwartz, who had worked with Belafonte in 1952. Schwartz collected everyday sounds: preachers, children, musicians and barkers, Puerto Rican and black church music, and nonprofessional singers of various backgrounds. In contrast, Belafonte's special would explore how zone 19's diverse cultures were expressed in musical performance.

Devoted to promoting cosmopolitan heterogeneity, Belafonte described the neighborhood as "a melting pot of races, creeds and nationalities—Negroes, Irish, Puerto Ri-cans, Jews." The neighborhood contained "the center of the theater, Broadway, Carnegie Hall, Madison Square Garden, and the Palladium dance hall, where the city dwellers of 1960 create their own folk music." Juxtaposing houses of worship with high and low music, Belafonte observed that "good men, bad men, great musicians—classical, jazz and popular—are all concentrated here."[91]

New York 19 would complement the cultural work of "Negro history in song" displayed in *Tonight with Belafonte* by dramatizing the foundational contributions of black music in varieties of American musical performance. In interviews preceding the broadcast, Belafonte categorized "spirituals, westerns, mountain and country melodies, rock and roll, and jazz . . . and the tunes of Broadway shows" as "urban folk music," stressing that "the most powerful influence of all, of course, has been the Negro . . . a great repository of our music. Here the strongest elements . . . influenced the melodic line of the English and Irish immigrants."[92]

Even though Belafonte's name was now indelibly tied to civil rights, television protocols and especially commercial sponsorship dictated the prohibition of "non-neutral" speech during a broadcast. Belafonte pushed against this limit, seizing invitations for interviews as opportunities for pointed criticism of commercial advertising pressures from Revlon and "Madison Avenue." He allowed as how "a sponsor has the right to identify himself with his product and the show," but insisted "a performer doesn't have to do it too." He acknowledged the limiting dynamic of industry protocol. Unlike the child who calls out the naked emperor, "I can't say he has no clothes on. I have to go with the others."[93]

Belafonte could be counted on to refer directly to the particular constraints facing black artists: "The Negro entertainer does not get a fair break on television." The few objections to the "mixed" cast of *Tonight with Belafonte* in

1959 did not come from the South, he observed, but from casting timidity by sponsors—despite evidence of whites' willingness to buy tickets to black entertainment, as well as the buying power of seventeen million Negroes in the country, 10 percent of the U.S. population. He repeated Nat King Cole's quip that "the men in grey flannel suits are afraid of the dark," adding that, "it's good to have Negroes on with white performers. It adds color."[94]

The performers of the *New York 19* broadcast highlighted black artistry, cultural heterogeneity, and musical versatility. Belafonte's numbers, which he sang alone or with black jazz singer Gloria Lynne, ranged from blues to children's songs to folk songs in Spanish and Hebrew, and included his first foray into "popular tunes," a medley from *My Fair Lady,* then running on Broadway.[95]

Combining the black virtuoso musicians of the Modern Jazz Quartet and the white classically trained musicians of the Contemporary String Quartet represented hybridity and exchange through jazz and classical fusion. The Modern Jazz Quartet first played "Django," written by *Odds against Tomorrow*'s composer John Lewis in tribute to the European Romany jazz guitarist Django Reinhardt, and then joined the Contemporary String Quartet. Herb Levy, a Jamaican pennywhistle player, accompanied Belafonte's rendition of "God Bless the Child"—a piece made famous by Billie Holiday—and the Cuban folk song "Guantanamera." The *New York Times* reviewer wrote that Levy made the pennywhistle sound "like an instrument of pure gold."[96]

Black dancers Arthur Mitchell and Mary Hinkson from *Tonight with Belafonte,* joined by Asian American ballet dancer Pat Dunn and Julie Robinson Belafonte, performed during Belafonte's singing of "Hava Nagila," "'Buked and Scorned," and "Django," as well as in "Palladium Dance," an homage to the Latin music and dance featured there. Sequences of enlarged photographs taken by Roy DeCarava, Belafonte's former CNA colleague, served the function of the Charles White drawings in the earlier special, introducing the different segments and "offering eloquent evidence of the diverse nationalities, institutions, and diversions" of the neighborhood. And at one point during the broadcast, Belafonte directly breached the informal rules of television's supposed neutrality by boldly calling out that "unfortunate legal anachronism, 'separate but equal.'"[97]

White reviewers responded by assessing *New York 19* in terms of what they labeled its "sociological" and "documentary" elements. They did not employ the superlatives they had used in responding to *Tonight with Belafonte,* although one Los Angeles critic praised *New York 19* as showing "more spirit, charm, and movement than you could find in a barrel of Ed Sullivans." A *Washington Post* critic, who had received both positive and negative letters about *Tonight with Belafonte*'s "social preachment," recognized that it was now hard to separate the urgency of Belafonte's performance from his stance as "spokesman for change."[98]

Black television reviewers, aware of Belafonte's unusual position as the "sole dictator of what goes and what doesn't go," were more divided about the shift from Negro history in song to New York's musical variety. They admired the quality of the artists, in particular Gloria Lynne, the Modern Jazz Quartet, and the dancers. One *Chicago Defender* critic was "disappointed." One *New York Amsterdam News* columnist found the show "superb"; he liked that "the little boys and girls were both Negro and white" and that the show was "unfettered by Madison Avenue clichés." A reviewer for the *Afro-American* understood that black critics might differ on "the subtle integration theme," but he personally thought that "showing us New York as a melting pot" was "fine entertainment."[99]

The show's ratings were high, and there was talk of another Emmy. Then in August 1961, Revlon canceled the remaining specials Belafonte had contracted to produce, ostensibly due to a "change in advertising policy." At first he avoided commenting publicly, beyond "expressing satisfaction" with the two completed shows and acknowledging that he had been well paid in compensation for the breach of contract.[100]

But to a sympathetic columnist Belafonte admitted his frustration. He had hoped to create television specials to make black diasporic culture familiar to American audiences. For example, "Africa Speaks" would have featured Miriam Makeba and performers from the continent. Another special on "legends of the Mississippi" would emphasize the centrality of black contributions within American culture by featuring interwoven white and black river lore, from Steven Foster songs to escapes from slavery. He hated to lose television's access to that mass audience, noting that it would take him twenty-five years of performing to reach the number of people who had tuned in for one hour of television.[101] Years later, during a 1968 debate on television's domination by "white supremacy concepts and racist attitudes," Belafonte analyzed the cancellation of his contract and payment of high fees as political censorship, a "major firm" paying him to stay "off the air, rather than to continue the series of specials in which I was using an interracial cast."[102]

Music and Politics in Changing Times

Belafonte knew that his high-profile musical celebrity attracted the audience for his political speech. He continued to perform in lucrative engagements at large concert venues and Las Vegas clubs, while scheduling appearances at civil rights protests and at benefits raising substantial sums for SCLC and SNCC.[103]

By the early 1960s, taste in commercial folk music was shifting from Belafonte's polished performance to unadorned versions of so-called traditional folk styles, shortly to be eclipsed by Bob Dylan's singer-songwriter combinations of folk and rock and roll. Belafonte's publicity began to describe him as a "balladeer" rather than folksinger. He defended his stylized performance against the critique of what he called the "purist cult" in folk music, emphasizing his artistic interpretation and the social significance of his selections.[104]

Belafonte attempted to keep his performance fresh by inviting other musicians to perform with him: the Belafonte Folk Singers (an independent group after 1960); Miriam Makeba; Appalachian singer Joan Toliver; Greek singer Nana Mouskouri; percussionist Ralph MacDonald, son of Trinidadian calypsonian MacBeth the Great; South African trumpeter Hugh Masekela; and the Trinidad Steel Band. With Lena Horne he recorded songs from *Porgy and Bess.* Other recordings included an album of chain gang songs that won the Grammy for Best Traditional Folk Recording in 1961; another calypso album, using some material written by Burgie; folk song collections, one track of which featured the young Bob Dylan on harmonica; and a live concert at Los Angeles's Greek Theater.[105]

Belafonte's live presence remained compelling and his live performances continued to sell out, but commercial success was more elusive. Calypso continued to sell, and the 1961 *Jump Up Calypso* album went gold, but other album sales were uneven. His 1965 collaboration with Makeba, singing about township struggles and protesting apartheid in Xhosa, Zulu, Sotho, and Swahili, won a Grammy for Best Folk Recording.

Whatever else he was doing, Belafonte made sure to periodically tour college campuses. College students were among his most consistent fans in this period, ranking Belafonte as their favorite male folksinger in *Billboard*'s college poll of 1963–1964. Many of the college campuses were seedbeds of civil rights activism.[106] Belafonte remained in close contact with young militant student activists, especially in SNCC, at the same time as being part of King's

Performing at an unidentified concert, ca. 1965. (Courtesy of Photographs and Prints Division, Schomburg Center for Research in Black Culture, the New York Public Library, Astor, Lenox and Tilden Foundations.)

inner circle. He often worked behind the scenes, and the SNCC students trusted him to watch their backs in strategy meetings with King's people, in negotiations with the Kennedy Justice Department, and to deliver emergency money to support front-line organizers. In 1963, he made sure the movement-based Freedom Singers appeared amid more well-known performers at a SNCC Carnegie Hall benefit and chartered the plane that enabled them to take part in the March on Washington.[107]

Belafonte's commitment, connections, and leadership skills kept him at the center of efforts to gather celebrity musicians to perform before, during, and after civil rights marches, even while some of these turned into police confrontations. In addition to the unquantifiable spirit and energy generated by these collective performances, Belafonte knew that the performers' presence helped to insure media attention to the marches. He also knew that being present and witnesses to the movement changed the artists themselves and that encouraging them to participate expanded the numbers of artists "identifying themselves . . . politically and socially."[108]

Belafonte's civil rights vision, built on wartime and postwar dreams of social transformation, was national and international. Belafonte spoke out against the Vietnam War in 1965 and stood with King in Paris in 1966, publicly opposing U.S. policy supporting the war in Southeast Asia and apartheid in South Africa.[109] By 1965, King's public positions on nonviolence and integration were under attack from many drawn to Malcolm X's militancy and to broad critiques of American society. Like James Baldwin and King himself, Belafonte worried about the problem of being "integrated into a burning house," although he remained a principled interracialist critical of racialized boundaries. In 1969, he would write that he didn't want to be "part of the integration in which one man helps another into the tottering tower of the Establishment."[110]

Belafonte's experience touring outside the United States further expanded his exposure to cultures that crossed national boundaries and deepened his awareness of the parochialism of racialized thinking at home.[111] Belafonte began to travel to Africa in 1962. He and Makeba performed at concerts to celebrate Kenya's formal independence in

With Martin Luther King, Jr., backstage at Madison Square Garden, and standing behind Coretta Scott King addressing the "Stars for Freedom" rally on the last night of the Selma to Montgomery march in support of voter rights in Montgomery, Alabama, March 24, 1965. (Madison Square Garden photograph courtesy of Photofest; "Stars for Freedom" photograph by Robert Abbott Sengstacke, courtesy of Getty Images.)

December 1963; he traveled to Senegal and Guinea in May 1964 to help plan an ambitious cultural center in Guinea.[112] Guinea was also the destination for a September 1964 trip he financed to revitalize a group of battle-weary SNCC activists. Wherever he performed with Makeba, they introduced their songs to emphasize the links between African liberation struggles, the movement to end apartheid in South Africa, and grassroots civil rights insurgency in the United States. In 1965, the two convinced a number of artists, writers, musicians, actors, and singers to join a cultural boycott, refusing to allow their work to be performed or displayed in South Africa while apartheid remained in place, an early part of a national campaign to pressure the United States to divest from South Africa.[113]

Still Seeking TV's Mass Audiences: Harlem History and Black Humor in TV's Snow White Land

Belafonte continued to strategize about how best to use television's public platform to serve a progressive agenda. Between 1960 and 1966, he made a few guest appearances on television that met his artistic conditions and resulted in what were described as "takeovers" of the shows in which he performed.[114] Drawing on his media savvy, he made sure that the celebrities he had gathered for the 1963 March on Washington were positioned so that TV cameras panning to them would include extensive coverage of the crowds of black and white marchers. When Dinah Shore planned an hour-long ABC tribute to the Peace Corps, Belafonte helped her sing in nine languages, including Swahili, Sotho, Chilean Spanish, Brazilian Portuguese, and Tagalog. Given any opportunity, in publicity or prebroadcast interviews, he continued to point out television's "fear of the dark."[115]

When CBS announced in 1965 that it would once again

Belafonte performing on soundstage with dancers, possibly for an appearance on Bell Telephone Hour, ca. 1964, and on Bell Telephone Hour, ca. 1960s. (Courtesy of Photographs and Prints Division, Schomburg Center for Research in Black Culture, the New York Public Library, Astor, Lenox and Tilden Foundations.)

air specials, Belafonte seized the opening to propose a broadcast featuring Harlem as a cultural mecca in the 1920s.[116] Harlem in 1965 was synonymous with bad news, as the scene of rioting in 1964 and a prime example for the Moynihan Report's "tangle of pathology," blaming black families and communities for perpetuating racial inequality. Press headlines and television airwaves insistently portrayed Harlem and other black neighborhoods as war zones of antisocial violence, criminality, and despair. Black radicals, even when troubled by violence in the streets, understood the riots, sparked initially by neighborhood protest against police brutality, as the product of institutional racial discrimination beyond the South.

Belafonte wanted to show the public another Harlem via a TV special to be written by poet and CNA colleague Langston Hughes. The black press recognized the strategic implications of Belafonte's all-star black cast as another wedge that might open the gates to "ease the discrimination that currently exists in TV programming."[117] Drawing on a blues idiom popularized by Hughes and Hughes's writing about Harlem in the 1920s, the special would depict Harlem as a magnet for southern migrants, as the sparkling epicenter of cultural forms that transformed modern life, and a source of black resilience.[118] Musical performances would tell the story with the help of the Stroller, whose poetic narration would situate the scenes as had Charles White's art and Roy DeCarava's photographs in the earlier specials.[119]

In prebroadcast interviews, Belafonte described *The Strollin' 20s* as "a glimpse of Negro life in Harlem in . . . a very prolific period," when black cultural expression was central to modernity. Referring to the Great Migration, to Hughes and Paul Laurence Dunbar, Duke Ellington, rent parties, and the Garvey movement, Belafonte observed that "the general American audience knew nothing about this splendid time in *our* history" (emphasis added). Else-

Langston Hughes on the set of The Strollin' 20s.
(Photograph by Rowland Scherman, courtesy of Getty Images.)

where he referred to the "recording of an untold chapter of Americana."[120]

Belafonte aimed to present this chapter of black history as a shared—and usable—American past. Above all, he wanted to "show another dimension of that ghetto," especially to television's white audiences, and to proclaim the ordinary humanity of the poor and working-class people who lived in impoverished black neighborhoods. They had become invisible in the national coverage of black rioting, including the battles unfolding in Los Angeles's Watts neighborhood in August 1965. Without diminishing the significance of these urban rebellions, he thought that there had been enough coverage of "contemporary hostility." He wanted to replace distance and distrust with empathy and identification: "Negro communities all over the U.S., like Watts, are on the path of head-on collision with the white world. Yet within the same ghetto, there is humor, love, and personality that remains unseen. . . . I found my own values in the Harlem ghetto, and I wanted to show that."[121]

To the disappointment of his fans, Belafonte did not perform in the special, other than in the introduction, where he invited viewers to rethink the Roaring Twenties as Harlem's "Strolling Twenties." Speaking in front of a series of historical photographs and old posters of Bessie Smith, Florence Mills, Josephine Baker, Bert Williams, and Fats Waller, Belafonte called attention to black contributions in radio, film, and recorded music, as well as to new kinds of entertainment in Prohibition-era nightclubs and speakeasies. *The Strollin' 20s* paid homage to the collective accomplishments of earlier performers; Belafonte pointed out that "no one in this show impersonates a Negro performer of the past; they all represent, collectively, the people of that exciting decade. Duke Ellington is the only one who plays himself."[122] Although this time Belafonte lost the battle on the number of ads, their placement was carefully structured to bookend rather than interrupt the musical narrative.

The musical prologue to *The Strollin' 20s* introduces different styles of blues emanating from the neighborhood, with children marking the beat on trash cans; jazz enhancing sexually charged encounters; and dancers, a full chorus, and orchestra evoking the larger community. The special presents strolling as a social display and interaction: singers and musicians mingle with neighbors at the market, while residents sitting on stoops provide a continuous audience.[123]

Both the musical selections and Hughes's narration, spoken by the Stroller, Sidney Poitier, embrace black working-class people and show sexual playfulness and pleasure as part of everyday life, depicting an easy sociability between performers and prostitutes, old-timers and newcomers. In an early scene set in a Harlem house party organized to raise rent money, comedians Nipsey Russell and George Kirby set up a card game; Brownie McGhee, the 1940s bluesman who appeared on the 1959 special, plays guitar as he sings verses that refer to political aspirations and black solidarity: "If I should catch me a 49, I'll help Marcus Garvey with that Black Star Line." Gloria Lynne, who sang with Belafonte in *New York 19*, performed a Bessie Smith blues song: "You been a good old wagon, Daddy, but you done broke down."

The Stroller explicitly admires the varied hues of black women working the street: "brown sugar, chestnut treat, honey gold . . . pecan spin . . . coffee and cream, chocolate . . . out of a midnight dream." The musical and dance numbers become more polished and formal, as Diahann Carroll, dressed in white feathers, belts out the blues anthem popularized by Billie Holiday, "Nobody Knows You When You're Down and Out." Ads before and after set off a sequence with Sammy Davis, Jr., performing virtuoso tap in tribute to veteran dancer Bill "Bojangles" Robinson and then singing Waller's "Ain't Misbehavin'" with Carroll, the chorus, and dancers.

The Stroller moves back into the neighborhood for a sequence showing the solace of Harlem family life. Hughes's narration introduces the pain of chronic black joblessness: "What does a man do when he aches in the morning and fakes at night, even in his dreams he aches; and when he faces the cold light of day and remembers the job he never could get and never could have and can't have now." The camera lights jazz and blues singer Joe Williams on a dark street with other aimless men, singing a blues lament, "Nobody Knows How I Feel This Morning." He returns to his tenement kitchen, where his wife and children revive his spirit by engaging him in a call-and-response song. The camera charts his journey from the periphery to the center of the family, offering an intimate glimpse of the strength of working-class black collectivity.

The final scene in The *Strollin' 20's* brings the neighbors and the entertainers together in the Savoy Ballroom, identified as "our place" in an era when "other places, the Cotton Club, aren't for colored folks." Duke Ellington at the piano is joined by the entire cast in a spirited rendition of his 1931 composition, "It Don't Mean a Thing If It Ain't Got That Swing," honoring communal bonds and Ellington's foundational contribution to American music in the 1930s and 1940s.

In the context of fierce street battles, welfare policy debates, and demands for black power that intertwined black militancy and masculinity, white and black viewers had conflicting responses to Belafonte and Hughes's love letter for a vanished Harlem. Some white critics saw a positive view of neighborhood culture as incompatible with outrage about contemporary problems. The *New York Times* music critic labeled the show "primly starched" and "lifeless," a "candy-colored Chamber of Commerce Valentine that might have been designed by Busby Berkeley for a movie of the 1930s." The *Variety* reviewer thought the "song and dance salute to the ghetto" would be appreciated by "absentee landlords"; the rent party was "full of chitlins and cornpone" that "came off like an ethnic commercial for Rheingold beer"; even the blues were "too clean."[124] Apparently, these reviewers were confused by the absence of explicit social critique and saw the effort to represent Harlem through everyday life as too sedate, robbing the neighborhood of its sexualized allure.

Other white television critics for the trade daily *Hollywood Reporter,* UPI, and AP admired the writing, the musical arrangements, the dancing, and the production values. They recognized how the special conveyed "love for its subject" and noticed the warmth of its characterizations, especially in the family sequence. But their language, describing "the Negro . . . refusing to let despair obliterate his love of life, music and laughter," veered dangerously close to the stereotype of the "happy darky."[125]

Black critics disagreed whether the glamorous stars and outstanding performances outweighed the vulnerability of exposing black urban working-class culture and public sexuality for all to see. One black critic from Los Angeles rated the show as the "TOP television special to date," but both the New York and Philadelphia black press covered black viewers' lack of unanimity. One New York black critic wrote that *The Strollin' 20s* "caused more comment" than any other show, with some letter writers seeing it as "light, nostalgic and fun-filled . . . timely entertainment" and others finding it "embarrassing, full of clichés . . . [that] left out so much." He thought the show would stimulate a "good argument in any crowd of over three people . . . stand back and watch the sparks fly."[126]

A Philadelphia black critic remarked on the special's unusual range, combining the "polish of a TV spectacular with the 'chit'lun and grits' atmosphere of a 'soul session.'" A New York viewer complained the show was "a souped up '66 version of the Roaring 20s": only the rent party seemed "authentic." The harshest critics, writing from Philadelphia, New York, and Los Angeles, worried about the dangers of depicting black working-class culture. By ignoring Harlem's wealthy residents and white-recognized literary and show business stars, the show might encourage the "kind of stereotype which made Amos and Andy famous."[127]

These conflicting responses revealed how much was at stake in presenting black culture and history to television's mass audience, after so many years of invisibility and in the midst of urban turmoil. A black press critic in Cleveland, who praised *The Strollin' 20s* as a presentation "the Negro could identify with and feel proud of," also recognized black viewers' special vulnerability. Familiar with John O. Killens's 1965 book of essays, *Black Man's Burden*, he reminded readers of the dangers of representing black people as rural folk outside of modernity, especially when American culture emphasized "freedom, wealth, equal opportunity and the idea of the melting pot." Television's power in communicating "representative social relations" had largely denied the Negro exposure that was "truly representative of his progress." He hoped that *The Strollin' 20s'* depiction of the Harlem Renaissance and black modernity as part of twentieth-century history demonstrated that "Negroes and whites are different in many ways and for many reasons, but their coming together and living in this country as they have done, has given them much in common."[128]

Belafonte, undeterred by the mixed reviews and lack of future interest from CBS, negotiated a deal to produce another special, this time exploring black humor, for ABC's *Stage 67* series. After working together on *The Strollin' 20s*, Belafonte had begun to perform with Nipsey Russell on college campuses and in Las Vegas. In the fall of 1966, they glimpsed a performance style that pushed the boundaries of racially provocative humor: the San Francisco Mime Troupe performing *A Minstrel Show, or Civil Rights in a Cracker Barrel*. A cast member spotted them in the audience "falling out of their chairs with laughter."[129] Credited as consulting "signifier," Russell helped to plan Belafonte's production *A Time for Laughter*, with individual sketches knit together by Belafonte's former CNA colleague and Sage partner, writer Bill Attaway.

Belafonte conceived of *A Time for Laughter* as offering an explicit critique of white assimilationist norms that made the few black characters on television indistinguishable from their white counterparts, such as Bill Cosby's part as a secret agent in *I Spy*. He approached actor friends Sidney Poitier, Diahann Carroll, Diana Sands, Godfrey Cambridge, and the comedians by emphasizing this angle: "Come on, let's do a show for us and about us and stop trying to play spies and stuff in the white world, but just be ourselves in our world." The demand that a black actor "submerge his identity . . . to find work" was no longer tolerable. Belafonte thought that even if there *were* Negro men in the CIA, "that has nothing to do with our life. . . . You never get to see a Negro villain or whore or priest except in a superficial caricature. The dilemma is to get into the guts of Negro life."[130] He hoped that black humor had the potential to reveal the sophisticated and skeptical subjectivities that helped resist the racial injuries of segregation and discrimination.

A Time for Laughter featured Russell's fellow comedians, whose sharp-edged humor, honed in front of black audiences, ranged from dizzying wordplay and double entendres to social and political satire. The oldest performers, Pigmeat Markham and Moms Mabley, had started out in the burlesque and blackface style common on the black vaudeville circuit. Markham had abandoned blackface by the 1940s; Mabley was one of the first comics to incorporate satire and direct social commentary into her astute grandmotherly monologues. George Kirby, featured with Russell on *The Strollin' 20s*, got his start singing blues on Chicago's South Side but became known for his impersonations of white and black entertainers. Redd Foxx was a black circuit performer who began to include social commentary in his act in the 1950s. Dick Gregory and Richard

Pryor, younger stand-up comics, gained success with humor suffused with sharp jabs at racial inequality.[131]

Belafonte saw black humor, like music, as a cultural resource, informing a white interviewer that "the American white can only become acquainted with the American Negro through his art." He was outraged that a community that had produced "Langston Hughes, Jimmy Baldwin, Lena Horne, Duke Ellington, [and] Ruby Dee" could be characterized as "culturally deprived" and turned the insult around. "If we're culturally deprived because we don't have 'Beverly Hillbillies' and 'Hello Dolly' then we're very rich. . . . You're the ones perpetuating mediocrity." His plans for the television specials were strategically political, in the spirit of the late 1940s progressive coalitions: to "unfold the realities of Negro life" so that white people would join with black allies in the struggle for justice, insisting that "we've all got to get committed" for American society to "make it."[132]

Even before the credits roll in *A Time for Laughter,* the performers appear in comic sketches that expose racialized assumptions. Moms Mabley, dressed up as a princess, looks into her mirror, but Redd Foxx tells her that the fairest of all is "still 'snow white' and don't you forget it!" George Kirby, in a black Santa outfit, chastises a black child for dreaming of a "white" Christmas. Diahann Carroll lies in a tub, waiting to be eaten by white "savages." Nurse Diana Sands assists Doctor Harry Belafonte in performing an elaborate surgical procedure on what turns out to be a watermelon.[133]

The special's opening segment offers an origin story for minstrelsy's distortions of black music and dance, choreographed by Walter Nicks. It begins with white performer Daddy Rice paying a pittance to black stable hand "Jim Crow" to teach him how to dance. Imitating the black performers' movement of "wheeling about," and their music "sweet and hot," the white performers put on blackface and dance to ragtime music in front of photographs of famous whites who blacked up: vaudeville performer Al Jolson and Amos 'n' Andy creators Freeman Gosden and Charles Correll. When Poitier repeats the final music refrain with heavy irony—"That's how darkies was born"—the phrase evokes the power of minstrelsy to normalize racial inequality.

By placing the comic performers in a range of black community settings, the middle section of *A Time for Laughter* offered television viewers an insider's vantage point. "Judge" Markham appears in divorce court, adjudicating marital problems between drifting Diahann Carroll and wayward Harry Belafonte. Redd Foxx holds forth in a poolroom, where despite his fast talk he ends up being "taken" by a chump. Novice clergyman Richard Pryor wildly improvises a eulogy in a funeral parlor. George Kirby holds forth on the subjects of *negritude* (a term used to refer to the black anticolonialist literary movement), politics, tokenism, and hair straightening, as he plays seven different characters cutting hair, dropping by, or appearing on television in a barbershop.

The final section directs its humor at what Poitier as the narrator calls "the price of integration." A sketch written by Godfrey Cambridge casts him and Diana Sands as pretentious, assimilationist, reactionary suburbanites who worry about "niggers" on the commuter line and how to manage their new black maid, Moms Mabley, who responds, "If this is what they call integration, maybe it ain't worth it." The final segment takes place in a jail cell, with demonstrator Dick Gregory offering edgy jokes about marchers, LBJ, Red China, and riffing on white and black uses of the term "nigger" (title of his 1963 autobiography). Gregory's joke, encouraging marchers bitten by dogs to bite back ("We'll come to their jails with rabies, and they'll go back to their masters singing 'We Shall Overcome'"), creates a bridge to the utopian finale. Belafonte manages to assemble everyone in the cell—black and white, adults and children—to join the singing of "Dogs," a rhythm-and-blues-influenced freedom song written by Nashville sit-in participants, a black-authored vision of multiracial community.[134]

A Time for Laughter's revealing exposé of white racial assumptions and insider black self-mockery attracted many viewers, according to its Nielsen ratings, and prompted critical debates.[135] The *New York Times* TV reviewer seemed uncomfortable with the show's racial explicitness, accusing the special of ignoring the "obvious truism" that "good entertainment neither knows nor pays any attention to the color line." He found individual sketches "dismal" and in "bad taste." In contrast, the TV reviewer for the *Oakland Tribune* welcomed the abandonment of a common television pretense that "differences between the races simply don't exist." *A Time for Laughter* showed that "Negroes have a history, a culture, and humor of their own," as well as the "history, culture, and humor they share with the rest of us." He agreed that white audiences were the ones who had been "culturally deprived" of the brilliance of Moms Mabley, Red Foxx, and Pigmeat Markham. Although he objected to the show's "Civil Righteousness," he praised its lampooning "well-to-do Negroes who imitated whites" and its taking aim at "white bigotry."[136]

Other white critics made varying and mostly unsuccessful efforts to separate their judgments on the show from its racial provocations. *Variety* claimed to put "racial considerations aside" in evaluating the special's "humor of the highest level." *Hollywood Reporter* judged it as the year's funniest show, especially the "honest and abrasive" humor of Foxx and Gregory, "sparkling with the spirit of self-deprecation and ironic insights that enable the socially deprived to survive." The AP reviewer rated it as "interesting" but found the humor "bitter, sharp, and stinging." To the UPI critic the show, although "erratic," was "a powerful weapon for exposing the over-sensitivity of various minority and majority groups."[137]

Black critics and viewers responded with mixed emotions to *A Time for Laughter.* Two black critics judged Dick Gregory's political humor as "off," while another thought his performance was stellar and his material "riotous."[138] Viewers who had felt exposed when 1920s Harlem street culture appeared in *The Strollin' 20s* were likely also unsettled by viewing insider black humor on television. A *Chicago Defender* columnist reported that some viewers felt the performers were "trying to ridicule the Negro race," but he personally defended the show for bringing "laughter to an entire nation." He saw this as a critical need in 1967, when racial temperatures were rising: "When people who used to say 'hi' to each other as they passed on their way to work in the morning are now crossing the street.... Those who want to be real are afraid they may be called a 'nigger lover' [or] a 'white man's nigger.'" His hope was that showing human beings "in their true light" would encourage others to "trade hate for laughter."[139]

In a letter to ABC that he forwarded to the *New York Amsterdam News,* an angry black minister in New Haven, Connecticut, denounced the show's "slander and mockery" of what he termed "an ethnic group." Concerned about televising black stereotypes, even in humor, he reported that after the broadcast, parents told him their children had been embarrassed at school by children "of other ethnic backgrounds." He was outraged by its use of "vulgar and offensive" terms and its resurrection of the minstrel show, and he called Dick Gregory a Negrophobe. The minister demanded a public apology from the network to "the black people of these United States."[140]

Expressing the opposite view, a black journalist with a syndicated column in Cleveland's black newspaper judged the production "a thing of pride for the Negro race." Like

Belafonte, he thought that if white people wanted to understand black people, they would have to recognize humor as key to black survival and resilience. He praised the comedians on *A Time for Laughter* for "truthfully [telling] whitey . . . the secret to our ability to absorb the murderous punishment they have for centuries heaped on us." Having "something to laugh at," in his view, kept "a switchblade out of our hands in futile retaliation for the wrongs perpetuated against us."[141]

Interviewed by the *New York Times* just before the broadcast of *A Time for Laughter*, Belafonte seemed to anticipate critical debate, racial polarization, and lack of conventionally measured success. But he held his ground. Looking ahead, he staked out two important principles to guide his efforts; first, not to squander the resources his celebrity provided him; and second, to take on projects that expressed his radical vision, independent of commercial considerations and naysayers. He found kindred spirits among 1960s countercultural rebels who were protesting materialism and affluence as well as racial inequality and militarism: "I must constantly ask myself . . . Do I really need another ten dollars? Do I really need another good review? . . . I've got something to say, something that I want to communicate. To do this, I have to shed myself of false ego and prideful pursuits . . . If that's romantic, if that's idealistic—that's me . . . To dissent? Sure! There's greater truth in the voice of the dissenter than those who cheer the going rates."[142]

No More "Playing It Safe": Filming *The Angel Levine*

After *A Time for Laughter*, Belafonte wanted to commit to a project that would express his dissenting voice without compromise. His pitch persuaded Chiz Schultz, a CBS television producer in Los Angeles who had worked on *New*

York 19, to leave Hollywood to work for Belafonte Enterprises in New York: "I hear you've sold your soul to the devil . . . You'll make a lot of money, have barbecues, drive a fancy car, and you'll do a lot of crap . . . Why don't you do some really good stuff with me?" Belafonte told a *Variety* columnist that he was "tired of playing it safe." He had "nixed all vid offers [for television]" because they were "all the same format." The fast pace of change made him bold. "These times are rich—the iconoclastic group is on the move."[143]

Belafonte hoped to turn from the comparatively more restricted format of network television to take advantage of what looked like new opportunities in independent filmmaking. New Wave filmmaking had thrown Hollywood conventions out the window, creating openings for experimentation in subject, style, and technique.[144] In August 1967, he announced plans for a return to moviemaking with a film adaptation of "Angel Levine," a fantastic short story by the writer Bernard Malamud about an impoverished Jewish tailor whose call for help from God is answered by a black Jewish angel from Harlem, Alexander Levine, a complex character Belafonte thought he could bring to life.[145]

Unlikely film material, Malamud's "Angel Levine" was published in 1955 and then revised for a 1958 collection of short stories that won the National Book Award. Reviewers compared Malamud's ne'er-do-well characters to those populating the stylized humorous tales of Yiddish writer Sholem Aleichem, a favorite of many on the left, including Belafonte.[146] The story's premise that the mutual need for recognition between an ordinary Jewish tailor and a formerly ordinary black Jewish angel could transform barriers into alliances particularly appealed to progressives. Marc Blitzstein considered it in 1961 when he began to work on *Tales of Malamud*, a series of one-act operas based on Malamud stories. Ossie Davis and the blacklisted actor Jack Gilford, both friends of Belafonte, had announced the first plans to film "Angel Levine" in 1962. Another scheme was to stage it in 1965 as part of a musical evening by Sheldon Harnick and Jerry Bock, responsible for the unexpectedly successful Broadway adaptation of Aleichem's Tevya stories, *Fiddler on the Roof*.[147] Belafonte's organization had picked up the film option, with backing from United Artists.[148]

Before he could fully launch this project, Belafonte received a television offer he couldn't refuse, as guest host of the most widely viewed show on late-night television—Johnny Carson's *Tonight*—for a week in February 1968. Belafonte would have complete control over many hours of valuable television time. He negotiated for the freedom to pick the guests and shift the format, replacing the opening comic monologue with a song. He refused to do commercials: they would be handled by Carson's sideman, Ed McMahon.

Belafonte's strategy for his week of television was to assemble high-powered black and white talent who could entertain and also address burning political questions in domestic and foreign policy. These included his close political allies Martin Luther King, Jr., and then senator Robert F. Kennedy; performer colleagues from left-wing circles in the late 1940s and early 1950s, including Sidney Poitier, Diahann Carroll, Lena Horne, Sonny Terry and Brownie McGhee, Leon Bibb, and Zero Mostel; his recent collaborator Nipsey Russell; film progressives Paul Newman, the Greek actress Melina Mercouri and her husband, blacklisted director Jules Dassin; rising stars of the 1960s, such as singers Robert Goulet, Aretha Franklin, Dionne Warwick, and Petula Clark; and comedians Bill Cosby and the Smothers Brothers.[149]

Belafonte's *Tonight* shows brought diverse voices of dissent onto television. A *Newsweek* reviewer described what *Tonight*'s vast audience heard: [guests] "denouncing government neglect of Negroes in Watts, mourning the high suicide rate among despondent Native Americans, and rebuking President Johnson over Vietnam." Robert Kennedy ignored the show's tobacco company sponsorship to accuse the cigarette industry of smoking-related deaths. The Smothers Brothers told jokes that had been censored by their own network.[150]

Belafonte's *Tonight* shows were revelatory for late-night viewers who knew Belafonte only as a singer-entertainer. The *New York Times* critic Jack Gould, a steadfast defender of a color-blind norm in television, admired Belafonte as a "witty and wise" host, an "adroit interviewer," and a "formidably persuasive recruiter of guests." He noted that Belafonte's guests included "Negro luminaries of the entertainment world," but he claimed that their race was inconsequential and that "quick minds and superior talent made racial considerations sublimely irrelevant."[151]

Many other commentators emphasized the racial significance of Belafonte's weeklong hosting. *Newsweek*'s reviewer, who tallied the numbers of black guests (fifteen out of twenty-five) wrote that the show "exuded color consciousness," with admissions of racial inequality driving the humor and suffusing personal commentary alongside multiple representations of easy interracial camaraderie. This reviewer gave examples: Zero Mostel's quip that Belafonte was "underpaying" just like a white capitalist; Belafonte's mocking an ad praising a product's "whitening" qualities; Belafonte reminiscing with Poitier about their narrow escape from the KKK when delivering emergency funds to voting rights organizers during Mississippi's Freedom Summer in 1964; the host's showing home movies of his interracial family and group of friends waterskiing on vacation. King's on-air reflections about threats on his life and his choice to emphasize not "how long you live" but "how well you live" reminded audiences of the racial violence and terrorist intimidation frequently mobilized in support of segregation's status quo.

The British critic W. J. Weatherby was astonished to see

how Belafonte's *Tonight* "became the tightest link between the streets and show business for a whole week. . . . [T]he eloquent fearless guests . . . discussed everything from soul food to Vietnam with no pulled punches." Belafonte's old friend at the *Chicago Defender* was particularly exuberant: "Harry Belafonte is Black Power." It was "the best damn show I have ever seen on TV," projecting "the power of being so respected that you can say anything that comes to your mind. The Power of being proud black and letting non-black know you're not putting him down if he too has soul. The power to joke about The Problem without being bitter but getting the message through."[152]

After Belafonte's triumphant week on *Tonight,* it must have been shocking one month later when a sponsor's representative demanded cuts of British singer Petula Clark touching Belafonte's arm when appearing on her NBC television special. Clark and the network program producer immediately objected, but both the sponsor's rep and the advertising agency claimed that if a "white girl touched a black man over network TV," they would not sell "one car in the South." Clark, who had kissed Belafonte on the cheek when she appeared as his guest on *Tonight,* was "flabbergasted." Although the sponsor's rep then retreated and apologized, claiming that his objection had no "racial connotation," Belafonte refused to keep quiet. He denounced the apology as coming "one hundred years too late," the ad agency personnel as "Gestapo troopers," and the incident as "the most outrageous case of racism I have ever seen in the business." The company backed down, the sponsor's representative was fired, and the show was broadcast as scheduled: sponsored and uncut.[153]

A black press account emphasized the persisting obstacles facing black artists on television: "how hard it is for a major company to properly school some of its employees in the hinterlands about the changing facts of life." *New York Times* critic Jack Gould, consistently anxious to avoid direct discussion of race, described the issue as "blown up" and criticized Belafonte's intervention as "divisive."[154]

When the *New York Times* invited Belafonte to respond to Gould, he delivered a devastating critique of television's depictions of black life and the scarcity of black artists onscreen or behind the cameras. The industry was "dominated by white supremacy concepts and racist attitudes" and driven by commercial imperatives to exclude "the reality of Negro life, with all its grievances, passions, and aspirations." At a time when "wars are being fought and nations destroyed over the issues of racism," he wrote, the only television images available to his son were either the "one-dimensional" Negroes in white adventure settings or "the Negro only as a rioter and a social problem, never as a whole human being." He detailed the celebrity straitjacket he faced as a token black star: to "go out and sing and look sexy.... Play a nice guy, drop dead, or maybe play a Supernegro who beats up Communists, who does not probe black-white relations, and maybe you'll have a chance on television."[155] Hammering away, building on CNA's late 1940s analysis of broadcasting and his own subsequent experiences, Belafonte became known for his willingness to "Jolt TV with . . . Frankness and Anger" and "Blast Mass Media for Racism." Black columnists called him a "superspokesman" for "telling it like it is."[156]

Just a few weeks later, in late March 1968, Martin Luther King was at the Belafontes' apartment in New York, planning his trip to Memphis to support striking sanitation workers and looking ahead to the Poor People's Campaign. Challenged by meeting with writer and activist Amiri Baraka (formerly LeRoi Jones) in Newark, King was worried about the direction of the movement; if integration was going into "a burning house," then nonviolent activists must "become firemen."[157] Just a few days later King was dead, killed by an assassin's bullet. Following his death, grief and rage drove black people into the streets, and cities across the country broke out in flames.

King's death was an enormous personal loss to Belafonte, ending a partnership profoundly meaningful to both of them. Within two months, his other eloquent *Tonight* guest, Robert Kennedy, would also be assassinated. Along with many others, Belafonte mourned the shocking deaths of these men whose efforts to end racial injustice, poverty, and the Vietnam War were beginning to converge. He did what he could to honor their memories through his own work, though he felt beaten down. To a reporter for the *Los Angeles Times* he said that he "wanted to 'stop answering questions as though I were a spokesman for my people. I hate marching and getting called at 3 a.m. to bail some cats out of jail, or sitting on panels and talking to reporters about America's racial problems.'"[158]

When Belafonte then returned to work on *The Angel Levine* in the fall of 1968, his deep sense of loss—of King's moral leadership, the values of nonviolence that motivated him, and the radical hopes of SNCC—infused the subsequent filmmaking. Malamud's story had registered the politics of 1940s antifascism, linking anti-Semitism and black exclusion as historically and economically driven forms of racism. Belafonte, like many black and Jewish progressives, continued to believe that blacks and Jews had common interests in opposing racialized discrimination, and he saw *The Angel Levine* as a way to dramatize these. But could a film in the late 1960s evoke the possibilities of that WWII progressive alliance many years later?

Over twenty years, black and Jewish political languages and strategic communal goals had shifted. Even when Jews looked back to the Nazi genocide to frame discussions of civil rights, there were heated and ongoing debates about whether the lesson learned was that they must stand up against any racialized forms of discrimination or that they had to prioritize their own communal survival above all other considerations. While Jewish lawyers worked on the *Brown v. Board of Education* legal team, everyday Jews were moving from Brooklyn to Levittown, from Newark to Short Hills. Cold war anticommunism, racially discriminatory mortgages and white suburban flight, battles over school and housing desegregation, internal debates in civil rights organizations, and new language of Black Power moved many Jews away from actual sites of contact with African Americans and eroded support for the formulation presuming shared interests. Closer to home, some black nationalists, some Jewish organizations, and the New York City teachers union were locked in a fierce battle in 1967 and 1968 over hiring and firing decisions made by the community-controlled, black majority Ocean Hill–Brownsville school board.[159]

Malamud's original story is framed by Jewish spirituality and kinship and plays lightly on the incongruity of a black Jew.[160] The offer to help the poor tailor, broken by misfortune, who prays to God to assist him and his sick wife, comes from a shabbily dressed black Jew "disincarnated into an angel." After the tailor refuses to accept Levine as a "bona fide angel of God," the disappointed angel returns to Harlem. In the end, the tailor does believe, Levine demands an apology, accompanies him home, and apparently ascends to Heaven, while the tailor's wife miraculously rises from her sickbed and resumes her cleaning duties. The tailor shares the revelation with his wife, "Believe me, there are Jews everywhere."[161]

In order to restage the Malamud story for the late 1960s, Belafonte turned to black theater and television actor and playwright Bill Gunn to revisit an earlier adaptation, with the specific mission to fill out black characterizations.[162] At this time Gunn was an accomplished writer with a produced play and a published novel among his credits. The film conception shifted the emotional tone from humor to a darker register and revised Malamud's story by questioning the racialized categories that impeded the recognition of interdependence.

The part of the Jewish tailor was written originally for Edward G. Robinson, the Jewish-born actor who had made a career playing ethnic gangsters and government agents by following Hollywood conventions that required him to mask his Jewishness.[163] Mishkin has a dying wife, chronic pain, mounting debts, and no hope. He is confronted with a fallen angel, a black Jewish hustler, played by Belafonte, who is killed that day while stealing a coat but given a chance to redeem himself if he can persuade Mishkin to accept him as an angel.

Levine's character was written to demand equality simply by his presence, like Johnny Ingram in *Odds against Tomorrow*. One sympathetic New York reviewer later described Belafonte's Levine in just those terms, as "surprisingly tough . . . and unyieldingly insistent upon the dignity that should be his."[164] The film dismisses shared religion as insufficient. The tailor must accept the black Jew as *kin and* be transformed by Levine's belief in the possibility of change, characterized by Lorraine Hansberry as "the strength of an incredible people who, historically, have simply refused to give up."[165]

The characters in *The Angel Levine* appeal to each other through cultural and racial particularity rather than universality. They are both flawed, unheroic; they are not everymen. They do not transcend their historical experience, nor do they deny their differences. Mishkin's pain results from his misfortunes, his self-pity and narrow parochialism. Levine's misguided hopes, his experience as a hustler, "runnin', runnin', always runnin' on somebody else's track," have left him unsettled and alone, unable to sustain a relationship with his girlfriend, played by actress Gloria Foster. The best Mishkin and Levine can offer each other is mutual recognition of their interdependency.

Belafonte conceived of *The Angel Levine* as an independent art-house film, and looked for directors outside Hollywood. After being turned down by British New Wave director Tony Richardson and not hearing back from Polish-born Roman Polanski, whose first American film, *Rosemary's Baby,* had just opened, he sent the script to Jan Kadar, a Hungarian-born Jew then working in Czech New Wave cinema. Kadar's *The Shop on Main Street* had won the Academy Award in 1965 for Best Foreign Language Film.[166] Kadar had spent World War II in a Nazi labor camp; his parents and sister died at Auschwitz. *The Shop on Main Street,* codirected with Elmar Klos, portrayed ordinary townspeople who witness Nazi abuse, persecution, and finally the deportation of their Jewish neighbors. After the August 1968 Soviet invasion of Czechoslovakia halted work on a film Kadar was making, he accepted the offer to direct *The Angel Levine.*[167] Kadar encouraged the casting of the internationally recognized Yiddish actress Ida Kaminska, the lead in The *Shop on Main Street,* as the tailor's wife, a part that had been expanded in Gunn's screenplay.[168] Just before filming began in February 1969, the director requested the services of a Jewish writer, playwright Ronald Ribman, for additional revisions to fill out the Jewish characterizations.[169]

Early publicity for *The Angel Levine* in the fall of 1968 emphasized the diversity of the collaborators, Belafonte, Edward G. Robinson, and expatriates Kadar and Kaminska, all drawn to Malamud's story and black screenwriter Bill Gunn's adaptation. In a report about "Belafonte's Comeback Film," *Variety* quoted the star's view that "the story is important because it illustrates the need for men to believe—and the need for someone to believe in men," and described Belafonte's embrace of "a part he could believe in."[170] Black press coverage focused on Gunn's screenplay, the location shooting planned for Harlem and New York City, and Hal De Windt, a black actor, stage manager, and director who had stepped into the role of assistant producer.[171]

During the same month that filming began on *Angel Levine*'s fable intertwining the fates of blacks and Jews, a number of prominent black artists went on record as questioning the goal of integration. Participating in a *New York Times* forum, "Can Black and White Artists Still Work Together?," most expressed doubts (writer James Baldwin: "The Price May Be Too High") and alternate priorities (actor and writer Julian Mayfield: "Explore Black Experience"; actress and director Barbara Ann Teer: "Who's Gonna Run the Show?"; director Douglas Turner Ward: "The Goal Is Autonomy"). Although he withheld support for integrating into "the tottering Tower of the Establishment," imagining instead "an integration which brings pride, fulfillment and meaning to all members of all races," Belafonte was one of only two willing to defend the need for black and white artists to learn from one another.[172]

For the film to provide opportunities for black artists behind the camera, Belafonte had to confront the history and union rules maintaining film production employment as all white. Belafonte turned to the Ford Foundation, then supporting other black theater efforts, for funds to train apprentices in a specially devised program, following the model of Bayard Rustin's program to train black workers for formerly all-white union jobs. Staying within union rules, twelve black and Puerto Rican young men and women got paid to work on the set with the film's assistant director, sound engineer, and script girl and in casting, publicity, wardrobe, and production. The apprenticeship program's effort to make headway against racial exclusion in the film industry also exposed the young people, as one commented, to thinking of films as more than entertainment, with potential to "change the social environment." *The Angel Levine* apprentices formed their own production company, ASONE, and began work on their own film, and other productions announced plans to train black apprentices.[173] Black press coverage of *The Angel Levine* showcased this apprenticeship program, and *Ebony* featured it prominently.[174]

When filming began in February 1969, Zero Mostel, fresh from performing musical comedy roles on Broadway, especially his star turn in the Jewish folk-tale musical *Fiddler on the Roof,* had replaced Edward G. Robinson. The black press reported on "Belafonte's Jewish Doctor Irishman" when Irish character actor Milo O'Shea joined the production. The photograph most often run by the black press reversed the supposed incongruity of Belafonte as a black Jew by showing a picture of Mostel posing in an exaggerated Afro wig, to the amusement of Belafonte and Kadar.[175]

Features in the *New York Times* and the *Los Angeles Times* both admired and doubted the film's unlikely racial-ethnic mélange. "Would You Believe Belafonte as a Jewish Angel?" queried the New York headline; the film, "with its allegorical themes and controversial probing of Black-Jewish distrust," would be an "advertising man's despair." But this reporter did recognize the potential for reigniting the spirit of 1940s antifascist solidarity, referring to Kaminska and Kadar's vulnerability as European Jews during World War II and amid recent political upheavals that brought them to the United States, and to Belafonte's and Foster's histories as black Americans. That "so many of the cast are well-rehearsed in the story of man's indifference to other men's fate" explained why "people of unusually disparate personality and background are working well together on this difficult script and hopelessly cramped set."[176]

The Los Angeles feature writer was also intrigued by a film about the "interdependence of human relationships" being made by "one of the most diversified contingents" on the Manhattan moviemaking scene, but he also worried about what might get lost in translation. He observed that director Kadar had little English, no familiarity with the filming locations, and no understanding of "the black situation in America."[177]

Kadar grouped *The Shop on Main Street* and *The Angel Levine* as "the same from the point of view of humanity, of our need to believe in each other, of how to reach each other with understanding." This framing revealed a lack of awareness of the different forms of social discrimination and racial oppression experienced by Jews and blacks in the United States, and the potential pitfalls of interpreting black experience through Jewish history.[178] When a reporter asked Belafonte about then current New York City school battles that had unleashed "Black anti-Semitism and Jewish anti-black feeling," he noted that planning for the film had preceded the eruption of tensions, and he expressed the hope that as a piece of art, it would survive what he termed "moments in history."[179]

The New York reporter doubted that a film about parallel despair and interdependent salvation would speak to contemporary viewers encouraged to think in terms of ethnic and racial difference. He wondered if Jewish groups might be offended by how Mishkin "failed to emphasize the nobler aspects of a Jewish community," and if "young Turks" from black neighborhoods in New York, Boston, and Los Angeles might view with scorn a film in which the black protagonist was a Jewish angel. He imagined "a box office nightmare," with opening night demonstrations called by Eldridge Cleaver and other Black Panthers refusing any "talk about miracles of communication" until "[imprisoned Black Panther leader] Huey Newton was set free."[180]

Other production problems were out of view to these reporters. In addition to fraught communication between actors and director, Kadar faced political pressure to return to Czechoslovakia midway through the shoot. Representatives from United Artists demanded extensive cuts from

New York film editor Carl Lerner. The pre-film-promotion strategy of the UA publicity obscured the film's racial provocations within an art-house auteurist appeal, publicizing director and actors.[181]

Belafonte knew that undertaking this film project at this historical moment exposed him to considerable risks. One New York feature writer described him as a "black Prince Hal, in his position as executive, public figure, prominent black capitalist and creative artist, he must at once keep his nerve ends free to possibility and his eyes out for those who would hustle and ambush him."[182] His judgment, both political and artistic, was on the line.

Belafonte used press interviews to spell out his version of the film's message, even if it meant giving away the ending: "We have two human beings who must believe in each other. The miracle is that they could. The drama is that Mishkin does believe, but he believes too late. . . . If they make it, humanity makes it. If they fail, humanity fails." He explicitly invoked recent history: "For me, the miracle in America was Martin Luther King. In the years that King and SNCC were coming to the people with love, the people didn't believe. They finally believed when it was too damn late."[183]

Belafonte's political sensibilities, taking for granted the compatibility between black pride and questioning the fixity of racial categories, suffused his interviews. The film "made his soul sing"; he was satisfied "beyond my wildest expectations." He continued to stand up for principled interracialism: "I have an intense belief in the brotherhood of man and I don't care who is turned off by that word." Referring in part to the apprenticeship program, he called *Angel* "the first picture where I could really do my black thing." He felt confident that white audiences would respond when apprentices learned the skills to film "what they wanted to do about the black condition," providing a "great service" to themselves and the black community and bringing "a new kind of truth and dimension for white people to look at, understand, and enjoy."[184] In his concept of internationalism, blackness involved world citizenship: "I think that after we have gone through a period of our blackness . . . we have to face the universe. No matter how much now we stick to finding our uniqueness, we'll find that we're just part of the human race and that this is a phase in the history of it all."[185]

As those feature writers feared, the film's appeal to 1940s progressive antifascist solidarity did not translate readily in the late 1960s. Black/white/Jewish interdependency was a hard sell when integration efforts were under fire and substantial evidence of racial equality remained elusive. A huge gap yawned between Belafonte's aspirations for *The Angel Levine*'s "message" and the UA press campaign; nothing in the promotion prepared audiences to think about the story in his terms. Early advertising for *The Angel Levine* featured Hebrew, a language beyond reach of even most Jewish moviegoers. The final press book offered oddly generic publicity, limited to the art-house/auteur focus on director and cast credits, and an ironic tagline for pictures of Belafonte with Mostel: "If He's an Angel, Imagine What God Is Like." Pitching the film as "tragicomic," the publicity campaign directed its efforts to colleges, hoping to reach film buffs and tap into Malamud's literary reputation. The press book's proposal to interest what it referred to as "Black/Jewish media" suggested post-screening panels of black and Jewish leaders debating the question, "Do You Still Believe in Miracles?"[186]

Belafonte's high-risk comeback film project did turn out to be an "advertising man's despair," with an outcome of critical and box office failure. When *The Angel Levine* opened in Los Angeles in mid-July and in New York at the end of the month, audiences didn't respond to the film's slippage between fantasy and "rigid old school New York squalid realism," mixing "colloquial Jewish humor" with "gutter language" and moments of tragedy.[187] One critic appreciated the film's effort to show "the world of the common man" on-screen, and a number of reviewers did praise Belafonte and the other principal actors. Even while noting the "strange and wistful mood" of the film, they still judged it "worth seeing." But they were troubled by shifts in emotional tone, the slight story, theatrical talkiness, "over length," and the jumbled Manhattan geography.[188] The harshest critics experienced Belafonte "ridiculous as an angel" and labeled the film "a failure of major proportions."[189]

Despite its carefully calibrated reversals, the film did not seem to unsettle conventional ethnic and racial categories. Some of the film's reversals included the Jewish tailor as a welfare supplicant facing a black welfare caseworker; Levine's actions in Mishkin's modest kitchen, helping him with medication, washing the dishes, putting away rather than stealing Mishkin's meager food money; Levine's appropriating the term "nigger" to insult Mishkin's parochial narrow-mindedness. Despite dialogue explicitly rejecting shared religion as a basis for kinship, the "Jewish" identification of Mishkin and Levine outweighed the few moments of imagined cross-racial mutuality. In 1970, the political ramifications at stake in representation for Jewish and black characters were very different. Even a miserable old and poor Jew could fit into new interest in Jewish immigrant culture and Jewish ethnic "roots." As appealing and compelling as Belafonte could make a black Jewish hustler reincarnated as an angel, he did not register along a spectrum of late 1960s blackness.[190] Belafonte's Levine was a powerful presence, but Mostel's Mishkin, and Kaminska's depiction of his dying wife, took over the film.

People who both liked and hated the film focused much more on Mishkin than Levine. One reviewer followed directorial evidence, observing how Kadar "dwelt lovingly

Publicity stills of tailor Mishkin (Zero Mostel) face-to-face with Belafonte's Alexander Levine in The Angel Levine *(1970). (Courtesy of Academy of Motion Picture Arts and Sciences, Ron Cohen Collection.)*

on the Jewishness of the old tailor." Others found the realist mode adopted in the final scenes, when Mishkin faces the approaching death of his wife, at odds with the fantastic narrative connected with Levine's accidental death and reincarnation. As one critic put it, "the core of the film, the sad acknowledgement that the death of a loved one is imminent, Kadar has realized with a tender compassion that is infinitely moving. It is the other-worldly aspects of the story that give him trouble, cause him to fumble."[191]

The Jewish framing dominated both critical and positive reviews. The critics noted that the "updating" in vocabulary and enlarged . . . ethnic scope" couldn't fix what seemed like a "cliché-ridden drama on a Jewish theme" and that "the Jewish ethnic bit is a much travelled road to which Kadar has brought no fresh point of view."[192] Reviewers familiar with Mostel's more well-known *Fiddler on the Roof* persona were perhaps disconcerted by his characterization of Mishkin's miseries: "Zero's comic genius cannot carry the lugubrious sermonizing about Black-Jewish relationships."[193] Reviewers seemed disoriented rather than intrigued by how Levine's combination of blackness and Jewishness complicated both identities. Other reviewers who were moved by Kadar's direction to feel empathy for Mishkin barely mentioned Levine.[194]

An interview with Belafonte published before the film opened in New York revealed worried soul-searching: "I hope I can hold my head up about *Angel Levine*. We went into it knowing it might not be a big commercial success. . . . But I had to make it. I had to make it."[195] Once again, trying to use film to challenge the racial status quo, to introduce black characters who could demand equality by their very presence, resulted in disappointment.

Significantly, much of the black press, which had showered attention on Belafonte's prior efforts, chose not to even review *The Angel Levine*. They reported on Belafonte's return to filmmaking and a few reprinted materials from the UA press book. One columnist for the *Amsterdam News* gave it a brief plug: "Don't pass up 'The Angel and Levine.'"[196] Black newspapers reviewed films that more clearly emphasized black subjectivity and black experience, for example Ossie Davis's film, *Cotton Comes to Harlem*. But they did not engage with *The Angel Levine*'s premise or evaluate Belafonte's efforts or acting.[197] Belafonte's "black thing" did not register as a film of interest to black critics or audiences.

When the film opened in New York, Belafonte was vacationing with his family in Brazil, where a columnist reported him as "spared" from reading the reviews. He knew that he could still please live audiences with the familiar songs, but this film project, undertaken with such high hopes, did not produce the desired outcome. Interviewed at this time, he admitted to being worried about "my inability to break through my own creative barriers."[198] The consistently contentious responses to the film and television he produced between 1959 and 1970 must have been unnerving, and *The Angel Levine* was the last effort of its kind.

The uncertain results of Belafonte's film and television producing efforts did not shake his commitment to making art to expand the political imagination. Even at this moment of failure, he articulated lessons he had learned from his movement experiences and his time in the limelight that could serve him in the years to come. One was that cultures outside the United States, African diasporic and others, could be a continuing source of inspiration; on this post–*Angel Levine* trip, he planned to soak up black and Latin culture in Brazilian music, painting, and poetry.

Another lesson was that he needed to have a dual vision for black arts inside and outside the commercial media. He had watched the "youth and civil rights movement" operating independently, attending free performances of political art by the San Francisco Mime Troupe and helping to support the SNCC-initiated Free Southern Theater. He reminded his interviewer, and perhaps himself, that the possibility of making politically provocative art also remained outside "the entertainment world": "If you're a writer and you cannot be published by one of the majors, mimeograph it, and get it out, into somebody's hands. . . . [I]f you can't break the back of monopoly theater and get on Broadway, then let's go off-Broadway and let's go in the churches or let's go in the barns or let's go anywhere."[199] Belafonte would keep fighting for access to commercial media, in order to speak to the broadest mass audience, but he would also continue to seek out venues for cultural expression unconstrained by establishment rules.

The third lesson was not to "bite his tongue," to continue to use any access to the press as an opportunity to speak the truths he knew. In a tribute to Martin Luther King, Jr., and W. E. B. Du Bois in January 1972, Belafonte paraphrased Du Bois's 1907 definition of the task of radicals: "to continually complain, and complain, and complain loudly."[200] Since 1956, at the height of his stardom, he had taken this mission to heart, seizing all opportunities to voice sharp political critique and articulate radical alternatives on subjects from racial representation in film and television to U.S. foreign policy. It would be a mission he would carry on into the twenty-first century.

There would be many more periods of doubt and uncertainty, projects initiated and left unfinished, failures as well as triumphs. But openness to change and solid political grounding in the postwar left and in new civil rights and countercultural activism nurtured Belafonte's resilience as a black artist and public radical. These would sustain continuing engagement in cultural activism and world citizenship through the decades to come.

AFTERWORD

If the audiences for *The Angel Levine* could have peered ahead to where Harry Belafonte's life would take him after 1970, no one would have been able to accuse him of staying buried in the past. He continued to respond to news and to move fast: in the summer of 2013, he would serve as one of three grand marshals at New York City's huge celebratory gay pride parade, following the Supreme Court decision invalidating the Defense of Marriage Act. Not long after, he would dash to the Florida state capital in Tallahassee to support the sit-in of a multiracial, multiethnic group of young people in response to black teenager Trayvon Martin's death at the hand of a self-appointed neighborhood watchman. There he joined them in demanding an end to "Stand Your Ground" laws, racial profiling, and school policies that send too many black children into the criminal justice system.

In the forty-plus years following *Angel Levine*, Belafonte would make more movies, speak out on a dizzying array of issues, and sing around the world as long as his voice held out. He would receive honors as a singer, as an actor, and as an internationalist, acknowledged by a wide spectrum of groups, from the music industry to the Folk Alliance; from the White House to the NAACP; from the Kennedy Center to the Black Filmmakers Hall of Fame; and from the UN to the international human rights advocacy group Global Exchange.

But if Belafonte did not remain stuck in the past, neither did he abandon the goals and values he established as a young artist and activist. Indeed, tracing Belafonte's path to "becoming" through the late 1940s, 1950s, and 1960s reveals the continuities running through the complex web of his commitments. Prioritizing black arts, black world citizenship, and social justice continued to shape his choices as he confronted the question of where to devote his considerable energies.

The black arts practice of the Committee for the Negro in the Arts, for instance, came to fruition in the multidisc historical musical archive released in 2001 as *The Long Walk to Freedom.* Belafonte first announced "the Negro Anthology" as a design for a traveling production in 1954. Then it became a plan for a boxed set of recordings to capture the magnificent variety of black musical expression—from African song traditions preceding U.S. slavery to prison songs and Gullah call-and-response spirituals and shouts from low-country South Carolina to the rich musical cross-fertilizations of New Orleans jazz. The first recording sessions took place in 1961 and continued for ten years. Langston Hughes was working on the liner notes when he died in 1967; Charles White produced the artwork and Roy DeCarava photographed the musicians. The renowned conductor Leonard de Paur arranged and conducted sessions recording Nigerian and Ghanaian drummers and singers, Georgia Sea Island singer Bessie Jones, as well as many who had already appeared in Belafonte productions: Odetta, Joe Williams, Sonny Terry and Brownie McGhee, Leon Bibb, and Gloria Lynne.[1] It would take more than thirty years, many musicians, and new technologies for this project to fulfill Belafonte's core commitment to producing black art featuring gifted black artists to teach black history's message of survival and resistance, using the highest quality resources he could muster, however long it took. Further, Belafonte's embrace of black musical traditions would prove to be far from static. In 1984, he produced a feature film about hip-hop culture, *Beat Street,* and he advocated for Cuban hip-hop artists at a 1999 meeting with Fidel Castro in Cuba.[2]

Likewise, when Belafonte helped organize Nelson Mandela's 1990 visit to the United States after twenty-seven years in prison—traveling with Mandela and introducing him to audiences across the country—it was a culmination of a fight against apartheid that Belafonte began in the 1950s in association with the American Committee on Africa. Belafonte heard Oliver Tambo, leader in exile of the African National Congress, speak at Africa Freedom Day in 1961 at Hunter College. In 1965, he and Miriam Makeba began to organize performing artists to refuse to let their work be performed or displayed in South Africa as long as apartheid remained in place. Eighteen years later, he and tennis champion Arthur Ashe would lead the effort to expand and publicize the cultural boycott as Artists and Athletes Against Apartheid. In 1977, he would help to found TransAfrica, an African American advocacy group dedicated to lobbying U.S. foreign policy; and in 1985, he would be arrested at a TransAfrica's Free South Africa picketing demonstration at the South African embassy in Washington, DC. In 1988, Belafonte's last studio album, *Paradise in Gazankulu,* would be recorded in Johannesburg with South African artists singing songs protesting apartheid.

The connections between "Negro life" and Africa that had been on Belafonte's mind since the late 1940s functioned as another line of continuity in Belafonte's cultural agenda. In the 1960s, he began to visit Guinea, Tanzania, and Zambia with the hopes of establishing musical and film collaborations between Africans and African Americans. In 1985, he would initiate the celebrity musical benefit performance of "We Are the World" and its worldwide simultaneous broadcast, and he would help to organize the ad-hoc group USA for Africa, particularly responding to famine in Ethiopia. In 1987, he would be appointed to serve as UNICEF goodwill ambassador, only the second American to hold this position, and to travel to Dakar, Senegal, as chair of the International Symposium of Artists and Intellectuals for African children. In 1994, he would undertake a mission to Rwanda to focus media attention on Rwandan children, and in 2001, he would travel to South Africa to support the campaign against HIV/AIDS.

Belafonte would also continue to embrace campaigns for racial justice as inseparable from campaigns for peace and economic and social justice. The contemporary blogosphere burns with Belafonte's scorching language as he uses his celebrity-based access to the media as a chance to rattle the cage, unsettling conventional political wisdom and challenging indifference in the face of widening social and economic inequality. In 2002, he would liken then secretary of state Colin Powell's position to that of "house slave," serving his master, in response to Powell's support for Bush's run-up to the war in Iraq. In 2006, he would refer to Homeland Security, with its ability to arrest without charge, as the new "Gestapo." In 2012, he would argue that instead of addressing the pressing problems of American society, powerful black celebrities such as Jay-Z and Beyoncé had "turned their back on social responsibility." With these pronouncements, he kept faith with his public promise in 1956 not to "bite his tongue when people around him, colored or white, express bigotry, narrow-mindedness, or chauvinism in any form."

In the twenty-first century United States, Belafonte's achievement at the crossroads between art and politics is nearly unrivaled, but, as he frequently points out, he has followed a path marked out by Paul Robeson ever since their first meeting in 1946. Because Robeson's career was powerfully foreshortened when the full weight of anticommunist blacklisting forced him from prominence to the margins, his name and work disappeared from view outside of radical and black Left circles. Starting in the early 1970s, when then president Nixon's trip to China signaled one ending to the Cold War, Belafonte would make sure to mention Robeson's name and credit his influence in his press and television interviews.[3] He would help produce the star-studded seventy-fifth birthday tribute in 1973, which Robeson was too fragile to attend. In 1979, Belafonte would perform a benefit concert for the new cultural project, Bread and Roses, started by the hospital workers union 1199 and devoted to encouraging and celebrating working people's own cultural creativity. This concert, his first in New York in seventeen years, represented a continuation of the labor-centered cultural politics to which Robeson first introduced him in the late 1940s. It was also an expression of the mission of his own musical attention to work songs and a central tenet of his own worldview as articulated in an interview in 2004, loosely paraphrasing a 1940s song: "My hands are mine to sell a major machine and they can stop them, too."[4]

Belafonte credits his own willingness to speak and act on his convictions as a byproduct of Robeson's teaching that "artists are the gatekeepers of truth . . . civilization's radical voices." As Belafonte indicated in 1960, his vision of the responsibilities of a radical citizen artist were shaped "once upon a time" when it was a "rich and common thing" for "the performer, the writer, the artist" to be welcomed "as an outspoken and free thinking man . . . part of an intellectual group that met in restaurants and went to meetings and participated in violent discussions."

The place he found in the late 1940s black and interracial Left gave Belafonte a formative experience of being part of an oppositional movement, joining with others to fight for their vision of a better world. This experience was amplified in his years with King and the civil rights struggle for "freedom now!" and through his commitments to world citizenship. His public acts and speech took multiple forms: he organized and appeared at rallies and benefits, showed up at demonstrations and picket lines, and joined strategy sessions about the best ways to keep up the pressure for social justice in the United States and around the world. He resisted efforts to represent his personal success across the color line as diminishing racial exclusion in U.S. society, refusing to confuse his own individual celebrity with progress toward racial or social equality. The story of Belafonte's "becoming," then, helps to reveal and document the collective resources he was able to draw upon to sustain his focus and commitments, and in doing so, illuminates why Belafonte's example continues to inspire those trying to rebalance the scales of justice and demonstrate the possibilities for multiracial democracy.

ABBREVIATIONS FOR NOTES

BLACK PRESS

AA	*Afro-American* (Baltimore)
ADW	*Atlanta Daily World*
BW	*Birmingham World*
CCP	*Cleveland Call and Post*
CE	*California Eagle*
CD	*Chicago Defender* (national edition)
CDD	*Chicago Defender* (daily edition)
KCC	*Kansas City Call*
LAS	*Los Angeles Sentinel*
LATr	*Los Angeles Tribune*
NJAG	*New Journal and Guide* (Norfolk, Virginia)
NYAN	*New York Amsterdam News*
PC	*Pittsburgh Courier*
PTr	*Philadelphia Tribune*

DAILY PRESS

CTr	*Chicago Tribune*
DW	*Daily Worker*
HCN	*Hollywood Citizen News*

LAE	*Los Angeles Examiner*
LAHE	*LA Herald Examiner*
LAMN	*Los Angeles Mirror News*
LAT	*Los Angeles Times*
NYDM	*New York Daily Mirror*
NYDN	*New York Daily News*
NYHT	*New York Herald Tribune*
NYHTBR	*New York Herald Tribune Book Review*
NYJA	*New York Journal American*
NYM	*New York Mirror*
NYMT	*New York Morning Telegraph*
NYP	*New York Post*
NYSN	*New York Sunday News*
NYT	*New York Times*
NYTBR	*New York Times Book Review*
NYTe	*New York Telegram*
NYTr	*New York Tribune*
NYWT	*New York World Telegram*
OTr	*Oakland Tribune*
WP	*Washington Post*
WPTH	*Washington Post and Times Herald*

NATIONAL WIRE SERVICES

ANP	Associated Negro Press
AP	Associated Press
INS	International News Service
UP	United Press Association
UPI	United Press International

TRADE PAPERS

BO	*Box Office*
HR	*Hollywood Reporter*
MPD	*Motion Picture Daily*
MPE	*Motion Picture Exhibitor*
MPH	*Motion Picture Herald*
VAR	*Variety* (weekly edition)
VAR(d)	*Variety* (daily edition)

ARCHIVAL COLLECTIONS

BRTC	Billy Rose Theater Collection, Lincoln Center for the Performing Arts, New York Public Library
CLACFC/TAM 148	Church League of America Collection of Files of *Counterattack*, the Wackenhut Corporation, and Karl Baarslag, Tamiment Library and Robert F. Wagner Archives, New York University
CVVP	Carl Van Vechten Papers, Yale Collection of American Literature, Beinecke Rare Books and Manuscript Library, Yale University
CVVPC	Carl Van Vechten Photography Collection, Yale Collection of American Literature, Beinecke Rare Books and Manuscript Library, Yale University
FOX/USC	Twentieth Century Fox Collection, University of Southern California Cinematic Arts Library
FSATC	Frank Schiffman Apollo Theater Collection, 1935–1985, National Museum of American history, Smithsonian Institution
HHC	Henry Hampton Collection, Washington University Film and Media archive
JPC/TAM 300	Janet Pinkard Collection, Tamiment Library and Robert F. Wagner Archives, New York University
LHP	Langston Hughes Papers, James Weldon Johnson Collection, Beinecke Library, Yale University
MGM/USC	Metro-Goldwyn-Mayer Collection, USC Cinematic Arts Library
MPAA/MH/AMPAS	Motion Picture Association of America files, Margaret Herrick Library, Academy of Motion Picture Arts and Sciences, Los Angeles

PCM/NYC	Paley Center for the Media, NYC
PE036	Printed Ephemera Collection, Tamiment Library and Robert F. Wagner Archives, New York University
RSS/LOC	Recorded Sound Section, Motion Picture, Broadcast and Recorded Sound Division, Library of Congress
SCRBC	Schomburg Center for Research in Black Culture, New York Public Library —ANT: American Negro Theater Scrapbook —BFC: Black Film Collection —CSC: Chiz Schultz Collection —Clipping Files on individuals and organizations —DDC: Davis-Dee Collection —MIRS: Moving Image and Recorded Sound Division
TB/HB	Taylor Branch interview with HB, March 6–7, 1985, in the Taylor Branch Papers, Southern Historical Collection, UNC-Chapel Hill
UAW65/WAG 006	United Automobile Workers District 65 Records, Tamiment Library and Robert F. Wagner Archives, New York University

NOTES

INTRODUCTION

1. Discussions of Belafonte's musical career and political contributions appear in Ronald D. Cohen, *Rainbow Quest: The Folk Music Revival and American Society, 1940–1970* (Amherst and Boston: University of Massachusetts Press, 2002); Elijah Wald, *How the Beatles Destroyed Rock and Roll: An Alternative History of American Popular Music* (New York: Oxford University Press, 2009); Brian Ward, *Just My Soul Responding: Rhythm and Blues, Black Consciousness, and Race Relations* (Berkeley: University of California Press, 1998); Colin Escott, *Island in the Sun* book accompanying Bear Family Recording Boxed Set, 2002; Taylor Branch, *Parting the Waters: America in the King Years, 1954–1963* (New York: Simon and Schuster, 1988), *Pillar of Fire: America in the King Years, 1963–1965* (New York: Simon and Schuster, 1998), and *At Canaan's Edge: America in the King Years, 1965–1968* (New York: Simon and Schuster, 2008); Steven J. Ross, "Politics in Black and White: Harry Belafonte," in *Hollywood Left and Right: How Movie Stars Shaped American Politics* (New York: Oxford University Press, 2011), 185–226. Discussion of his relationship to Caribbean music and politics appears in Michele Stevens, "The First Negro Matinee Idol: Harry Belafonte and American Culture in the 1950s," in *Left of the Color Line: Race, Radicalism, and Twentieth Century Literature of the United States*, ed. Bill V. Mullen and James Smethurst(Chapel Hill: University of North Carolina Press, 2003), 223–237; Lisa D. McGill,

Constructing Black Selves: Caribbean American Narratives and the Second Generation (New York: New York University Press, 2005); Gordon Rohlehr, "Calypso Reinvents Itself," in *Carnival: Culture in Action—The Trinidad Experience*, ed. Milla Cozart Riggio (New York: Routledge, 2004); Shane Vogel, "*Jamaica* on Broadway: the Popular Caribbean and Mock Transnational Performance," *Theatre Journal* 62 (2010):1–21; Ray Funk and Donald R. Hill, "'Will Calypso Doom Rock 'n' Roll?': The U.S. Calypso Craze of 1957," in *Trinidad Carnival: The Cultural Politics of a Transnational Festival*, ed. Garth L. Green and Philip W. Scher (Bloomington: Indiana University Press, 2007), 178–197. Some discussions of Belafonte's films appear in *Abraham Polonsky's Odds against Tomorrow: The Critical Edition (Film as Literature)*, ed. John Schultheiss (Northridge, CA: Center for Telecommunications Studies, 1999); Arthur Knight, "Movies and the Racial Divide," in *American Cinema of the 1950s: Themes and Variations*, ed. Murray Pomerance (New Brunswick, NJ: Rutgers University Press, 2005), 211–244.

2. Janny Scott, *A Singular Woman: The Untold Story of Barack Obama's Mother* (New York: Riverhead Books, 2011), 4; Barack Obama, *Dreams from My Father: A Story of Race and Inheritance* (New York: Three Rivers Press, 2004), 51; Thurston Moore interview with Patti Smith, *Bomb* 54 (Winter 1996); Gil Scott-Heron, *The Last Holiday: A Memoir* (New York: Grove Press, 2012), 44; Joan Baez in *Joan Baez: How Sweet the Sound* (American Masters Documentary, 2009); Bob Dylan, *Chronicles*: Volume 1, (New York: Simon and Schuster, 2004), 69; Ahmed Kathrada, *No Bread for Mandela: Memoirs of Ahmed Kathrada, Prisoner No. 468/64* (2004; repr., Lexington: University Press of Kentucky, 2010), 263.

3. Arnold Shaw, *Belafonte: An Unauthorized Biography* (New York: Pyramid Books, 1960); Ronald D. Cohen, "Arnold Shaw," in *American National Biography*, vol. 19, ed. John A. Garraty and Mark C. Carnes (New York: Oxford University Press, 1999), 373–378. First published in the Black American series for Holloway House in 1980, updated in 2008, Genia Fogelson's *Harry Belafonte: Singer and Actor* followed Belafonte's career into the 1970s and 1980s, using much of Shaw's material and replicating his omissions.

4. James Smethurst, *The African American Roots of Modernism: From Reconstruction to the Harlem Renaissance* (Chapel Hill: University of North Carolina Press, 2011); Cedric Robinson, *Forgeries of Memory and Meaning: Blacks and the Regimes of Race in Amer-*

ican Theater and Film Before World War II (Chapel Hill: University of North Carolina press, 2007); Karl Hagstrom Miller, *Segregating Sound: Inventing Folk and Pop Music in the Age of Jim Crow* (Durham, NC: Duke University Press, 2010); Michele Hilmes, *Radio Voices: American Broadcasting, 1922–1952* (Minneapolis: University of Minnesota Press, 1997), 75–96; J. Fred MacDonald, *Don't Touch That Dial!: Radio Programming in American Life from 1920 to 1960* (Chicago: Nelson-Hall, 1979), 327–370.

CHAPTER ONE

1. Harry Belafonte, *My Song* (New York: Knopf, 2011), 12–16. Melvine Love was born ca. 12/19/06; Harold George Bellanfanti, ca. June 3, 1899, according to Colin Escott, *Island in the Sun*, book for Bear Family Recording Boxed CD Set, 2002, 4.

2. Belafonte, *My Song*, 13–30, 43. White music-fans continued to attend the Apollo until the rioting in Harlem in 1943, after which white audiences significantly diminished. See the histories of the Apollo by Ted Fox, *Showtime at the Apollo* (New York: Holt, Rinehart and Winston, 1983) and *Ain't Nothing Like the Real Thing: How the Apollo Theater Shaped American Entertainment*, ed. Richard Carlin and Kinshasha Holman Conwill (Washington, DC: Smithsonian Books, 2010).

3. Belafonte, *My Song*, 12, 18–19; David Gelman, "Belafonte: Profile-II," *NYP*, 4/16/57. On black and white working-class survival strategies more generally, see Susan Porter Benson, *Household Accounts: Working-Class Family Economies in the Interwar United States* (Ithaca, NY: Cornell University Press, 2007).

4. Belafonte, *My Song*, 18.

5. Jonathan Gill, *Harlem* (New York: Grove Press, 2011), 283–284; Belafonte, *My Song*, 20–24.

6. Gill, *Harlem*, 282–283; Arnold Shaw, *Belafonte: An Unauthorized Biography* (New York: Pyramid Books, 1960), 30; Gelman, "Profile-II"; Belafonte, *My Song*, 25; *Sing Your Song* (2011).

7. Belafonte, *My Song*, 23–25, 32–35.

8. Robin Kelley, "Place Is the Space: The 'Hood as a Locus of Jazz History,'" seminar paper presented at Harvard University, Cambridge, MA, 2/4/2011, in author's possession.

9. Belafonte, *My Song*, 28–30. Ella Fitzgerald first appeared at the Apollo in 1934; Billie Holiday in 1935, Duke Ellington in 1936;

Fox, *Showtime at the Apollo* and the timelines in *Ain't Nothing Like the Real Thing*, ed. Carlin and Conwill.

10. Belafonte, *My Song*, 37–41.

11. Gelman, "Profile-II."

12. Maurice Zolotow, "Belafonte," *The American Weekly*, 5/10/59, 11; Belafonte, *My Song*, 37–41. Langston Hughes turned this exclusion into a metaphor for national Jim Crow in his poem, "I, Too, Sing America," "I am the darker brother / They send me to eat in the kitchen / When company comes," written in 1924, published in *The Weary Blues* in 1926, and recorded by Hughes on Folkways in 1955.

13. David Gelman, "Belafonte: Profile-III," *NYP*, 4/17/57.

14. Brad Fredericks, "American Rhythm and Blues Influence on Early Jamaican Musical Styles," *The Dread Library* at http://www.uvm.edu/`debate/dreadlibrary/fredericks.html, accessed 7/4/2008; Robert Witmer, "'Local' and 'Foreign': The Popular Music Culture of Kingston, Jamaica, before Ska, Rock Steady, and Reggae," *Latin American Music Review/Revista de Música Latino Americana* 8, no. 1 (Spring–Summer, 1987): 1–25; Gordon Rohlehr, "Calypso Reinvents Itself," in *Carnival: Culture in Action—The Trinidad Experience*, ed. Milla Cozart Riggio (New York: Routledge, 2004), 214–215; 1940 observer cited by Donald Hill, *Calypso Calaloo: Early Carnival Music in Trinidad* (Gainesville: University of Florida Press, 1993), 130.

15. Gill, *Harlem*, 326–333; Hughes, "Down Under in Harlem," *New Republic*, 3/27/44, 405.

16. Gelman, "Profile-II"; John Leland, "The Way We Live Now: Questions for Harry Belafonte; Sing Out Strong," *NYT*, 8/26/2001; Belafonte, *My Song*, 42.

17. Belafonte, *My Song*, 42–43.

18. Gelman, "Profile-II"; Belafonte, *My Song*, 45–46.

19. Belafonte, *My Song*, 45–48; Richard Dalfiume, "The 'Forgotten Years' of the Negro Revolution," *Journal of American History* 55, no. 1 (1968): 90–106.

20. Fred Hift, "Harry Belafonte: Calypso's Top Banana," *Weekend Magazine*, 11/25/57 (BRTC); Leonard Katz, "Harry Belafonte: A Human Being First," *NYP*, 11/11/56; "Lead Man Holler," *Time*, 3/2/59.

21. W. E. B. Du Bois, *Dusk of Dawn: An Essay toward an Autobiography of a Race Concept* (1940; repr., New Brunswick, NJ: Transaction Press, 2006), 117, 153; Shaw, *Belafonte*, 42.

22. Rayford Logan, ed., *What the Negro Wants* (1944; repr., Notre Dame, IN: University of Notre Dame Press, 2001), 135.

23. W. E. B. Du Bois, *Color and Democracy: Colonies and Peace* (New York: Harcourt, Brace, 1945), 91, 108, 113; Metz Lochard, editor in chief of the *Chicago Defender*, as quoted by Penny Von Eschen, *Race against Empire: Black Americans and Anti-Colonialism, 1937–1957* (Ithaca, NY: Cornell University Press, 1997), 78.

24. Belafonte, *My Song*, 49–56; Cornell West, 1996 interview with Belafonte in *Restoring Hope*, ed. Kelvin Shawn Sealey (Boston: Beacon Press, 1997),13–14; Michael Eldridge, "Remains of the Day-O: A Conversation with Harry Belafonte," *Transition*, no. 92 (2002): 117–118.

25. Michael Denning, *The Cultural Front: The Laboring of American Culture in the Twentieth Century* (London: Verso, 1996), 3–50, poll data on 4; editorial, *Chicago Defender*, September 12, 1942, as cited in Bill V. Mullen, *Popular Fronts: Chicago and African American Cultural Politics, 1935–1946* (Urbana: University of Illinois Press, 1999), 2.

26. See Denning, *Cultural Front*, and Judith E. Smith, *Visions of Belonging: Families Stories, Popular Culture, and Postwar Democracy, 1940–1960* (New York: Columbia University Press, 2004), 1–27.

27. On the importance of the Harlem Left in New York's Popular Front and of radical Harlem theater, see Denning, *Cultural Front*, 15, 369–370; Gelman, "Profile-III."

28. Errol G. Hill and James V. Hatch, *A History of African American Theatre* (Cambridge: Cambridge University Press, 2003), 307–334.

29. Hill and Hatch, *History*, 335–374; Ethel Pitts Walker, "The American Negro Theatre," in *The Theatre of Black Americans: A Collection of Critical Essays*, ed. Errol Hill (New York: Applause Theater Book Publishers, 1987), 247–260; Ossie Davis and Ruby Dee, *With Ossie and Ruby: In This Life Together* (New York: William Morrow, 1998), 96; Hill quoted by Walker, 251; Belafonte interviewed by Tracy Heather Strain, 2/25/2009.

30. Reviews, in American Negro Theatre Scrapbook, SCRBC; Jay Thomas, "Dashing Elwood Smith Deserved Better Treatment Than ANT's New Play Offered," *NYAN*, 12/29/45.

31. "New Anti-Fascist Play Is Due Soon," *NYAN*, 11/24/45; "'Home Is the Hunter; Opens; the American Negro Theatre Dec 20," *Age*, 12/22/45, ANT Scrapbook, SCRBC; Denning, *Cultural Front*,

4–50; Smith, *Visions of Belonging,* 109–139, 208–215, and 281–327; Glenda Gilmore, *Defying Dixie: The Radical Roots of Civil Rights, 1919–1950* (New York: Norton, 2008) 157–200, 346–399.

32. Jeanne Van Holmes, "Belafonte Gives It All He's Got," *Saturday Evening Post,* 4/29/57, 69, 73; Davis and Dee, *With Ossie and Ruby,* 122–123.

33. Holmes, "Belafonte," 73; Osceola Archer interview, quoted in Shaw, *Belafonte,* 47–48.

34. Belafonte described the ANT actors' adoption of a "Caribbean brogue" in author's interview, 4/17/2010. John Hudson Jones, "An Evaluation of the ANT," *Daily Worker,* 8/25/46.

35. Holmes, "Belafonte," 73.

36. Martin Duberman, *Paul Robeson* (New York: Ballantine, 1990), 263–295, and Paul Robeson, Jr., *The Undiscovered Paul Robeson: Quest for Freedom, 1939–1976* (New York: John Wiley, 2010); "Eight Thousand to Honor Robeson," *New York Times,* 4/13/44, 25; "Paul Robeson Honored With Spingarn Medal by NAACP," *NYT,* 10/19/45.

37. Author's interview with Belafonte, 4/17/2010. On Robeson's significance for Belafonte, see Guy Flatley, "Be Thankful You're Not as Handsome as Harry," *NYT,* 7/2/72; M. Cordell Thompson, "Belafonte Bounces Back, Big and Black," *Jet,* 7/6/72, 59; West's 1996 interview with Belafonte in *Restoring Hope,* 15.

38. Duberman, *Robeson,* 296–311; Gerald Horne, *Communist Front? The Civil Rights Congress, 1946–1956* (London: Associated University Presses, 1988), 13–58.

39. Von Eschen, *Race against Empire,* 70–95; Duberman, *Robeson,* 301-305; James H. Meriwether, *Proudly We Can Be Africans: Black Americans and Africa, 1935–1961* (Chapel Hill: University of North Carolina Press, 2002), 61–62.

40. Von Eschen, *Race against Empire,* 103–104.

41. Andrew Hemingway, *Artists on the Left: American Artists and the Communist Movement, 1926–1956* (New Haven, CT: Yale University Press, 2002), 195–196; Robson, Jr., *Undiscovered Paul Robeson,* 41–110; see also the ICCASP materials in Box 5, Folders 6 and 7, CLACFC/TAM 148.

42. Shaw, *Belafonte,* 50.

43. "Protests Grow as Hate Shock Grips Nation," *CD,* 8/10/46, 1; Horne, *Communist Front?,* 56; "UNAVA" in *Organizing Black America,* ed. Nina Mjagkij (New York: Garland, 2001), 668–669, and Keith

Gilyard, *John Oliver Killens: A Life of Black Literary Activism* (Athens: University of Georgia Press, 2010), 69–70; "Vets Seek to End US Fascism," *CD*, 5/25/46, 13. UNAVA conveners included Coleman Young and George B. Murphy, Jr.; white vet Bertram Alves chaired, Joe Louis was honorary chair.

44. Davis and Dee, *With Ossie and Ruby*, 178; Martha Biondi, *To Stand and Fight: The Struggle for Civil Rights in Postwar New York City* (Cambridge, MA: Harvard University Press, 2003), 61–68; Simon Callow, *Orson Welles: Hello Americans* (London: Vintage, 2007), 323–343.

45. Duberman, *Robeson*, 305; John C. Culver and John Hyde, *American Dreamer: A Life of Henry Wallace* (New York: Norton, 2000), 419–425; "Protests Grow as Hate Shock Grips Nation," *CD*, 8/10/46, 1; "Wallace to Speak Here," *NYT*, 9/8/46, 14; leaflet for 9/12/46 rally, in Box 5, Folder 6 on PCA/ICCASP 1945–1946, in CLACFC/TAM 148; "Truman Balks at Lynch Action," and "Nation's Liberals Back Wallace Peace Stand," *CD*, 9/28/46, 1.

46. Shaw, *Belafonte*, 48; Belafonte, *My Song*, 67.

47. "Erwin Piscator," *Current Biography Yearbook, 1942* (Bronx, NY: H. W. Wilson, 1942), 665–667; John Willett, "Erwin Piscator: New York and the Dramatic Workshop, 1939–1951," *Performing Arts Journal* 2, no.3 (Winter 1978): 3–16. By 1949, Jay Gorney, the radical theater and film composer and songwriter was teaching the class in musical theater; 12/16/49, report on the "Dramatic Workshop," in Box 9, Folder 3, "Dramatic Workshop," CLACFC/TAM 148; Sondra Gorney, *Brother Can You Spare a Dime: The Life of Composer Jay Gorney* (New York: Scarecrow Press, 2005), 49–52.

48. Marlon Brando, *Current Biography Yearbook, 1951* (Bronx, NY: H. W. Wilson, 1951), 62–63; Patricia Bosworth, *Marlon Brando* (New York: Viking, 2001), 16–27; Belafonte, *My Song*, 68–70. In 1945, Dunham, a modern dancer and an anthropologist who did her fieldwork in Haiti and the Caribbean, opened her New York dance school, specializing in Afro-Cuban and Afro-Caribbean dance and rhythms, located near Times Square. Dunham's career was followed closely in *Ebony*, with articles in January 1947, June 1953, December 1954, August 1955, and October 1956; see also VeVe Clark and Sara E. Johnson, *Kaiso! Writings by and about Katherine Dunham* (Madison: University of Wisconsin Press, 2005).

49. Willett, "Erwin Piscator," 9, 15. Student productions were staged in the President Theater in the theater district at 247 West

48th Street, and in a larger space, the Rooftop Theater, 111 East Houston Street on the edge of the Lower East Side.

50. Eldridge, "Remains of the Day-O," 119.

51. Julie Robinson was teaching at the school by 1947; VeVe Clark, "An Anthropological Band of Beings: An Interview with Julie Robinson Belafonte," in *Kaiso!*, 364–381; Harry Belafonte, "Why I Married Julie," *Ebony*, July 1957, 91.

52. Denning, *Cultural Front*, 283–322; Arnold Rampersad, *The Life of Langston Hughes*, vol. 1 (1986; repr., New York: Oxford University Press, 2002), 355–360.

53. Lead Belly, born in 1888 and performing for money since 1903, was first recorded by the folk song collector John Lomax and his son Alan in 1933 in the Angola Prison Farm in Louisiana. Thelma Ruby and Peter Frye, *Double or Nothing: Two Lives in the Theatre* (London: Janus Publishing Company, 1997), 69–75, 142–147, 154–161, 168–173; Belafonte, *My Song*, 72–73.

54. On cabaret blues, see Denning, *The Cultural Front*, 323–361; opening in 1938, Cafe Society was the city's first racially mixed night club, drawing progressive audiences for jazz as well as left-wing political satire, blues, and gospel performance; "Cafe Society's Biggest Act, ["its own Fair Employment Practices Act"], *Ebony*, December 1946, 36–41; David Stowe, "The Politics of Cafe Society," *Journal of American History* 84, no. 4 (1998): 1384-1406.

55. Shaw heard Belafonte perform this song in the Dramatic Workshop production and cited these lyrics, which were not included when the song was recorded in 1949; *Belafonte*, 61–64. Ellen Holly, *One Life: The Autobiography of an African American Actress* (New York: Kodansha International, 1996), 47–48.

56. A prior musical adaptation of Gay's opera by Bertolt Brecht and Kurt Weill had opened in Germany in 1928, translated into English as *Threepenny Opera*. Prominent African American actors in The *Beggar's Holiday* included Avon Long, Archie Savage, and Mildred Joanne Smith. The premiere was a benefit for the Council on African Affairs; the show ran for 111 performances; Harvey G. Cohen, *Duke Ellington's America* (Chicago: University of Chicago Press, 2010), 272–275.

57. Miles M. Jefferson, "The Negro on Broadway, 1945–1946," and "1946–1947," *Phylon* 7, no. 2 (1946): 187–188; 8, no. 2 (1947): 147–152.

58. On the emergence of bebop, see David Stowe, *Swing Changes:*

Big Band Jazz in New Deal America (Cambridge, MA: Harvard University Press, 1994), 206; Scott DeVeaux, *The Birth of Bebop: A Social and Musical History* (Berkeley: University of California Press, 1997).

59. On the particular interracial character of 52nd Street, see Arnold Shaw, *Fifty-Second Street: the Street of Jazz* (1971; repr., New York: De Capo, 1977), 204–205; Patrick Burke, *Come in and Hear the Truth: Jazz and Race on 52nd Street* (Chicago: University of Chicago Press, 2008), 156–200. The success of the interracial night spots (52nd Street, the Zanzibar, the two Cafe Societies, the Village Vanguard) in drawing black and white customers encouraged the modernizing of nightclubs in Harlem: "Harlem Night Club Boom," *Ebony*, November 1946, 28.

60. Lewis Erenberg, *Swingin' the Dream: Big Band Jazz and the Rebirth of American Culture* (Chicago: University of Chicago Press, 1998), 235–236; Gillespie quoted in Shaw, *52nd Street*, 263. On jazz and Africa, see Robin Kelley, *Africa Speaks, American Answers: Modern Jazz in Revolutionary Times* (Cambridge, MA: Harvard University Press, 2012); on bebop and Afro-Cuban music, see Geoffrey Jacques, "Cubop! Afro-Cuban Music and Mid-Twentieth-Century American Culture," in *Between Race and Empire: African Americans and Cubans before the Cuban Revolution*, ed. Lisa Brock and Digna Castaneda Fuertes (Philadelphia: Temple University Press, 1991), 249–265; Dizzy Gillespie, *Dizzy: To Be or Not to Bop* (London: Quartet, 1982), 317–325, 347–350; Donald L. Maggin, *Dizzy: The Life and Times of John Birks Gillespie* (New York: Harper Collins, 2005), 215–224.

61. Erenberg, *Swingin' the Dream*, 235; Shaw, *52nd Street*, 272–273 (quote on 272); Stowe, *Swing Changes*, 214–215.

62. Belafonte interview (1996) in *Restoring Hope*, 16–17; Belafonte, *My Song*, 72–73; Dorham interviewed by Arthur Taylor, 11/12/71, in *Notes and Tones: Musician to Musician Interviews* (New York: Da Capo, 1993), 232.

63. Belafonte interview (1996) in *Restoring Hope*, 16–17; Sidney Finkelstein, *Jazz: a People's Music* (1948; repr., New York: International, 1989), 146, 150; Denning, *Cultural Front*, 328–329, 334–335.

64. "Program of Jazz Traces Its History," *NYT*, 1/2/46, 28; Stowe, *Swing Changes*, 70. "January 1945–June 1946 Report on ICCASP Activities," in Box 5, Folder 6 on PCA/ICCASP 1945–1946, CLACFC/

TAM 148; "Negro Unit Accuses South's Postmasters," *NYT*, 6/1/47, 45; "UNAVA to Honor Jackie and Ingrid," *NYAN*, 5/17/47, 9.

65. Lead Belly, Burl Ives, and Woody Guthrie all had their own radio shows in the 1940s, on network and commercially supported programs. Lead Belly, Josh White, the Golden Gate Quartet, Burl Ives, and Woody Guthrie also appeared regularly on Alan Lomax's radio programs in 1940 and 1941. Ronald Cohen, *Rainbow Quest: The Folk Music Revival and American Society, 1940–1970* (Amherst: University of Massachusetts Press, 2002); Benjamin Filene, *Romancing the Folk: Public Memory and American Roots Music* (Chapel Hill: University of North Carolina Press, 2000), 47–71; John Szwed, *Alan Lomax: The Man Who Recorded the World* (New York: Viking, 2010), 43–167; Ed Cray, *Ramblin' Man: The Life and Times of Woody Guthrie* (New York: Norton, 2004) 48–227.

66. David King Dunaway, *How Can I Keep from Singing?: The Ballad of Pete Seeger* (New York: Random House, 2008), 124; Davis and Dee, *With Ossie and Ruby*, 131; Irving Burgie, *Day-O!!!: The Autobiography of Irving Burgie* (New York: Caribe Publishing, 2006), 43, 111–113.

67. Cohen, *Rainbow Quest*, 8–40; "Hyde Park Party, *Ebony*, March 1946, 3–7; Cray, *Ramblin' Man*, 239; Ronald Cohen and Dave Samuelson, *Songs for Political Action*, book for Bear Family Records Boxed CD Set, 1996), 77–96.

68. Duberman, *Robeson*, 175–178; quote on 178;Sheila Tully Boyle and Andrew Bunie, *Paul Robeson: The Years of Promise and Achievement* (Amherst: University of Massachusetts Press, 2001), 288–291; Millard Lampell, "The Lonesome Train," in *Radio Drama in Action*, ed. Eric Barnouw (New York: Rinehart, 1945), 240–250.

69. Asch recorded Ukrainian, Italian, Greek, Negro, Hebrew, and calypso songs; Cohen, *Rainbow Quest*, 36–37, 40. Alan Lomax recorded Carl Sandburg, Richard Dyer-Bennett, Josh White, and Burl Ives for Decca; Szwed, *Alan Lomax*, 219–223; author's interview with Robert DeCormier, June 16, 2010.

70. Lomax, "The Best of the Ballads," *Vogue*, 12/1/46, 208; E. Y. Harburg and Fred Saidy, *Finian's Rainbow: A Musical Satire* (New York: Random House, 1947), 3, 21, 22.

71. Edwin E. Gordon, "Cultivating Songs of the People, *New York Times*, August 25, 1946, 53; Dunaway, *How Can I Keep*, 132–138; Cohen, *Rainbow Quest*, 42–47; Robbie Lieberman, *My Song Is My Weapon: People's Songs, American Communism, and the Politics of*

Culture, 1930–1950 (Urbana: University of Illinois Press, 1989), 83–124; Richard A. Reuss with Jo Anne C. Reuss, *American Folk Music and Left-Wing Politics, 1927–1957* (Lanham, MD: Scarecrow Press, 2000), 179–220.

72. Author's interviews with Robert DeCormier, 7/29/2008, and 6/16/2010.

73. "Hootenanny," *Time,* 4/15/46; Lord Invader had already begun to sing a version of Trinidadian Lord Pretender's hit song "God Made Us All" with its refrain, "Nobody better than us," which he brought to the United States as "Ode to the Negro Race." Invader sang it, introduced by Pete Seeger, at a Union Hootenanny NYC, 5/6/46; it was published in the July 1946 issue of *People's Songs* (liner notes for *Lord Invader Calypso in New York: The Asch Recordings, 1946–1961,* reissued by Smithsonian Folkways Recordings, 2000). The song was praised in "Calypso Songs Use Biting Satire to Criticize Colonial Rule," *Freedom* 1, no. 2 (February 1951): 6; Cohen and Samuelson, *Songs,* 159.

74. "People's Songs Designed to Fight Discrimination," *AA* (Baltimore), 5/4/46, 5; "This Week's Programs," *NYT,* 8/25/46, 53; "Music Notes," *NYT,* 9/4/46, 34; "Music Notes," *NYT,* 9/25/46, 47.

75. "Second Hootenanny: Songs of Freedom of Various Origins Sung at Town Hall," *NYT,* 5/17/46, 14; Program for "Freedom Sings," 5/24/46, in Box 1, Folder 9, JPC/TAM 300; "Jefferson Chorus Heard," *NYT,* 5/25/46, 22. One of the songs was Langston Hughes's poem-song "Freedom's Plow," originally recited on the radio in 1943 by Paul Muni, with musical accompaniment by the Golden Gate Quartet and an orchestral score written and conducted by the African American composer Dean Dixon; Rampersad, *Hughes,* vol. 2 , 58.

76. Cohen, *Rainbow Quest,* 51, 42–47; Szwed, *Lomax,* 225–228; "The Programs of the Week," *NYT,* 11/9/46; "Blues Are Featured in Midnight Concert," *NYT,* 11/11/46; "Programs of the Week," *NYT,* 12/15/46.

77. Clipping from *PM,* a 1940s Left-oriented New York City afternoon newspaper, reproduced in Cohen and Samuelson, *Songs,* 32.

78. Danny Glover's interview with Belafonte for History Makers, 2000; author's interview with Belafonte on 4/17/2010.

79. Shaw, *Belafonte,* 50–51; Belafonte, *My Song,* 73.

80. Smith, *Becoming Something,* 217–223

81. Atkinson, "At the Theatre," *NYT,* 4/22/48, 35; Jefferson, "The Negro on Broadway, 1947–8," 107.

82. Katz, "Belafonte Close-Up"; Holmes, "Belafonte," 73.

83. "Reunion in Hollywood: Schoolmates Harry Belafonte and Tony Curtis Meet Again after Both Become Successful," *Ebony*, July 1953, 26–30.

84. On the cantata, see Lampell, "Lonesome Train," in *Radio Drama in Action*, 242–250, quote on 248; Earl Robinson with Eric Gordon, *Ballad of an American: The Autobiography of Earl Robinson* (Lanham, MD: Scarecrow Press, 1998), 133–140.Notices of the upcoming production appeared in *PM, NYP*, and *NYT* on the days preceding the event (2/6–14/48); also "Program Honors Lincoln: CIO Chorus Sings Robinson's 'Lonesome Train' Cantata," *NYT*, 2/15/48.

85. Cohen and Samuelson, *Songs*, 28. Waldemar Hille, a classically trained musician who helped produce the organization's publication beginning in 1946, remembered criticizing Belafonte when he stopped by the People's Songs office. It was a "sectarian" response, he later admitted; in Lieberman, *My Song Is My Weapon*, 89.

86. Author's interviews with Robert DeCormier, 7/29/2008, and 6/16/2010; Oscar Brand, *Ballad Mongers: Rise of Modern Folk Song* (New York: Funk and Wagnalls, 1962) 140–142; Belafonte quoted in Marcy Ellis, "Folk Songs Pay Off for Harry Belafonte," *NYP*, 4/5/52.

87. Phil Gordon (the winning deejay), "Salute to Show Business," *California Eagle*, 10/29/59; author's communication with Eric Foner, 1/28/2012.

88. Shaw, *Belafonte*, 53–54; Belafonte, *My Song*, 73–76.

89. For prominent black and white supporters of Wallace, see "Arts, Sciences and Professions for May Day" notice in *PM*, 4/30/47; "PCA Put Notables on Suckers List," *NYWT*, 5/29/47; Report on PCA meeting at Madison Square Garden, 9/11/47, all in Box 5, Folder 7, CLACFC/TAM 148; Notice of Speakers at Literature, Theater and Music and Arts divisions, PCA Conference, October 25–26, 1947; "Open Letter to the Motion Picture Industry," in *VAR*, 12/10/47, both in Box 5, Folder 8, CLACFC/TAM 148; "We Are for Wallace" advertisement from the National Council of Arts, Sciences and Professions appearing in *NYT*, 10/20/48, in Box 8, Folder 30, CLACFC/TAM 148. See also Rampersad, *Hughes*, 167–170; Hemingway, *Artists*, 194.

90. Culver and Hyde, *American Dreamer*, 457; Gerald Horne, *Black and Red: W. E. B. Du Bois and the Afro-American Response to the Cold War, 1944–1963* (Albany: State University of New York Press, 1986), 83–95; Gerald Horne, *Race Woman: the Lives of Shirley*

Graham Du Bois (New York: New York University Press, 2000), 13–114; David Levering Lewis, *W. E. B. Du Bois: the Fight for Equality in the American Century, 1919–1963* (New York: Norton, 2000), 532–557; Duberman, *Robeson*, 316–414; Clayborn Carson, *The Papers of Dr. Martin Luther King, Jr.*, vol. 2 (Berkeley: University of California Press, 1992), 13 and photograph.

91. Margaret Wilkerson, "Political Radicalism and Artistic Innovation in the Works of Lorraine Hansberry," *African American Performance and Theater History*, ed. Harry Elam and David Krasner (New York: Oxford University Press, 2000), 45; materials in Box 6, Folder 32, "Young Progressives of America," CLACFC/TAM 148.

92. Curtis D. MacDougall, *Gideon's Army* (New York: Marzani and Munsell, 1965), 112, 596.

93. Author's interview with DeCormier, 6/16/2010; West-Belafonte interview (1996) in *Restoring Hope*, 17.

94. "48,000 Hear Wallace Assert Prejudice Will Fail in South," and "Rally Combines Revival, Song Fest," *NYT*, 9/11/48.

95. MacDougal, *Gideon's Army*, 844–850; "Wallace Prepares Last Speeches," *NYT*, 10/24/48, 51.

96. Cohen and Samuelson, *Songs*, 180; Reuss and Reuss, *American Folk Music*, 198–204.

97. Biondi, *To Stand and Fight*, 47, 54, 209–211.

98. Shaw, *Belafonte*, 58; Belafonte, *My Song*, 75–76.

CHAPTER TWO

1. "Bop Comes Home to Roost: Monk, Dizzy—Ooh, Vop!" *Billboard*, 5/29/48, 20; Ken Vail, *Bird's Diary: The Life of Charlie Parker, 1945–1955* (Chessington, Surrey, UK: Castle, 1996), 41–49; ticket for Royal Roost, Thursday, January 20, 1949, on 49; Belafonte, *My Song*, 77–81. The rhythm and blues vocalists were Dinah Washington and the Ravens; the Charlie Ventura group was also on the bill.

2. Shaw, *Belafonte*, 58–62.

3. Billy Rowe, "Harry Belafonte Makes Good Just as He Was about to Give Up Hope," *PC*, 1/22/49; JEG, "Unknown Belafonte Just Sang Self Into Roost Job," *Down Beat*, 3/11/49, 12; Shaw, *Belafonte*, 62.

4. Ingrid Monson, *Freedom Sounds: Civil Rights Call Out to Jazz and Africa* (New York: Oxford University Press, 2007), 5–6; Paul

Dennis, "The Negro Makes Advances," *Billboard*, 1/2/43, 28, 80; Elijah Wald, *How the Beatles Destroyed Rock and Roll: An Alternative History of American Popular Music* (New York: Oxford University Press, 2009) 144–148.

5. Shaw, *Belafonte*, 62–63; Belafonte, *My Song*, 77–82. Eckstine had led a hot jazz band before beginning to sing solo in 1947; Rowe, "Harry Belafonte Makes Good" and JEG, "Unknown Belafonte."

6. This concert took place on 2/20/49; Leonard Feathers, *The Jazz Years: Eyewitness to an Era* (New York: Da Capo, 1987), 102.

7. Belafonte played the Apollo on 3/4/49; Christopher Washburn, "Latin Music at the Apollo," in Carlin and Conwill, *Ain't Nothing Like the Real Thing*, 223; Machito's card in FSATC.

8. *DW*, 1/19/49; Dave Samuelson, *The Weavers 1949–1953*, Bear Family Boxed CD Set, 2000, 10–11.

9. *DW*, 3/6/49; "People's Song Unit in Carnegie Concert," *NYT*, 3/8/49, 30; Cohen, *Rainbow Quest*, 58; and Szwed, *Alan Lomax*, 238. In this period "Palestinian" likely referred to the British-designated Palestine Mandate, then including the present-day Israel and the West Bank.

10. Materials in Box 20, Folder 44, "Young Progressives of America," 1948–1950, CLACFC/TAM 148.

11. "Wallace Scores Pact as Promoting War," *NYT*, 4/12/49, 4; leaflet announcing "Meeting of Forest Hills Young Progressives" in Box 20, Folder 44, "Young Progressives of America," 1948–1950, CLACFC/TAM 148; ad in *DW*, 4/8/49 for "Youth Salute to FDR" ("speakers and performers including Henry Wallace, Harry Belafonte, Jack Gilford, Art Hodes Band, and others, at Manhattan Center, April 18, 1949").

12. "Salute to FDR" flyer, April 18, 1949, in Box 20, Folder 44, "Young Progressives of America," 1948–1950, CLACFC/TAM 148. Several of the featured musicians had also played at the People's Songs Carnegie Hall benefit concert where Belafonte had appeared the previous month. Gilford's performance noted in "Wallace Prepares for Last Speeches," *NYT*, 10/24/48, 51.

13. Wald, *Alternative History*, 126–128, 138–165; "Many Trends Combine to Give Folk Music a Wider Audience," *Billboard*, 2/27/43.

14. "Recognition" sold ten thousand copies; Arnold Shaw, *Belafonte*, 63; Belafonte, *My Song*, 82.

15. Shaw, *Belafonte*, 64–65; Belafonte, *My Song*, 81–85. Mrs. Byrd

would remain as part of the household until they moved to Elmhurst in late 1953.

16. Larry Ceplair and Steven Englund, *The Inquisition in Hollywood: Politics in the Film Community, 1930–1960* (Berkeley: University of California Press, 1983); David Everitt, *A Shadow of Red: Communism and the Blacklist in Radio and Television* (New York: Ivan Dee, 2007), 3–28.

17. Everitt, *A Shadow of Red*, 3–28; Elizabeth Fones-Wolf, *Waves of Opposition: Labor and the Struggle for Democratic Radio* (Urbana: University of Illinois Press, 2006), 125–201.

18. Wald, *Josh White*, 148–149; Duberman, *Robeson*, 336–362; Smith, *Becoming Something*, 251–296.

19. "Sponsors of the World Peace Conference," *NYT*, 3/24/49, 4. This conference was planned as a meeting of artists and scientists from thirty countries, including the USSR, in New York. Among the 1940s radicals who signed the call to sponsor the conference was Peter Neubauer, who would be Belafonte's psychoanalyst from 1957 until he died. Lee made efforts to publicly remove his name from this list: Smith, *Becoming Something*, 340. In "Red Visitors Cause Rumpus," *Life*, 4/4/49, 39–43, twenty-one of the fifty people pictured had *not* signed on as sponsors of this conference.

20. Duberman, *Robeson*, 341–362; Robeson, Jr., *The Undiscovered Paul Robeson*, 142–146, 156–164; Arnold Rampersad, *Jackie Robinson: A Biography* (New York: Ballantine, 1997), 210–216; Smith, *Becoming Something*, 190–191; Gerald Nachman, *Right Here on Our Stage Tonight: Ed Sullivan's America* (Berkeley: University of California Press, 2009), 318.

21. "Canada Lee Explains," *NYT*, 7/7/49, 31.

22. "Call to a Conference on Radio, Television, and the Negro People," copy of printed announcement provided to me by Terry Signaigo, in Box 24, Folder "Committee for the Negro in the Arts," PE 036.

23. In addition to Belafonte, black sponsors included classically trained musicians and singers Lawrence Brown, Larry Winters, Hope Foye, Aubrey Pankey, Muriel Smith Kenneth Spencer; jazz musicians Eddie Barefield, Cyril Haynes, Andy Kirk; conductors Dean Dixon, Leonard de Paur, and Hall Johnson; artists Ernest Crichlow, Jacob Lawrence, Norman Lewis, and Charles White; stage and screen actors Georgia Burke, James Edwards, Georgette

Harvey, Gordon Heath, Juano Hernandez, Earl Jones, Canada Lee, Abbie Mitchell, Frederick O'Neal, Virgil Richardson, Paul Robeson, Wardell Saunders, Fredi Washington, Ellsworth Wright; Broadway set designer and producer Perry Watkins; intellectuals W. E. B. Du Bois, Howard University professor Alain Locke, former Schomburg Library curator and Atlanta University professor Dr. Lawrence Reddick; writers Shirley Graham, Langston Hughes, Theodore Ward, *Pittsburgh Courier*'s Billy Rowe; tap dancers Fayard and Harold Nicholas; ballet dancer Janet Collins and modern dancers Pearl Primus, Archie Savage, and Jean Destine; lawyer Hope Stevens; prominent Harlem minister Sheldon Hale Bishop.

24. On the prehistory of what became of CNA, see Terry Signaigo, "Committee for the Negro in the Arts" (master's essay, University of Massachusetts, 2005); "Organizational Report," n.d., ca. 1949, in CNA clippings file, SCRBC; also materials in Box 5, Folders 17–18, National Negro Congress, 1941–1947, CLACFC/TAM 300; John O. Killens, "He [Charles White]Took His Art More Seriously Than Himself," *Freedomways* (Summer 1980): 193; Brian Dolinar, *The Black Cultural Front: Black Writers and Artists of the Depression Generation* (Jackson: University Press of Mississippi, 2012), 60–64; Laurence Jackson, *The Indignant Generation: A Narrative History of African American Writers and Critics* (Princeton, NJ: Princeton University Press, 2011), 309–310.

25. "Radio Held Biased on Negro Problem," *NYT*, 7/10/49, 31; "Networks That Foul the Air," *AA*, 6/18/49, and Harold Cruse, "Progressives in Radio Map Plans to Defeat Industry Blacklist," *DW*, 8/17/49, 11. Quoted passages from "Negro Stereotypes on Air, Lack of Job Chances Scored by Canada Lee," *VAR*, 7/13/49, 35.

26. Looking back in 1980, the writer John O. Killens identified CNA with the "wonderful days in Harlem in the Fifties, when all of us were young and everything was possible, even liberation, even socialism!" He recalled "Ernie Crichlow and Roy DeCarava and Charles [White] and Ruth [Jett] and Thelma [Dale] and John [Henrik] Clark and Walter [Christmas] and Sidney [Poitier] and Harry [Belafonte] and Julian [Mayfield] and Lorraine [Hansberry] and the rest of us in the CNA . . . with Paul Robeson as the inspiration and guiding spirit for all of us. . . . In the arts, he was for most of us a patron saint." "He [Charles White] Took His Art More Seriously," 193. Belafonte's relationships with writers John O. Killens and William

Attaway, artist Charles White, and actor Frank Silvera persisted through the 1950s and into the 1960s.

27. The concert was planned as a benefit for the Harlem chapter of the Civil Rights Congress, publicized as "disloyal" by the Attorney General's list in December 1947; Duberman, *Robeson*, 363–375; Robeson, Jr., *The Undiscovered Paul Robeson*, 165–178; Samuelson, *The Weavers*, 11; "Weed Out Campaign Widens," *VAR*, 9/28/49, 23. Belafonte placed himself in the audience of the rescheduled concert in *My Song*, 83–84.

28. The recording-marketing categories that had segregated sound shifted in 1949 when *Billboard* charts used the new term "rhythm and blues" to refer to music made by black musicians for black audiences. Some musicians and some labels began to direct conscious efforts to produce a popular form of rhythm and blues that could be played for, and marketed to, both black and white audiences; Wald, *Alternative History*, 137, 148; Shaw, *Belafonte*, 66; "Belafonte's Wax Works Out Soon," *PC*, 8/27/49, 19; Vail, *Bird's Diary*, 65; *DW*, 9/6/49; Vail, *Dizzy Gillespie*, 79.

29. Harry Castleman and Walter J. Podrazik, *Watching TV: Six Decades of American Television*, 2nd ed. (Syracuse, NY: Syracuse University Press, 2003), 36–38; MacDonald, *Blacks and White TV*, 20–21; Donald Bogle, *Prime Time Blues: African Americans on Network Television* (New York: Farrar, Straus and Giroux, 2001), 14–15.

30. "CBS Throws in Towel in Bid to Compete with Berle; 'Sugar Hill' Shifts," *VAR*, 10/5/49, 1, 55.

31. Vail, *Bird's Diary*, 65, 69; "Birdland Bistro Fails to Open, No Liquor OK," *Billboard*, 9/17/49, 18; Billy Shaw to Frank Schiffman, 10/20/49, Frank Schiffman to Shaw Artists Corporation, 11/11/49 in FSATC; Carlin and Conwill, *Ain't Nothing Like the Real Thing*, 73–74, 82–83, 146, 196.

32. Vail, *Bird's Diary*, 69; "Goings On About Town," *New Yorker*, 12/31/49, 4; Jerry Wexler, "Birdland goes to Cooler Jazz: Garner on 88," *Billboard*, 1/28/50, 14.

33. David Hajdu, *Lush Life: A Biography of Billy Strayhorn* (New York: North Point Press, 1997), 114–117. Many of these artists were homosexuals; Neal remembered sexuality as an "understood thing," not a topic of discussion. Others who attended occasionally included the composer John Cage and the singer Eartha Kitt.

34. Reminiscence by Craig Work, 1/2/2007, as part of biogra-

phies connected with the Manumit School, http://manumitschool.com/ManumitBios/work.html; accessed 2/27/2012. Fred Norman's 1940s career detailed in "Negroes Make Advances," *Billboard*,1/2/43, 2, and William Grant Still, "The Men behind American Music," *The Crisis* (January 1944): 14.

35. William Attaway, author of two important and well-received novels in 1939 and 1941, was part of the black theater world in NYC; Alan Wald, *Exiles from a Future Time: The Forging of the Mid-Twentieth-Century Literary Left* (Chapel Hill: University of North Carolina Press, 2002), 281–283; Richard Yarborough, "William Attaway," in *Writers of the Black Chicago Renaissance*, ed. Steven C. Tracy (Urbana: University of Illinois Press, 2011), 30–52; Shaw, *Belafonte*, 67–68; Birdland review in *Variety* quoted in Escott, *Belafonte*, 7; Gelman, "Profile-III."

36. Oscar Brand described the Lead Belly memorial concert in *Ballad Mongers*, 142–143.

37. Kay quoted by Shaw, *Belafonte*, 71–72; Jeanne Van Holmes, "Belafonte Gives It All He's Got," *Saturday Evening Post*, 4/29/57, 75.

38. Holly, *One Life*, 51. At this time, Belafonte was part of a Harlem cultural scene that included actors Frederick O'Neal, Alice Childress, Maxwell Glanville, Ruby Dee, Sidney Poitier, and Ossie Davis; artists Charles White, Ernest Crichlow, and Roy DeCarava; and writers John O. Killens, John Henrik Clarke, and Harold Cruse, according to Gilyard, *Killens*, 80.

39. Programs, CNA Clipping file, SCRBC.

40. Belafonte joined other CNA supporters, including Alice Childress, Sidney Poitier, and the lyricist Yip Harburg, in signing a letter circulated by writer Shirley Graham calling for the firing of May Quinn, a New York teacher with a long history of expressing anti-Semitic and racist sentiment in her classroom; Gerald Horne, *Race Woman: The Lives of Shirley Graham* (New York: New York University Press, 2002), 114. Belafonte and many of those who had signed the radio conference call in 1949 were listed as sponsors on CNA letterhead on a letter from Charles White, 8/15/50, asking for help in publicizing twenty art scholarships for young people; CNA clipping file, SCRBC.

41. *DW*, 3/26/50 and *Counterattack*, 1/8/54; Moe Foner and Dan Forth, *Not for Bread Alone: A Memoir* (Ithaca, NY: Cornell University Press, 2002), 26–27 and *Counterattack*, 2/12/54; *DW*, 4/9/50; Burgie, *Day-O!!!!*, 160.

42. Shaw, *Belafonte*, 66; ad for Hart's Record Shop in *Lima News*, Lima Ohio, 2/17/50, 10.

43. Three Deuces [including Barry Ulanov],"Record Reviews," *Metronome* (April 1950):25 and (July 1950):27.

44. Jose, "Harry Belafonte," *VAR*, 3/31/50, 53; Barry Ulanov, "Voices and Modern Jazz; Frank [Sinatra], Sarah [Vaughan], and Harry [Belafonte], Lennie [Tristano], Pete [Rugolo], and Woody [Herman]," *Metronome* (June 1950):29. Anticommunist pressures had forced out the original owner of Cafe Society, Barney Josephson, as of March 2, 1949; Barney Josephson with Terry Trilling-Josephson, *Cafe Society: The Wrong Place for the Right People* (Urbana: University of Illinois Press, 2009), 232–266.

45. *Counterattack*, June 9, 1950, in Samuelson, *The Weavers*, 19.

46. American Business Consultants, *Red Channels: The Report of Communist Influence in Radio and Television*, June 1950; Erik Barnouw, *Tube of Plenty: Evolution of American Television* (New York: Oxford University Press, 1990), 122–124.

47. Robbie Lieberman, *My Song Is My Weapon*, 122; Cohen, *Rainbow Quest*, 72–73.

48. Wald, *Josh White*, 177–195; Josh White, "I Was a Sucker for the Communists," *Negro Digest* (December 1950): 26–31; Cohen, *Rainbow Quest*, 80.

49. Samuelson, *The Weavers*, 14–27.

50. "Goings on about Town," *New Yorker*, 8/19/50, 6.

51. On Jack Rollins, see references in Sam Zolotow's theater columns, *NYT*, 1/12/49 and 3/4/49; Phil Berger, "The Business of Comedy," *NYT Magazine*, 6/9/85, 54ff.; and the loving character based on him played by his longtime client Woody Allen in *Broadway Danny Rose* (1984). See also "Reminiscence by Craig Work," 1/2/2007; Escott, *Island*, 7.

52. "Head of the Family," *Ridgefield (CT)Press*, 9/13/50; "Harry Belafonte Seen to Advantage in Try-Out Production of 'Head of the Family,'" *NYAN*, 12/2/50; Etta Moten's 1956 radio interview with Harry Belafonte for WMAQ in Chicago, n.d., ca. sometime between May 15 and May 21; MIRS, SCRBC. Moten, married to Claude Barnett, the Chicago journalist who had founded the Associated Negro Press wire service, had by 1950 traveled with Barnett to Liberia, Gambia, Sierra Leone, Gold Coast, and Nigeria.

53. Before going to Miami, Belafonte also appeared in a "birth of the blues" show at a nightclub on Broadway and 49th Street in No-

vember 1950: *New Yorker*, 11/4/50, 6, and 11/11/50, 6. On Miami, see Shaw, *Belafonte*, 66–68, 71–73; Belafonte, *My Song*, 87–88.

54. Shaw, *Belafonte*, 75–82; Belafonte, *My Song*, 90–99.

55. "Biographical note," Gordon Heath Papers, Special collections, W. E. B. Du Bois Library, University of Massachusetts Amherst; Goudsouzian, *Sidney Poitier*, 91–100.

56. Belafonte, *My Song*, 90–93; these are listed among the spaces open to black customers in "Harlem Night Club Boom," *Ebony*, November 1946, 28.

57. David McAdoo, 34 Bedford Street, quoted by Allan Morrison in "Twilight for Greenwich Village," *Negro Digest* (January 1949), 35. On Richard Wright's move to Greenwich Village see Hazel Rowley, *Richard Wright: The Life and Times* (New York: Henry Holt, 2001), 297.

58. Morrison, "Twilight for Greenwich Village," 27–37; quoted material on 28–29; Delaney quoted on 30–32. Other Village residents interviewed include the philosopher Alain Locke, who had recently bought a house at 12 Grove Street; artist Joe Delaney, younger brother of Beauford, and jazz trumpeter Frankie Newton. Morrison was married to the actress Ruth Attaway, sister of Belafonte's close friend and Sage partner Bill Attaway.

59. James Smethurst, *The African American Roots of Modernism: From Reconstruction to the Harlem Renaissance* (Chapel Hill: University of North Carolina Press, 2011), 200–216. Other black artists residing in the Village included Charles White, Elizabeth Catlett, and Richmond Barthé. The writer James Baldwin moved to the Village in 1943, stayed until 1948, and then returned in 1958 and stayed until 1963; Lorraine Hansberry moved to the Village with her husband Bob Nemiroff in 1953; Audre Lord moved there in 1953; LeRoi Jones, who later took the name Amiri Baraka, lived there from 1955 to 1965, with Hettie Cohen after 1957. In the 1950s, the actor Glynn Turman moved with his actress and post-office-worker mother from Harlem to a small apartment around the corner from where Hansberry and Baldwin lived. Turman described his mother as "very, very progressive in thought." She moved to "that different place, it was an art mecca" because "that place had a different freedom . . . her friends were from all walks of life . . . transgender, gay, straight, white, black . . . these people . . . were all embraced by my mother. They all had a sense of self and none were cast aside"

http://www.scpr.org/programs/storycorps/2011/06/16/25194 /storycorps-griot-glynn-turman-with-daughter-delena.

60. Szwed, *Lomax,* 251–305; Duberman, *Robeson,* 381–403; "Du Bois Is Shocked," *NYT,* 2/10/51, 6; "Protest Du Bois Indictment," *NYT,* 2/13/51, 35; Lewis, *Du Bois, 1919–1963,* 548–549; TB/HB, 3/7/85.

61. Belafonte, *My Song,* 91–98.

62. "Stage, Radio, Film Stars Win Scrolls, *ADW,* 6/1/51, 3; CNA clippings file, SCRBC.

63. Club Baron was the biggest of the new "first-rate" nightclubs opened in Harlem in 1946 catering to black as well as to white customers; "Harlem Night Club Boom," *Ebony,* November 1946, 28–30. It was "built like a theater with balcony and box seats overlooking the stage" and could accommodate a crowd of 350. Its white owner, Herman Baron, had founded the American Contemporary Artists Galleries in 1932.

64. Hughes's collection of columns, *Simple Speaks His Mind,* was published in 1950. Program for CNA production "Just a Little Simple," in Box 1, Folder 6, "Committee for the Negro in the Arts," JPC/TAM 300. "Revue at the Club Baron," *NYT,* 9/15/50, 30; "Club Baron Revue Extended," *NYT,* 10/3/50, 33; "Show to Aid Hospital," *NYT,* 11/14/50, 38; "Christmas Shows in Hospitals," *NYT,* 12/27/50, 27; Goudsouzian, *Poitier,* 90–91. Poitier and Frank Silvera were part of the CNA subcommittee on unemployment, chaired by actor and writer Julian Mayfield, in July 1951, CNA Summer Bulletin, CNA Clippings File, SCRBC.

65. Sentenced originally in 1945, McGee was a black truck driver, whose rape conviction followed a four-year relationship with Willette Hawkins. The Civil Rights Congress organized around his legal defense; young lawyer Bella Abzug worked on his case. Other events in New York included a meeting at the Abyssinian Baptist Church with Willie McGee's wife, Rosalie, and a rally at St. Nicholas arena on April 16, 1951; in Box 217, "Civil Rights—general" Folder, UAWD65/WAG 006.

66. *CD,* 4/3/51, 20; Jim Hudson Jones, "Harlem's Vigorous New Variety Show," *DW,* 4/26/51, CNA clippings file, SCRBC; Geoffrey Jacques, "Cubop! Afro-Cuban music and Mid-Twentieth-Century American Culture," in *Between Race and Empire: African-Americans and Cubans Before the Cuban Revolution,* ed. Lisa

Brock and Digna Castañeda Fuertes (Philadelphia: Temple University Press, 1991), 255; Lewis Finke, "Gossip of the Rialto," *NYT*, 2/11/51, 93.

67. Belafonte, *My Song*, 93; Shaw, *Belafonte*, 77–88; Work, "Reminiscence," 2007; *Lowell Sun*, 2/25/51, 55; Three Deuces, "Record Reviews," *Metronome* (April 1951): 26. Belafonte's version of "Venezuela" followed recordings by Burl Ives in 1949 and Richard Dyer Benner in 1946; the song was written in 1918 by American ballad singer John Jacob Niles, inspired by Barbados sailors in Marseilles singing a song about a girl they had met in Venezuela.

68. Shaw, *Belafonte*, 85; "Music Inn: Chronological Notes," http://musicinnfilm.net/history/chronology.html; accessed August 29, 2011; http://www.musicinn.org/history-of-the-music-inn.html; accessed March 24, 2012; John Gennari, *Blowin' Hot and Cool: Jazz and Its Critics* (Chicago: University of Chicago Press, 2006), 216–218; Bill Coss, "The Weavers: These Modern Folk-Singers Speak Up for Jazz," *Metronome* (October 1951): 14.

69. Rollins officially became Belafonte's agent in December 1951, according to the publicity in his later lawsuit: Alfred Albelli and Harry Schlegel, "Suit Charges Singer Belafonte Switched Agents in Mid-Dream," *NYDN*, 9/20/55; Shaw, *Belafonte*, 78, 86–87; Belafonte, *My Song*, 96–97; Garren, "William Attaway," *Dictionary of Literary Biography*, Vol. 76, 4–6.

70. Shaw, *Belafonte*, 86.

71. Max Gordon, *Live at the Village Vanguard* (New York: St. Martin's Press, 1980), 86–89; Gilbert Millstein "O Tempora O Vanguard," *NYT Magazine*, 1/16/57; Shaw, *Belafonte*, 92.

72. Shaw, *Belafonte*, 91; Work, "Reminiscence" (2007).

73. Dorothy O'Leary, "Regarding Miss Jo Stafford," *NYT*, 1/7/48, 11; Millstein, "Very Good Night," *NYT*, 10/15/50, 21 (versions in "pop, race, hill-billy and ballad style"); Wald, *Alternative History*, 159; Cohen, *Rainbow Quest*, 67–92.

74. "Going on about Town, 10/27/51, 8; "New Acts" [Jose.] *VAR*, 10/31/51; "Belafonte in a New Role," *Down Beat*, 11/16/51; Barry Ulanov, "In Person: Harry Belafonte," *Metronome* (January 1952): 17. For examples of syndicated columns, see Dorothy Kilgallen, "Voice of Broadway," *Mansfield (Ohio) News Journal*, 11/20/51; "open door" comment in Mark Barron, "Broadway: Harry Belafonte, New Folk Singer," *Denton (TX) Record Chronicle*, 11/22/51, 4, and *Daily Sun* (Corsicana, TX), 12/1/51, 4.

75. *Counterattack*, 11/30/51.

76. Wald, *Josh White*, 150–152, 158–161; "New Acts," *VAR*, 10/31/51, and Barron, "Broadway: Harry Belafonte, New Folk Singer."

77. Ulanov, "In Person," 17; Barron, "Broadway."

78. Ibid. When writing jazz criticism, "Ulanov tended to use the term 'primitive' as a synonym for 'folk,'" in Gennari, *Blowin' Hot and Cool*, 137–144.

79. Robin Kelley, "Place Is the Space." A popular Decca single of "Sly Mongoose," a Jamaican mento-jazz hybrid first recorded by Sam Manning, was credited by New York barrelhouse pianist and journalist Dan Burley as starting the calypso craze, "getting the topical folk song style" off the ground in 1939, although Burley noted that "calypso has been part of Harlem music since the days of Marcus Garvey"; "Dan Burley's Back Door Stuff," *NYAN*, 4/27/57, 13.

80. "Music: Calypso Boom," *Time*, 8/29/38; calypso music was featured in an essay in *Esquire* in September 1937, and in the *New Yorker*, 5/6/39; Wenzell Brown, "How Calypso Was Born," *Negro Digest* (June 1947): 52–59; Harvey R. Neptune, *Caliban and the Yankees: Trinidad and the United States Occupation* (Chapel Hill: University of North Carolina Press, 2007), 43–50, 129–157; Rohlehr, "Calypso Reinvents Itself," 215–217; Donald Hill, "'I am Happy Just to Be in This Sweet Land of Liberty': The New York City Calypso Craze of the 1930s and 1940s," in *Island Sounds in the Global City: Caribbean Popular Music and Identity in New York*, ed. Ray Allen and Lois Wilckin (New York: New York Folklore Society and Institute for Studies in American Music, 1998), 74–92. Opened in 1943, the Calypso restaurant on Macdougal Street in Greenwich Village became a meeting place for musicians, actors, writers, and progressive West Indians, including James Baldwin and C. L. R. James; Stan Weir and George Lipsitz, *Singlejack Solidarity* (Minneapolis: University of Minnesota Press, 2004), 3–16.

81. Hill, "I Am Happy," 87; Szwed, *Alan Lomax*, 226–227; Donald R. Hill and John H. Cowley, "Liner Notes" for rerelease of the recordings of the December 21, 1946, "Midnight Special Concert: Calypso at Midnight," Rounder Records, 1999. *Ebony* reported on Trinidad calypso in articles appearing July 1946, 39, and March 1947, 19–22. MacBeth the Great and the Calypso Serenaders played "Hold 'Em Joe" and "Man Smart, Woman Smarter" at a Monk concert in Harlem, 4/30/48: Robin Kelley, *Thelonious Monk*, (New York:

Free Press, 2009), 136–137. A version of "Hold 'Em Joe" had been recorded by Sam Manning in Trinidad in 1927; Louis Farrakhan also recorded this song under his Calypsonian name, the Charmer, in 1954. "Man Smart" was originally recorded by the Trinidadian calypsonian Norman Span, called King Radio, in New York for Decca in 1936; MacBeth recorded it in 1945 for Guild.

82. Maya Angelou had to fight to sing calypso in a folk set at a San Francisco nightclub in 1953; *Singing and Swinging and Getting Merry Like Christmas* (New York: Random House, 2009), 95–99. Trinidadian dancer and artist Geoffrey Holder described how British colonial values trivialized Trinidad folk arts; Jennifer Dunning, *Geoffrey Holder: A Life in Theater, Dance and Art* (New York: Harry N. Abrams, 2001), 32–34.

83. Shaw, *Belafonte*, 95–96; Work, "Reminiscence," 2007.

84. The cover of the convention program featured Langston Hughes's 1940 lament "You've taken my blues and gone," CNA clipping file, SRBC. In the poem, "Notes on Commercial Theater," the speaker comments, "you sing 'em on Broadway . . . and you fixed 'em, So they don't sound like me." Later in the poem he promises that ". . . someday somebody'll / Stand up and talk about me / And write about me / Black and beautiful / And sing about me . . . I reckon it'll be / Me Myself"; Rampersad, *Langston Hughes*, 380–381.

85. CNA clipping file, SCRBC; John Hudson Jones, "Evening in the Arts Stirs CNA Convention," *DW*, 1/31/52; "Cultural Festival in Celebration of Negro History Month," *Freedom* (February 1952): 8; Michael Anderson, "Lorraine Hansberry's Freedom Family," in *Red Activists and Black Freedom*, ed. David Levering Lewis, Michael H. Nash, and Daniel J. Leab (New York: Routledge, 2010), 95; *Freedom* (May 1952): 2.

86. Marcy Elias, "Folk Songs Pay Off for Harry Belafonte," *NYP*, 4/8/52.

87. Belafonte appeared on pop singer Peggy Lee's radio show "Dial Twisting," *San Mateo (CA) Times*, 1/1/52, 13; and on Don Ameche's revamped Musical Playhouse; *AA*, 2/2/52; "Blue Angel," *VAR*, 2/20/52, 53; 3/12/52, 53; 4/9/53, 60; *NYAN*, 3/1/52, 12; CNA clipping file, SCRBC; Kilgallen, "Kilgallen on Broadway," *Charlestown Gazette* (WV), 5/6/52, 12; "Radio and Television," *CD*, 6/14/52, 22.

88. Robert M. Lichtman and Ronald D. Cohen, *Deadly Farce: Harvey Matusow and the Informer System in the McCarthy Era* (Ur-

bana: University of Illinois Press, 2004), 21–60; Dunaway, *How Can I Keep*, 149–150, 185–188; Constance Jackson, *Red Hope? The Blacklisting of Hope Foye* (documentary film, 2012); Cohen, *Rainbow Quest*, 79–80; Smith, *Becoming Something*, 289–351.

89. Duberman, *Robeson*, 398–403, Robeson, Jr., *Undiscovered Paul Robeson*, 224.

90. The group of younger artists who accompanied Robeson at this time included Belafonte, Poitier, Ossie Davis, Julian Mayfield, and Leon Bibb; Ron Ramdin, *Paul Robeson: The Man and His Mission* (London: Peter Owen, 1987), 171. Coleman Young and Lonnie Wheeler, *Hard Stuff: The Autobiography of Coleman Young* (New York: Viking, 1994), 133.

91. Later Belafonte would frequently credit Robeson's guidance for adopting this strategy: "Get them to sing your song, and they'll want to know who you are"; Belafonte interview with Leonard Lopate, WNYC, 12/20/2011.

92. Smith, *Visions of Belonging*, 197–202; Donald Bogle, *Bright Boulevards, Bold Dreams: The Story of Black Hollywood* (New York: Ballantine, 2006), 287–293.

93. "MGM Starts Filming Vroman Pic," *LATr*, 8/8/52, 14. The writer Mary Elizabeth Vroman was born in the United States but raised partly in Antigua, and her story drew in part on her own experiences teaching in an Alabama black public school; E. B. Rea, "Teacher Novelist Proves What One Person can Do," *AA*, 11/22/52, 9; Edith Blicksilver, "Mary Elizabeth Vroman," *Dictionary of Literary Biography*, Vol. 33, 255–258.

94. Bob Thomas, "The Hollywood Scene" (syndicated column), *Cumberland (MD) Evening Times*, 8/26/52, 4; "'How They Run' Cited Gamble, but MGM Is Taking a Chance," *AA*, 9/27/52, 6.

95. Dandridge's letter of July 11, 1952, "clearing" and defending herself is reproduced in Bogle, *Dorothy Dandridge*, 221–222. Belafonte probably wrote a similar letter, noted in his exchange with *Counterattack* published 2/12/54. He described this defense in Victor Navasky, *Naming Names* (New York: Penguin, 1981), 192–193.

96. The photograph pictures Leigh with one arm around Belafonte and the other around her husband Curtis; *Ebony*, July 1953, also "Reunion in Hollywood," 26–30. Early 1950s Los Angeles segregation described in Bogle, *Bright Boulevard*, 275–277; Sidney Poitier, *This Life* (New York: Ballantine, 1980), 127; Davis and Dee, *With Ossie and Ruby*, 195.

97. Richard Griffith's review, *LAT*, 5/11/53; Harry Levette, "Sororities Cool over 'Bright Victory'[sic] Film," *AA* (ANP), 5/9/53; Richard A. Jackson, "This Viewer Liked 'Bright Road,'" *KCC*, and "Critics Divided Over 'Bright Road,'" *KCC* (ANP), both 5/15/53.

98. Shaw, *Belafonte*, 99–102; see also Kelley, *Thelonious Monk*; Bogle, *Dandridge*; James Gavin, *Stormy Weather: The Life of Lena Horne* (New York: Atria, 2010).

99. Hal Rothman, *Neon Metropolis: How Las Vegas Started the Twenty-first Century* (New York: Routledge, 2002), 40–42; Eugene P. Moehring, *Resort City in the Sunbelt: Las Vegas, 1930–2000* (Reno: University of Nevada Press, 2000), 177–183. Monte Kaye's friend Pete Kameron helped Belafonte and Millard Thomas get access to a motel room by introducing them to the Yiddish-speaking manager as "Latin"; Shaw, *Belafonte*, 100.

100. *Variety*, January 1953, cited by Shaw, *Belafonte*, 109; Kilgallen, "Voice of Broadway," *Pottstown (PA) Mercury*, 11/1/52, 4; Freeman, "Sharp or Square, They All Like Harry Belafonte's Art in Song," *Down Beat*, 5/6/53, 2; [nat.], "Caught in the Act," *Down Beat*, 11/4/53, 2; Shaw, *Belafonte*, 79–80. "Hava Nagila," a Zionist creation of the early twentieth century, had become a popular Jewish wedding song in the 1940s. Adding this to his repertoire, Belafonte was following a long tradition of black artists (Ethel Waters, Jules Bledsoe, Paul Robeson) singing Yiddish and Hebrew songs; see Jeffrey Melnick, *A Right to Sing the Blues: African Americans, Jews, and American Popular Song* (Cambridge, MA: Harvard University Press, 1999), 180–181. "Matilda" was first performed by Norman Span, King Radio, during Carnival in Trinidad in the 1930s, and recorded by him.

101. Tony Schwartz, *The Responsive Chord* (Garden City, NY: Anchor Press, 1973), xii. Schwartz recorded Belafonte 1/1/52; 5/11/52; 6/18/52 (performance at the Village Vanguard); 8/1/52; 9/19/52; 1/3/53; first appearance on Ed Sullivan 10/11/53; tapes in RSS/LOC. Belafonte credited Schwartz with helping him to master recording: "Technically all that is heard on record I have learned from Tony Schwartz"; recorded 9/19/52.

102. "Popular Singles," *Capital-Times*(Madison, WI), 9/12/52,4; "Belafonte in Pair Waxings," *CD*, 9/27/52, 23.

103. Robert DeCormier was singled out by *Counterattack* in February 1953; in March, Ruby Dee faced public censure after she spoke at a rally in support of clemency for the Rosenbergs, facing the death

penalty for allegedly passing atomic secrets to the Soviet Union; Davis and Dee, *With Ossie and Ruby,* 222–251; in April, Langston Hughes faced a HUAC hearing.

104. Wald, *Alternative History,* 172–173; Alan Nadel, *Television in Black and White America* (Lawrence: University of Kansas Press, 2004), 8. "Television," *Ebony,* June 1950, 23; Ed Sullivan, "Can TV Crack America's Color Line?"; *Ebony,* May 1951, 60–61; Gerald Nachman, *Right Here on Our Stage Tonight! Ed Sullivan's America* (Berkeley: University of California Press, 2009), 311–328; Navasky, *Naming Names,* 193.

105. Tony Schwartz tape of Sullivan and Belafonte's segment of *Toast of the Town,* October 11, 1953;RSS/LOC.

106. Anderson had been creating and producing spectacle on Broadway, for Ringling Brothers circuses, Billy Rose aquacades, movie-house stage shows, and nightclub shows since 1919; "Gilbert Millstein, "Anderson of 'Almanac,'" *NYT,* 1/24/54, X1; Brooks Atkinson, "First Night at the Theatre," *NYT,* 12/11/53, 42, "Almanac for 1954," *NYT,* 1/3/54, X1, and "Made with Music," *NYT,* 3/31/54, X1. Van Vechten photographed "Harry Belafonte in John Murray Anderson's Almanac," 2/18/54; 36 images in CVVPC; letter from "Harry" to "Carl," thanking him for the "pictures you sent me," 5/15/54, in "Letters in James Weldon Johnson–Van Vechten Box B-Be," CVVP.

107. Howard Taubman, "A Folk Singer's Style," *NYT,* 2/7/54, X7; "Audrey Hepburn Wins Stage Tony," *NYT,* 3/29/54, 23. Belafonte was the first black actor to win a Tony.

108. The Supreme Court announced its decision on 5/17/54; *Freedom* (August 1954): 1.

109. "Box Office Hits of 1953," *Billboard,* 12/19/53, 19.

110. Shaw, *Belafonte,* 118–120.

111. *Counterattack,* 1/8/54, 4; Navasky, *Naming Names,* 193; Belafonte described his negotiations with Sullivan in the documentary *Scandalize My Name: Stories from the Blacklist* (1998) and in *My Song,* 115–117.

112. *Counterattack,* 2/12/54, 3–4.

113. Belafonte, *My Song,* 118–120; "US Adds Twenty Groups to Subversive List," *NYT,* 7/22/54, 4. Rather than engage in lengthy and expensive court cases, many groups listed as "subversive" simply dissolved and disappeared rather than register and turn over membership lists to the Subversive Activities Control Board.

114. Arts Festival the week of 7/12/53, noted in *Musical Magazine/Musical Courier* 147–148:11. At the time Belafonte met Jay Richard Kennedy, he had created a very long-running and successful radio serial, *The Man Called X*, running from 1948 through 1952, had written the screenplay for a 1948 film called *To the Ends of the Earth*, reviewed favorably in *PM* (2/13/48, 20), and a well-received "inside Hollywood" novel, *Prince Bart*, (New York: Farrar, Straus and Young, 1953), reviewed in the *NYT*, 3/8/53, and 3/11/53. Janet Alterman Kennedy's research appeared in *Psychiatry* 115, no. 3 (August 1952): 313–327. In 1985, Belafonte recalled meeting them: "And by this time, this whole political thing is getting much more difficult and much more problematic. . . . I just went to her for some advice and the advice led to therapy and the therapy led to analysis . . . and maybe she could prevail on her husband to just help me with my financial problems . . . So I went to see him, and I told him about my life, and he wept at the desk, tears came to his eyes. I'll never forget it." TB/HB, 3/7/85.

115. TB/HB, 3/7/85.

116. Shaw, *Belafonte*, 139–140; Kilgallen, "Voice of Broadway: Broadway Bulletin Board," *Anderson [IN] Daily Bulletin*, 12/30/54.

117. Shaw, *Belafonte*, 125; "Splash with a Song," *Newsweek*, 3/9/54.

118. "Audrey Hepburn Wins Tony," *NYT*, 3/29/54, 23. Shaw quoted Belafonte as ambivalent about receiving an acting award for singing: "Instead of bringing me closer to the goal I was shooting for, I had the oppressive feeling that I might be doomed forever to go on as a singer"; *Belafonte*, 123.

119. Belafonte was cast nearly a month before Dandridge; "Preminger to Meg All-Colored Cast in 'Carmen Jones,'" *VAR*(d), 12/23/53; "To Film 'Carmen Jones' as Preminger Indie: Hammerstein Scripting," *VAR*(d), 3/3/54; Thomas M. Pryor, "Belafonte Signs to Star in Film," *NYT*, 4/30/54, 28; Bogle, *Dandridge*, 275.

120. "A Picture Finish," *NYSN*, 10/3/54, in *Carmen Jones* clipping file, SCRBC.

121. Belafonte quoted in Bogle, *Dandridge*, 278; author's telephone interview with Olga James, 9/26/2011.

122. Diahann Carroll and Ross Firestone, *Diahann!*," (Boston: Little Brown, 1986); 47; see similar comments by Brock Peters, interviewed in 2004, in Chris Fujiwara, *The World and Its Double:*

the Life and Work of Otto Preminger (New York: Faber and Faber, 2008), 166.

123. "On the 'Bright Road' of 'Carmen' and 'Joe,'" *NYT*, 10/30/54, X5.

124. "Of Local Origin," *NYT*, 11/9/54, 30; "'Carmen Jones' Threat to Box Offices in Most Cities It Has Played," *CD*, 12/4/54, 6. The film's budget was about $750,000, and it eventually made $9,812,000 in rentals; this is fairly close to the box office returns on initial costs for *On the Waterfront* (cost $910,000; rentals $9,600,000). *AA* hoped the box office success "will fling somewhat wider the gates of opportunity for colored entertainers;" 1/29/55.

125. "Hollywood's Newest Love Team," *Jet*, 9/30/54, as cited in Bogle, *Dandridge*, 298; Aline Mosby, "Film Censor Code Grows Up at Last," *Bakersfield Californian*, 1/17/55, 21; "Carmen Jones," *Cue*, 10/30/54; "New Films: Carmen Jones," *Newsweek*, 10/25/54; Bosley Crowther, "Negroes in a Film," *NYT*, 10/31/54; Ruth Waterbury, "Carmen Jones Tears Heart," *LAE*, 11/2/54; Bosley Crowther, "Screen in Review: Carmen Jones," *NYT*, 10/29/54; Juan Herron, "Carmen Jones Outdoes Nature, Bizet, and All Reason," *LATr*, 11/12/54, 17c.

126. Nineteen fifty-four tour plans in Thomas M. Pryor, "Universal Buys Novel by Goertz," *NYT*, 7/5/54, 6; also elaborated more fully in *VAR*, 7/7/54, 57.

127. Shari Belafonte was born 9/22/54: Shaw, *Belafonte*, 131–133, 142; "Tele Follow Up Comment," *VAR*, 9/29/54, 30; Eleanor Harris, "The Stormy Success of Harry Belafonte," *Redbook*, May 1958, 104.

128. The film opened in NYC on 10/28/54. "Dorothy D, Pearl Stars of Show There," *AA*, 11/6/54, 7.

129. These included "Mark Twain," "Scarlet Ribbons," Lead Belly's "Sylvie," the spiritual "Take My Mother Home," "Matilda," and the New Orleans anthem, "When the Saints Come Marching In"; some of these would appear on his second album, *Belafonte*; Helen Gould, "Unusual Musical: Director of '3 for Tonight' Finds his Offering Hard to Classify," *NYT*, 4/3/55, X3.

130. "Singer Belafonte 'Sees' Bias Via Dirty Glasses," *CD*, 4/23/55, 6; Belafonte [guest columnist for Dorothy Kilgallen], "The Voice of Broadway: Giant Strides for U.S. Negro," *NYJA*, 5/31/55, 13; Belafonte, *My Song*, 129–135. The Champions signed on to this tour

before Belafonte: "Champions Signed," *Billboard*, 5/29/54, 25; Louis Calta, "Harry Belafonte to Star in Musical," *NYT*, 9/18/54.

131. Helen Gould, "Unusual Musical"; Kerr, "'3 for Tonight,'" *NYTr*, 4/7/55; Atkinson, "Theatre: Song and Dance Diversion," *NYT*, 4/7/55.

132. "Plans for 'Negro Anthology'" in Sol Padlibsky, "Of All Things," *Charleston (WV) Daily Mail*, 12/31/54, 7.

133. Belafonte's retrospective description of his psychic state in Harris, "Stormy Success," 104; similar comments in Gelman, "Profile-I," *NYP*, 4/15/57.

CHAPTER THREE

1. Horace R. Cayton, *Long Old Road: An Autobiography* (Seattle, University of Washington Press, 1972), 368–369.

2. Cayton, *Long Road*, 368–369; Brenda Gayle Plummer, *Rising Wind: Black Americans and U.S. Foreign Affairs, 1935–1960* (Chapel Hill: University of North Carolina Press, 1996); Mary Dudziak, *Cold War Civil Rights: Race and the Image of American Democracy* (Princeton, NJ: Princeton University Press, 2000).

3. Gene Roberts and Hank Klibanoff, *The Race Beat: The Press, the Civil Rights Struggle, and the Awakening of a Nation* (New York: Knopf, 2006); J. Fred MacDonald, *Don't Touch That Dial! Radio Programming in American Life, 1920–1960* (Chicago: Nelson Hall, 1979); Michele Hilmes, *Radio Voices: American Broadcasting, 1922–1952* (Minneapolis: University of Minnesota Press, 1997); Steve Classen, *Watching Jim Crow: The Struggle Over Mississippi TV, 1955–1969* (Durham, NC: Duke University Press, 2004).

4. Montgomery boycott described in Taylor Branch, *Parting the Waters: America in the King Years, 1954–1963* (New York: Simon and Schuster, 1988), 143–205.

5. Barbara Ransby, *Ella Baker and the Black Freedom Movement* (Chapel Hill: University of North Carolina Press, 2003), 162–167; John D'Emilio, *Lost Prophet: the Life and Times of Bayard Rustin* (Chicago: University of Chicago Press, 2004), 224–225. Other people in the coalition included District 65 officer Cleve Robinson and Reverend Thomas Kilgore, the minister at Baker's Harlem church, Friendship Baptist.

6. Hansberry, "Destruction of a Heritage"; for Hansberry's thinking on these questions, see *Visions*, 290–322. For an overview

of black writers' concerns in this period, see Lawrence P. Jackson, *The Indignant Generation: A Narrative History of African American Writers and Criticism, 1934–1960* (Princeton, NJ: Princeton University Press, 2011), 379–509. On renewed pressures for respectability, see Thaddeus Russell, "The Color of Discipline: Civil Rights and Black Sexuality," *American Quarterly* 60, no. 1 (March 2008): 101–128.

7. Dorothy Masters, "The Belafonte Story: $70 Weekly to $7,000," *NYSN*, 5/1/55.

8. Brian Ward, *Just My Soul Responding: Rhythm and Blues, Black Consciousness and Race Relations* (Berkeley: University of California Press, 1998), 2.

9. "Lead Man Holler," cover story in *Time*, 3/2/59, 40.

10. Dave McAleer, *Hit Singles: Top Twenty Charts from 1954 to the Present* (San Francisco: Backbeat, 2000), 34–44; Wald, *Alternative History*, 184–198.

11. Wald, *Alternative History*, 195. Belafonte would eventually have six gold albums (representing one million sales) during the period from 1956 to 1961.

12. "Kids Dig Pop Vocals Most But Don't Always Buy Them," *Billboard*, 12/15/56, 31; Wald, *Alternative History*, 182–183; "Presley loses Out to Harry Belafonte in Marquette Student Union," *Ogden (UT) Standard Examiner*, 12/10/56, 2.

13. Belafonte, "The Voice of Broadway: Giant Strides of U.S. Negro," *NYJA*, 5/31/55, 13.

14. Ross Parmenter, "Folk Song Collecting in the Field," *NYT*, 11/2/52, X39; Sigmund Spaeth, "Folk Music to the Fore," *Theatre Arts* (July 1953): 10–11; Oscar Brand, "The Authentic Version," *Saturday Review*, 8/29/53, 54; Duncan Emrich, "Letter in Response to 'the Authentic Version,'" *SR*, 11/28/53, 96–97; Cohen, *Rainbow Quest*, 87–92.

15. Charles Edward Smith, "Folk Music, the Roots of Jazz," *Saturday Review* 7/29/50, 35ff., and his liner notes for the Folkways series of jazz recordings in the early 1950s, especially on *Jazz: Volume 1: The South* (1950), and the jazz seminars at the Music Inn, Ch. 2, n68. Interviewed in *Down Beat*, Belafonte emphasized the folk roots of jazz: Dom Cerulli, "Belafonte: the Responsibility of the Artist," 3/6/57, 18. See also Monson, *Freedom Sounds*, and Gennari, *Blowin' Hot and Cool*.

16. See Smith's liner notes and the essays collected to accom-

pany the 1997 Smithsonian reissue of *The Anthology of American Folk Music*; Christopher A. Waterman, "Race Music: Bo Chatmon, 'Corrine, Corrina,' and the Excluded Middle," in *Music and the Racial Imagination*, ed. Ronald Radano and Philip V. Bohlman (Chicago: University of Chicago Press, 2000), 167–205.

17. Mark Barron, "Broadway: Harry Belafonte, New Folk Singer, Reminds One of Burl Ives, Others," *Fitchburg (MA) Sentinel*, 11/16/51, 6; press release published as John Callaghan, "Words and Music" *Long Beach (CA) Telegram*, 10/1/53, 47; also John Ricche, "Words and Music," *Altoona (PA) Mirror*, 10/5/53, 5.

18. Scott quoted by Shaw, *Belafonte*, 152; Scott's comments on Belafonte in Dom Cerulli, "Belafonte: Where Do We Go From Here?," *Down Beat*, 4/4/57, 17.

19. Arnold Shaw's "unauthorized" 1960 star biography would further protect Belafonte by carefully providing an extensive account of Belafonte's life and career cleansed of any clues that could tie him to the postwar Left. Born Arnold Shukatoff, and employed in the English department at City College in the 1930s, he had been one of the forty radical and union activist faculty and administrators fired in 1942 after investigations by the New York state legislature's anticommunist Rapp-Coudert Committee. By 1944, Shaw had taken his new name and begun a new career in the music publishing industry; Ronald Cohen, "Arnold Shaw," *American National Biography*, vol. 19 (New York: Oxford University Press, 1999), 737–738.

20. Don Freeman, "Sharp or Square, They All like Harry Belafonte's Art in Song," *Down Beat*, May 1953, 2; Brooks Atkinson praised Belafonte's performance in *3 for Tonight* for "not playing footsie with the audience" in "Theatre: Song and Dance Diversion," *NYT*, 4/7/55.

21. Freeman, "Sharp or Square," 2; Brooks Atkinson, "Almanac for 1954," *NYT*, 1/3/54, X1; Howard Taubman, "A Folk Singer's Style: Personality and Integrity Worth More Than Cultivated Voice to Belafonte," *NYT*, 2/7/54, X7; B.C. [Bill Coss], "Harry," *Metronome*, June 1954, 20; Jim Kerins, "The Wax Works," *Monmouth College (IL) Oracle*, 5/14/55, 2.

22. Taubman, "A Folk Singer's Style."

23. Atkinson, "3 for Tonight"; still Gibbs termed Belafonte as "an artist of great and growing consequence"; Wolcott Gibbs, "The Theatre: A Matter of Definition," *New Yorker*, 4/16/1955, 74; Walter

Kerr's praise, "This young man is an artist" in "Theatre: '3 for Tonight,'" *NYTr*, 4/7/55.

24. Robert Cantwell explored the folk song movement as a liminal realm in *When We Were Good: The Folk Revival* (Cambridge, MA: Harvard University Press, 1996), esp. 142–149; see also Burgie, *Day-O!!!!*; Richie Havens with Steve Davidowitz, *They Can't Hide Us Anymore* (New York: Spike, 1999); Len Chandler's interview in Denise Sullivan, *Keep on Pushing: Black Power Music from Blues to Hip Hop* (Chicago: Lawrence Hill Books, 2011), and Odetta, interviewed by Tony Schwartz, 2/1/52, and by Studs Terkel, in 1956 and 9/4/57, in RSS/LOC.

25. Bob Reisman, *I Feel So Good: The Life and Times of Big Bill Broonzy* (Chicago: University of Chicago Press, 2011) 124–138, 139–166, 180–182.

26. Sol Padlibsky, "Of All things," *Charleston (WV) Daily Mail*, 1/11/55, 18; Emily Beisner, "In Hollywood; Singer Laments 'Pathetic' Today's Lack of Heroes," *El Paso (TX) Herald Post*, 8/17/55, 24; Jay Rogers, "Just Roving; Ballad Lands Almost Gone," *Denton (TX) Record Chronicle*, 12/18/55, 17; Belafonte, "Folk Singer Gathers Music from Everywhere," in Aline Mosby's UP syndicated column, *Nevada State Journal*, 9/8/56, 5.

27. Belafonte, "Folk Singer Gathers Music from Everywhere"; Faye Emerson, "Belafonte Favors Show on U.S. Negro History," *Albuquerque (NM) Tribune*, 6/22/55, 11; Belafonte, "My Repertory Must Have Roots," as told to Nat Hentoff, *HiFi/Stereo Review* 2 (January 1959): 42–43.

28. Dorothy Kilgallen, "Around New York," *Mansfield (OH) News Journal*, 2/3/55, 23; Sidney Skolsky, "Hollywood Is My Beat," *NYP*, 8/19/56. By 1958, Belafonte's trademark costume no longer registered as folk-singing garb. When Columbia University classical music student Len Chandler was invited by poet Hugh Romney to sing folk music with him at the Gaslight on MacDougal Street, Chandler planned to approximate Belafonte's costume until Romney advised him that the now-preferred folk outfit consisted of black jeans, a blue chambray work shirt, and a red bandana: author's interview with Len Chandler, 9/15/2011.

29. Alfred Duckett, "Backstage with Harry Belafonte: Belafonte Tells Ideas about Race," *CD*, 8/23/56, 8; Shaw, *Belafonte*, 156.

30. For example, *LATr*, 6/11/54, 2; *AA*, 1/29/55; "Harry Belafonte

Gets Own TV Hit," *CD*, 10/8/55, 6; Al Munroe, "Swinging the News," *CD*, 11/19/55.

31. According to a 1957 account, black waiters found him in the lobby and brought him back to the stage, Gelman, "Post Profile: Belafonte," *NYP*, 4/15/57; in *My Song*, Belafonte wrote that Hilton hotels executive Muriel Abbott retrieved him and confronted the maître d', 143–144.

32. Shaw, *Belafonte*, 150–158, 167–169. In *My Song*, 108–109, Belafonte dated the swimming pool/Thunderbird desegregation in 1952, but the Scotts were traveling and working with him in the summer and fall of 1955.

33. "He's Brother Harry Belafonte Now," *Hotel*, 11/7/55; *DW*, 11/22/55. The former president of Local 6, Charles Collins was an important labor radical and antiracist activist in New York City; Biondi, *To Stand and Fight*, 147–148. Belafonte later explained that the person who booked him to perform at the Waldorf hired many black, Hispanic, and Asian waiters at the same time: *My Song*, 140.

34. Castleman and Podrazik, *Watching TV*, 63; Smith, *Visions of Belonging*, 256–258. O'Neal quoted in Estelle Edmerson for her master's thesis, "A descriptive Study of the American Negro in U.S. Professional Radio, 1922–1953" (UCLA, 1954), 389. Julian Bond described "family alerts" as common practice in the 1950s in *Sing Your Song* (2011); Patricia Turner remembered them in the early 1960s in *Ceramic Uncles and Celluloid Mammies: Black Images and Their Influences on Culture* (1992; repr., Charlottesville: University of Virginia Press, 2002), xi-xiv.

35. Kinescope of this episode of *Cavalcade of Stars*, PCM/NYC. Belafonte sang "Hold 'Em Joe" in *John Murray Anderson's Almanac*, recorded it as an RCA single in January 1954, and sang it on his third appearance on Ed Sullivan's television show, 9/26/54. The song was also recorded in the early 1950s by Louis Farrakhan, then a Calypsonian.

36. *Counterattack*, 11/30/51.

37. Belafonte appeared on *Toast of the Town*, 10/11/53; 1/17/54; 9/26/54; 4/24/55; Nachman, *Ed Sullivan's America*; Wald, *An Alternative History*, 172–173.

38. Hy Gardner, "The Editor's Corner," *NYHTr TV and Radio Magazine*, 9/18/55, back cover; Steve Allen "Talent Is Color Blind: NBC TV Humorist Tells Why He Uses Many Negro Performers," *Eb-*

ony, September 1955, 41–49; Emerson, "Belafonte Favors Show on U.S. Negro History," *Albuquerque (NM) Tribune,* 6/22/55, 11.

39. Emerson, "Belafonte Favors."

40. Later Belafonte recalled that Attaway recommended Burgie as "the black Alan Lomax, a walking library of songs from the islands," *My Song,* 155.

41. Burgie, *Day-O!!!,* 111–115, 123–128, 134–136, 165–180; Escott, *Island,* 30; Music Inn chronology; author's interviews with Burgie, 11/4/2011 and 4/3/2012. On the South Side Community Arts Center, see Mullen, *Popular Fronts,* 75–105. Lord Burgess and his Calypso Serenaders recorded *Folk Songs of Haiti, Jamaica and Trinidad* for Stinson in 1954. Burgie signed up with the left-wing booking agency People's Artists in 1954 and 1955; in the early months of 1955 he performed at a Robeson concert in Chicago; 172–177. On People's Artists, see Cohen, *Rainbow Quest,* 42–45, 78, 104.

42. William Ewald, "Belafonte Series to Start Sunday," *Racine (WI) Journal Times,* 10/1/55, 8: "Harry Belafonte Gets Own TV Hit," *CD,* 10/8/55, 6. "Day De Light" was a Jamaican work song originating among the men loading the banana boats on the Kingston docks, collected and published in 1952, recorded on a small British label by a West Indian actor in 1954, and at some point in the early 1950s by a Jamaican close harmony group, the Frats Quinte; Escott, *Island,* 31. Belafonte recorded his version two weeks after the television performance, but RCA did not release it as a single until after a different version of "Banana Boat Song" by the Tarriers, an interracial folk group, hit on the pop charts. On "Winner by decision," see Bogle, *Prime Time Blues,* 68.

43. Lawrence Witte, "TV-Radio News Bits," *Evening Independent* (Massillon, OH), 9/21/55, 14.

44. Escott, *Island,* 31.

45. Wald, *Alternative History,* 195. See also "Belafonte Album, Best Seller, Aids Latest Acclaim," *CD,* 9/29/56, 14, which noted that *Calypso* and *Belafonte* were among the Top 10 best-selling albums of the season, ahead of the *King and I* soundtrack, and the seventh most played album by disc jockeys.

46. Mercer, "TV Displays Timidity toward Negro, Is View," *Racine (WI) Journal Times,* 10/5/55, 21. In actuality, writer Robert Alan Aurthur, struck by Poitier's resemblance to a black West Indian longshoremen he had known, had written the part specifi-

cally for him. The program staff took advantage of this being the final broadcast for Philco-Goodyear Playhouse to boldly defy network racial and censorship practices by casting Poitier for a supposedly racially unmarked character without requiring him to sign a loyalty statement or renounce Robeson. Southern defenders of segregation protested, but the show was already off the air; Smith, *Visions,* 267–273.

47. Belafonte quoted in Mercer, "TV Displays Timidity."

48. Belafonte, "The Negro Star in Television," *NYHTr TV and Radio Magazine,* 6/24/56.

49. "No Dough-Re-Mi Man," *NYDN,* 6/8/58; Sid Shalit, "TV/Radio What's On: Singer Works for $500 After Turning Down 45Gs," *NYDN,* 8/6/57.

50. Gelman, "Profile-I and IV," *NYP,* 4/15/57, 4/18/57.

51. Gelman, "Profile-IV." Even when in New York, Belafonte stayed elsewhere, often with Bill Attaway; Shaw, *Belafonte,* 177. Rumors of marital discord appeared in *NYAN,* 2/12/55 cited by Shaw, *Belafonte,* 142; in Walter Winchell, "On Broadway," *Humboldt Standard* (Eureka, CA), 6/28/55, 4, with a disavowal from Belafonte's press agent cited in Winchell's column, *Charleston (WV) Daily News,* 7/10/55, 6; Al Munroe, "Swinging the News,"*CD,*11/19/55; Harry Levette, "Gossip of the Movie Lot," (ANP), *ADW,* 7/24/56, 4; Betty Granger "Conversation Pieces," *NYAN,* 12/22/56, 10.

52. "Belafonte Boom," *Look,* 8/21/1956.

53. Their financial involvement began in May 1954; Kennedy's share of ownership in Belafonte's royalties increased in May and June 1955; Al Hall, "Belafonte, Ex-Agent in Court Fight," *NYAN,* 4/20/57, 1, 35. Shaw, *Belafonte,* 161–167; Belafonte, *My Song,* 135–139; "Belafonte's Best Year: Singer's Popularity and Income Soar" and "Millionaire Steers Folk Singer to Fame," both in *Ebony,* March 1956, 56–58, 58–59; Eleanor Harris, "The Stormy Success of Harry Belafonte," *Redbook,* May 1958, 104.

54. "Never a Judas to My People, Belafonte Says," *ADW,* 12/23/55, 4.

55. *NYT* coverage of Kennedy cited in Ch. 2, n114. In May 1956, Belafonte described their relationship: "With great persuasion, I got Kennedy to take over my career, mainly from the economic point of view, because he's an economic advisor . . . he also became my artistic advisor. He'd written a screenplay . . . which got all the awards, and he had a radio series, . . . got all the awards, and he also . . . wrote a

best seller called *Prince Bart*." Etta Moten interview with Belafonte, on WMAQ (NBC) in Chicago [n.d., ca. May 1956], MIRS, SCRBC.

56. EVW, "Music: Belafonte Will Star in 'Sing, Man, Sing,'" *Syracuse (NY) Herald American*, 3/25/56, 24.

57. Lincoln Haynes, "Theater," *Pasadena (CA) Independent*, 12/22/55, 28; Special *Sing, Man, Sing* program, containing complete words of songs and script, Paramount Theater, Toledo, Ohio.

58. Jacob Deschin, "'Family of Man': Museum of Modern Art Prepares Global Collection for January Opening," *NYT*, 1/12/54, X19. See also Deschin's review, "'Family of Man,'" *NYT*, 1/30/55, X17. Some critics expressed concern about the exhibit's sentimentality and universalizing erasure of history; "Symposium: the Family of Man," *Aperture* 3, no. 2 (1955): 8–27; Roland Barthes, "The Great Family of Man," in *Mythologies* (1957; repr., New York: Hill and Wang, 1972), 100–103. See also Eric Sandeen, *Picturing an Exhibition: The Family of Man and 1950s America* (Albuquerque: University of New Mexico Press, 1995); Rob Kroes, *Photographic Memories: Private Pictures, Public Images, and American History* (Hanover, NH: University Press of New England, 2007), 120–134.

59. Leon Levinstein's warm and intimate portrait of motherhood depicting a delighted black mother cuddling an adoring child on a picnic blanket accompanied the *NYT* coverage of the exhibit, 1/12/54, X19; the Urban League honored the exhibit: "Cited by Urban League," *NYT*, 5/1/55, 78. DeCarava quoted in Peter Gelassi, *Roy DeCarava, A Retrospective* (New York, Museum of Modern Art, 1996), 19; Max Kozloff, et al., *New York: Capital of Photography* (New Haven, CT: Yale University Press, 2002), 55. Belafonte's inscription to William Attaway, August 1955, on a copy of the exhibit catalogue expressed his identification with the exhibit: "Perhaps, however, through my art, whatever strong, positive things you may see, know that you have, through your understanding, your strength, and your great kindness contributed to that art and therefore to me and therefore to 'The Family of Man' [signed] your devoted brother, Harry"; Shaw, *Belafonte*, 159. Belafonte's son David framed his father's divided loyalties between his political commitments and his domestic life using the exhibit title: "You had two families, us, and the family of man, [and you were] running back and forth between the two like a maniac"; *Sing Your Song* (2011).

60. These lines appear in a poem called "Timesweep," written by Sandburg, identified for me with the help of Philip Chassler and Ste-

phen J. Whitfield. Richard L. Coe, "One More on the Aisle: Belafonte IS This Revue," *WPTH*, 4/25/56, 22.

61. Shaw, *Belafonte*, 173; Seymour Raven, "Bright Belafonte Walks into Trap in This Musical," *CTr*, 5/15/56, B5; Special *Sing, Man, Sing* program.

62. *CDD* favorable review 5/15/56, 15; majority negative opinion reported in "'Mr. Wonderful,' 'Sing, Man, Sing' Defying Critics," 5/21/56, 22; in *CDD*, "'Sing Man' Is Uncertain As to Its Future," 5/22/56, 19; Lee Blackwell's praise in "Off the Record," 5/28/56, 10. Hughes, "Notes on Commercial Theater," cited by Arnold Rampersad, *Langston Hughes*, vol. 1, 380–381.

63. Ralph Matthews, "Faces Big Decision: Will Belafonte Dare Take His Mixed Show South?," *CCP*, 4/28/56, 1C. The ANP wire service article, *LAS*, 5/24/56, A17, described the finale: "'I don't want a handout, I just want a hand,' says Belafonte as a beggar. 'Get lost, brother,' snaps the other man. 'We're all lost,' cries a deep voice in the background, then the members of the interracial company get hep to the solution and clasp hands and slap shoulders like mad."

64. "Harry Belafonte Brilliant," *CCP*, 4/7/56, 9C; Coe, "Belafonte IS This Revue"; Pitts, "Belafonte Show," *PC*, 4/25/1956, A35; Belafonte, *My Song*, 152–153; Raven, "Bright Belafonte,"*CTr*, 5/15/56, B5; Herb Lyon, "Town Ticker," *CTr*, 5/17/56, B2.

65. Belafonte, *My Song*, 152–153, 160–161.

66. Belafonte, *My Song*, 159–162; David J. Garrow, *The FBI and Martin Luther King, Jr.: From "Solo" to Memphis* (New York: Norton, 1981), 30–31.

67. David Garrow interviewed Jay Richard Kennedy because of his connection to Stanley Levison, King's trusted associate whose left-wing past was used to justify FBI surveillance of King; *The FBI and Martin Luther King*, 29–34, 139–144. The CIA memos quoted by Garrow were dated 6/9/, 7/7, and 7/21/65, 141–143. Belafonte's FBI file contained repeated mention of Kennedy, although conflicting dates for the years when Kennedy was directly reporting to the FBI, and some questions about how much they valued his information; *My Song*, 160–162; 282–284. Belafonte and Levison did not discover their shared connection to Janet Alterman Kennedy until 1963, *My Song*, 282–282.

68. Through the summer of 1956, Belafonte continued to promote "the strength and integrity of the Belafonte-Kennedy team"

and to dismiss the criticism of *Sing, Man, Sing* as "dislike for the mixed cast and the clear message of the show," in the "Backstage with Belafonte" *CDD* series, 8/21–23/56. News of the ended partnership was in the Broadway columns by the end of October, 1956; see Kilgallen, "Around New York," *Mansfield (OH) News Journal*, 10/23/56, 4; Earl Wilson, *Hammond (IN) Times*, 10/25/56, 17; Al Hall, "Belafonte, Ex-Agent in Court Fight," *NYAN*, 4/20/57, 1, 35; Shaw, *Belafonte*, 165–167.

69. "Music: Stadium Record," *NYT*, 6/29/56, 17; Harriet Johnson, "Words and Music: Belafonte Breaks Stadium Record," *NYP*, 6/29/56. His playlist included "John Henry," "Mark Twain," "Jamaica Farewell," "Water Boy," "Hava Nagila" (an Israeli folk song sung in Hebrew), "Merci Bon Dieu" (a Haitian Creole Harvest Prayer), the ballads "Shenandoah" and "Scarlet Ribbons," and various calypsos, including "Man Smart," "Man Piaba," "Matilda," "Love, Love, Alone"; "He's Shocking the World: $1 Million a Year," *AA*, 12/29/56, 27.

70. "Who Will Be Harry Belafonte's Next Wife?," *Jet*, 1/17/57, 60–62; "Belafonte's Wife Off to Reno," *AA*, 1/19/57, 7.

71. "Harry Belafonte Divorced," (UPI); *NYT*, 3/1/57, 14; "Mrs. Belafonte Wins Divorce from Singer," *NYAN*, 3/9/57, 12; Betty Granger, "Belafonte Settlement: Maggie Got Everything but Harry in Divorce," *NYAN*, 4/6/57, 1.

72. VeVe Clark, "An Anthropological Band of Beings: An Interview with Julie Robinson Belafonte," in *Kaiso!*, 364–381; Constance Valis Hill, "Katherine Dunham's *Southland*: Protest in the Face of Repression," *Dance Research Journal* 26, no. 2 (Fall 1994): 1–10. Belafonte highlighted Robinson's "interest in anthropology, in the struggle of the Negro people, in folk dancing and folk culture"; Harris, "Stormy Success," 104; see also Belafonte, *My Song*, 126.

73. Robinson taught at the Phillips Fort dance studio in 1955, started by two former Dunham teacher-dancers after the Dunham school closed; Shaw, *Belafonte*, 173; Agnes Murphy, "At Home with Mrs. Harry Belafonte" [n.d., but probably *NYDN*, ca. Dec. 1959], Belafonte clipping file, SCRBC; Beverly Solochek, "At Home with Julie Belafonte," *NYP*, 7/27/70, 37.

74. Earl Wilson, "Around New York," *Hammond (IN) Times*, 10/25/56, 17; Kilgallen, "Voice of Broadway," *Weirton (WV) Daily Times*, 10/31/56, 16. Belafonte's new management structure in "Be-

lafonte Becomes 'Big Business,'" *Ebony*, February 1958, 17–24; Harris, "Stormy Success," 105; Emily Coleman, "Organization Man Named Belafonte," *NYT*, 12/13/59; SM 35, 37–38, 40, 42.

75. TB/HB, 3/6/85.

76. Belafonte recalled King's approach to him as "Look, I know of your commitment to the struggle. You have been outspoken," TB/HB, 3/6/85.

77. Ward, *Just My Soul*, 102–103. Belafonte's appearances on southern stages with Marge Champion in 1954 did not generate this kind of response.

78. *AA*, 4/21/56, 6, cited by Ward, *Just My Soul*, 130.

79. According to the *AA*'s coverage, Cole's immediate response *was* to quit the tour: "I'm not going through with the rest of my tour. You can put that in the papers. I'm through with the South." But he was talked out of that stance: "Cole had changed his plans after talking with his manager, Bob Schwartz, and would complete his present tour": Emory Jackson, "Attack Puzzles Nat King Cole," 4/21/56, 6.

80. *CD*, 4/21/56, 10, cited by Ward, *Just My Soul*, 131; Praise for musicians Duke Ellington, Benny Goodman, Stan Kenton, Lena Horne, Dorothy Dandridge, and Eartha Kitt for refusing to play "Dixie dance and concert halls"; "Nice Guy Victim; Other Nice Guys Avoid Challenge," *CD*, 4/21/56, 15.

81. "Cole Leaves Us Cold!," *NYAN*, 4/21/56, 1, 25.

82. Milton Mallory, "Sidewalk Interviews," *NYAN*, 4/21/56, 9.

83. Editorial in *Carolina Times*, 4/21/56, 1, cited by Ward, *Just My Soul*, 133–134; "King Cole Now NAACP Life Member, *NYAN*, 4/28/56, 1, 26; Cyd Reid, "Mrs. Nat Says King 'Appeased' NAACP with $500," *NYAN*, 5/5/56, 1, 24.

84. "Belafonte's Troubles Piling Up!," *PC*, 5/5/56, 12; "Probe Police Investigation with Washington Show," *ADW*, 5/8/56, 2; "Suggested Cast Changes May Void 'Sing, Man, Sing' for Air: Ask Belafonte, All Sepia Aid on Air Starrer," *CDD*, 5/28/56, 19.

85. "Through with Pacifier, Says Abernathy at Rally," *CDD*, 5/28/56, 5. Mahalia Jackson and Thomas A. Dorsey and his Celestian Gospel Trio performed for the two thousand attending the 5/25/56 gathering.

86. Excerpts from Khrushchev's speech to the Twentieth Congress of the Soviet Communist Party appeared in the *NYT*, 2/16/56, 10; "The World: Russia's New Course Attack Stalin Impact of Meet-

ings," *NYT*, 2/26/56, E1; Schrecker, *Many Are the Crimes*, 15–20; D'Emilio, *Lost Prophet*, 31–38; 250–278; Ransby, *Ella Baker*, 148–195; Branch, *Parting the Waters*, 208–212; *Climbin' Jacob's Ladder: The Black Freedom Movement Writings of Jack O'Dell*, ed. Nikhil Singh (Berkeley: University of California Press, 2010), 27.

87. Later, Belafonte obliquely would refer to these connections in "Belafonte Hits 'Escapist' Show Bizites; Asks More Political Action, Less Pools," *VAR*, 8/10/60, 48–49; "Artists Should Not Dodge Issues, Belafonte Declares," *VAR*(d), 8/20/60, 15.

88. "Civil Rights Rally Slated for Garden," *AA*, 5/12/56, 17; "Civil Rights Lag Scored at Rally," *NYT*, 5/25/56, 8; D'Emilio, *Lost Prophet*, 240. Daniel Levine identified Belafonte as singing at this rally, but I was not able to find confirmation; in Levine, *Bayard Rustin and the Civil Rights Movement* (New Brunswick, NJ: Rutgers University Press, 2000), 89–90.

89. "Belafonte on Program for Montgomery," *NYAN*, 12/1/56, 12; Ransby, *Ella Baker*, 167. Belafonte contributed his performance and paid some of the expenses of putting on the event, with all the advertising paid for by Levison, TB/HB, 3/6/85.

90. Alfred Duckett, "Backstage with Belafonte: Speaks Language of Great and Humble," *CDD*, 8/21/56, 7. Duckett identified himself as a public relations representative for Belafonte in a letter to Killens, 8/22/56, cited in Gilyard, *Killens*, 129n24, 348.

91. Duckett, "Backstage with Belafonte: Big Gamble Pays Off for Harry," *CDD*, 8/22/56, 7.

92. Duckett, "Backstage with Belafonte: Belafonte Tells Ideas about Race," *CDD*, 8/23/56, 8. Belafonte's use of the term "chauvinism" here could have revealed Belafonte's left-wing past to a knowing reader: "white chauvinism" was the term Communist Party members used to critique evidence of unexamined racist forms of thinking. In the postwar period, women in the party began to use the term "male chauvinism" to critique the unexamined attitudes of male supremacy.

93. Duckett, "Belafonte Tells Ideas about Race," 8.

94. Ibid.

95. Harold Cruse, "Letter to the *Amsterdam News*," 4/19/56, reprinted in William Jelani Cobb, *The Essential Harold Cruse: A Reader* (New York: Palgrave, 2002), 36–42.

96. Leonard Katz, "Close-up: Belafonte: A Human Being First," *NYP*, 11/11/56; A Reader, "Open Letter to Harry Belafonte," submit-

ted to the *NYP*, 11/11/56, reprinted in Cobb, *The Essential Harold Cruse*, 43–45.

97. Cruse later developed these arguments in *The Crisis of the Negro Intellectual (1967)*; on Cruse and Belafonte, see Jackson, *The Indignant Generation*, 309–318, 465–466.

98. Lee Blackwell, "Off the Record," *CD*, 10/15/57, 10; Thomas W. Pryor, "Film about Indies Is Planned by Fox," *NYT*, 5/2/55, 17; Stephen Watts, "Hove to on 'Island in the Sun,'" *NYT*, 1/20/57. Alec Waugh crowed over its financial success: "I made more in one month with *Island in the Sun* than I did in forty years of writing with thirty-eight books and countless stories," cited in Edwin McDowell, Obituary: Alec Waugh, 83, Author of 'Island in the Sun,'" *NYT*, 9/4/81, A12.

99. "Pix Code Brought Up to Date," *VAR*, 9/9/53, 5, 18; "Revised Pix Code OKs Miscegenation, Drinking, Smuggling If 'In Good Taste,'" *VAR*, 9/15/54, 3, 16; "Dope, Kidnapping and Other Tabu Plots OK Under Revised Film Code," *VAR*, 12/12/56, 1–20; Thomas Doherty, *Hollywood's Censor: Joseph I. Breen and the Production Code Administration* (New York: Columbia University Press, 2007), 319. On these 1949 films, see Smith, *Visions*, 117–123, 166–204. Geoffrey Shurlock to Harry Cohn, Columbia Studios, 5/13/55, in the *Island in the Sun* folder, MPAA/MH/AMPAS.

100. Daryl Zanuck's comments at the conference on the screenplay, October 25, 1955, in "Island in the Sun" script materials, FOX/USC. Filming in Grenada did not unsettle this limited understanding. The director Robert Rossen was quoted saying that "to ignore the race problem in the West Indies would be like trying to ignore the bananas"; Watts, "Hove to on 'Island in the Sun.'"

101. Daryl Zanuck's comments at the conference on the screenplay, 10/25/55, and the story conference on the final screenplay, 1/16/56, in *Island in the Sun* script materials, FOX/USC.

102. "Izzie Rowe's Notebook, *PC*, 1/14/56, B30; Bogle, *Dandridge*, 343–360; Bob Thomas, "Singer Harry Belafonte's One-Man Show 'Smash Hit,'" *Corpus Christi (TX) Times*, 7/13/56, 33. Truman Gibson to Frank McCarthy, 7/19/56; Frank McCarthy to Geoffrey Shurlock, 7/26/56, in *Island in the Sun* folder, MPAA/MH/AMPAS. Screenwriter Alfred Hayes recalled that his script was rewritten during filming: "Harry Belafonte wouldn't play a certain kind of character . . . Belafonte says, 'I don't want to play a sharpie,' so they rewrite the part," interview, 8/18/80, in *Contemporary Authors Online* in *Gale Biography in Context*, "Harry Belafonte Expects to be

Tapped for *Island in the Sun,*" *Coshocton (OH) County Democrat,* 8/22/56, 6.

103. Bogle, *Dandridge,* 358–365. Zanuck personally supervised the final edit, after Rossen's work was completed; Don Ross, "Negroes and Whites Are Linked in 'Island in the Sun' Romance," *NYHTr,* 6/2/57; "'To Kiss or Not to Kiss' Is Question Which Upset Cast," *Ebony,* July 1957, 34.

104. "He's Shocking the World: $1 Million a Year," *AA,* 12/29/56, 27; Hilda See, "The Dandridge Story: 'Island in Sun' Defies Old Rule with Dot, Justin," *CD,* 2/2/57, 14; Edward Scobie, "Two Interracial Romances Help Make Pix Unique," *CD,* 2/9/57, 8; "Belafonte Gets Dixie Threats for Movie Role," *Jet,* 1/3/57. *DW* repeated *Jet*'s claim, also noting the film's criticism of colonialism and the fact that "a Negro emerges as the winner in an explosive political situation" despite the film's "last tinge of color consciousness"; David Platt, "Boy Meets Girl in Mixed Romance," 2/3/57.

105. *Citizen's Council,* 2, no. 4 (February 1957); "Harry Belafonte Receives Threats," (UP) *Fairbanks (AK) News,* 12/14/56, 12; "Dixie Segregationists Attack 'Island in the Sun,'" *VAR* (d), 4/4/1956; "'Island in the Sun' Faces Legal Ban in S.C., *AA,* 5/4/157; "Nothing Could Be Fiercer in Carolina than Belafonte: Zanuck Offer Passed By," *VAR,* 5/15/157, 1; "Memphis Bans 'Island in the Sun,'" *AA,* 5/20/57; "Dixie Fights 'Island' Film As It Did 'Chillun',"' *AA,* 6/13/57, 8; "Cops Guard Joan Fontaine, Poison Pen 'Sun' Burn Victim, at Pic's Preem," *VAR*(d), 7/14/57, and Fontaine, *No Bed of Roses* (New York: William Morrow, 1978), 216. Fontaine also received letters that were more "startled" than "critical," in "Belafonte-Fontaine Dance Photo Startles Fans," *Jet,* 1/24/57, 62.

106. Jack Hamilton, "The Storm Over Belafonte," *Look,* 1/25/57; "Belafonte Told to Keep Quiet," (UP), *San Mateo (CA) Times,* 6/11/57, 15; "Belafonte Told to 'Keep Quiet' About Romance Theme in Film," *ADW,* 6/13/57, 2; "Belafonte Silenced by Studios: Told to Keep Quiet about Interracial Romance Depicted in the Movie," *PC,* 6/15/57, 3; Bosley Crowther, "Color or Class: Are Issues Evaded in 'Island in the Sun'?" *NYT,* 6/23/57, drew on arguments provided by a New York–born Grenadian that "only an American with a fertile imagination and a background in race relations in the U.S. could write about the West Indies in terms of racial conflict" rather than focusing on the problems of "poverty, social welfare, lack of schools, class prejudice . . . distinctions of economic status more than of race."

107. Archer Winston, *NYP*, 6/13/57, 34; Bosley Crowther, *NYT*, 6/13/57; *VAR*(d), 6/13/57; "'Island in the Sun' Faces the Race Issue," *OTr*, 6/14/57, 33, and "'Island in the Sun' Is Controversial, But Strong and Absorbing Theater," 6/16/57, B2–B3. Black press criticism in *Arkansas State Press*, 1/28/57, 7; *LATr*, 7/10/57, 17, 20; *LATr*, 7/17/57, 1; Wilbert E. Hemming, "'Stereotype' Casting Leads to Jamaican Film Ban Threats," *AA*, 8/20/57, 10; Wilbert E. Hamming[sic], "Jamaica's Governor Explains Why Pix 'Island in the Sun' Was Banned," *CD*, 8/24/57, 19; "Jamaicans Resent 'Island' as Lie," *AA*, 9/28/57, 8; Albert Johnson, "Black Brown and Beige," *Film Quarterly* 13, no. 1 (Autumn 1959): 39–41.

108. "The white residents of the island are made the aggressors, guilty of terrible crimes and mistreatment, while the black people are shown as fine and upright," *(Hollywood) CN*, 7/16/57; press book for "Island in the Sun," USC archives. "Belafonte Silenced by Studios: Told to Keep Quiet about Interracial Romance depicted in the Movie," *PC*, 6/15/57, 3: "'Sun' A Terrible Pic, Says Belafonte" in "Hollywood's Summer Films Tackle Some Sweaty Topics with Varying Success," *Life*, 7/22/57.

109. *NYAN*, 4/13/57, 1.

110. "Belafonte Wed Secretly South of the Border," *NYP*, 4/10/57.

111. Betty Granger, "Will Harry's Marriage Affect His Status As Matinee Idol?" and "Rumors vs. Facts in the Big Story," *NYAN*, 4/20/57, 1, 35.

112. "Belafonte Salute Could be 'Greatest,'" *NYAN*, 4/20/57, 4; Jimmy Booker, "Uptown Lowdown," *NYAN*, 5/4/57, 9, describing mobs of autograph-seeking teenagers catching him on 156th Street en route to introducing Julie to his mother; "Nation's Top Calypso Artist," *AA*, 5/4/57, 5.

113. Gelman, "Belafonte: Profile I-VI, 4/15–21/1957; Jeanne Van Holmes, "Belafonte Gives It All He's Got," *Saturday Evening Post*, 5/29/57; "Belafonte: Close-Up: 'I Wonder Why Nobody Don't Like Me,'" *Life*, 5/27/57; Jack Hamilton, "The Storm over Belafonte," *Look*, 6/25/57; "Wild about Harry," *Time*, 7/1/57; Harry Belafonte, "Why I Married Julie," *Ebony*, July 1957, 90–95. As described in *My Song*, Belafonte's sessions with Dr. Peter Neubauer, a Jewish psychoanalyst and child psychiatrist from Austria, a sponsor for the 1949 Peace Conference, continued from 1957 until Neubauer's death in 2008.

114. "Harry Ought to Fall," Elaine Campbell to *AA*, 5/18/57, 4;

"I'm for Belafonte," Harold R. Woodhouse to *AA*, 6/1/57, 4; Dan Burley, "Harry Belafonte: 'Takes Two to Tango,'" includes letter from Frederick Vincent Seabrook, in Dan Burley's "Back Door Stuff," *NYAN*, 6/1/57, 15; letters to *Ebony*, September 1957, 9–11.

115. Belafonte, "Why I Married Julie," 90–91, including statements from columnist George Schuyler, Mahalia Jackson, and Tallahassee, Florida, boycott leader Rev. G. K. Steele.

116. Letters to *Ebony*, September 1957, 9–11; "The Tragedy of Divorce," *Ebony*, August 1958, 25–32; and letters in response in *Ebony*, October 1958, 8. After the divorce, Marguerite worked as women's news editor at the *NYAN*, broadcaster on a daily local women's radio show, and as fund-raiser for the NAACP Freedom Fund.

117. In the *NYP*, see Murray Kempton, "The Ghetto," 10/5/58; Gael Greene, "Belafonte: The Doors Slammed Shut," 10/12/58; Helen Dudar, "The Belafontes Find a Place to Live," 11/1/58.

118. Rohlehr, "Calypso Reinvents Itself," in *Carnival*, 215–217.

119. Ned Soublette, "The Kingsmen and the Cha-Cha-Cha," in *Listening In: A Momentary History of Pop Music*, ed. Eric Weisbard (Durham, NC: Duke University Press, 2007), 69–84; Reebee Garofalo, "Off the Charts: Outrage and Exclusion in the Eruption of Rock and Roll," in *American Popular Music*, ed. Rachel Rubin and Jeffrey Melnick (Amherst: University of Massachusetts Press, 2001), 111–126, esp. 118–124.

120. Ray Funk and Donald R. Hill, "'Will Calypso Doom Rock 'n' Roll?' The U.S. Calypso Craze of 1957," in *Trinidad Carnival: The Cultural Politics of a Transnational Festival*, ed. Garth L. Green and Philip W. Scher (Bloomington: Indiana University Press, 2007) 178–197; Michael S. Eldridge, "Bob Girl Goes Calypso: Containing Race and Youth Culture in Cold War America," *Anthurium: A Caribbean Studies Journal* 3, no. 2 (2005): Article 2, accessed from scholarlyrepository.miami.edu/anthurium/vol3/iss2/2.

121. "Calypso Craze taking Spotlight," *ADW*, 2/1/57, 2; "Calypsomania," *Time*, 3/25/57, 55–56; Arthur Gelb, "Hide and Seek to Open Tonight," *NYT*, 4/2/57, 37; Geoffrey Holder, "That Fad from Trinidad," *NYT*, 4/21/57; SM 14, 60; "The Fad from Trinidad" and "Chicago's Blue Angel Nightclub Is the Oldest Calypso Club in the U.S., in *Ebony*, June 1957, 48, 51–52; John Wilson, "Belafonte and Others in Calypso Variety," *NYT*, 5/5/57, 145; "Music: Tornado from Trinidad [Geoffrey Holder]," *Time*, 5/6/57 "Belafonte Leaves Musical," *NYT*, 2/5/57, 27; Shane Vogel, "*Jamaica* on Broadway: The Popular Carib-

bean and Mock Transnational Performance," *Theatre Journal* 62 (2010): 1–21.

122. "Belafonte, Riding on Calypso Craze, Wants No Part in It," (UP), *Ogden (UT) Standard Examiner*, 1/17/57, 2; "Belafonte Says Today's Calypso 'Synthetic,'" *AA*, 2/16/57, 7; Harry Belafonte, "Belafonte's Lament: I Want No Part of Calypso Craze" (as told to Dick Kleiner, NEA Staff Correspondent), *Amarillo (TX) Globe Times*, 3/5/57, 2; Dom Cerulli, "The Responsibility of the Artist" and "Belafonte: Where to from Here?" *Down Beat*, 3/6/57, 18, and 4/4/57, 17. Belafonte's colleague Bill Attaway's *Calypso Song Book* was organized as a "cross-section of Caribbean island music," providing a general history of calypso variations and revision as well as histories of the individual songs (New York: McGraw Hill, 1957).

123. Burgie's name appeared at the bottom of the staff listing in the Fox press book, but most film promotion credited only Belafonte and did not acknowledge Burgie's authorship; "Controversial Movie Premieres Next Week," *AA*, 5/25/57, 8, and Robert Rossen's description "He [Belafonte] sings two calypsos . . . he wrote both for the film" in Don Ross, "Negroes and Whites Are Linked in 'Island in the Sun' Romances," *NYHTr*, 6/2/57, 1B.

124. Belafonte remembered a Trinidadian journalist directly challenging his usage during the making of *Island: My Song*, 165–166; "U.S.-Type Calypsos Annoying to Purists," *Press Telegram* (Long Beach, CA), 4/3/57, 3; "'Jamaican Variations' Not Calypso, says Trinidadians," *LATr*, 4/10/57, 18. Robert Mitchum's version of "Momma Look at Bubu" won first prize at Trinidad's 1957 calypso carnival competition, over Belafonte and an assortment of Trinidad champions"; Dick Kleiner, "The Record Beat," *Corpus Christi (TX) Times*, 5/17/57, 40.

125. "Nation's Top Calypso Artist," *AA*, 5/4/57; Jesse H. Walker, "Theatricals," *NYAN*, 5/4/57, 14.

126. Hamilton, "Storm over Belafonte," *Look*, 6/25/57.

127. *PC*, 6/22/57, 1; Bob Thomas, "Harry Belafonte Blazes a Trail" (AP), *Cedar Rapids (IA) Gazette*, 8/6/57, 16.

128. Rob Roy, "Attention Hollywood: Make 'Em, Don't Just Promise Sepia Pics," *CD*, 3/24/56, 15; Gilyard, *Killens*, 129; John O. Killens, "Hollywood in Black and White," *The Nation*, 9/20/65, 158–159; Louella Parsons syndicated column in *Anderson (IN) Daily Bulletin*, 2/13/57, 12.

129. "A Word or Two from Mr. Belafonte, *NYP*, 7/10/57.

130. "Belafonte Puts Rap on Movies," *AA*, 7/20/57, 10; Dolores Calvin, "Seein' Stars," *Arkansas State Press*, 8/2/57, 7.

131. *NYMT*, 7/24/57, as cited by Steven J. Ross, *Hollywood Left and Right: How Movie Stars Shaped American Politics* (New York: Oxford University Press, 2011), 201.

132. Sam Lacy, "It Was an Accident!," *AA*, 7/2/157, 1.

133. Associated Press wire service Hollywood reporter Bob Thomas's two-part article on Belafonte's rise appeared in different lengths with different headlines, guiding different readers of the same interview toward different interpretations: for example: "Former Negro Janitor Is Now a Millionaire," "Only Fancy Thing about Entertainer Is His High Salary and the Steep Taxes He Pays on It," "Money Is Comfort but It Hasn't Changed Belafonte." Quotations cited in "Harry Belafonte Soars to Top Flight of Entertainers: One Time Janitor Now Earning Millions," *News Palladium* (Benton Harbor, MI), 8/7/57, 12.

134. Ibid.

135. Killens to Belafonte, 12/26/56, cited in Gilyard, *Killens*, 129n25, 348.

136. Louella Parsons, "Belafonte to Star in His Own Film," *ADW*, 8/26/57, 5; Pictures of Belafonte with "Robert Korman" [DeCormier] making the Caribbean album, *Arkansas State Press*, 12/13/57, 2; Gilyard, *Killens*, 129–130; Robert DeCormier interview, 6/16/2010.

137. Hy Steirman, ed., *Harry Belafonte: His Complete Life Story* (New York: Hillman Publications, 1957) is reproduced in Escott, *Island*, 40–77; Terrance Van Wort, "When Belafonte Tried to 'Pass,'" [September 1957] and Max Maxwell, "Harry Belafonte's Big Problem ['the white gals just won't leave the guy alone!']," October 1957; in HB clippings, BRTC (Lester Sweyd Collection). See also "The Belafonte Secret," *Teen* (July 1957); "Tommy Sands vs. Belafonte and Elvis" [1957], "Who's The Greatest? Elvis, Pat, Tab, Belafonte," *16*, July 1957, and "The Harry Belafonte Story," *Calypso Stars* 1 (1957), fan magazine covers collected and provided to me by Ronald Cohen.

138. Taylor Branch and Steven Ross have documented many aspects of Belafonte's political involvements, particularly his close relationship with King, his contributions to strategic decision-making and strategy for SCLC and for SNCC, his extensive fund-raising, his role as a mediator between these two organizations, and between

these organizations and Robert Kennedy, throughout Branch's three volumes history of King, and in Ross, *Hollywood Left and Right*, 185–226.

139. Stevenson's civil rights stance in *PC*, 6/30/56, as cited in "The Negro Should Support Stevenson," *The Crisis*, October 1956, 461–462; Alfred Duckett, "Harry Belafonte Endorses Adlai," *CDD*, 10/8/56, 6; Lee Blackwell, "Off the Record," *CDD*, 10/9/56, 8; "Democrats Plan Closed Circuit TV Show," *NYT*, 10/18/56, 25; Mattie Smith Colin for ANP, "Political Pot-Pourri," *Plain Dealer* (Kansas City, KS), 10/19/56, 6; Alfred Duckett, "One Thousand See Closed TV for Adlai," *CDD*, 10/22/56. "The House I Live In" (music by Earl Robinson, lyrics by Lewis Allan/Abe Meeropol) was recorded by Paul Robeson, Josh White, and Frank Sinatra and sung by Mahalia Jackson; Belafonte also sang it on a closed-circuit labor broadcast for Stevenson; "Victor Reisel Sees Party by Labor After Vote Study," *Portsmouth (OH) Times*, 11/8/56, 22.

140. JFK 1960 campaign spots with Harry Belafonte, IFP, 135–158 (5 minutes) and F 80 (1 minute), JFK Library; Belafonte, *My Song*, 214–219; Branch, *Parting the Water*, 306–307, 314, 365–366; 369; "I Feel Like a Real Champion Now" and "Editorial: Great Race Relations Day," *AA*, 7/2/60, 6 and 8. The *AA*'s endorsement of Kennedy included a picture of Belafonte with Kennedy, 10/28/60, A4. Discussion of African issues appeared frequently in the 1960 presidential campaign: see James H. Meriwether, "'Worth a Lot of Negro Votes': Black Voters, Africa, and the 1960 Presidential campaign," *Journal of American History* 95, no. 3 (2008): 737–763.

141. Chisholm was the first black woman in Congress and the first woman to run for president; Shirley Chisholm, *Unbought and Unbossed* (Boston: Houghton Mifflin, 1970), 47–48.

142. Ransby, *Ella Baker*, 172–178; D'Emilio, *Lost Prophet*, 262–264; Letter from Kilgore, Rustin, and Baker to James Hicks, *NYAN*, June 4, 1957, SCLC files, cited by Ransby, 176; "All Roads Lead to D.C. for Prayer Pilgrimage," *Plain Dealer* (Kansas City, KS), 5/10/57, 1; "Prayer Pilgrimage to Washington," *Ebony*, August 1957, 17; Betty Granger, "Conversation Piece," *NYAN*, 5/23/57, 10; Belafonte, *My Song*, 172; Duberman, *Robeson*, 446–447; Robeson, Jr., *Undiscovered Paul Robeson*, 263–264. Ella Baker remembered NAACP's Roy Wilkins red-baiting Belafonte around the prayer pilgrimage; in Ward, *Just My Soul Responding*, 318–319. Belafonte, worried about the implications of his "red" impact on King's movement, was reas-

sured by Ossie Davis in a letter to Belafonte [n.d., ca. summer 1958], in Box 1, Folder 2, in DDC, SCRBC.

143. "Belafonte, Mrs. Martin King Head 'Youth March,'" *LATr*, 10/24/58; "White, Negro Youths Rally for Integration," *Newport (RI) Daily News*, 10/25/58, 13; "Harry Belafonte, Jackie Robinson Lead Integrated-Schools March," *WPATH*, 10/26/58, A17; Evelyn Cunningham, "White House 'Silent' Before Greatest Rally: 10,000 Jam Capital for 'Youth March,'" *PC*, 11/1/58, A21; "Eisenhower Refused Them," *LATr*, 11/7/58, 5; "Youth March for Freedom," *AA*, 11/8/58, 20.

144. "Dr. Martin L. King to Join Youth Marchers in Capital," *AA*, 4/11/59, 1; Steve W. Duncan," 20,000 Due in D.C.," *AA*, 4/18/59, 1; Hamilton Bims, "Youth Integration Yellers Really Opened Up This Time," *AA*, 4/25/59, 2; Mary Stratford, "'We'll be Back,' Shout Marchers," *AA*, 4/25/59, 1; "26,000 at Youth Meeting," *AA*, 5/2/59, 8.

145. D'Emilio, *Lost Prophet*, 276–278; *Sit In*, NBC white paper documentary about the Nashville student movement, broadcast December 20, 1960; Freedom Riders version of "Day-O" reprised at the SNCC 50th Anniversary Conference, 4/17/2010; Leigh Raiford, *Imprisoned in a Luminous Glare: Photography and the African American Freedom Struggle* (Chapel Hill: University of North Carolina Press, 2011), 90.

146. Branch details Belafonte's work with SNCC in *Parting the Waters* and *Pillars of Fire*, including 1964 trip to Africa; see also Stokely Carmichael with Ekwueme Michael Thelwell, *Ready for Revolution: The Life and Struggles of Stokely Carmichael (Kwame Ture)* (New York: Scribner, 2005) 11, 213–214, 222, 305; Tanarive Due and Patricia Stephens Due, *Freedom in the Family: A Mother-Daughter Memoir of the Fight for Civil Rights* (New York: Ballantine/One World, 2004); support for darkrooms in Raiford, *Imprisoned*, 72; see also Belafonte's description of the trip to Africa in "Interview with Harry Belafonte for *Eyes on the Prize II*, 5/15 and 5/22/89, in HHC/WU. Belafonte told President Sekou Toure that SNCC represented "the kind of militant leadership that was needed in the liberation struggle in the US," that was previously associated with Du Bois and Robeson: in James Forman, "Brief Report on Guinea," *Eyes on the Prize Civil Rights Reader*, ed. Clayborn Carson, et al. (New York: Penguin, 1991), 192.

147. These labor leaders included the UAW's Walter Reuther; Mike Quill, the left-wing head of the Transport Workers Union;

Harry Van Arsdale, the head of New York's Central labor council; and Arnold Zander and Jerry Wulf from the public employees union, AFSCME. "In Person: Harry Belafonte: Noted Star to Join Outstanding Program, October 1" [*probably RWDSU Record*], 7/20/58, in Belafonte clipping file, SCRBC; "Morris Kaplan, "Mayor Supports Stronger Union," *NYT*, 10/22/58; "15,000 Attend Garment Center Civil Rights Rally," *NYT*, 4/18/60, 22.

148. "N.A.A.C.P. Benefit Show Set," *NYT*, 4/3/57, 26; Gilyard, *Killens*, 129.

149. Steve W. Duncan, "$7,400 Is Pledged for King Fight," *NYT*, 3/5/60; letter from Belafonte to Langston Hughes to join the Committee for the Defense of MLK and the Struggle for Southern Freedom, 3/15/60, Langston Hughes Papers, JWJ/MSS 26, Box 13, Folder 306; letter from Stanley Levison to King, March 1960, in *Martin Luther King Papers*, vol. 5, 381; "Heed Their Rising Voices" political ad, *NYT*, 3/29/60, 25; "King Committee Won't Retreat," *ADW*, 4/13/60, 1; "No Retreat on Ala. Ad," *AA*, 4/23/60, 9.

150. "Top Screen Stars in Benefit Show," *AA*, 4/16/60, 15; "Belafonte, Poitier, Shelly Winters Entertain at May 17 Rights Benefit," *NYAN*, 4/16/60, 3; "Benefit Show to Support Sitdowners," *AA*, 4/23/60, 7; "Dr. King to Address Armory Spectacular," *NYAN*, 5/14/60, 2, 15; "Thousands of Students March for Civil Rights," *Berkshire Eagle*, 5/18/60, 3; "15,000 Attend Garment Center Civil Rights Rally," *NYT*, 5/18/60, 22; "Cold Fury: New Negro Is Key in Struggle", *NYAN*, 5/21/60, 1. Stanley Levison praised the significance of Belafonte's leadership in a letter to King cited above in n149, and James L. Hicks described it in "'Let's Do It Ourselves' Is Attitude," "The Spirit of the 60's," *NYAN*, 5/21/60, 1, and in "New Leadership," *NYAN*, 5/28/60, 11. See also George E. Pitts, "Harry Belafonte in Thick of Rights Fight," *PC*, 6/11/60, 23.

151. Ad for Rally, "Harry Belafonte Sings for Peace," *NYP*, 5/18/60; "NY Rally Against A-bomb Ends in Mass March to UN," *Berkshire Eagle*, 5/20/60, 3; "Madison Square Garden Rally Calls for an End of U.S.-Soviet Arms Race," *AA*, 5/21/60, 9.

152. "While Belafonte Bids for His Crown," *News Chronicle* (UK), August 11, 1958, 3; Howard Taubman, "Belafonte Sings at Brussels Fair," *NYT*, 9/6/58, and Eleanor Roosevelt, "My Day," *NYP*, 9/12/58.

153. "Newsflash," *AA*, 10/4/58, 1; "Great Dictator: British TV Columnist Reveals Belafonte Pact," *AA*, 1/17/59, 15; see also Belafonte's

mention of the "Notting Hill Troubles" and his copy of the judge's ruling in "Three Belafontes Reported 'Seeing Our Psychiatrist,'" *AA*,10/3/59,15.

154. Kathleen Teltsch, "Mboya of Kenya Cautions Britain," *NYT*, 4/9/59, 10; Clayton Knowles, "African Leader Asks Democracy," *NYT*, 4/26/59, 8; Rampersad, *Langston Hughes*, vol. 2, 299; "Who Speaks for Africa?" A Report on the Activities of the American Committee on Africa" [1959], accessed from the African Activist Archive, Michigan State University, July 15, 2012. On ACOA, see George M. Hauser, *No One Can Stop the Rain: Glimpses of Africa's Liberation Struggle* (New York: Pilgrim Press, 1989).

155. "81 Kenyans to Hold U.S. Scholarships," *NYT*, 8/6/159; Belafonte, Robinson, and Poitier to Carl Van Vechten, 8/26/59, in Box A, African American Students Foundation, CVVPC; "Give to Young Africa" (letter from Belafonte, Robinson and Poitier), *AA*, 9/5/59, 4. The senior Barack Obama was one of the Kenyan students, although not a recipient of this airlift travel. The Sharpeville massacre, where the police opened fire on unarmed demonstrators and killed sixty-nine people, had just occurred two weeks before, March 21, 1960. "April 13 Announced as 'Africa Freedom Day,'" *ADW*, 4/7/60, 1; "Boycott in U.S. Asked on Africa," *NYT*, 4/14/60, 5; "Annual Report American Committee on Africa, June 1, 1959 to May 31, 1960," accessed from the African Activist Archive, Michigan State University, July 15, 2012; Meriwether, *Proudly We Can Be Africans*, 191. Right after Sharpeville, ACOA demonstrators picketed Woolworth's in solidarity with the southern students and then marched to demonstrate at the South African consulate; "South Africans 'Out to Lunch' as Shooting Is Protested," *NYT*, 3/24/60, 8. Looking back, Belafonte commented that internationalism was a critical resource for the U.S. civil rights movement: the only hope "to get the cause full protected, in a way, would be for us to have powerful external alliances, Europe, Africa . . .," in TB/HB, 3/6/85.

156. Lionel Rogosin, *Come Back Africa—A Man Possessed* (2004); Belafonte, *My Song*, 201–202, and interview with Leonard Lopate, WNYC, 1/27/2012.

157. Makeba performed extensively as a professional singer in South Africa, and her early repertoire included songs in English, Xhosa, and Yiddish, the latter acquired from a Jewish show business colleague in South Africa; "Belafonte Protégée [Makeba]," *NYAN*, 12/5/59; Milton Bracker, "Xhosa Songstress," *NYT*, 2/28/60,

SM 32; Makeba's memoir, *Makeba: My Story*, with James Hall (New York: New American Library, 1987), and Ruth Feldstein, "Screening Anti-Apartheid: Miriam Makeba, *Come Back, Africa*, and the Transnational Circulation of Black Culture and Politics," *Feminist Studies* 39, no. 1 (2013): 12–39, and *How It Feels to Be Free: Black Women Entertainers and the Civil Rights Movement* (New York: Oxford University Press, 2013).

CHAPTER FOUR

1. "Africans Oppose JFK's Peace Corps," *AA*, 4/8/61, 15. In contrast to Peace Corps advertising directed at Ivy league college graduates described by Molly Geidel in "The Point of the Lance: Gender, Development, and the 1960s Peace Corps" (doctoral dissertation, Boston University, 2011), 44–45, Belafonte encouraged recruits without a high school diploma; transcript of HB on *Tonight Show*, February 28, 1966, provided by Geidel.

2. Dolores Calvin, "Harry Belafonte Put Money Where Mouth Is, An Old Legend, for Pix," *CDD*, 11/13/58, 19; Belafonte quoted in Murray Schumach, "Hollywood Patterns," *NYT*, 7/26/59, X5; Richard W. Nason, "Evaluating the Odds: Harry Belafonte Tries Broad Racial Approach in Locally Made Feature," *NYT*, 3/15/59; "Independent Production" in Peter Lev, *The Fifties* (Berkeley: University of California Press, 2003), 24–32, esp. 25.

3. Gilyard, *Killens*, 129.

4. Robert J. Landry, "Sensational 10 Year Upsurge of Negro Market," *VAR*, 1/27/54, 1, 69; and "'Race': Box Office But Booby-Trapped, *VAR*, 1/8/58, 15.

5. W. E. B. Du Bois, "Human Rights for All Minorities' (1945), cited in Nikhil Pal Singh, "Culture/Wars: Recoding Empire in an Age of Democracy," *American Quarterly* 50, no.3 (1998): 483.

6. Richard Durham, interviewed by Hugh Cordier in "A History and Analysis of *Destination Freedom*" (unpublished seminar paper, Northwestern University, 1949), 24–25.

7. For examples of this kind of criticism, see Brooks Atkinson, "'Giant Step' Negro Dramatist tells an American Story," *NYT*, 10/4/53, X1; Nan Robertson, "Dramatist against the Odds," *NYT*, 3/8/59, X3, and "Her Dream Came True: Lorraine Hansberry," *NYT*, 4/9/59, 37; "With a Wallop" and "Surprise" *Newsweek*, 3/23/59, 76 and 4/20/59, 75; Smith, *Visions of Belonging*, 310–322.

8. Jack Hamilton, "The Storm over Belafonte," *Look*, 6/25/59; Thomas Pryor, "Belafonte's Firm Plans First Film," *NYT*, 9/26/57, 21. *Brothers* was still under discussion as a Belafonte Enterprises project in 1968: Folder 2-3, Box 1, CSC, SCRBC.

9. The novel *The Purple Cloud*, written by the British West Indian writer M. P. Shiel in 1901–1902, was sold to a Hollywood studio in 1927. Ferdinand Reyher, a writer who translated and promoted the work of Bertolt Brecht, prepared several story treatments for Paramount between 1939 and 1947; Introduction to the Reyher papers, Special collections, University of Maryland Libraries; "World Flesh and the Devil" script materials, MGM/USC. Siegel bought the rights in 1956; printed MGM program, The *World, the Flesh and the Devil* production file, MH/AMPAS. On the Siegel/Harbel partnership, Pryor, "Belafonte's Firm Plans First Film," and Louella Parsons, "Belafonte to Star in Own Film," *ADW*, 9/26/57, 5. Sol Siegel, "Project for 3," 9/9/57; treatments/scripts by Rand MacDougall, a radio dramatist turned Hollywood screenwriter, who had begun to direct films in the mid-1950s, beginning 10/2/57; black character appears in 2/1/58 script, in The *World, the Flesh and the Devil* scripts material, MGM/USC.

10. Schultheiss interview with Belafonte, 9/2/98, in *Abraham Polonsky's Odds against Tomorrow: Critical Edition*, ed. John Schultheiss (Northridge, CA: Center for Telecommunications Studies, 1999), 236.

11. Belafonte [guest columnist for Kilgallen, "The Voice of Broadway"],"New Era A-Dawning for the Negro," *NYJA*, 10/24/57, 20.

12. "Joe Hyams in Hollywood: Negro Stars Are Coming Into Their Own," *NYHT*, 4/14/58, 15. In "Belafonte Becomes 'Big Business,'" *Ebony*, June 1958, the film was still *The End of the World*, and the plan was to exhibit it through "art houses," 18.

13. *End of the World*, RM notes to SS, 8/18/58, in The *World, Flesh and the Devil* script materials, MGM/USC.

14. A. H. Weiler, "By Way of Report: Back Again," *NYT*, 11/2/58, X7; "My Life, by Harry Belafonte, As Told to Anthony Carthew," *Daily Herald*(London), 12/5/59,4; Schultheiss interview with Belafonte, *OAT: Critical Edition*, 235–236.

15. *MPH*, 4/11/1959; Ivan Spear, "World, Flesh and the Devil" review, *BO*, 4/13/59.

16. Stan Anderson, "Stage and Screen: 'World, Flesh and the

Devil' Is Film You Shouldn't Miss," *Cleveland Press,* 4/22/59; W. Ward Marsh, "This World Ends—Last 3 on Earth Find Loneliness," *Cleveland Plain Dealer,* 4/23/59; in MGM press book, BFC, SCRBC.

17. For example, "Emperor" in MGM press materials, and in Jean Beaver, "Film Fare," *Lima (OH) News,* 6/6/59, 21; "Black Adam," in *Time,* 6/2/59. See also *VAR,* 4/8/59; Alton Cooke, "End of the World Is with Us Again," *NYTe,* 5/21/59.

18. MGM printed program, production file, MH/AMPAS; Paul V. Beckley, "World, Flesh and the Devil," *NYHT,* 5/21/59; John L. Scott, "'World, Flesh Devil' Gripping Film Drama," *LAT,* 5/30/59.

19. Effie Burrus, "Belafonte, The Producer, Makes a Better Singer," *CCP,* 4/4/59, 6C; MGM printed program, production file, MH/AMPAS; "Midwest Paper Cool to New Belafonte Picture Cleveland," *LATr,* 4/24/59, 18; Hollis Alpert, "Saturday Review Goes to the Movies," *Saturday Review,* 5/2/59.

20. "Trite triangle" in Bob Thomas's syndicated column in *The Herald-Press* (St. Joseph, MI), 3/25/59, 8; Archer Winston, "Reviewing Stand," *NYP,* 5/21/59; *Newsweek,* 5/25/59; "mishmash of clichés," in John McCarten, *New Yorker,* 5/30/59; "silly example," in *Time,* 6/1/59; Dick Williams, "Great Start, Poor End for 'Flesh, Devil,'" *LAMN,* 6/1/59; Bosley Crowther, "Screen: Radioactive City," *NYT,* 5/21/59; Robert Hatch, "Films," *The Nation,* 6/13/59 (Hatch did admit that he had "rarely so enjoyed a picture so deplorable").

21. Slightly different versions of the MGM press kit are at USC and at BFC, SCRBC; black newspapers reproducing the film's own publicity materials included *CD,* 5/16/59, 18; *NYAN,* 5/23/59, 14; *ADW,* 5/24/59, 9; *PC,* 5/30/59, 24; *NJAG,* 6/6/59, 18; *LAS,* 6/11/59, C1.

22. Al Monroe, "So They Say," *CD,* 4/4/59, 19; "Belafonte's New Wrinkle Almost Solves 'Problem,'" *CD,* 4/11/59, 18; "Is This for Real?," *CDD,* 5/21/59, 15; "Belafonte's First Starring Pix Role Wins Chicago Fans," *CD,* 8/1/59, 19.

23. Kerry Jackson, "New Films, *LATr,* 5/29/59, 18; Albert Johnson, "Black Brown and Beige," *Film Quarterly* 13, no. 1 (Autumn 1959): 43. The black press covered Johnson's critique: "U of C editor Says Films on Race Mixing Phony," in *LATr,* 10/23/59, 20, and *AA,* 10/24/59, 1. Belafonte seconded Johnson's criticisms in a Cleveland interview: Charles L. Sanders, "Harry Belafonte Says: Screen Portrayals of Mixed Marriages False," *CCP,* 10/24/59, 1A.

24. Al Monroe, "So They Say," *CDD*, 5/26/59, 18; "Belafonte's First Starring Pix Role Wins Chicago Fans," *CD*, 8/1/59, 19; Al Monroe, "So They Say," *CDD*, 7/30/59, 22.

25. "Bob Thomas Writes about Belafonte's Films," in *Laurel (MS) Leader Call*, 7/9/59, 8; "My Life, by Harry Belafonte," 4.

26. "Protest Stops Showing of Film Starring Belafonte," *BW*, 9/2/59.

27. Harbel negotiated with both Twentieth Century Fox and United Artists before working out the financing and distribution for *OAT*, announced in October 1958; a six-picture deal at UA worked out with Max Youngstein, then head of production, announced in March 1959; "Belafonte May Portray Rev. King," *Plain Dealer* (Kansas City, KS), 10/25/57, 8; "Belafonte Becomes 'Big Business,'" *Ebony*, June 1958, 18–19; Hazel Washington, "Richard Widmark Will Star in Belafonte Film as Owner," *CD*, 10/18/58, 19; Nason, "Evaluating the Odds," X7; Geoffrey Shurlock to Phil Stein (at Harbel), 2/18/59, requesting script revisions, *Odds against Tomorrow* file, MPAA/MH/AMPAS.

28. Anthony Boucher, "Aftermath of a Crime," *NYTBR*, 11/3/57, 54; James Sandoe, "Odds against Tomorrow," *NYHTBR*, 1/27/57, 13.

29. On the differences between novel and film, see *OAT: Critical Edition*, 245–259.

30. Thom Anderson, "Red Hollywood," 257–263, and the other essays in Frank Krutnik, et al., *"Un-American" Hollywood: Politics and Film in the Blacklist Era* (New Brunswick, NJ: Rutgers University Press, 2007).

31. Polonsky and Belafonte were clients of the same left-wing lawyer, Sidney M. Davis; Schultheiss interview with Belafonte, *OAT: Critical Edition*, 238.

32. Polonsky's friend Walter Bernstein remembered Killens's name on a preliminary script; *Inside Out: A Memoir of the Blacklist* (1996; repr., New York: De Capo, 2000), 241. In 1953–1954, Killens and Polonsky served together on the editorial board of a short-lived left-wing journal, *The Contemporary Reader*, along with Millard Lampell, Ring Lardner, Jr., Lester Cole, Ellsworth Wright, Paule Marshall, and Julian Mayfield; Paul Buhle and Dave Wagner, *A Very Dangerous Citizen: Abraham Lincoln Polonsky and the Hollywood Left* (Berkeley: University of California Press, 2001), 167–168; *OAT: Critical Edition*, 245.

33. JOK to HB, December 12/3/57, Polonsky diaries, 3–7, 1958, and JOK to HB, 4/7/59, cited in Gilyard, *Killens*, 137, 142.

144. *Ebony* described him as "Belafonte's film editor" in "Belafonte Becomes 'Big Business,'" June 1958.

34. Lillian Fisher, "Hollywood Scratchpad, "*LATr*, 10/16/59, 20; "New Pictures," *Time*, 10/26/59; Almena Lomax, "Notes for Showfolks," *LATr*, 11/6/59, 19.

35. Eric Sherman and Martin Rubin, eds., *The Director's Event: Interviews with Five American Filmmakers* (New York: Atheneum, 1970), 10; Schultheiss interview with Polonsky 7/7/98, *OAT: Critical Edition*, 191.

36. Schultheiss interview with Belafonte, *OAT: Critical Edition*, 250–252.

37. *OAT: Critical Edition*, 93.

38. Bernstein, *Inside Out*, 241, 273–274; Buhle and Wagner *Polonsky*, 179–180; George Hickenlooper interview with Wise in *Reel Conversations* (New York: Citadel, 1991), 173; Schultheiss interview with Robert Wise, 2/11/98, *OAT: Critical Edition*, 137; Robert Ryan, "I Didn't Want to Play a Bigot," *Ebony*, November 1959, 68–72.

39. Ches Washington, "Uncovering Kim Hamilton" *PC* [n.d. but ca. August 1960].

40. Joseph Brun, *American Cinematographer*, August 1959; Murray Schumach, "Movie Director Explains Method," *NYT*, 10/5/59, 26.

41. John Nichols, "Three Movie Scores Issued on LP Disks: They Show How Films Are Using Jazz by Ellington, Lewis and Davis," *NYT*, 12/20/59, X15; "John Lewis, Highbrow Jazz Man," *AA*, 12/31/60, A5.

42. Nason, "Evaluating the Odds," X7; Irene Thirer, "Movie Spotlight," *NYP*, 4/5/59. Black newspaper columnists also noted the significance of Belafonte's path-breaking position: "Belafonte to Begin Shooting Next Film, OAT, Soon," *CDD*, 10/19/58, 19; Calvin, "HB Put Money Where Mouth Is," 19.

43. Nason, "Evaluating the Odds"; Jessie Zunser, "Young Man in a Hurry," *Cue*, 4/25/59.

44. "Lead Man Holler," *Time*, 3/2/59, 40–44, esp. 41.

45. Maurice Zolotow, "Belafonte," *American Weekly*, distributed with the *NYJA*, 5/10/59, 9–14. Prepublication ads shouted "Belafonte—Hero or Heel? What has Belafonte done to alienate himself from the people who helped him to the top? Why are the Negro peo-

ple who hailed him as the symbol of their aspirations disappointed in him?" *Denton (MD) Journal*, 5/8/59, 2.

46. Jesse H. Walker referred to the *American Weekly* article as a "hatchet job" in "Theatricals," *NYAN*, 5/10/59, 37; Jackie Robinson, *NYP*, 5/14/59. Robinson wrote his column with the assistance of William Branch, an African American playwright whose work had been staged by CNA in 1951. See also sympathetic *Variety* columnist Armand Archerd's warm profile "Harry Belafonte, Battling Eye Ailment, Again Reaches Top," *Lancaster (OH) Eagle Gazette*, 6/11/59; and *Ebony*, July 1959, 94–100.

47. Nason, "Evaluating the Odds"; Zunser, "Young Man in a Hurry"; "Negroes Human Beings in Film at Viking," *PTr*, 11/3/59, 8; "No Made to Order Stories for Negroes-Belafonte," *NJAG*, 11/28/59, A17.

48. Langston Hughes, "Too Much of Race," in *Good Morning Revolution: Uncollected Social Protest Writings of Langston Hughes*, ed. Faith Berry (1973; repr., Secaucus, NJ: Carol, 1992); Nason, "Evaluating the Odds"; "Belafonte Seeks Films without Race Conflict," *AA*, 3/21/59, 15.

49. "For Harry For Belafonte," *NYAN*, 9/5/59,15; Kate Cameron, "Singer, Actor, Now a Film Producer," *NYSN*, 10/4/59, sec. 1; "Belafonte Barnstorming Here and O'Seas to Work Up Bigger Ante on 'Odds,'" *VAR* [n.d., ca. 9/9/59].

50. "Tomorrow's Music Man," *NYT*, 10/13/50; "Movie Music Is by John Lewis," *NJAG*, 10/10/59, 22. UA also promoted two albums of Lewis's music, an orchestral version of the soundtrack as well as one performed by the MJQ; *Odds* clipping file, SCRBC.

51. Advertising in *NYP*, 10/9/59, and *OTr*, 10/28/59, 41; in *Hayward (CA) Daily Review*, 11/23/59, 39; *Bakersfield Californian*, 12/30/59, 13; *Clearfield (PA) Progress*, 12/30/59, 10; "Hollywood Told Lunch Sitdowns Hurt Bookings," *CDD*, 7/18/60, A17.

52. Reviews in *VAR*(d), 10/2/59 and 10/7/59; *MPH*, 10/3/59; *Film Daily*, 10/5/59; *NYDM*, 10/16/59; *Knickerbocker News*, 10/16/59; *Box Office Estimate* [n.d., ca. October 1959]; *HCN*, 11/12/59. Black press commentary includes "New Belafonte Film 'Bank Robbery' Sock," *CDD*, 9/1/59, 18; "Press See, Hail Latest Harry Belafonte Film," *CD*, 9/12/59, 20; Jesse H. Walker, "Theatricals," *NYAN*, 10/3/59, 16; Darcey DeMille, "Data 'n' Chatter," *AA*, 10/10/59, 12; A. L. Foster, "Other People's Business," *CD*, 10/17/59, 4; George E. Pitts, "Odds Favor Belafonte's 'Odds Against,'" *PC*, 11/21/59, 18.

53. *VAR*(d) reviews, 10/2/59 and 10/7/59; *NYP*, 10/16/59; *NYDM*, 10/16/59. The Motion Picture Production Code administrator had objected to the seductive mob henchman ("seems quite obviously to be a fairy" with "effeminate mannerisms") as "unacceptable in the finished picture" but the film *was* approved 6/29/59; Geoffrey Shurlock to Philip Stein, 2/23/59 and other materials on the film in the MPAA/MH/AMPAS.

54. *VAR* reviews (d), 10/2/59 and (w) 10/7/59; *LATr*, 10/2/1959, 18; Photo of "The 'On Screen' Belafonte Family" in *NYAN*, 7/4/59, 14, and *CD*, 7/4/59, 19; photos of "Child Friendly Set" and "A Most Happy Father," in *CCP*, 7/18/59, 1C; *CDD*, 8/25/59, 18.

55. Reviews in *MPH*, 10/3/59; *VAR*(d) 10/2/59 and 10/7/59; *NYT*, 10/16/59, 27, and 10/22/59, X1; *LAT*, 11/1/1959; *LAMN*, 11/11/59.

56. Geoffrey Warren, "'Odds Against' Bitter New Racial Drama," *LAT*, 11/12/59; Hollis Alpert, "Odds against Tomorrow: D for Effort," *Saturday Review*, 10/3/59.

57. Alpert, "Odds"; Mickey Pilley, "Odds Hailed for Photography," *Knickerbocker News*, 10/16/59.

58. "Belafonte Film Just Good Suspense, Says People's World Reviewer," in *LATr*, 11/20/59, 19; Ruth Waterbury, "'Odds' Is Startling Picture," *LAE*, 11/12/59; Archer Winston, "Reviewing Stand," *NYP*, 10/16/59; *Time*, 10/26/59.

59. Almena Lomax, "Belafonte's 'Odds against Tomorrow' May Mark 'Return to Reality' for Films," *LATr*, 10/2/59, 18; "Supported by 'Saturday Review,'" *LATr*, 10/16/59, 9.

60. Lomax, "Belafonte's 'Odds'"; Crowther, "Screen," *NYT*, 10/16/59, 27.

61. "George Gilbert Says: Don't Get the Message," *Salina (KS) Journal*, 2/8/60, 8.

62. George E. Pitts, "Harry Belafonte Wears a Smile of Success," *PC*, 10/31/59, 18.

63. A. S. "Doc" Young, "Short Takes," *LAS*, 10/22/59, C1; *OAT: Critical Edition*, 180; "Porgy 'N' Bess" also "clicked" in Melbourne and Sidney, Australia; *CDD*, 9/1/60, 8.

64. "Murder, Robbery Films Spotlight Sepia Stars," *CDD*, 10/13/59, 16; Joy Tunstall, "A Little Bit of Everything," *PC*, 10/24/59, 13.

65. "Frank Quinn's Movies: Belafonte His Toughest Critic," *NYM*, 1/31/60.

66. Hamilton, "Storm Over Belafonte," *Look*, 6/25/57; "OAT Belafonte Pix Due Soon," *CDD*, 3/16/59, 19; Delores Calvin, "HB Introduces Plan to Rate Sepians," *CDD*, 3/18/59, 18; "Belafonte Seeks Films without Racial Conflict,"15; "Movie-Maker Belafonte," *Ebony*, July 1959, 98; "HB Signs TC Contract with BBC," *AA*, 8/8/59, 15; Hal Boyle, "Belafonte Crusade Seeks New Role for Negro," *NYWT*, 9/14/59; Cameron, "Singer, Actor, Now a Film Producer." Jesse Walker announced an MGM plan for Belafonte to star as the beloved mixed-race French writer in a filmed "Life of Alexandre Dumas" (father), in "Theatricals," *NYAN*, 5/10/59, 37. Belafonte was still talking up his Pushkin biopic to be filmed in Russia on "Youth Want to Know," (NBC) as noted in "Tele Follow-Up Comment, *VAR*, 8/26/59, 31; in Al Monroe, "So They Say," *CDD*, 10/27/59, 16; "Belafonte Reveals Plan to Film Pushkin, Western [Exodusters]," (ANP) *AA*, 11/7/59, 15.

67. Harbel bid for but did not get the rights to film *Raisin*, eventually produced by David Susskind's company for Columbia; Thirer, "Movie Spotlight."

68. Jessie Zunser, "Young Man in a Hurry."

69. *Belafonte at Carnegie Hall* stayed on the pop charts for three years. The second live album, *Belafonte Returns to Carnegie Hall* (1960) also included selections sung by Miriam Makeba, Odetta, the renamed and now independent group, the Belafonte Folk Singers, and the Chad Mitchell Trio.

70. Hal Boyle, "Belafonte Crusade Seeks New Role for Negro," *LAMN*, 9/14/59 (a shorter version appeared first in *NYWT*, 9/1/59).

71. May Okon, "No Dough-Re-Mi Man," *NYDN*, 6/8/58; John P. Shanley, "Belafonte with Allen," *NYT*, 11/10/58, 59; "Tele Follow-Up Comment," *VAR*, 11/12/58, 27; "Belafonte Is Cut Off,' *NYT*, 11/10/58, 59.

72. "Meet Harry Belafonte, Stage's 'Mr. Wisdom,'" *CD*, 1/3/59, 18; *TV Guide*, 1/10–16/59; Charles Mercer, "Mercer Pans 'Adventures in Music: Harry Belafonte's Songs Only Part Thoroughly Enjoyed," (UP), *Appleton (WI) Post-Crescent*, 1/13/59, 38; Jack Gould, "Television: A Bell Ringer," *NYT*, 1/13/59; "Bell Telephone Hour," *VAR*, 1/4/59, 39.

73. Television specials began to be produced in 1954: Castleman and Podrazik, *Watching TV*, 90–91.

74. "Foreign TV Reviews," *VAR*, 8/27/58, 29.

75. "'Great Dictator;' British TV Columnist Reveals Belafonte Pact," *AA*, 1/17/59, 18; Richard Shepard, "Belafonte Signed for Special on TV," *NYT*, 8/27/59.

76. Emily Coleman, "Organization Man Named Belafonte," *NYT*, 12/13/59, 35.

77. "CBS-TV Slates Belafonte for Hour Show," *CD*, 9/5/59, 19; Kay Gardella, "Specs Aren't Special Says Star Belafonte," *NYSN*, 12/6/59; "Tonight with Belafonte," *Lima County (OH) Daily Times*, 12/5/59, 36; "An Evening with Harry Belafonte," *TV Guide*, 12/5–11/59; *Tonight with Belafonte* broadcast, PCM/NYC.

78. Nat Hentoff, "The Faces of Harry Belafonte," *The Reporter*, July 1959.

79. "Odetta to be Heard on Television November 15," *CDD*, 11/9/59, 20. Hinkson and Nicks worked on *Sing, Man, Sing*. Mitchell's dance with a white female company member on a 1958 television broadcast of Balanchine's *Nutcracker* generated controversy; author's interview with Chiz Schultz, 7/30/2012.

80. John P. Shanley, "TV: Tonight with Belafonte Offered," *NYT*, 12/12/59.

81. A few days after the TV special, Belafonte opened in a one-man show at the Palace, a former vaudeville theater in New York City. New York drama critic Walter Kerr contrasted Belafonte's entrance with other entertainers: most "breeze onto the stage with a great big smile, a waving of the hands and a welcome-home air of having done the world a great big favor. The most striking thing about Harry Belafonte is that he enters glowering"; quoted in *AA*, 12/26/59, 15.

82. Shanley, "TV: Tonight with Belafonte"; Larry Wolters, "Belafonte Gives TV a Fine Hour," and "TV Mailbag," *CTr*, 12/11/59, 6, and 1/6/1960, C22; Fred Danzig, "Night with Belafonte Wins Praise of TV Fans," (UPI) *CDD*, 12/14/59, A17; "Television Reviews: Tonight with Belafonte," *VAR*, 12/16/59, 27; Richard Coe, "1959: A Year to Grow On," *WP*, 12/27/59, H3.

83. *CD*, 12/19/59, 19; Young, "The Big Beat," *LAS*, 12/17/59, C1.

84. Young, "Big Beat"; [Ziggy Johnson], "Zig and Zag," *CD*, 1/9/60, 18; Chestyn Everette, "Tonight with Belafonte, or, Odetta saves the Day," *LATr*, 12/18/59, 19; Young, "Big Beat."

85. "Belafonte 'Tonight' Cops Sylvania Video Award," *AA*, 1/30/60, 15; "Emmy Award Winners," *NYP*, 6/21/60; Chazz Crawford, "Belafonte First to Win TV's Emmy," *CE*, 6/23/60, 1; Television

"Trendex" ratings in Bob Salmaggi, "Madison Ave. Is Dead End—Harry," *LAT*, 11/18/60, A12.

86. "Belafonte Arrives in Japan for Tour," *Stars and Stripes*, July 10, 1960; http://park18.wakwak.com/~chanki/belafonte/e_belafonte.html, accessed and translated for me by Toru Shinoda, 7/2/2013.

87. "Belafonte Hits 'Escapist' Show Bizites; Asks More Political Action, Less Pools," *VAR*, 8/10/60; "Afro Readers Say," *AA*, 4/16/60, 4.

88. "Belafonte on Four Shows for Revlon," *CE*, 3/31/60, 9; "Harry Seeks New Talent While Abroad," *NYAN*, 7/23/60, 16; "Belafonte OKs Two TV Specials," *AA*, 10/1/60, 5.

89. Richard F. Shepard, "Two Music Specials Due on Television," *NYT*, 10/15/60, 47; newspaper advertisement, *NYT*, 11/20/60. Postal zone 19 extended from 48th to 59th Streets and from Fifth Avenue to the Hudson River.

90. "Belafonte's New York 19 Gives Folk Singing Bounce," (UPI, *ADW*, 11/16/60, 2.

91. Ben Gross, "Harry Belafonte Discusses Russian and U.S. Folk Music," *NYSN*, in section 2, What's On? TV-Radio, 11/20/60.

92. Gross, "Harry Belafonte Discusses Russian and U.S. Folk Music."

93. Quinn, "Belafonte His Toughest Critic"; John Crosby, "Mr. Belafonte and Madison Avenue," *NYHT*, 11/13/60; "Belafonte, Revlon Hit Snag on Video Commercial Set-Up," 11/14/60, 22; Salmaggi, "Madison Ave Is Dead End."

94. Gross, "Harry Belafonte Discusses Russia and U.S. Folk Music."

95. "Belafonte Sings 'Popular' 1st Time," *PTr*, 11/15/60, 5.

96. Shanley, "Belafonte on the Town," *NYT*, 11/21/60, 59.

97. Lawrence Laurent, "Radio and Television: Harry's Husky Urgency Gives Any Show Pace," *WP*, 11/22/60, A17.

98. Shanley, "Belafonte on the Town"; Cecil Smith, "Belafonte: Man of Charm, Spirit," *LAT*, 11/22/60, A8; Laurent, "Harry's Husky Urgency"; "Television Reviews," *VAR*, 11/23/60.

99. Sam Lacy, "Star Gazing: Belafonte TV Show Among Finalists for Top Award," *AA*, 1/16/60, 15; Lori Nails, "Belafonte 19 Was Almost 20, Par for Star's Future Shows," *CDD*, 11/23/60, 21; Jesse H. Walker, "'Theatricals,' *NYAN*, 11/26/60, 15; Ralph Mason, "TV Notes and Notices: Bright Spot in a So-So Season," *AA*, 12/3/60, A5.

100. Val Adams, "Sponsor Cancels Belafonte Shows: Revlon Says New TV Show Plans Eliminate Two Specials," *NYT*, 8/1/61; "Report Handsome Payoff in TV Cancellations," (ANP), *AA*, 8/26/61, 15.

101. Cecil Smith, "The TV Scene—Why No Niche for Belafonte?," *LAT*, 8/28/61.

102. Harry Belafonte, "Belafonte: 'Look, They tell Me, Don't Rock the Boat,'" *NYT*, 4/21/68, D21, reprinted as "TV a Nightmare for Blacks," in *PC*, 5/4/68, 13.

103. TB/HB, 3/6/1985; Ward, *Just My Soul Responding*, 315–325.

104. Belafonte (as told to Nat Hentoff), "My Repertory Must Have Roots," *Hi-Fi Review*, January 1959, 42–43 and Belafonte's forward in *Songs Belafonte Sings* (New York: Duell, Sloan and Pearce, 1962), vii–x.

105. The recording session with Dylan took place in the summer of 1961. Dylan offered a backhanded tribute to Belafonte's repertoire with "Talkin' Hava Negilah Blues," which he introduced as "a foreign song I learned in Utah," sung in folk clubs in the Village in 1961 and recorded 4/25/62 on a demo tape. Dylan wrote an effusive account of Belafonte's influence on him in *Chronicles* (New York: Simon and Schuster, 2004), 68–69. *Belafonte at the Greek Theater* (1964) was his last album to break into the Top 40.

106. Cohen, *Rainbow Quest*, 213.

107. "Belafonte Concert to Benefit 'Riders,'" *AA*, 9/23/61, 15; Robert Shelton, "Negro Songs Here Aid Rights Drive," *NYT*, 6/23/63, 15; Bernice Johnson Reagon interview with Amy Goodman on *Democracy Now!*, 12/30/2008; Belafonte's work with SCLC, SNCC, and King covered in Taylor Branch's three volumes; see also Stokely Carmichael's memoir, *Ready for Revolution*, 213-222. Once the FBI began to focus on King's close relationship with Stanley Levison, Belafonte's friendship with Stanley Levison and his proximity to King also placed him under FBI scrutiny; Garrow, *The FBI and MLK*, 40–60. Belafonte urged King to resist anticommunist witch-hunting; Branch, *Parting the Waters*, 844–845.

108. "Sellout NY Crowd Greets 'Summit' at King Benefit," *AA*, 2/4/61, 15; Belafonte organized a special performers' benefit at midnight at the Apollo before the buses left for the March on Washington on 8/23/1963; D'Emilio, *Rustin*, 353; Frank Hunt, "30,000 Roar as King declares 'Freedom' War," *AA*, 4/3/65, 1. Belafonte managed both the logistics and the community spirit in orchestrating the celebrity performances in support of the third Selma to Montgomery

March in 1965; Gertrude Wilson, "How the Stars Fared at Montgomery Rally," *NYAN*, 4/3/65, 2; see also Renata Adler's long "Letter from Selma," *New Yorker*, 4/10/65, 121–157.

109. Belafonte's opposition to the Vietnam War reported in *The Worker* 7/18/65, cited by Ross, *Hollywood Left and Right*, 219; Belafonte in Paris Assails Policy of U.S. in Vietnam," *NYT*, 3/25/66, 37; "Vietnam Splits King's Paris Backers," *AA*, 4/9/66, 14; Ollie Stewart, "Report from Europe," *AA*, 4/16/66, 8.

110. *The Fire Next Time* (1963; repr., New York: Laurel, 1988), 127; TB/HB, 3/16/85; Belafonte, "What Kind of Integration," *NYT*, 2/2/69, D9.

111. "Harry Belafonte Raps Sorry Colored Leaders, U.S. Lethargy, Hails Need for Colored Press," *AA*, 7/5/61, 8.

112. "Belafontes on Short Trip to Africa, Italy," *AA*, 2/24/62, 15; "Belafonte Marks Nairobi Freedom," *AA*, 12/21/63, 11; "Belafonte in Dakar," *AA*, 5/9/64, 12; Elizabeth M. Oliver, "They Came 3,000 Miles, from Mississippi to the Boardwalk to Rewrite History," *AA*, 9/12/64, A6; "Belafonte, Dr. King, Get Rhodesia Bids," *AA*, 10/24/64, 12.

113. Miriam Makeba and HB to Langston Hughes, February 10, 1965, in Box 16, Folder 306, LHP; "We Say No to Apartheid: A Declaration of American Artists, distributed by the American Committee on Africa, [1965]," accessed at http://africanactivist.msu.edu/document_metadata.php?objectid+32–130-FC3, 7/14/2012.

114. "Belafonte, Makeba to Visit Sullivan," *AA*, 4/21/62, 15; "Tele Follow-Up Comment," *VAR*, 4/27/1963, 31, 49, and 4/3/64, 41; Doc Quigg, "HB Makes Rare TV Appearance: Singer Generally Finds Commercial Television Terribly Limiting," (UPI) *Independent Press Telegram* (Long Beach, CA), 4/7/63, 125; Alta Baer, "Scene and Heard," *NYJA*, 3/22/65.

115. Lawyer and King associate Clarence Jones interviewed on *Fresh Air*, NPR, 1/17/2011; "Belafonte to Join Dinah on TV Special He Planned," *AA*, 2/13/65, 11; Bernard Weintraub, "Harry and Dinah Sing for the Peace Corps" and "Salute to Peace Corps," *NYT*, 2/14/65, X13, and 2/16/65, 71.

116. Alta Baer, "Scene and Heard," *NYJA*, 3/22/64; "Belafonte to Host one Hour TV Special," *HR*, 4/26/65; "Belafonte Plans Musical," *NYT*, 4/26/65, A1; Val Adams, "CBS Will Offer Specials Again," *NYT*, 6/2/65, 91.

117. "Negro Life in Harlem," *CDD*, 5/11/65, 18; "Belafonte to Re-

create Harlem Hey-Day on All-Tan TV Show," *PTr*, 5/11/65, 13. Donald McKayle, a CNA colleague, choreographed the dancing in *The Strollin' 20s*.

118. "Belafonte Plans Musical"; "Book Gave Belafonte Idea for Harlem Spec," *NYSN*, 2/20/66. Hughes occasionally pitched songs to Belafonte's organization, and wrote the liner notes for Belafonte's 1959 album, *My Lord What a Mornin'*. Hughes worked on the script for *The Strollin' 20s* between May and December, 1965, writing that it had been "wonderful working with you on Strollin' 20's and I am most grateful to you for the privilege . . . You have a way of making everyone around you feel needed— which therefore makes everyone want to do his best for you"; Rampersad, *Hughes II*, 266, 302, 392, 394, 398; letters in Folders 305, 306, Box 13, drafts of the liner notes in Folder 5984, Box 370, LHP.

119. Hughes produced "six or eight drafts before we were satisfied"; "A Big Star Stomp through Old Time Harlem," *Life*, 2/4/66, 76.

120. "Harry Belafonte: Sentimental Journey," *NYT*, 2/20/66; "Book Gave Belafonte the Idea"; "A Big Star Stomp," 76.

121. "Harry Belafonte: Sentimental Journey"; "A Big Star Stomp," 76; "Book Gave Belafonte the Idea."

122. "Book Gave Belafonte Idea."

123. *The Strollin' 20s* broadcast, PCM/NYC.

124. John S. Wilson, "TV: 'The Strollin' 20s' Limp Sadly in CBS Version," *NYT*, 2/22/66, 35; "Television Reviews," *VAR*, 2/23/66. The theatrical reviewer for the *NYAN* tallied up the daily press in New York as "5 minuses, one half plus, and only one plus"; Jessie H. Walker, "Theatricals," 2/26/66, 19.

125. Hank Grant, "TV Review: The Strollin' 20s," *HR*, 2/23/66; Rick Du Brow, "'Strollin' 20s' Takes High Harlem Road," (UPI), *LAT*, 2/23/66, C15; reprinted in many newspapers, for example, *Cumberland (MD) Evening News*, 2/22/66; 5; *AA* 3/5/66, 11; *NJAG*, 2/26/66, A2; Cynthia Lowry, "Harlem Memoir Pleasant Viewing," (AP), *Athens (OH) Messenger*, 2/22/66, 7; also widely reprinted.

126. Gertrude Gipson, "Belafonte Produces: The Strollin' 20s and the Harlem of Yesteryear," *LAS*, 2/24/66, B10; Jessie Walker, "Theatricals, *NYAN*, 3/5/66, 18.

127. Jacob Sherman, "Reviewers Have Mixed Emotions," and E. W. Rhodes, "Stereotypes Distasteful," *PTr*, 2/26/66, 19; Mrs. G. Prescott's letter to *NYAN*, 5/21/66, 31; E. W. Rhode and Ivan Harold

Browning, letter to *NYAN* quoted in Walker, "Theatricals," 3/12/66, 18, and letter to *PC*, 4/16/66, 9B, possibly responding to a *PC* columnist who had written that although the show was panned by critics, "the man on the street . . . was loud in his applause"; 3/12/66, 5B.

128. Joseph L. Turner, "Strolling Twenties Called Sleeper," *CCP*, 3/19/66, 3C.

129. "Harry Belafonte Tops Star Cast 'Stage 67,'" *LAS*, 1/5/67, B5; Paul Gardner, "Dark Laughter in Snow White Land," *NYT*, 4/2/67, 117; Russell and Belafonte's 1966 tour information on http://www.nanamouskouri.qc.ca/concerts/concerts_1966.html, accessed 7/16/2012; Russell's *VAR* ad, 4/19/67, 95; Peter Coyote, *Sleeping Where I Fall: A Chronicle* (Washington, DC: Counterpoint, 1998), 44. Belafonte's plans to produce an off-Broadway version of the Mime Troupe show between 1968 and 1971 in Folder 2, Memos 1968–1976, Box 1, CSC, SCRBC.

130. Gardner, "Dark Laughter in Snow White Land."

131. Mel Watkins, "Pioneering Comedians," and "Stand-Up Comedy," in *There's Nothing Like the Real Thing*, 112–117, 186–192; Bob Hull, "TV Talk: Belafonte Leads Negro Cast in 'Time for Laughter' Show," *LAHE*, 4/5/67. Mabley was born in 1894; Markham in 1904; Foxx, Kirby, and Russell in the early 1920s; Gregory in 1932, and Pryor in 1940.

132. Gardner, "Dark Laughter in Snow White Land."

133. *A Time for Laughter* broadcast, PCM/NYC.

134. "Dog, Dog," also called "My Dog Loves Your Dog" and "The Dog Song," was written in 1959 by students at the American Baptist Theological seminary in Nashville, then sung in jail during the Nashville sit-in movement. The Nashville Quartet sang it on the 1960 album *The Nashville Sit-In Story*. The SNCC Freedom Singers sang it on their 1963 album *We Shall Overcome*. Belafonte recorded a version on his 1967 album, *Belafonte on Campus*.

135. *A Time for Laughter* was one of the highest-ranked shows in ABC's Stage 67 series; "Poitier Red Hot in TV Ratings," *VAR*, 4/19/67, 1.

136. Jack Gould, "TV: 'Time for Laughter,'" *NYT*, 4/7/67, 74; Bob MacKenzie, "TV: The Color of a Laugh," *OTr*, 4/7/67, 24; Hazel Garland, "Video Vignettes," *PC*, 5/23/68, 13.

137. "Tele Follow-Up Comment," *VAR*, 4/12/67; "TV Review, *HR*, 4/7/67; Cynthia Lowry, "Radio-TV Highlights," (AP), *News* (Fred-

erick, MD), 4/7/67, 8; Rick Du Brow, "Negro Humor Show Called Erratic Yet Important," (UPI), *Tipton (IN) Tribune*, 4/7/67, 2, and *NJAG*, 4/15/67, 14.

138. M.B. comments, *PTr*, 4/11/67, 11; Jesse H. Walker, "Theatricals," *NYAN*, 4/15/67, 20; Lee Ivory, "Among the Stars," (NPI), *CCP*, 4/29/67, 3B.

139. Ziggy Johnson, "Zagging with Ziggy," *CD*, 4/22/67, 24A.

140. Harold A. L. Clement, "Pulse of NY's Public: Mourn, Don't Laugh," *NYAN*, 4/22/67, 14.

141. Lee Ivory, "Among the Stars."

142. Gardner, "Dark Laughter in Snow White Land."

143. Author's interview with Chiz Schultz, 7/30/2012; Army Archerd, "Just for Variety," *VAR*, 8/16/67.

144. Paul Monaco, *History of the American Cinema: The Sixties, 1960–1969* (Berkeley: University of California Press, 2003), 20–45, 54–55.

145. Archerd, "Just for Variety."

146. Malamud, "Angel Levine," *Commentary* 20, no 6 (December 1955): 534–540; revised for *The Magic Barrel* (Philadelphia: The Jewish Publication Society of America, 1958), 43–56; "Old Men of the Sea: *The Magic Barrel*," *Time*, 5/12/58, 104. Based on short stories, "The World of Sholom Aleichem" had a successful off-Broadway run in 1953 that supported a number of blacklisted artists, Ossie Davis, Ruby Dee, and Robert DeCormier among them. In 1967, a film adaptation of Malamud's prize-winning 1966 novel, *The Fixer*, was under way, directed by John Frankenheimer, with screenplay by formerly blacklisted writer Dalton Trumbo; it would be released in December 1968.

147. Howard Pollack, *Marc Blitzstein: His Life, His Work, His World* (New York: Oxford University Press, 2012), 487; A. H. Weiler, "Passing Picture Scene: The Angel Levine to Face Cameras Here," *NYT*, 3/11/62; "Films to Shoot in New York," *Back Stage*, 5/25/62; A. H. Weiler, "Local View," *NYT*, 2/23/64, X9. The planned production crew other leftists: Gilford's wife, actress Madeline Lee; documentary filmmaker Haskell Wexler; blacklisted writer Saul Levitt; and industrial and documentary film director Victor D. Solow. Harnick and Bock plan noted in Lewis Funke, "The Rialto: Guild Gets Going," *NYT*, 6/27/65, X1. Later Malamud would regain the musical rights for a Jewish opera version produced by Elie Siegmeister that premiered in 1985.

148. The *Angel Levine* film was green-lighted by David Picker, UA vice president in charge of production, credited with the James Bond series, the Beatles films, and the risky and unconventional film *Midnight Cowboy*; author's interview with Schultz, 7/30/2012.

149. Belafonte's conditions and the lists of guests appeared in daily newspaper TV announcements; "Belafonte Power," *Newsweek*, 2/19/68, 161; Hal Humphrey, "Belafonte Makes It Big as a Host for 'Tonight,'" *Courier Journal* (Louisville, KY, 3/10/68).

150. "Belafonte Power"; Belafonte, *My Song*, 322–325.

151. Jack Gould, "TV: Belafonte Reinvigorates the Late Night Show," *NYT*, 2/7/68, 95, and reprinted elsewhere, for example, *Hutchinson (KS) News*, 2/8/68.

152. Weatherby, "Green Power—and Black—on Broadway," *Manchester Guardian*, 4/4/68; Duckett in *CDD*, 3/2/68, 11.

153. Bob Williams, "Belafonte and Petula Clark Touch a Sponsor's Nerve," *NYP*, 3/6/68; Robert E. Dallos, "Incident at TV Taping Irks Belafonte," *NYT*, 3/7/68, 87; "Auto Aide Relieved in Belafonte Case," *NYT*, 3/11/68, 82; "The Touch," *Newsweek*, 3/18/68; author's interview with Schultz, 7/30/2012.

154. Bill Lane, "Inside Story: Clean Up," *LAS*, 3/14/68, B10; Jack Gould, "TV: Petula Clark with a Network Hour of her Own," *NYT*, 4/3/68, 95.

155. Harry Belafonte, "Look, They Tell Me, Don't Rock the Boat," *NYT*, 4/21/68, D21, reprinted as "TV a Nightmare for Blacks," *PC*, 5/4/68, 13.

156. Rick Du Brow, "Four Jolt TV," (UPI), *NJAG*, 7/6/68, 14; Earl Calloway, "Theatre Wing," *CDD*, 7/3/68, 17; Hazel Garland, "Video Vignettes," *PC*, 7/12/68, 13; "C.B.S. Leads in TV Race to Probe Race," *PTr*, 7/13/68, 20.

157. TB/HB, 3/6/85, TBC.

158. *LAT*, 8/7/68, as cited in Ross, *Hollywood Left and Right*, 223. A similar statement appeared in Belafonte, "Control and Conscience," *Films and Filming* 18, no.12 (September 1972), 27.

159. Michael Staub, *Torn at the Roots: The Crisis of Jewish Liberalism in Postwar America* (New York: Columbia University Press, 2002); Wendell Pritchett, *Brownsville, Brooklyn: Blacks, Jews, and the Changing Face of the Ghetto* (Chicago: University of Chicago Press, 2002); Jerald Podair, *The Strike that Changed NY: Blacks, Whites, and the Ocean-Hill Brownsville Crisis* (New Haven: Yale University Press, 2004).

160. One review criticized the original story as not as rewarding as the "old Jewish joke on which it was based"; *Time*, 5/12/58, 104.

161. Malamud, "The Angel Levine," in *The Magic Barrel*, 46, 56.

162. Gunn was hired by Belafonte Enterprises to rewrite an earlier script written by Joe Sargent. Gunn's 1968 script was admired by UA's David Picker; author's interviews with Alice Spivak, 5/6/2012, and Chiz Schultz, 7/30/2012.

163. On Robinson's gangster masking, see Rachel Rubin and Jeffrey Melnick, *Immigrants and American Popular Culture* (New York: New York University Press, 2007), 30–34.

164. "The Angel Levine," *Cue*, 8/1/1970.

165. Hansberry, "Willy Loman, Walter Younger, and He Who Must Live," *Village Voice*, 8/12/59, reprinted in *Women in Theater: Compassion and Hope*, ed. Karen Malpede (New York: Drama, 1983), 170.

166. Memo from Chiz Schultz to HB, 9/5/68, Folder 2, Box 1, CSC, SCRBC.

167. Kimmis Hendrick, "'One Red Thread' in Kadar's Films," *Christian Science Monitor*, 9/30/67; "The Czechs in Exile," *Newsweek*, 7/27/70; Jerry Tallmer, "Film Director Jan Kadar," *NYP*, 6/26/71, 15.

168. Before WWII, Kaminska founded and directed two Yiddish theater companies in Warsaw. After the Nazi invasion of Poland, she fled to the Soviet Union, returning to Warsaw at the end of WWII to found another Yiddish performing company, the Jewish State Theater, to keep Yiddish culture alive after the destruction of most of the Polish Jewish communities. A new wave of attacks on Polish Jews, including Kaminska's company, after the Six-Day War in June 1967 encouraged her to bring her company to tour in the United States and then to leave Poland permanently in 1968.

169. Memos to HB from Chiz Schultz, 5/13/68; 6/6/68 in Box 1, Folder 2, CSC, SCRBC; Nick Browne, "Would You Believe Harry Belafonte as a Jewish Angel?," *NYT*, 4/27/69; author's interview with Schultz, 7/30/2012.

170. A. H. Weiler, "Paging Ethel Waters," *NYT*, 11/24/68, D18; Robert B. Frederick, "Belafonte's 'Comeback' Film: He Long Nixed Wrongo Roles," *VAR*, 12/18/68, 5, 18.

171. "Cinema Happenings," *CDD*, 12/14/68, 17; Jesse Walker, "Theatricals," *NYAN*, 12/21/68.

172. Dick Gregory, John O'Neal, Julian Mayfield, Barbara Ann

Teer, Douglas Turner Ward, James Baldwin, Vinnette Carroll, Harold Cruse, Harry Belafonte, Alice Childress, "Can Black and White Artists Still Work Together?," *NYT*, 2/2/69, D1.

173. Donal Henahan, "A Grant Opens Door to Film Apprentices," *NYT*, 4/2/69, 38; Rustin-initiated program described in Levine, *Bayard Rustin*, 218–219.

174. "Raymond St. Jacques, Godfrey Cambridge in 'Private Eye' Movies," *PTr*, 4/15/69; "Brown [*AL* apprentice] Associate Producer," *NYAN*, 7/18/70, 20; "Chicago's Film Workshop into High Gear," *CDD*, 7/17/70, 2; "Belafonte Plays Angel On and Off the Screen," *Ebony*, October 1969, 76–82.

175. "Belafonte to Star in Movie with Zero Mostel," *PTr*, 2/11/69, 30; "Hues and Cries," *AA*, 2/22/69, 10; "Billy Rowe's Notebook," *NYAN*, 2/22/69, 21; "Belafonte's Jewish Doctor Irishman," *AA*, 3/8/69, 10; "Gloria Foster Has Key Role in New Belafonte Movie," *PTr*, 3/8/69, 19; "Barbara Ann Teer Cast in Belafonte Vehicle," *AA*, 3/29/69, 10. The picture appeared on 6/14/69 in *AA*, *CCP*, *NJAG*; *PC*, 6/28/69.

176. Browne, "Would You Believe Harry Belafonte as a Jewish Angel?"

177. Wolfe, "A Melting Pot Cast."

178. "Czech Director of Harry Belafonte's New Film Learned English from Cast," *PTr*, 4/4/70, 22; Kadar quoted in Wanda Hale, "Angel Levine—That's Belafonte," *NYSN*, 7/27/70; Melnick, *A Right to Sing the Blues*, 9.

179. Brown, "Would You Believe Harry Belafonte as a Jewish Angel?"

180. Brown, "Would You Believe Harry Belafonte as a Jewish Angel?"

181. Author's interview with Schultz, 7/30/2012; memos from Schultz to HB and from David Payne to Schultz, 3/6/70 and 3/27/70, Box 1, Folder 2, CSC, SCRBC. Examples of this publicity include "Mostel, Belafonte Starrer Roles February 27," *HR*, 2/6/69; "Belafonte to Star in Movie with Zero Mostel," *PTr*, 2/22/69, 10; "Belafonte-Mostel Film Completes Major Work," *AA*, 6/7/69, 9.

182. Browne, "Would You Believe Harry Belafonte as a Jewish Angel?"

183. Browne, "Would You Believe Harry Belafonte as a Jewish Angel?"

184. "Harry Belafonte Says He Once Considered Quitting the

Movies," *PTr*, 10/18/69, 24; "Belafonte Doing Something Special," *CCP*, 10/25/69, 5B; "Belafonte Plays Angel On and Off Screen," 80, 77.

185. "Belafonte Plays Angel On and Off Screen," 80.

186. Memo to HB from Chiz Schultz, 3/6/70, in Folder 2, Box 1, CSC, SCRBC; author's interview with Schultz, 7/30/2012; "United Artists Pressbook for *The Angel Levine*," BFC, SCRBC; "Harry Belafonte's New Movie Reunites Many Old Friends," *PTr*, 2/7/70, 22; "'The Angel Levine' to Open next Month," *NYAN*, 3/7/70, 19; "'The Angel Levine' Opening on July 30," *NYAN*, 7/25/70, 19; "'The Angel Levine' Prize Winner [Kadar]'s Film," *NYAN*, 8/1/70, 21; "Belafonte Plays Rogue 'Angel' in Newest Movie," *PTr*, 8/15/70, 2.

187. These phrases appear in Kevin Thomas, "'Angel Levine' Opens Run," *LAT*, 7/15/70, and "Review," *MPD*, 7/14/70, 14.

188. Arthur Knight, "It Suffers in Translation," *Saturday Review*, 8/1/70; *VAR*(d), 7/14/70; *HR*, 7/15/70; *MPD*; Thomas, "Angel Levine Opens Run"; Winifred Blevins, "Belafonte, Mostel Perfect in 'Angel,'" *LAHE*, 7/17/70; "Showman's Trade Reviews: The Angel Levine," *MPE*, 7/22/70; "Reviews," *MPH*, 7/29/70; "Miracle in the Ghetto," *Newsweek*, 8/3/70.

189. Leo Guild, "'Angel Levine' Stars Belafonte," *HCN*, 7/17/70; Roger Greenspun, "Screen: Kadar's 'The Angel Levine,'" *NYT*, 7/29/70, 32.

190. Author's interview with Schultz, 7/30/2012; "Showman's Trade Reviews"; see also Matthew Frye Jacobson, *Roots Too: White Ethnic Revival in Post–Civil Rights America* (Cambridge, MA: Harvard University Press, 2006); James Edward Smethurst, *The Black Arts Movement: Literary Nationalism in the 1960s and 1970s* (Chapel Hill: University of North Carolina Press, 2005).

191. Arthur Knight, "It Suffers in the Translation," *Saturday Review*, 8/1/70.

192. "Showman's Trade Reviews."

193. Mark Goodman, "Meshugge," *Time*, 8/3/70, 68.

194. Knight, "It Suffers in the Translation"; Deac Rossell, "'Angel Levine:' A Movie Miracle," *Boston After Dark*, 9/1/1970.

195. Wanda Hale, "'Angel Levine'—That's Belafonte," *NYSN*, 7/26/70, S7.

196. Vernon Scott, "A Decade Brings Return of Belafonte to Movies," *NJAG*, 8/1/70, 14, titled "Belafonte Relents, Now Ready for More Movies," *AA*, 8/1/70, 11; Les Mathews, "Mr. 1-2-5 Street," 8/1/70, 6.

197. *Cotton Comes to Harlem*, based on a detective novel by African American writer Chester Himes, was reviewed in *CD* and *NYAN*; *LATr* had ceased publication by the summer of 1970; *NYAN* and *PTr* reprinted the UA press book release 8/1/70, 21, and 8/15/70, 22; no reviews in *LAS*, *PC*, *CCP*, *AA*, *NJAG*, or *ADW*.

198. Ralph Blumenfeld, "A Talk with Harry Belafonte," *NYP*, 8/1/70, 11.

199. Blumenfeld, "A Talk."

200. Harry Belafonte, "Martin Luther King and W. E. B. Du Bois: A Personal Tribute," remarks from 1/30/72, printed in *Freedomways* 2, no. 1 (1972): 21.

AFTERWORD

1. "St. Jacques, Belafonte, Pioneer in 'Self Help,' *LAS*, 9/11/69, E1. Recording sessions took place in 1961, 1962, 1967, 1968, 1970, and 1971. De Paur had worked with the Hall Johnson choir from 1932 to 1940, directed music for the NYC Negro Unit of the FTP, and conducted the WWII Infantry Chorus that toured throughout the world until 1968, releasing an album of African music in 1965.

2. *Beat Street* was produced with support from David Picker, the UA executive who had been willing to take a chance on *The Angel Levine*. Its fictional account of hip-hop culture was shot in the Bronx and features actor-musician Guy Davis (son of Ossie Davis and Ruby Dee), actor Rae Dawn Chong (daughter of Tommy Chong), and appearances by hip-hop pioneers Kool Herc, Afrika Bambaataa, and Grandmaster Melle Mel. Belafonte's advocacy helped establish a special division on hip-hop within Cuba's Ministry of Culture.

3. For example, M. Cordell Thompson, "Belafonte Bounces Back Big and Black," *Jet*, 7/6/72, 59; Dorothy Gilliam, "Harry Belafonte," *WP*, 11/20/78, D1ff.; "TV: Belafonte Interviewed," *NYAN*, 2/2/79; "Belafonte Sours on Films, Disco, Music, TV, Racism, Backsliding Blacks," *Jet*, 4/26/79, 33.

4. Belafonte interviewed on *Democracy Now*, 6/15/2004, referring to People's Songs musician Bernie Asbel's 1945 "Song of My Hands" and the verse "I made your machines, I made each one / But without my hands, no machine could run," *Songs for Political Action*, 139.

INDEX

Page numbers followed by the letter *f* indicate figures. Titles in bold indicate works performed or produced by Harry Belafonte. Unless otherwise indicated, entries in quotation marks are songs. The abbreviation HB in subheadings refers to Harry Belafonte.

ABC. *See* American Business Consultants
Abernathy, Ralph, 142
Abzug, Bella, 281n65
"A Dollar Ain't a Dollar Anymore," 45
Afro-American newspaper, 43, 174, 208, 211; HB profile in, 154, 159–160
Ailey, Alvin, 104, 134
Aleichem, Sholem, 32, 232, 233
All the King's Men (stage play, 1948), 31
Almanac Singers, 40
"A Man Is Ten Feet Tall" (television drama, 1955), 127
American Business Consultants (ABC), 62. See also *Counterattack* newsletter
American Committee for Yugoslav Relief, 38
American Committee on Africa, 173, 253
American Labor Party, 53
American Legion, 67
American Negro Theater (ANT), 19–24, 25–26, 46–47; HB and, 19, 20–24, 24f, 25–26, 30, 46–47, 179; dissolution of, 47, 66
Amos 'n' Andy, 65, 67, 124, 225, 228. *See also* minstrelsy
Amsterdam News. See *New York Amsterdam News*
Anderson, Marian, 45
"And God Made Us All" (Lord Invader), 43
Andrews Sisters, 88

"Angel Levine" (Malamud short story), 232. See also ***The Angel Levine*** (film)
Angelou, Maya, 156, 284n82
Anna Lucasta (stage play, 1944), 20–21, 78
ANT. *See* American Negro Theater
Anthology of American Folk Music (album, 1952), 115–116
anticommunism in America: and Taft-Hartley Act, 49–50; broadcasting and film industries as particular targets of, 62, 91; and civil rights organizations, 62–63, 142, 308n142; black radical resistance to, 63; *Life* magazine "Dupes and Fellow Travelers" photo spread, 63; Ed Sullivan denouncing Canada Lee, 64; Robeson as target of, 67–68, 92, 255; McCarthy claiming Communist "infestation," 72; and legislative investigations, 79, 292n19; and white gang attacks in Greenwich Village, 79; and McCarran Act, 79–80; HB dealing with, 86, 92, 93–94, 98–99, 101–102, 123, 136, 147, 236; HB discussion with King on, 322n107. *See also* blacklisting
antifascism, 25–26, 38, 41, 53, 237
antisegregation protests: during World War II, 6, 15–17; in late 1940s, 18, 26, 28–30, 38, 43, 45; Robeson and, 25–29, 28f, 49, 52; in 1950s, 111–112, 139–141, 164–167, 165f; young people in, 164–167, 165f, 167, 169, 170f (*see also* SNCC). *See also* King, Martin Luther, Jr.; NAACP; *under* Belafonte, Harry: political and cultural activism of
AP. *See* Associated Press
Apollo Theater, 9, 11, 64, 69, 88–89, 158, 263n9; racial composition of audience at, 9, 263n2; HB appearances at, 58, 69
Archer, Osceola, 22, 46–47
**"A Rovin'," **71, 97
Associated Press (AP), 127, 168, 224, 229–230
A Time for Laughter (television special, 1967), 225–231
Atkinson, Brooks, 47, 100, 118
Atlantic Charter (1941), 17
Attaway, William, 71, 81, 278n35, 280n58, 306n122; as HB friend, 71, 77, 83, 84, 124, 162, 276–277n; as writer, 81, 83, 124, 126, 162, 226
Aurthur, Robert Alan, 295–296n46

Baker, Ella, 112, 142–143, 308n142
"Bald-Headed Woman," 205
Baldwin, James, 70, 215, 241, 280n59, 328n172
"Ballad for Americans," 40
Bal Negre (dance revue, 1946), 35
"Banana Boat Song." *See* **"Day-O"**
Baraka, Amiri (LeRoi Jones), 236, 280n59

Barnes, Mae, 196
Barrajanos, Danny, 138
Bartók, Béla, 115
Basie, Count, 25, 31
Bates, Daisy, 166
Bauzá, Mario, 37
Beat Street (film, 1984), 253, 331n2
Beaver Lodge, 48–49
bebop jazz, 36–38, 55–57, 68–69
Beetlejuice (film, 1988), 1
Beggar's Holiday (musical, 1946), 35
Belafonte (album, 1955), 113
Belafonte, Gina, 2
Belafonte, Harry, comments by: on what influenced him, 32, 45, 83–84, 120, 255, 285n91; on jazz as protest, 38; on barriers for black actors, 47, 105, 158–159, 191–192; on folk music, 83–84, 120, 144, 157; on pressure of success, 103, 109, 158, 288n118; on ***Carmen Jones***, 104; on race and television, 127–128, 209–210, 212, 236; on Montgomery boycott and meeting Martin Luther King, Jr., 140; in 1956 *Chicago Defender* series, 143–146; on speaking out, 145, 160–161, 207–208, 231, 250, 254; on race consciousness, 145–146; on ***Island in the Sun***, 150, 152, 158–159, 160; on ***The World, the Flesh and the Devil***, 181, 182, 184–185, 188; on ***Odds against Tomorrow***, 193, 194, 200; on black community strengths, 219–221, 227; on King and RFK assassinations, 237, 244; on ***The Angel Levine***, 244–245, 248, 249; on black arts outside "the establishment," 249–250; on U.S. in early 2000s, 254
Belafonte, Harry, personal life of: birth and early childhood in Harlem and Jamaica, 8–14; Navy service (1944–1945), 15–18, 19; finding American Negro Theater, 19–24; studying at the Dramatic Workshop, 30–34; courtship and marriage with Marguerite Byrd, 16, 27, 45–46, 48–49, 54, 61, 103–104; children born to, 54, 55, 61, 103–104, 138; opening Sage restaurant, 77–78; buying house in Elmhurst, 101; Janet Alterman Kennedy as psychoanalyst (1954–1955), 102–103, 129–130, 135, 136, 288n114; relationship with Julie Robinson, 104, 107; marital tension and divorce; 103–104, 107, 129, 137; marriage to Robinson (1957), 137–138, 153, 154–155
Belafonte, Harry, political and cultural activism of: in late 1940s, 27–28, 29, 49–53, 59–60, 60f, 65; and CNA, 65, 72, 81–82, 89–90; performing at labor events, 73, 82, 168, 255; protesting Du Bois's indictment, 80; and *Counterattack* (1951), 86, 89, 101–102, 123; Robeson advice to distance himself, 92; respond-

Belafonte, Harry, political and cultural activism of (*cont.*) ing to *Counterattack* (1954), 101–102; challenging racial conventions in his profession, 121–122, 127–128, 142, 145, 158–159, 162, 191–192, 204–206, 212, 236; in television, 124, 127–128, 235–236; and Martin Luther King, Jr., 140, 164, 169, 174, 215, 216f, 233, 234, 236–237; fundraising for civil rights movement, 143, 168–169, 172; using fame to support civil rights protest, 163–172, 165f, 168f, 170f, 171f, 206; endorsing Stevenson and JFK, 163–164; and Kennedy administration, 164, 177, 214; particular aid to youth marches and SNCC in civil rights work, 165–167, 172, 212, 217, 249, 309n146; opposition to nuclear weapons, 172; anti-apartheid activism, 173–175, 174f, 217, 253; supporting other liberation struggles in Africa, 173–174, 174f, 215–217, 253–254; speaking against Vietnam War (1965), 177–178, 215; in aftermath of King and RFK assassinations (1968), 236–237; in 1970s and after, 251, 253, 255

Belafonte, Harry, professional career of: in ***Sojourner Truth*** (stage play 1948), 46–47; performing jazz, 55–59, 61, 68–70, 76–77; recording **"Recognition"** (1949), 61; Capitol Records recording sessions (1949), 68; network television appearances, 69–70, 85–86, 123, 124–126; expanding repertoire, 70–72; performing folk music live, 71, 72, 84–89, 96, 116–118, 120; dropped by Capitol, 73; signing with Jubilee Records, 75–76; in ***Head of the Family*** (stage play, 1950), 76; Belafonte Folk Singers (1951), 82–83; contract with RCA Victor (1952), 90, 97; in ***Bright Road*** (1952), 93–95, 94f, 95f; on Ed Sullivan's *Toast of the Town*, 98–99, 99f, 107, 123; in ***John Murray Anderson's Almanac*** (1953), 98, 100, 100f; *Billboard* honor roll (1953), 101; Tony award (1954), 101, 103, 288n118; in ***Carmen Jones*** (1954), 103–107, 106f, 113, 138, 159; in ***3 for Tonight*** (1955), 108, 118, 124; topping charts (1956–1957), 113–114; release of ***Calypso*** album (1956), 126, 137; Jay Richard Kennedy as advisor (1956), 129–131, 135–136, 296–297n55; in ***Sing, Man, Sing*** (1955), 131–135; creating Belafonte Enterprises (1956), 138; in ***Island in the Sun*** (1957), 147–153, 151f; working with Robert DeCormier, 161f, 162, 201, 204; as first black Hollywood movie producer (1957–1959), 178–180 (see also ***Odds against Tomorrow***; ***The***

World, the Flesh and the Devil); Carnegie Hall benefit concerts (1959, 1960), 201; BBC and CBS contracts (1959), 203; ***Tonight with Belafonte*** (1959), 203–206; Emmy and Sylvania awards (1959), 206; ***New York 19*** (1960), 208–212; Grammy award (1965), 213; ***Strolling 20s*** Harlem tribute (1966), 217–225, 230; ***A Time for Laughter*** (1967), 225–231; in ***The Angel Levine*** (1970), 231, 237–249; guest hosting ***Tonight Show*** (1968), 233–235; ***Long Walk to Freedom*** (2001), 252; ***Beat Street*** (1984), 253, 331n2; ***Paradise in Gazankulu*** (1988), 253

Belafonte, Julie Robinson. *See* Robinson (Belafonte), Julie

Belafonte, Marguerite Byrd. *See* Byrd (Belafonte), Marguerite

Belafonte Folk Singers (after 1960), 98, 169, 213, 319n69

Belafonte Singers (1950–1951, also known as Belafonte Folk Singers), 76, 82

Belafonte Sings of the Caribbean (album, 1957), 157, 162

Bellanfanti, Harold George (HB's father), 8

Bell Telephone Hour television show, 202, 218f

Bibb, Leon, 162, 233, 252, 285n90

Bilbo, Theodore, 28–29

Billboard magazine, 40, 101, 113–114, 213

Birdland nightclub, 69, 71, 75, 89, 97

"Birds and Bees," 96

Black Filmmakers Hall of Fame, 252

blacklisting, 20, 62, 74–75, 93, 98, 162, 255, 286n103, 326n146; threat of, for HB, 4, 23, 86, 89, 98, 101–102, 123, 189, 190–191; of Canada Lee, 64, 91; of Robert DeCormier, 98, 162, 326n146. See also *Counterattack* newsletter

Black Man's Burden (Killens), 225

"blackness as problem" framework, 179–180

Black Power, 176–177, 235, 237–238, 241

black press, 16–17, 21, 64, 177; on HB's career, 6, 121, 125, 152–153, 157–158, 196, 203, 205–206, 219, 242, 248–249; on antisegregation struggles, 111, 141, 219; on HB's personal life. See also *Afro-American; Amsterdam News; Carolina Times; Chicago Defender; Ebony; Freedom; Jet; Pittsburgh Courier*

Blitzstein, Marc, 33, 53, 232

Blue Angel nightclub (Chicago), 125

Blue Angel nightclub (New York), 84, 89, 90, 91, 96

bohemian culture, 78–79, 88, 144. *See also* Greenwich Village

Box Office trade paper, 185

Boyle, Johnny, 22, 24

Brand, Oscar, 47–48, 73, 74
Brando, Marlon, 31, 32, 104, 129, 138, 163, 180
Bretton Woods agreements, 17
Bright Road (film, 1953), 93–95, 94f, 95f, 113, 159
Broadway, 34–35, 37, 41, 98
Broonzy, Big Bill, 43–45, 88, 118–120
"Brothers" (unproduced film), 180, 200
"Brown-Skinned Gal," 82
Brown v. Board of Education, 6, 94, 101, 110, 163–164, 23; anniversaries of, 168, 168f, 169–170, 171f
"Buked and Scorned," 210
Burgie, Irving (Lord Burgess), 39, 73, 124; and Caribbean folk music, 124–125, 295n41; as composer, 126, 134, 155, 157, 213, 306n123; part of HB recording sessions, 126, 162
Byrd, Marguerite (Belafonte), 102, 129, 137, 154, 155, 305n116; family background of, 16, 46; courtship of, with HB, 16, 27, 45; early married life of, 48–49, 54, 61; as teacher and initial primary wage earner, 54, 61; and marital tensions, 103–104, 107, 129, 137, 154; after divorce, 155, 305n116

CAA. *See* Council on African Affairs
Cafe Society nightclub, 34, 63, 73, 78, 268n54, 269n59, 279n44
calypso, 13, 39, 87–88; HB's style of, 3, 86, 88–89, 97, 125–126, 156–157; growing popularity of, 13, 39–40, 83, 87–88, 155–156, 157–158; embraced by People's Songs, 43; performed by HB before 1955, 72, 84–85, 96–97, 99, 100, 107, 123; Irving Burgie and, 124–125; on HB albums, 157–158, 162, 213 (see also ***Harry Belafonte: Calypso***). *See also* Duke of Iron; ***"Hold 'Em Joe"***; Trinidadian calypso
Calypso (album). See ***Harry Belafonte: Calypso***
"Calypso at Midnight" concert (1946), 44, 88
Camp Unity, 33, 51, 125
Carmen Jones (film, 1954), 103–107, 106f, 113, 138, 159, 289n124
Carmen Jones (musical, 1943), 33, 35, 47
Carolina Times, 141–142
Carroll, Diahann, 104–105, 222, 226, 228, 233
Casseus, Franz, 72, 126
Cayton, Horace, 110–111
Champion, Gower, 108, 118
Champion, Marge, 108, 118, 300n77
Charles, Ray, 98
"chauvinism," uses of term, 145, 254, 301n92
Chicago Conference for Brotherhood, 130, 142
Chicago Defender newspaper, 81, 230; on fight against segregation, 18, 141; on HB's ris-

ing career, 90–91; on HB stage and TV performances, 97, 134, 206, 211, 235; HB interviews in (1956), 143–145, 158, 163; on HB films, 187, 188, 200
Chicago Federal Theater Project (FTP), 20
Chicago Tribune, 135
Childress, Alice, 72, 81, 89–90, 278nn38,39
"Chimney Smoke," 97
Chisholm, Shirley, 164, 308n41
"Cinderella Gentleman," Belafonte as, 56
CIO. *See* Congress of Industrial Organizations
citizenship, U.S., 8
Clark, Petula, 233, 235
"Close Your Eyes," 73
Club Baron, 81–82, 90, 281n63
CNA. *See* Committee for the Negro in the Arts
Cocoanut Grove Lounge, 96, 121
Cold War: progressive movement opposition to, 29, 49, 59; intensification of, 49–50, 62–64, 72; impact of, on *Brown* decision, 110–111; and Family of Man exhibit, 132–133. *See also* anticommunism in America
Cole, Nat King, 88, 140–142, 146–147, 210; HB and, 58, 128, 145, 147; marketing of, as mainstream pop singer, 68; attacked at Birmingham concert, 134, 140, 300n79; and segregated audiences, 134, 141–142, 145; and NAACP, 141, 142
Color and Democracy (Du Bois), 17, 26
Come Back, Africa (film, 1959), 175
Committee for the Negro in the Arts (CNA), 64–66, 146, 252, 276n26; events sponsored by, 64–66, 72, 80–82, 89–90; HB and, 65, 68, 72–73, 80–82, 89–90, 91–92, 102, 145, 179, 252; Robeson and, 66, 68, 91–92, 276n26
"common denominator songs," 39
Communist Party USA, 19, 62–63, 140, 142, 301n92; laws targeting, 53, 79–80; and civil rights organizations, 62–63, 142, 308n142. *See also* anticommunism in America
Condon, Eddie, 59–60
Congress of Industrial Organizations (CIO), 38, 45; chorus sponsored by, 27, 29, 42, 47
Correll, Charles, 65, 66f, 228. See also *Amos 'n' Andy*
Cosby, Bill, 226, 233
Council on African Affairs (CAA), 26–27, 91, 268n56
Counterattack newsletter, 62, 74, 75, 286n103; and HB, 86, 89, 101–102, 123
Cradle Will Rock (musical, 1937), 33
Crossroads Africa, 177
Crowther, Bosley, 105, 187, 199
Cruse, Harold, 146–147, 276n25, 278n38, 328n172
Cry the Beloved Country (Paton), 46

"Cubano Be, Cubano Bop," 81–82
Cultural and Scientific Conference for World Peace, 63, 275n19, 304n113
Cultural Committee to Defend Martin Luther King and the Struggle for Freedom, 169
Curtis, Tony, 31, 47, 94

Daily Worker newspaper, 23, 136
Dandridge, Dorothy, 93–94, 94f, 104–105, 106f, 149–150, 169
"Danny Boy," 203
Davis, Miles, 37–38, 55, 68
Davis, Ossie, 39, 168–169, 232, 249, 278n38, 326n146, 331n2; and HB, 29, 168–169; and Robeson, 285n90
Davis, Sammy, Jr., 154–155, 165, 222
"Day-O" ("Banana Boat Song"), 1, 125, 157, 167, 295n42
Days of Our Youth (stage play, 1946), 22
DeCarava, Roy, 132–133, 210–211, 219, 252, 276n26, 278n38
DeCormier, Robert, 41, 42–43, 47, 48, 51; and CIO chorus, 42, 47; and HB, 42–43, 48, 161f, 162, 201, 204; blacklisting of, 98, 162, 326n146
Dee, Ruby, 165, 227, 278n38, 347n2; and American Negro Theater, 20, 22; blacklisting of, 98, 286n103, 326n146
Deep Are the Roots (stage play, 1946), 34
Defense of Marriage Act, 251
De Lavallade, Carmen, 104, 196
de Paur, Leonard, 78, 252, 275n23, 331n1
Destiné, Jean-Léon, 125
De Windt, Hal, 240–241
District 65, 45, 71, 73, 101, 168
"Django," 210
"Dogs," 229, 325n134
Don't You Want to be Free? (stage play, 1938), 33
Double Victory campaign, 6, 15
Down Beat magazine, 56, 96
Dramatic Workshop, 30–35, 38, 41–42
Du Bois, Shirley Graham. *See* Graham, Shirley
Du Bois, W. E. B., 16, 34, 140; HB and, 16, 80, 102, 140, 250; political activism of, 17, 26, 49, 50, 52; redbaiting of, 63, 140
Duckett, Alfred, 144, 301n90, 327n152
Duke of Iron, 44, 51, 73, 88, 156
Dumbarton Oaks Conference (1944), 17
Dunham, Katherine, 31–32, 35, 125, 138, 267n48; dancers influenced by, 70, 104, 134, 138, 153, 299n73
Dusk of Dawn (Du Bois), 16
Dyer-Bennett, Richard, 40, 74, 86
Dylan, Bob, 4, 212–213, 322n105

Ebony magazine, 40, 78, 98, 242; on HB, 94, 154, 167, 193; on interracial marriage, 154–155
Eden Roc Hotel, Miami, 121
Eisenhower, Dwight, 166, 207
Ellington, Duke, 11, 33, 35, 69,

70, 154–155, 227; political associations of, 25, 27, 38, 143; and racial conventions, 35, 191, 300n80; and ***The Strollin' 20s***, 219, 221, 223
Ellington, Mercer, 38
Elliot, Ramblin' Jack, 119f
Emperor Jones (proposed film), 158, 179
End of the World. See ***The World, the Flesh and the Devil***

Fair Employment Practices Commission (FEPC), 26, 28, 29, 49
"Family of Man" photographic exhibit, 131–133, 297n59
FBI, 92, 102, 136
Federal Theater Project (FTP), 301; in New York, 20, 331n1
FEPC. *See* Fair Employment Practices Commission
Ferrer, Mel, 182, 183, 184f, 187
Finian's Rainbow (musical, 1947), 35, 41, 126
Fitzgerald, Ella, 11, 88
Five O'Clock Club, 76
Flies (stage play, 1947), 31
Florence (stage play, 1950), 81
folk musics: HB and, 33–34, 41, 71, 81–84, 90, 116–117, 120, 144, 157; in 1940s New York City, 39–45; Robeson and, 40–41, 72, 97; performing race in, 115–120, 119f; racial boundary crossing in, 115–120, 119f
Fontaine, Joan, 150, 151f, 152, 182
Ford Foundation, 241
"For Lincoln and Liberty" (People's Songs concert, 1948), 47–48
Foster, Gloria, 239, 242
Foxx, Redd, 226–229
Foye, Hope, 80, 91, 275n23
Fraternal Clubhouse, 48th Street, 45
Free Southern Theater (SNCC), 249
Freedom newspaper, 80, 89, 91–92, 101
Freedom Riders, 167
Freedom Singers, 214–215
Freeman, Mort, 82, 96
Frye, Peter, 33–34
Fur and Leather Workers union, 67

Garvey, Marcus, 8, 9. *See also* Garveyite movement
Garveyite movement, 9, 125, 219, 222
Gassner, John, 31–32
Gibbs, Wolcott, 118
Gibson, Truman, 150
GI Bill, 45
Gilford, Jack, 60, 232
Gillespie, Dizzy, 36, 37, 38, 68, 81
Gleason, Jackie, 85, 101, 123
"God Bless the Child," 210
Golden Gate Ballroom, 52
Golden Gate Quartet, 40, 270n65, 271n75
Gold through the Trees (stage play, 1952), 90
"Gomen Nasai," 97
"Goodnight Irene," 33
Gordon, Max, 84, 89, 125
Gorelik, Mordecai, 30

Gorney, Jay, 53, 267n47
Gosden, Freeman, 65, 66f, 228. See also *Amos 'n' Andy*
Gould, Jack, 234, 235–236
Graham, Shirley, 20, 49–50, 63, 278n40
Grant, Rupert. *See* Lord Invader
Greene, Alan, 48, 61
Greenwich Village, 77–84
Gregory, Dick, 226–228, 229, 230
Gregory, Paul, 107–108
Gunn, Bill, 238–239, 240, 328n162
Guthrie, Woody, 34, 39–43, 75, 83, 270n65

Hamilton, Kim, 191, 199
Hammerstein, Oscar II, 25, 27, 33, 163
Hansberry, Lorraine, 90, 112, 125, 180, 239, 280n59; political activism of, 51, 174
Harbel production company, 162, 178–179, 181, 188–189, 191, 201, 319n67. See also ***Odds against Tomorrow***; ***The World, the Flesh and the Devil***
Harburg, Yip, 35, 53, 278n40
Harlem: HB's youth in, 8–11, 13, 30, 32, 39; racial confinement in, 10, 13–14, 78; bebop jazz in, 36; Savoy Ballroom in, 36, 80, 223; calypso in, 39, 87–89, 158, 283n79; Wallace rallies in, 52; Theresa Hotel in, 64, 66, 78; CNA programs in, 72, 81, 276n26; and black arts radicals, 80–82; DeCarava's photographic exploration of, 132–133; Abyssinian Baptist Church in, 140; Armory Freedom Rally in (1960), 169–172, 171f; as shown in ***The Strollin' 20s***, 219–225, 230; and ***The Angel Levine***, 232, 238, 240. *See also* Apollo Theater
Harlem Jubilee (television show, 1949), 69
Harrington, Oliver, 29
Harry Belafonte: Calypso (album, 1956), 137, 153, 155, 157–158; origin of, 113–114, 124, 126; popularity of, 113–114, 126, 127–128, 137, 153, 155, 157–158, 213
Harry Belafonte Singers (1957–1960), 162, 201, 204
"Hava Nagila," 96, 172, 203, 210, 286n100, 299n69
Hayes, Alfred, 149, 302n102
Hayes, Lee, 39, 40, 42, 44, 59
Head of the Family (stage play, 1950), 76, 113
Heath, Gordon, 78, 276n23
Hentoff, Nat, 96
Hepburn, Philip, 93
Herman, Woody, 58
Hicks, James, 170–171
Hill, Abram, 20, 22, 31–32
"hillbilly" music, 40
Hinkson, Mary, 134, 204, 205, 210, 320n79
"Hold 'Em Joe," 88, 96, 100, 107, 123, 283–284n81, 294n35
Holiday, Billie, 11, 34, 210, 222

"Holiday in Trinidad" (television show, 1955), 125–126
Holly, Ellen, 34, 72
Hollywood Reporter, 224, 229
Home Is the Hunter (stage play, 1946), 19, 21–22
"Hootenanny" People's Songs concerts, 42
Horne, Lena, 49, 156, 213, 227, 233
"Hosanna," 134
HUAC (House Committee on Un-American Activities), 63, 64, 75; Hollywood hearings of, 50, 91; and HB, 102
Hubley, John and Faith, 191
Hughes, Langston, 14, 81, 173, 193, 204, 264n12; stage productions by, 33, 35; and CNA, 49, 63, 80, 276n23; redbaiting and blacklisting of, 63, 98, 287n103; HB and, 109, 204, 252; "You've taken my blues" by, 134, 284n84; and ***The Strollin' 20s***, 219, 220f, 222–223, 324n118

ICCASP (Independent Citizens Committee of the Arts, Sciences, and the Professions), 27, 38, 60, 65; HB and, 27, 29; and Wallace campaign, 49, 51; on attorney general's list, 62
"I Come for to Sing," 118
"I Found Me," 135
In Friendship, 112, 139, 142–143, 164, 169
Island in the Sun (film, 1957), 147–153, 151f, 157, 182, 303n104; HB comments on, 150, 152, 158–159, 160
Ives, Burl, 39–41, 52, 74–75, 91, 115, 270n65

Jackson, Mahalia, 154–155, 164
Jamaica, 12–13; HB in, as child, 10, 11–13, 32; music of, 120, 125–126, 157, 210, 295n42 (*see also* calypso)
Jamaica (musical, 1957), 156, 262n1
"Jamaica Farewell," 4, 157
Japan tour (1960), 206
Jeb (stage play, 1946), 34
Jefferson, Miles, 47
Jeffries, Herb, 156
Jenkins, Gordon, 75
Jet magazine, 150–152
Jim Crow. *See* racial segregation
"John Henry," 73, 82, 145, 179
John Henry (musical, 1940), 41
John Murray Anderson's Almanac (musical revue, 1953), 98, 100–101, 103
Jones, Bessie, 252
Jones, Claudia, 173
Jones, LeRoi. *See* Baraka, Amiri
Jones, Robert Earl, 196
Jordan, Louis, 36, 44, 88
Jump for Joy (musical revue, 1941), 33
"Jump in the Line," 1
Juno and the Paycock (stage play, 1946), 22–24, 23f, 24f, 25, 70
Just A Little Simple (stage play, 1950), 81

Kadar, Jan, 240, 242–243, 246–248
Kaminska, Ida, 240, 242, 246, 328n168
Kay, Monte, 37–38, 55–56, 57–58, 61, 68–71
Kennedy, Janet Alterman, 102–103, 129–130, 135, 136, 288n14
Kennedy, Jay Richard (Samuel Richard Solomonick), 102, 136, 192, 288n114; as influential HB advisor, 102–103, 129–130, 131, 133, 137, 288n114, 296–297n55; and ***Sing, Man, Sing***, 131–135; as FBI informant, 135–136, 298n67
Kennedy, John F., 164, 177, 214
Kennedy, Robert F., 233, 234, 237, 307–308n138
Killens, John O., 89–90, 189, 225; collaborations of, with HB, 158, 161–162, 179, 189, 276–277n26
King, Coretta Scott. *See* Scott (King), Coretta
King, Martin Luther, Jr., 244; and 1950s desegregation efforts, 112, 139–140, 164, 166–167; and HB, 140, 164, 169, 174, 215, 216f, 233, 234, 236–237; and Vietnam war, 215; death of, 236–237; FBI and, 298n67, 322n107
"King of Calypso" title, 1, 155, 159
Kirby, George, 222, 226, 227, 228
Kitt, Eartha, 154–155
Kootz, Samuel, 21
Korean conflict, 74, 86
labor unions. *See* unions
Lacy, Sam, 159–160
Lampell, Millard, 40, 47–48. See also ***Lonesome Train***
Landau, Felix, 43
Lawrence, Jacob, 49, 275–276n23
"Lead Man Holler," 152
"Lean on Me," 61
Ledbetter, Huddie (Lead Belly), 33–34, 71, 75, 204, 268n53; influence of, on HB, 39, 42–43, 45; memorial concert for, 71
Lee, Canada, 27, 46, 49, 63, 64, 67, 91; blacklisting of, 64, 91
Levison, Stanley, 112, 136, 142–143, 298n67, 322n107
Levy, Herb, 126, 210
Lewis, John, 191, 210
Life magazine, 63, 154
"Little Lyric (of Great Importance)," 204
Little Rock, Arkansas, school desegregation conflict, 111, 165–166, 172–173, 183
Lomax, Alan, 41, 71, 88, 270n65; and People's Songs, 42–44, 51, 59; redbaiting of, 80; field recordings by, 83, 107, 268n53
Lomax, Almena, 198–199
Lonesome Train (folk cantata), 40, 47–48, 89, 90, 96
Long, Avon, 52, 76
Longshoremen's union, 67
Long Walk to Freedom, The, 252. *See also* **"Negro Anthology"/*Long Walk to Freedom*** project
Look magazine, 129, 152, 154, 158

Lord Flea, 125, 156
Lord Invader (Rupert Grant), 39, 43, 44, 51, 88, 271n73
Los Angeles Times, 95, 237, 242–243
Lost in the Stars (musical, 1949), 46
Love, Jane, 10–11
Love, Melvine "Millie" (HB's mother), 8–12, 14–15
Lucy, Autherine, 139, 143
Lynne, Gloria, 210, 211, 222, 252
Lysistrata (stage play, 1946), 35, 46

Mabley, Moms, 226–229
Macbeth, Harlem performance of (1936), 20
MacBeth the Great, 44, 88, 213, 283n81
MacDonald, Ralph, 213
MacDougall, Curtis, 51
MacDougall, Rand, 183
Machito, 58, 61
Makeba, Miriam, 174f, 175, 212, 253, 311n157; joint performances of, with HB, 213, 215–217
Malamud, Barnard, 232, 237–238, 245
Malcolm X, 215
"Mama, Look a Booboo Dey," 157
Mandela, Nelson, 4, 253
"Man Smart, Woman Smarter," 4, 88, 97, 134
March on Washington (1963), 215, 217, 322n108
March on Washington movement (1941), 15, 143
Markham, Pigmeat, 226, 228–229
"Mark Twain," 99–100, 107, 117
Mark Twain (album, 1954), 113
Marshall, William, 89
Martin, Trayvon, 251
Martinez, Louis "Sabu," 81–82
"Mary Ann," 157
"Mary's Boy Child," 1, 203
Masekela, Hugh, 213
Maslow, Sophie, 72
"Matilda," 96, 97, 99
Mayfield, Julian, 46, 125, 241
McCarran Act, 79, 91
McCarthy, Joseph, 72
McGee, Willie, 81, 281n65
McGhee, Brownie, 39, 40, 88, 204, 222, 233, 252; and People's Songs, 42, 43, 44, 51
McGivern, William, 188–189
Mento music (Jamaica), 13, 125
Mercer, Charles, 127
Mercer, Johnny, 68
Mercouri, Melina, 233
Metronome magazine, 73–74, 82–83, 86
Middleman, What Now? (dramatic revue, 1947), 34
"Midnight Special" Town Hall concerts, 44
minstrelsy, 67, 111, 192, 227–228. See also *Amos 'n' Andy*
Mitchell, Arthur, 204, 210, 320n79
Modern Jazz Quartet, 191, 210, 211
Monk, Thelonious, 36, 283n81
Montgomery bus boycott, 111–112, 139, 143

Morrison, Allan, 78–79, 280n58
Mostel, Zero, 25, 29, 233, 234; in ***The Angel Levine***, 242, 246–248, 247f
Motion Picture Herald, 185, 196
Moynihan Report, 219
My Song (HB memoir, 2011), 2

NAACP: 28f, 50, 112, 143; Nat King Cole and, 141, 142; barring of Communists by, 142, 308n142
Nation, 187
National Negro Congress (NNC), 26, 65
National Negro Labor Council (NNLC), 91, 92, 102
Nazism, 21, 240; parallels of U.S. white supremacy to, 17, 172–173, 237–238
"Negro Anthology"/*Long Walk to Freedom* project, 107–109, 124, 203, 252
Negro History Week programs, 66, 72
New School for Social Research. *See* Dramatic Workshop
Newsweek magazine, 103, 233–234
New York Amsterdam News, 21, 29, 34, 141, 211, 230, 249; on HB, 153, 154, 170–172
"New York: A Musical Tapestry" (People's Songs benefit concert, 1949), 59
New York Federal Theater Project, Harlem Unit, 20, 331n1
New York music scene in 1940s: Broadway, 34–35; bebop jazz, 36–38; folk music genres, 39–45
New York 19 (television special, 1960), 208–212
New York Post, 90, 147, 153, 154, 192
New York Times: list of Cultural and Scientific Conference for World Peace sponsors published by, 63; performance reviews of HB in, 100–101, 234; full-page ad supporting Martin Luther King in, organized by HB, 169; film reviews and features, 187, 242; on significance of Harbel production company, 191; Jack Gould criticism and HB's response in, 223, 229, 234, 235–236; "Dark Laughter in Snow White Land" interview in, 231; "Can Black and White Artists Still Work Together?" in, 241
Nicks, Walter, 134, 204, 227
Night of the Stars for Civil Rights (benefit, 1957), 168–169
92nd Street Y, 47
NNC. *See* National Negro Congress
NNLC. *See* National Negro Labor Council
"No, No, No Discrimination," 45
"Noah," 134
Norman, Fred, 71, 75–76
Notting Hill riots, 173
nuclear weapons, ban on testing of, 172, 177

Oakland Tribune, 229
Obama, Barack, 4
O'Casey, Sean, 22–23, 25, 32
Odds Against Tomorrow (film, 1959), 188–191, 193–201, 194f, 195f, 197f, 198f, 239; HB comments on, 193, 194, 200
Odetta, 169, 204, 205, 252
Of Mice and Men (stage play), 33–34, 41
Oklahoma! (musical, 1943), 33
Olatunji, Babatunde, 169, 173
"old time" music, 40
O'Neal, Frederick, 20, 76, 122
O'Neill, Eugene, 179, 185
"On Radio, Television and the Negro People" conference (1949), 65–66, 66f
On Strivers Row (stage play, 1946), 22, 23f
On Whitman Avenue (stage play, 1946), 34

"Palladium Dance," 210
Palladium dance hall, 58, 209
Palmer House, 121, 144
Paradise in Gazankulu (album, 1988), 253
Parker, Charlie "Bird," 36, 38, 52, 55, 61, 68
Parks, Rosa, 111
PCA. *See* Progressive Citizens of America
People's Songs, 43–45, 51; interracial mission of, 43–45; concerts held by, 44, 45, 47–48, 59; HB and, 47–48, 59; red-baiting of, 63, 74, 91
Peters, Brock, 70, 78, 104, 126, 162
Phylon journal, 47
Piedmont-style blues, 40
Pins and Needles (musical revue, 1937), 33
Piscator, Erwin, 30, 31, 191
Pittsburgh Courier, 15, 56, 68, 110, 158, 163
Poitier, Sidney, 22, 46, 174, 233; as stage actor, 46, 78, 81, 82, 127; film roles of, 78, 158, 191, 199; civil rights/arts activism of, with HB, 81, 89–90, 168–170, 278n40; breaking of TV racial conventions by, 127, 295–296n46; as narrator in HB productions, 222, 228
Polonsky, Abraham, 189–190
Porgy and Bess, 52, 70, 76, 95, 126, 158, 200, 213; HB's rejection of role in, 158
Powell, Adam Clayton, Jr., 63, 140, 143
Pozo, Chano, 37, 82
Prayer Pilgrimage (SCLC, 1957), 164
Primus, Pearl, 25, 29, 125, 276n23
Progressive Citizens of America (PCA), 49
Progressive Party, 29, 51, 52, 63, 88, 91. *See also* Wallace, Henry
Pryor, Richard, 226–228
Puente, Tito, 156

racial segregation, 122, 142, 145, 264; in the military, 15–18;

racial segregation (*continued*)
HB's experiences of, 15–18, 76–77, 94–96, 108, 121–122, 142, 150–152, 235; in theater, 19–20, 46; violent enforcement of, 29, 111, 139, 140–141, 143; in accommodations, 57, 76–77, 95–96, 108, 115, 121–122; in film industry, 94–95, 104–105, 147–148, 150–152, 187–188, 241–242; HB's challenges to, in his work, 121–122, 127–128, 142, 145, 158–159, 162, 191–192, 204–206, 212, 236; in television, 124, 127–128, 235–236. *See also* antisegregation protests
Raisin in the Sun, A (Hansberry), 180, 201
Randolph, A. Philip, 17, 112, 155, 165f, 172, 173; and March on Washington movement, 15, 143
"Recognition," 34, 56, 61, 72–73
red-baiting. *See* anticommunism in America
Red Channels, 74, 75. See also *Counterattack* newsletter
Reinhardt, Django, 210
Ribman, Ronald, 240
Rice, Elmer, 35
Roach, Max, 55, 68
Robbins, Fred, 60
Robeson, Paul: public stature of, in 1940s, 24–25, 27; and HB, 24–26, 66, 92, 102, 140, 254–255, 285n91; political and cultural activism of, 25–27, 28f, 29, 49–52, 63, 80, 89, 91–92, 101; folk music repertoire of, 40–41, 52, 72, 97; targeted by government and conservatives, 63–64, 67–68, 80, 92, 102–103, 136, 296n46; stature of, among black artists, 66, 276n26, 285n90
Robinson, Bill "Bojangles," 69, 222
Robinson, Earl, 28f, 40, 47–48, 52, 74
Robinson, Edward G., 239, 240, 242
Robinson, Jackie, 64, 69, 164–165, 165f, 192–193, 317n46
Robinson (Belafonte), Julie, 137–138, 164; as dancer and dance teacher, 32, 134, 138, 210, 268n51, 299n73; and Marlon Brando, 32, 104, 138; relationship with HB and his divorce, 104, 107, 137, 138; as artistic collaborator with HB, 137–138, 162, 210; at Youth March, 165f
Rodgers, Richard, 33
Rogosin, Lionel, 175
Rohlehr, Gordon, 155–156
Rollins, Jack, 76, 82–84, 90, 103, 116
Rome, Harold, 33, 53
Roosevelt, Eleanor, 21, 40, 143, 172, 174
Roosevelt, Franklin (FDR), 19, 26, 30, 40, 59–60, 60f
"Round and Round Hitler's Grave", 40
Royal Roost nightclub, 37–38, 52, 55–59, 61, 69

Russell, Nipsy, 222, 225–226, 233
Rustin, Bayard, 112, 139, 142, 164–165, 175, 241
Ryan, Robert, 163, 190, 198f

Sage restaurant, 77–78, 80, 82, 84
Sahara (film, 1943), 15
"Salute to FDR" event (1949), 59–60, 60f
"Salute to Negro Veterans" (UNAVA benefit, 1947), 38
San Francisco Mime Troupe, 225, 249
Sandburg, Carl, 48, 75, 132, 133, 270n69, 297–298n60
Sands, Diana, 196, 226–228
SANE rally (1960), 172
Saturday Evening Post, 154
Savoy Ballroom, Harlem, 36, 80, 223
"Scarlet Ribbons," 96–97, 99
Schultz, Chiz, 231–232
Schwartz, Bernard. *See* Curtis, Tony
SCLC. *See* Southern Christian Leadership Conference
Scott (King), Coretta, 50, 143, 216f
Scott, Fran Settele, 84, 103, 121–122
Scott, Tony, 82–83, 97, 116, 121–122; as HB friend, 82, 84, 97, 103, 107, 116, 121–122
Scott-Heron, Gil, 4
Sebree, Charles, 70
Seeger, Pete, 39–40, 42–44, 51–52, 59, 74, 83
segregation. *See* antisegregation movements; racial segregation
Senate Internal Security Committee, 79
Settele, Fran. *See* Scott, Fran Settele
Shaw, Arnold, 4, 61, 292n19
Shaw, Artie, 31, 59–60, 74
"Shenandoah," 97, 205
Shore, Dinah, 217
Show Boat (musical revival, 1946), 35
Schwartz, Tony, 97, 208, 286n101
Siegel, Sol, 181, 183–184
Silvera, Frank, 72, 101, 107, 276n26, 281n64
Sinatra, Frank, 31, 85, 101, 114, 308n39
Sing, Man, Sing (musical production, 1956), 131–135, 137, 142
Sing Out, Sweet Land (musical, 1945), 41
Sing Your Song (film, 2011), 2
Sir Lancelot, 43, 51–52, 88
Smith, Bessie, 222
Smith, Harry, 115–116
Smothers Brothers, 233, 234
SNCC (Student Nonviolent Coordinating Committee), 237, 244, 309n146; HB's help to, 167, 172, 212, 217, 249, 309n146
Sojourner Truth (stage play, 1948), 46–47
Solomonick, Samuel Richard. *See* Kennedy, Jay Richard
"Sometimes I Feel Like a Motherless Child," 72–73

Songs for Political Action (People's Songs album, 1946), 44–45
Southern Christian Leadership Conference (SCLC), 164, 167, 172, 212
Southland (ballet, 1951), 138
Stafford, Jo, 40, 68, 85, 96
"Stand Your Ground" laws, 251
Stevens, Inger, 182, 184–187, 184f, 186f
Stevenson, Adlai, 163–164
St. Louis Woman (musical, 1946), 35
"Strange Fruit" (Billie Holiday song), 34
Strange Fruit (stage play, 1945), 34
Street Scene (opera, 1947), 35
Stritch, Samuel, Cardinal, 130–131
Strollin' 20s. See ***The Strollin' 20s***
Subversive Activities Control Board, 79
Sugar Hill Times (television show, 1949), 69
Sullivan, Ed, 64, 98, 128, 211; hosting of HB by, 98–99, 99f, 101, 107, 123, 128, 194f
"Sylvie," 4, 205
"Symphony Sid" (Sid Torin), 37, 55–58, 61, 69

Taft-Hartley Act (1947), 49–50
"Take My Mother Home," 118
Taylor, Clarice, 19, 21–22, 89
Terry, Sonny, 39, 40, 88, 204, 233, 252; and People's Songs, 42, 43, 44
The Angel Levine (film, 1970), 231–233, 237–249, 247f, 251, 326n147, 327n148
"The Blues Is Man," 134
"The House I Live In," 163
Theresa Hotel, 64, 66, 78
The Strollin' 20s (television special, 1966), 219–225, 230
The World, the Flesh and the Devil (film, 1959), 181–188, 184f, 186f; HB comments on, 181, 182, 184–185, 188
Thomas, Millard, 71, 82–83, 89, 108, 115, 134
Three Deuces nightclub, 37
3 for Tonight (musical revue, 1954), 108, 115, 118, 124
Thurmond, Strom, 53
Till, Emmett, 111
"Timber," 96–97
Tin Pan Alley, 11, 33, 39, 53, 117
Tonight (television show, 1968), 233–235
Tonight with Belafonte (television special, 1959), 203–206
Torin, Sid. *See* "Symphony Sid"
Trinidadian calypso, 13, 87–89, 155–157, 284n81; and American occupation, 82; sung by Belafonte, 82, 123, 157
Trinidad Steel Band, 213
Truman, Harry, 29–30, 49–50, 52, 53, 79
TV Guide, 202
Tynes, Margaret, 126, 134

Ulanov, Barry, 73–74, 86–87, 283n78
UNAVA (United Negro and Al-

lied Veterans of America), 28–29, 38, 62
unions: of sleeping car porters, 9; Robeson and, 25, 27, 67, 91–92, 101; and folk songs, 40, 42, 44–45, 48; Taft-Hartley Act restrictions on, 49–50; CNA and, 65, 67, 91; HB support of, 73, 101, 255; supporting civil rights, 112, 143, 165–168, 168f, 169–170, 255; and support for HB, 122; all-white, in film industry, 241–242. *See also* District 65
United Fruit Company, 8, 11
UPI (United Press International) reviews, 224, 230
Uptown Jubilee (television show, 1949), 69

Van Vechten, Carl, 100, 100f
Variety newspaper, 67, 90, 193–194, 317n46; reviews of HB's singing in, 71, 73; HB interviewed by, 193–194, 207–208, 232, 240; critique of ***The Strollin' 20s*** in, 223–224; praise for ***A Time for Laughter*** in, 229
"Venezuela," 82, 97, 282n67
vernacular music, 35, 39–41, 118. *See also* folk musics
Veterans of Foreign Wars, 28, 67
Village Vanguard, 75, 78, 101, 123, 125; HB performances at, 84–85, 87, 89, 101

Waldorf Astoria, 121–122
"Walk in Peace" (Sir Lancelot), 43
Wallace, Henry, 49–54, 59–60, 63
Ward, Brian, 113
Ward, Douglas Turner, 241
Ward, Theodore, 20–21, 49, 63, 80, 275–276n23
Warfield, William, 169
Washington, Fredi, 80, 275–276n23
Washington Post, 211
"Water Boy," 205
Waters, Ethel, 126, 286n100
Weatherby, W. J., 234–235
Weavers, 59, 74–75, 84, 91, 97
Welles, Orson, 20, 27, 29, 163
"Whispering," 73
White, Charles, 49, 252, 276–277n26, 280n59; and CNA, 80, 275n23, 276n26, 278n40; and HB television special, 204, 219
White, Josh, 84; music of, 34, 39, 40–41, 45, 83–84, 86, 96; and People's Songs, 43, 44, 63, 74; distancing himself from Left, 63, 74–75; redbaiting of, 74–75
White Citizens' Councils, 111, 140–141, 152
Wickes, Virginia, 57, 61, 90
Williams, Joe, 223, 252
Williams, Mary Lou, 25, 80
Wilson, Earl, 68
Winchell, Walter, 68
Winters, Shelley, 190
Wise, Robert, 190
Woodard, Isaac, 29
Work, Craig, 71, 76, 82, 85, 89, 97, 123

World, the Flesh and the Devil. See ***The World, the Flesh and the Devil***
World War II, 39, 82, 240, 242, 328n168; Double Victory campaign in, 6, 15; HB's Navy service in, 15–18; black critique of colonialism in, 16–17; veterans of, in Dramatic Workshop, 30–31
Wright, Bishop R., 50
Young, Lester, 37–38, 69
Young Progressives of America, 51–52, 59, 60f, 97, 101, 142
Youth Marches for Integrated Schools, 165–167

Zanuck, Darryl, 148–150, 152